The Soviet Theory of
International Relations

The Soviet Theory of International Relations

Margot Light

Lecturer in International Relations
University of Surrey

ST. MARTIN'S PRESS
New York

First published in the United States of America in 1988

Printed in Great Britain

ISBN 0-312-01889-4 (cl.)
    0-312-01891-6 (pbk.)

Library of Congress Cataloging-in-Publication Data

Light, Margot.
    The Soviet theory of international relations/by Margot Light.
        p.   cm.
    Bibliography: p.
    Includes index.
    ISBN 0-312-01889-4: $39.95 (est.).   ISBN 0-312-01891-6
    (pbk.):
  $15.95 (est.)
    1. Soviet Union—Foreign relations—1917–
    2. International law and socialism.   I. Title.
JX1555.Z5 1988   87-34021
327.47—dc 19   CIP

Contents

For Girlie

Acknowledgements

This book is the product of many years of studying and teaching. I am grateful to my teachers and my students who provided the intellectual stimulus that made me embark on the project. I would not have completed it without the advice and patient encouragement of three teachers who became colleagues, critics and friends and who read the manuscript chapter by chapter: Michael Banks, Otto Pick and Tony de Reuck. I would like to record my indebtedness to them.

I benefited from the help and advice of many other colleagues and friends who read part or all of the manuscript. I would like in particular to thank Fred Halliday, John Erickson, James Mayall and Edwin Lichtenstein. The generosity of Debra, Linda, Eva, Elisabeth, Leonie, Miriam, Richard and Wendy who helped me beat a deadline by proof reading for word processor and personal quirks is gratefully acknowledged.

Most of the writing was done during a sabbatical year granted by the University of Surrey. I spent one term at the University of Kent and two terms and a summer at the Centre for International Studies, London School of Economics and Political Science. I am indebted to the University of Surrey for granting me time and freedom, and to Kent and CIS for hospitality and an ambience conducive to writing. The British Library of Political and Economic Science provided most of my sources. But I would like to thank Jenny Brine and Jackie Johnson, librarians at the Centre for Russian and East European Studies, University of Birmingham, for their courteous, speedy and efficient replies to urgent telephone enquiries.

Finally, I owe profound gratitude to my mother for patiently enduring my preoccupation with theory.

June 1987, University of Surrey.

1 Introduction

Soviet policy-makers and scholars argue that the foreign policy of the Soviet Union is based on an explicit philosophy and theory. This is a study of their claim. What is the theoretical framework which is said to underlie their policy? Is it powerful enough to fulfil the role which is claimed for it?

All policy reflects theory, whether or not that theory is articulated or recognized by those who make policy. Western foreign policies are usually based on ideas about the utility of power as a means of maximizing national interest and assuring international order. However, the formulation of theory in the West, and the use to which theory is put, differ vastly from Soviet practice. For one thing, Western theories are not well articulated by policy-makers. Policy is usually only explained in terms of theory on ceremonial occasions. For another, more often than not, theorizing takes place in a plural system which discourages the notion that there can be a monopoly of truth. Competing political parties promise alternative policies, and scholars propose different theories which, they believe, are either a better reflection of reality or will lead to a better reality. Western theories can, none the less, be extrapolated, particularly since there is a strong tradition of criticizing both policy and the assumptions or theory on which it is presumed to be based.

Soviet policy-makers tend to legitimize their policies by claiming a conscious attempt to base their practice on theory. Their theory is, therefore, more frequently articulated than Western theory. It is, Soviet politicians and scholars argue, Marxist-Leninist theory. There is a large body of academic,

1

popular scientific and programmatic literature explaining the theory and relating it to Soviet foreign policy and international relations. There is, however, no tradition of criticism of either theory or practice in the Soviet Union. As a result, debates about alternative policies or theories are rarely found in Soviet literature. There is very little open and published discussion of when and where the existing theory has been found to be inadequate. And there is no mention of occasions when practice has diverged from theory.

In Western analyses of the Soviet Union the question is perennially posed whether Soviet foreign policy is motivated by Marxist-Leninist ideology, as Soviet leaders insist, or by power. The question is considered important because if Soviet foreign policy is based on an explicit theory, accurate interpretation of past and present and reliable prediction of future Soviet policy would perhaps be possible. It is far less common, however, to find in Western literature a detailed consideration of the contents of Soviet theory and the way in which Soviet decision-makers and theorists describe the international system and the Soviet role within it.

This study, therefore, aims to reconstruct the Soviet view of the world by examining the theories used to analyse key aspects of international relations. The themes which will be considered are first, the development of the inevitably conflictual relations between opposing social systems into peaceful coexistence; second, the Soviet view of the Third World and its relationship to the socialist system; third, proletarian internationalism (or relations between socialists) and the development of this concept into socialist internationalism (or relations between socialist states); fourth, questions of war and peace and the Soviet attitude to neutrality and non-alignment; and fifth, the nature of the present international system and the new correlation of forces within it.

It must be stressed that this is not a study of Soviet foreign policy *per se*. Nor is it an examination of the differences between Soviet political actions and theoretical statements, although from time to time it will be apparent that there have been and are differences. It should also be emphasized that although this is a critical study, it is not concerned with making value judgements about the moral rightness or wrongness of Soviet theory or policy. The aim is to examine Soviet theory in two ways. First, the origins and development of the theory relating to the key aspects listed above will be described and, second, the theory will be considered critically in terms of its usefulness in the role which Soviet theorists say that it plays. In other words, an attempt will be made to investigate whether the claims that are made by Soviet theorists and policy-makers for their theory are justified. In the final chapter some suggestions will also be offered about other, unacknowledged roles that are played by Soviet theory.

Before any judgement can be made about whether Soviet theory justifies the claims made for it by theorists and policy-makers, the functions it is said to fulfil must be understood. This in turn requires some conception of the importance accorded to theory in the Soviet Union and the connection between theory and ideology. It also requires an understanding of who makes theory, particularly since the task is not left entirely to scholars. Soviet political leaders often use public occasions to enunciate or reiterate aspects of Soviet theory, signalling the acceptability of certain interpretations and the inadmissability of others. This affects the nature of the sources that an analyst needs to use in studying Soviet theory. These are the questions which will be considered in the rest of this chapter. First the nature and status of theory in the Soviet Union will be discussed. This will be followed by a brief consideration of who makes theory in the USSR, which in turn will lead to an explanation of the sources which have been used in this study. The chapter will end with a summary of the structure of the rest of the work.

THE NATURE AND STATUS OF INTERNATIONAL RELATIONS THEORY IN THE SOVIET UNION

In the West the phenomenon of the politician (or indeed the academic) who denies the usefulness of theory is common. In the Soviet Union the reverse is true. All published scholars work within the framework of officially accepted philosophy, doing what Kuhn (1970) termed 'normal science'. All politicians maintain that they make their foreign-policy decisions on the basis of the Marxist-Leninist theory of international relations. Indeed, a distinction between theory and practice would not be accepted in Soviet philosophy. One of the methodological principles which forms the cornerstone of that philosophy is the unity of theory and practice. Marxist social science is said by Soviet theorists to be characterized by unity, since it contains 'a close fusion of theory and practice and . . . unity of theoretical and empirical levels of research' (Rumyantsev 1984: 83). Theory and practice are considered interdependent: there can be no practice without theory and no valid theory without practice. Soviet philosophers believe that theory fulfils the function of organizing, mobilizing and transforming. It is also the means of foreseeing the outlines of future development and therefore of being able to pursue a scientifically grounded policy (Kharin 1981: 41–8). Soviet writers often quote Lenin's dictum that 'without a revolutionary theory there can be no revolutionary movement' (Lenin 1902: 369) to indicate the importance of theory. Stalin maintained that theory gives

confidence, the power of orientation, and an understanding of the inherent connection between surrounding events; . . . it alone can help practice to discern not only how and in which direction classes are moving at the present time, but also how and in which direction they will move in the near future.

(Stalin 1924a: 15)

Although Stalin has seldom been cited by name since 1956, Soviet scholars have continued to use similar phraseology to explain the value of theory (see, for example, Il'ichev *et al.* 1958: 101).

But theory, in turn, must be closely connected to practice. The classical thinkers discovered the general laws of society. Society, however, changes, and Soviet philosophers believe that it is the task of theoreticians to incorporate the changes into new theoretical generalizations (Rumyantsev 1984: 129). In other words, the empirical facts which arise from practice are vital in updating theory. Soviet scholars accept that facts can be misused, for example by selecting them carefully to support existing theory. One prominent theorist, in defending himself against criticism when his conclusions about the probable future developments of the capitalist economy offended Stalin, warned that 'it is not a matter of enumerating all the facts so that they inevitably lead to the former conclusions of Marxism-Leninism, but to use the Marxist-Leninist method in studying these facts' (Varga, cited in Hoffmann and Fleron 1980: 286).

The Marxist-Leninist method which Soviet scholars use to study facts is called dialectical materialism, defined as 'a materialist approach to all real phenomena (society included), and the dialectical method of cognizing these phenomena' (Rumyantsev 1984: 128–9). In relation to international relations, the dialectical method 'shows the diversity and contradictory nature of international developments in their interconnection, interdependence and constant movement and the dialectical unity of all the counteracting factors' (Israelyan 1967: 48).[1]

The close connection between theory and practice is said by Soviet theorists to apply equally to international relations theory and the practice of Soviet foreign policy:

If the theory of the foreign policy of socialism, based on the teachings of Marxism-Leninism, has become the political compass which determined and determines the concrete foreign policy actions of the Soviet Union in the world arena, the practice of Soviet foreign policy has not only been a school for testing the accuracy of theoretical concepts, but also the basis for working out a number of theoretical propositions and conclusions which are in complete accordance with the theory of scientific communism.

(Sanakoyev and Kapchenko 1977: 263)

The unity of theory and practice and the fact that political actions are based on theory are considered to be great strengths of Soviet foreign policy and amongst the advantages that the socialist system has over the capitalist (Petrenko and Popov 1981: 8). It gives to Soviet foreign policy 'the strength of an orientation which is absent from bourgeois policy' (Il'ichev *et al.*, 1958: 101).

It is not, however, just the unity of policy and theory and the basing of policy on theory that are considered strengths by Soviet academics and decision-makers. The particular nature of the theory is even more important. It is Marxist-Leninist theory and it is, therefore, *scientific*, capable of transforming reality and accurate. It is axiomatic, in Soviet thinking, that Marxism-Leninism is scientific. Marxist-Leninist philosophy, for example, is defined as:

a science studying regularities in the relationship between matter and consciousness, the universal laws of nature, society, and thought, and developing a world outlook and a method of cognising and transforming reality.

(Sheptulin 1978: 27)

Marx's belief that philosophers should do more than just interpret the world, but should endeavour to change it (Marx 1845: 421–3) is thus an integral part of the function of philosophy in Soviet thinking. But Marxism-Leninism consists of more than philosophy. It is said to be 'a scientifically-based system of philosophical, economic and socio-political views' (Rumyantsev 1984: 128). Because it is scientific, it is thought to reflect the objective laws inherent in any particular manifestation of social life (Sokolovskiy 1963: 385). It is this that makes it accurate and enables it to give 'correct scientific answers about the origin and essence of politics in general and of foreign policy in particular' (Selektor 1955: 34).

The fact that the theory has, according to Soviet scholars, withstood the test of time attests to its accuracy. As both theory and method it has been proven by life itself (Trush 1977: 6). As one scholar expressed it, 'history has, in fact, authoritatively certified the truth of scientific communism' (Shakhnazarov 1982: 8). In other words, the predictions made by the founders of Marxism-Leninism are thought to have been realized and this proves that the theory is accurate: the proof of the accuracy of any scientific theory lies in its ability to predict the course of historical development (Varga 1953: 11). It is believed, moreover, to be self-evidently the *only* system of thought that is accurate. One theorist has contended, for example, that 'there is no need to prove the obvious truth that an analysis of international relations can be correct only if it is based on the Leninist methodology' (Gantman, in 'The Moscow Meeting' 1969: 55). The absence of such a methodology in bourgeois analyses and the avoidance of a class approach makes Western foreign-policy theories and concepts 'pseudo-scientific' (Sanakoyev 1975: 108).

The usefulness of Marxism-Leninism is not confined to providing a methodology for historical or contemporary analysis. Its value lies also in its ability to transform or to influence historical development successfully. Soviet theorists maintain that Marxist-Leninist theory has enabled, and still does enable, Soviet politicians to influence the international environment. It does this by giving guidance on which to base current policy and to analyse the correct foreign-policy course for the long-term future (Sanakoyev and Kapchenko 1977: 296). It makes possible the successful forecasting of future international conditions (Kokoshin 1978: 3–10).

Soviet policy-makers and theorists contend that because their policy is based upon a scientific theory, the policy itself is 'a model of scientific objectivity' (Ermolenko 1977: 17).[2] This makes it different from (and more efficacious than) bourgeois foreign policy. The diplomacy of the capitalist states, for example, cannot be considered scientific. It both fails to take proper account of the existing state of affairs and it has aims which contradict the objective laws which determine social development. Indeed, it usually goes against the course of that development and this is the main reason why there have been so many foreign policy miscalculations by the Western countries since the Second World War. Soviet diplomacy, on the other hand, is scientific:

It is built on the foundation of Marxist-Leninist theory, it wields the powerful weapon of a Marxist, i.e. a genuinely scientific, analysis of reality and of knowledge of the laws of historical development.
(Gromyko *et al.* 1960–4, vol. 1:459)[3]

The past successes of Soviet foreign policy are attributed to the scientific nature of policy and theory. It is this that will also guarantee future success, up to and including 'the final historical victory' (Sanakoyev and Kapchenko 1977: 287), in other words, the creation of a socialist world.

Some Western scholars believe that the deference which is paid to theory by Soviet decision-makers makes it important to know what the theory is, or at least what it is said to be (see, for example, McLane 1966: 3 and Boersner 1982: xii). Few of them, however, agree with the Soviet depiction of the relationship between Soviet theory and foreign policy. Opinions differ about whether there is any relationship at all. The expatriate (and ex-Marxist) Polish philosopher Kolakowski believes that 'Marxism has become simply a rhetorical dressing for the Realpolitik of the Soviet empire (Kolakowski 1978, vol. 3: 105). Other non-Soviet scholars maintain that theory fulfils important roles, but that Soviet foreign policy is essentially pragmatic (see, for example, Kennan 1961: 258; McLane 1966: 2; Semmel 1981: 18).

Whatever role Soviet theory is thought to play, however, considerable scepticism has been expressed in the West about whether it retains much connection to Marxist theory or to the methodology of dialectical materialism. As a result of his investigation into Soviet philosophy, Wetter, for example, concludes that 'there is very little left of dialectics . . . it consists, rather, of a materialistic evolutionism decked out in dialectical terminology (Wetter 1958: xi). Similar criticisms have been made of other aspects of Marxism-Leninism, including international relations theory. In relation to the latter, Kennan maintained that Communist doctrine had acquired a 'rubbery consistency' which allowed it to be used as an 'infinitely flexible rationalization for anything whatever the regime finds it advantageous to do' (Kennan 1961: 258). Even less credence is accorded to the claim that Marxism-Leninism, the international relations theory which derives from it and the foreign policy which is based upon it are scientific. Western scholars tend to refer not to Soviet theory but to doctrine or ideology. In non-Soviet definitions 'ideology' is a term which automatically precludes science.

Soviet scholars also often use the terms 'ideology' or 'doctrine', but they use the words as synonyms of 'theory'. They see no contradiction between these terms and science. Socialist ideology is invariably called scientific. One political philosopher defines socialist ideology as 'a scientific system of political, philosophical, legal, moral and aesthetic views' (Mshvenieradze 1981: 122). Elsewhere it has been defined as 'a truly scientific world outlook' (Milovidov 1977: 221). One of the reasons why non-Marxist scholars would disagree with these definitions is their strongly held belief that science ought to be, or at least to strive to be, objective and value-free. While Soviet scholars believe that Marxism-Leninism reveals the objective laws of social development and that dialectical materialism makes it possible to avoid 'deviations from objective truth' (*Marxism-Leninism on War and the Army*

1972: 387),[4] the notion of objectivity implied here differs greatly from Western definitions of the concept. Soviet theorists reject the idea that theory or science can be value-free in the Western sense. They believe that bourgeois scholars who proclaim the objectivity of their scientific thought are merely concealing their partisanship. All systems of ideas are the product of social consciousness and all consciousness is class consciousness. Far from pretending to be non-partisan, dialectical materialism is said to include partisanship in that it 'enjoins the direct and open adoption of the standpoint of a definite social group in any assessment of events' (Lenin 1894: 401). But there is a great difference between bourgeois partisanship and working-class partisanship. The subjectivism of working-class partisanship is not thought to preclude objectivity. On the contrary, the subjective interests of the proletariat (the class whose consciousness is reflected in socialist ideology) coincide with the objective laws of development. Thus proletarian partisanship is not thought to contradict the scientific character of the ideology of the working-class (Milovidov 1977: 220–1).

To summarize, Soviet theorists claim that Soviet international relations theory both forms the basis of Soviet foreign policy and is adjusted as a result of that policy. It is a scientific Marxist-Leninist theory which reflects the objective laws of historical development. But it also influences that development. It allows Soviet foreign policy to be formed and executed in accordance with objective laws, and it gives to policy short- and long-term aims which are concordant with the interests and demands of social progress. In short, it is a means of interpreting the past, a reliable guide to action in the present and an accurate method for forecasting future developments.

The claims made for Soviet theory are thus rather large. Let us leave aside the insistence that Soviet theory and policy are scientific on the grounds that the explanation of what makes them scientific is, in the final analysis, a circular argument. It can be reduced to the contention that the theory is scientific because it is true and accurate and it is true and accurate because it is scientific. It is also scientific because it reflects objective laws. The only proof of the objectivity of the laws, however, is that they have been observed in the past to hold true. But non-Marxist analysts could equally well point to events in the past where they have not held true. In other words, the Soviet view of what constitutes scientific methodology and science is so self-evidently far from Western concepts of science that it is simpler to agree to disagree—arguments about first principles can rarely be resolved. In any case, there is a long-standing debate in the West about whether social science, including international relations, can really be scientific, whether it be Soviet Marxist-Leninist or Western capitalist.

But the other claims made for Soviet theory are no less extensive. They imply a theory which is sufficiently flexible to explain, deal with or encompass any change which occurs in the international system. They also imply a theory which is general enough to incorporate new phenomena in international relations and powerful enough to influence the way in which international relations develop. In fact, Soviet theory has often found it difficult to adapt to change. There has tended to be a considerable lag between change in the real world and the adaptation of theory to reflect it. It has also experienced problems in incorporating new phenomena. While the *existence* of the Soviet Union has influenced the way in which international relations have developed, it is much less clear that the application of Soviet theory has played any part in the developments, except in so far as Soviet foreign policy has been based on theory. The relationship between theory and practice, however, has been far less simple and immediate than Soviet theorists suggest. Moreover, concurrent with the prodigious claims made for existing Soviet theory, there have been continual demands over the years for more and better theory (see, for example, Butenko 1975: 39–84; Ermolenko 1977: 12; Brezhnev 1976a: 86). This suggests that Soviet international relations theory is less comprehensive and less useful than has been claimed. It can also be argued that Soviet foreign policy has been less successful than Soviet theorists would have us believe. If it has, indeed, been based on theory, then the theory must sometimes have turned out to be less than infallible. In examining the key aspects of international relations theory which form the contents of the rest of this study, some of the reasons why Soviet theory has fallen short of the claims made for it will become clear.

WHO FORMULATES SOVIET INTERNATIONAL RELATIONS THEORY?

To say that Soviet theory has responded slowly to change is not to imply that contemporary theory is indistinguishable from the original writing of Marx and Lenin. Soviet international relations theory has, of course, changed over the years and it is these changes that form the subject-matter of this study. In some respects, the result has sometimes been a theory which seems to have little in common with its origins, although Soviet writers continue to insist that the works of Marx, Engels and Lenin are vital ingredients of contemporary theory. Sometimes, previously accepted aspects of theory have been discarded or repudiated. What makes this confusing for analysts of Soviet theory is that rejections have rarely been made explicit (except when they have been part of a power struggle in which the defeat of the vanquished has included ritual public criticism and the insistence on recantation). It is rare to find in Soviet literature an explanation that a particular aspect of theory turned out to be mistaken, or an analysis of why it was wrong. Instead, that particular aspect will merely be omitted, or a new interpretation will be presented as if that has always been the way in which it has been interpreted.[5]

On the other hand, when changes have occurred and have seemed to be dramatically new—the revisions announced by Khrushchev at the Twentieth Congress of the Communist Party of the Soviet Union (CPSU) are a case in point—they can often be seen in retrospect to have been incubating for some time before their public proclamation. This, too, is confusing, in that it is rarely possible to follow the genesis and development of new ideas as they occur. A further confusion arises from the fact that new aspects of theory have sometimes been added which are inconsistent with older theoretical premises. The latter have not, however, been discarded. Moreover, explanations have sometimes been transferred from one level of analysis to others where, to non-Soviet theorists at least, they seem to fit less well, if at all. But one looks in vain for critical responses from other Soviet scholars. The consequence is that theoretical debate is rare in Soviet literature. The cause, in part, is the way in which Soviet theory is formulated.

It can be argued that there was very little Soviet international relations theory before the Brezhnev era. Political science is a young subject in the Soviet Union, international relations an even younger branch of it. In the 1950s and 1960s, while Western scholars were polemizing in the traditional–behavioural debate (see, for example, Knorr and Rosenau 1969), their Soviet would-be counterparts were arguing over the establishment of international relations as an independent field of enquiry. The previous official position had been that Marxism-Leninism *was* political science and provided a ready-made theory of international relations. If Stalinism imposed an official line and made dissent impossible in subjects like linguistics and genetics, what need could there be for academic research, debate and writing on politics or international relations?[6] And how could opposing views possibly exist? It was only in the Brezhnev era that a group of respectable and respected international relations specialists (called *mezhdunarodniki*) emerged and international relations became a recognized and established field of academic study.[7] There had always been Soviet books and articles on international relations, but they were the works of politicians or exegetists of Marxist-Leninist doctrine (with the occasional contribution by historians or international lawyers). In the late 1960s and 1970s, the number of books and articles on international relations multiplied, the range of topics they covered was greatly extended and many of them were the work of professional *mezhdunarodniki*. However, although the discipline had become an independent field of study, the theory was still said to be based on Marxism-Leninism. And since some of the most influential professional theorists worked in the Central Committee apparatus, international relations theory remained primarily the preserve of the CPSU.

These two facts—that international relations theory was once formulated by specialists in Marxist-Leninist ideology and that it has remained primarily the preserve of the Party—have led to the curious way in which theory changes in the

Soviet Union. Perhaps the most descriptive term to use for it is 'democratic centralism'. Originally, democratic centralism was the organizational principle on which Lenin based his vision of the Bolshevik Party. After 1921, when the decree on Party Unity effectively made all opposition disloyal (Carr 1966 vol. 1: 206–19), it gradually became the way in which the whole of Soviet society was organized. As an organizational principle it implied strict subordination of lower Party organs to higher. It permitted free discussion (about policy or theory) until a decision had been reached, after which the decision would be binding on everyone. Under Stalin the element of free discussion eventually disappeared. There sometimes *was* discussion, but it tended to be orchestrated rather than free (a good example is the publication of the 1936 Constitution as a draft discussion document before it became law). The people who had participated in the free discussions of the 1920s paid a high price in the 1930s; those who had taken positions opposed to Stalin's became early victims of the purges. From then onwards the correct theory or opinion was handed down, and it became the only possible theory or opinion. After Stalin's death the penalty for holding opinions and theories which diverged from those of the leader and therefore from accepted conventional wisdom became far less severe. But there *were* penalties and, in any case, the habits of controversy and non-conformity had been lost. Thus, while democratic centralism does not operate with the same ferocity as it did in Stalin's time, to a considerable (and, to those unfamiliar with the Soviet Union, surprising) extent this is still the way that Soviet society works.[8]

As a model of how theory has been and is formulated and changed in the Soviet Union, democratic centralism implies that it is not that theoretical change does not occur, but that it is centrally directed and it occurs uniformly. In practical terms this means that a close reading of the work of prominent theorists (particularly those who hold positions in the Central Committee apparatus) may give some intimation that theoretical change is likely to occur. But it is only after a particular aspect of theory has been given an imprimatur by the political leadership that it will be taken up widely. It will then be binding on all theorists. Explaining that particular phenomenon or event (or analogous phenomena and events) in any other way will not be acceptable (and is unlikely to be printed). One Western scholar describes the process in this way:

Of course . . . even in the Soviet Communist Party, opinions change. What was heresy yesterday is orthodoxy today. But . . . the Party takes care to make the position plain . . . *at any one moment* it teaches the *same thing* throughout the length and breadth of the Soviet Union.

(Vigor 1975: 4)*

This is not to suggest that the political leadership necessarily has either the time or the ability to indulge in theoretical development, innovation and amendment. Theory almost certainly originates amongst theorists. But to be successfully accepted and widely known, it needs to capture the attention of an important political leader (best of all, the General Secretary of the CPSU, but the 'ideological secretary' is almost as good; Suslov, for example, was extremely influential in formulating the Soviet view of the Sino-Soviet dispute). If it does so, it will be publicized in political speeches or be embedded in the contents of political programmes and communiqués. The publicity will act as a signal that a particular concept or interpretation is acceptable. It will then be taken up by theorists and receive the status of conventional wisdom. The political leader or the political document in which it was first publicly mentioned will usually be given the credit for formulating the theory in the introduction to countless articles which develop it.[9] New efforts in theory building have been initiated in the same way, first being mentioned in speeches in which the need for work in a particular field is expressed (see, for example, Brezhnev's Central Committee report to the Twenty-Fifth Party Congress, in Brezhnev 1976a: 86–7) and then being taken up by theorists.

This description of how theoretical change usually takes place in the Soviet Union refers, of course, to important concepts which are too close to the essence of Marxist-Leninist teaching to be left entirely to theorists. More peripheral theoretical concerns can be and are left to them. Differences of opinion occur and theoretical debates can be

---

*Emphasis original unless otherwise stated.

found about less important aspects of theory. This is not, however, to imply that the theories so produced would necessarily not meet with the approval of the political leadership. For one thing, the parameters of the debate will, of course, be provided by Marxism-Leninism. For another, the distinction between the political and academic establishments which often seems so total in the West, is far less marked in the Soviet Union. Most theorists (certainly the more influential amongst them) are members of the CPSU; a few are members or candidate members of the Central Committee. Whether or not this allows them a direct input into foreign-policy decision-making (and they probably have little to do with day-to-day policy), it means that they almost certainly share the values and the perceptions of the political leadership. As far as more momentous subjects are concerned, like the inevitability of war (before Stalin's death), the need for peaceful coexistence (after Stalin's death) or the definition of what characterizes the present historical era, the analyst looks in vain for different 'schools of thought'.

Thus theory building and elaboration in the Soviet Union probably does take place in the specialist international relations institutes and in the Central Committee apparatus, where some prominent theorists work.[10] But the theory is communicated upwards, and only if it is acceptable there will it be publicized to the academic and the wider community. But before that happens, it is likely that it will have been taken up by the political leadership and it may later seem to have originated at the top level of the political hierarchy. This has important consequences for the kinds of sources which must be used in studying Soviet international relations theory. Something needs to be said, therefore, about the sources which have been used in this study.

THE SOURCES USED TO EXAMINE SOVIET INTERNATIONAL RELATIONS THEORY

Since one of the aims of this study has been to examine the development of Soviet international relations theory, amongst the major sources that have been used in preparing it have been those writings of Marx, Engels and Lenin which, according to past and contemporary theorists, form the basis of contemporary theory. This study is not, however, an attempt to extrapolate an international relations theory from the entire *oeuvre* of these authors.[11] The subject of this study is *Soviet* international relations theory, and Soviet theorists use the Marxist-Leninist classics selectively. Attention has thus been concentrated on those ideas in the work of the classical Marxist-Leninist writers which are said by contemporary theorists to be relevant. Occasionally, however, it has been necessary to examine the context in which the classical theorists have expressed particular points of view or to see whether they have expressed alternative views at other times. It has also sometimes seemed important to check whether and why Soviet theorists have selected certain aspects of the theory and ignored others, or exalted as theory something which was clearly an *ad hoc* statement.[12] This has particularly been the case with references to Lenin's writings, where Soviet writers quite often use the term 'theory' to refer to post-1917 statements that were patently made in response to the pressure of events and have little in common with carefully thought-out theory. It is interesting, in this connection, to compare what Chicherin said about Lenin and foreign policy:

Vladimir Il'ich himself never outlined the Soviet republic's foreign policy in its entirety and in the form of a systematically worked out plan. Its structure and development were in his head . . . Only some general principles, some basic concepts of his foreign policy were set out by him in a general form.

(Chicherin 1961: 276)

with what modern scholars claim for him:

By the time the socialist revolution occurred in Russia Lenin had scientifically elaborated the main principles and trends of socialism's foreign policy. He solved the primary problems of the Communist Party's strategy and tactics, and expounded his views on the main issues of the working class's international policy. Consequently, by the time the Russian proletariat took power, the Party had already been equipped with a Marxist-Leninist doctrine of socialist foreign policy.

(Sanakoyev 1972: 176)

From what has been said about the way in which theory is formulated and changed in the Soviet Union it will be clear that it is not just the writings of academic theorists which are of interest to the analyst of Soviet theory. Political speeches, communiqués and Party reports are equally relevant. Indeed, they are often referred to by Soviet authors as the place where Marxist-Leninist international relations theory is best expressed and most creatively developed. After the 1969 International Meeting of Communist and Workers' Parties, for example, the editorial board of *International Affairs* held a seminar to discuss the meeting. Most speakers commented on the proceedings in words similar to these:

The material of the Moscow Meeting . . . contains propositions and conclusions which are a further development of Marxist-Leninist theory and scientifically elaborate the chief issues of our time, in particular the pressing problems of present-day international relations.

('The Moscow Meeting' 1969: 53)

Similar claims have been made for other declarations and statements issued after international meetings of Communist Parties (see, for example, Sovetov 1964). One of the theorists who participated in the *International Affairs* seminar later maintained that the documents of Party Congresses and plenary meetings, joint statements by government and Party leaders of socialist states, documents of the international communist movement, contain 'theoretical generalizations' and 'a profound analysis of the alignment of class and political forces' which 'contribute to the theoretical elaboration of foreign policy' (Sanakoyev 1975: 118). Another theorist similarly claimed that scientific research into the new type of international relations which resulted from the formation of a socialist system was based on the theory in the classics of Marxism-Leninism and the documents of the Communist and Workers' Parties of the socialist countries and of the international communist movement (Butenko 1975: 39). To the list of Party documents and Congress reports, other theorists add the speeches of Brezhnev, Suslov, Gromyko, Ponomarev and other political leaders (Petrenko and Popov 1981: 147–53). This may, of course, merely be an elaborate form of lip-service, but since such importance is attributed to these documents by Soviet theorists, it behoves non-Soviet scholars to consult them, and they have formed one of the sources which have been used in the preparation of this study.

Most of the sources used in describing contemporary theory

have, however, been articles and books written by Soviet *mezhdunarodniki* themselves. An attempt has been made to use as wide a selection as possible of different sources for any particular period of history or any one theme. Sometimes, however, one scholar is so dominant in a particular period or in relation to a particular aspect of theory that it has been difficult to find alternative sources to demonstrate that a point of view is generally shared by the Soviet academic community. English versions have usually been cited when they are available (and therefore the publication dates which appear in the text and bibliography are sometimes a couple of years later than the publication dates of the original Russian books).

THE STRUCTURE OF THE REST OF THIS STUDY

To apply terms which are commonly used in linguistics, this is both a diachronic and a synchronic study. It is diachronic because it examines the historical, or classical, writings which, according to contemporary Soviet theorists, form the basis of current Soviet theory and looks at some of the changes which have occurred in the way classical theory is interpreted. It is synchronic in that it pays particular attention to the theory of a particular period of Soviet history, namely the period that spans the tenure as General Secretary of the CPSU, first of Nikita Khrushchev and then of Leonid Brezhnev.

The starting point of the study was dictated by Soviet theorists. Since they claim direct descent from Marx and Engels, this is where the analysis begins. The initial cut-off point was intended to be the death of Brezhnev. However, there are indications that the theoretical changes which have begun under Gorbachev will continue and will seem as radical as the revisions in Marxism-Leninism announced by Khrushchev at the Twentieth Party Congress in 1956. And just as the genesis of Khrushchev's changes were later seen to predate Stalin's demise, in time it will probably be clear that the origins of the new theory are to be sought before Gorbachev's accession to the general secretaryship. The study, therefore, ends with a brief examination of the origins and present state of Gorbachev's 'new political thinking'. The reason for concentrating on the period during which Khrushchev and Brezhnev were, in turn, General Secretary of the CPSU is that it was then that international relations became an independent discipline and that Soviet scholars began to interest themselves seriously in international relations theory. In the chapters that follow, key aspects of Soviet theory will be examined to see what changes have occurred and to consider whether the theory can, as Soviet scholars claim, explain the past, guide the present and predict the future.

In choosing which aspects of theory to analyse, the intention has been to provide as full a picture as possible of the Soviet view of the world. Soviet theorists contend that the relations which occur at an international level between socialist and capitalist states are cardinally different from those which are enjoyed among socialist states or between socialist states and newly independent, less-developed countries (LDCs). Accordingly, these three kinds of international relations are examined separately in the following three pairs of chapters. The first chapter of each pair deals with pre-1956 theory and the second with the Khrushchev and Brezhnev period.

The question of the order in which to examine the three kinds of relations turned out to be awkard. In practice the three kinds of relations have taken place simultaneously. Historically, they were all established at the same time (although socialist–socialist state relations were established last, Party relations predated them and influenced in significant ways the conception of acceptable socialist inter-state relations). Each seemingly logical choice of which category should begin the analysis produced illogical side-effects because of the inevitable overlap and interaction between categories. The order which has finally been chosen may seem idiosyncratic in terms of the importance of the three types of state to the Soviet Union. It has been based on two criteria: first, the immediate salience of relations with capitalist states after the revolution and, second, the central role of China in the development of Soviet theory. Relations between socialist and capitalist states are thus dealt with first. And since Soviet theory about the Chinese revolution prior to 1949 falls into the category of relations with LDCs, these relations are examined before inter-socialist relations (which include relations with China after the revolution).

Chapters 2 and 3 deal with the development of peaceful coexistence. In 1956 Khrushchev proclaimed that peaceful coexistence was the basis of Soviet relations with the capitalist countries. Moreover, he maintained that the Soviet Union had always based its relations on that principle. It was defined as the absence of military conflict, together with continuing competition in the economic and ideological spheres. Peaceful coexistence is not, in the Soviet view, inconsistent with Soviet support for the capitalist working class and international revolution. The origin of the concept and practice of peaceful coexistence is examined in Chapter 2, while its development into one of the twin pillars of Soviet foreign policy is traced in Chapter 3.

When decolonization began after the Second World War, the Soviet Union was in the throes of post-war reconstruction and preoccupied by the deteriorating state of relations among the erstwhile allies. To begin with, little notice was taken of the cracks in the pre-war empires (except for those countries which had immediately begun fighting to become socialist). When more serious attention began to be directed towards the colonies, Soviet theorists became convinced that Lenin's predictions about imperialism being the final stage of a moribund capitalism were proving true. They expected that many of the newly independent countries would become socialist. By the late 1960s, however, there was some disillusion with developments in the Third World (indeed, the fact that there *was* a Third World was, in itself, disappointing). By the late 1970s it had become debatable whether profoundly underdeveloped states could or should attempt to embark on a socialist path. This is the area of Soviet theory where both theoretical and practical problems have been most intractable. Chapter 4 considers the attitudes of Marx and Engels towards the colonies and Lenin's expectations of the national liberation movement. The theoretical dilemmas after decolonization form the subject-matter of Chapter 5.

One of the most frequently encountered assertions in Soviet writing is that relations among socialist states are 'a new type of international relations', distinct in important ways from relations between capitalist states or between capitalist and socialist states. The theoretical explanation of what characterizes the new type of international relations has involved transposing the principle of proletarian internationalism (which governs relations between socialists and between socialist parties) to the inter-state level, where it is called socialist internationalism. Yet the history of inter-socialist relations and the theoretical debates that have arisen from the various crises which have occurred in the socialist commonwealth suggest that the transposition has not occurred without practical and theoretical difficulty. The evolution from proletarian to socialist internationalism is examined in Chapters 6 and 7. Here, too, the first of the two chapters considers the theory before 1956, and the second looks at the theoretical and practical problems of relations within the socialist system after de-Stalinization.

Chapters 8 and 9 are thematic rather than geographic. Both concern the way in which Soviet theory has adapted to, incorporated and posited change in the international system. According to Soviet policy-makers and theorists, avoidance of war and preservation of peace have always been the highest priority goals of Soviet foreign policy. These aims have co-existed, however, with the deep conviction that war is inevitable and the belief (seemingly confirmed by the 1917 Revolution and the changes which occurred after 1945) that war can have the effect of speeding up socialist revolution. The combination of these two sets of views presented a paradox to Soviet theory which was only partially resolved by the recognition in 1956 that war could not be inevitable in a nuclear age. A further problem has been encountered in incorporating the theory and practice of neutrality, particularly in its modern manifestations of permanent neutrality (or neutralism) and non-alignment, in what is essentially a dichotomous view of the world. Chapter 8 deals with the changes that have occurred in the Soviet theory of war and peace and in attitudes towards neutrality.

The importance accorded to the correlation of forces is relatively recent. Soviet theorists and policy-makers maintain that the correlation has changed since the Second World War and that it is continuing to change in favour of socialism. They assert that the concept differs in significant ways from Western balance of power ideas. In Chapter 9 the way in which they characterize the differences are examined, as well as their reasons for saying that the correlation of forces has changed in favour of socialism. The implications of Gorbachev's 'new political thinking' for Soviet international relations theory are considered in Chaper 10. Finally, an endeavour is made to evaluate the methodology and content of Soviet theory so as to consider whether it can fulfil the role ascribed to it. The study ends with some suggestions about why theory is so important in the Soviet Union.

NOTES

1.　Wetter points out that until Stalin's work on dialectical materialism in 1938, Soviet philosophy adopted Engels' interpretation and three basic laws of dialectical materialism: the law of the mutual inter-penetration of opposites; the law of the transformation of quantity into quality; and the law of the negation of the negation (Wetter 1958: 310–18). Stalin laid down four features of dialectical materialism: the general connection between phenomena in nature and society; the continuous movement and development of phenomena in nature and society; development as the transition from quantitative to qualitative change; development as the struggle between opposites (Stalin 1938: 591–618). Historical materialism was 'the extension of the principles of dialectical materialism . . . to the study of society and of its history' (Stalin 1938: 591). It was important to use the historical mode in investigating social phenomena. The combination of an historical approach and the dialectical method enabled history to become 'as precise a science as . . . biology' (Stalin 1938: 601). In this way history made scientific prediction of the future possible and could be used for practical purposes. In the late 1940s dialectical materialism was seen as a universal methodology without which no science could exist. It was 'an instrument of scientific investigation, a method penetrating all natural and social sciences' (Zhdanov 1947b: 10). It is still called 'the universal method of modern science', but a warning is added that 'analysis of the facts cannot be replaced by references to general propositions of dialectics' (Kharin 1981: 249, 251).

2.　The claim that Soviet foreign policy is scientific can be found in most Soviet books on international relations, whether they are historical or theoretical. See Gromyko *et al.*, (1960, vol. 1: 458), *Milestones* (1967: 10) and Sanakoyev and Kapchenko (1973: 6) for other examples. Petrenko and Popov (1981) called the first section of their book 'The Scientific and Theoretical Basis of the International Politics of the CPSU and the Soviet State'.

3.　This quote comes from the first edition of *Diplomatichesky slovar'* (Diplomatic Dictionary). The fourth edition (1984, vol. 1; 1985, vol. 2;

edited by A. A. Gromyko, A. G. Kovalev, P. P. Sevost'yanov and S. L. Tikhvinsky) does not mention whether or not bourgeois diplomacy is scientific. But Soviet diplomacy is still said to be built on a scientific basis, that is 'Marxism-Leninism, the principles of dialectical and historical materialism' (1984, vol. 1: 328).

4. Wetter distinguishes between Engels, who rejected the idea that there was an ultimate truth that could be discovered and the Soviet view that absolute truth is attainable by dialectical materialism (Wetter 1958: 52–3). Absolute truth, once attained, leaves no room for theoretical development, however. Since Stalin, some philosophers have retreated from claiming absolute truth. The truth and irrevocability of the fundamental propositions of Marxism-Leninism have been proved, but this 'in no way signifies that every tenet put forward by Marxists is an absolute truth in its final form' (Rumyantsev 1984: 219).

5. There is a similar problem with changes in Soviet policy. Changes do, of course, occur, but they are infrequently admitted to be changes. It is even rarer to find an admission that a previous policy was mistaken. The laborious and lengthy process of theoretical change is described by Hough, who cogently sums up Soviet reluctance to admit that change has taken place: 'Any change in Soviet policy, when acknowledged at all, is described as the natural response of a perfectly consistent program to differences in conditions' (Hough 1980: 509).

6. In 1950 Stalin wrote 'Marxism and Linguistics' (1950: 407–44) to put an end to the dominance of the theories of N. Y. Marr (who maintained that language has a class structure and therefore was part of the superstructure). As far as genetics were concerned, Stalin supported T. D. Lysenko (who held that acquired characteristics could be inherited), who completely controlled Soviet biology, agricultural science and genetics until 1965. For an account of the effects of Lysenko on Soviet science, see Zhores A. Medvedev (1969) and David Joravsky (1970). Berki (1971) offers an interesting analysis of why international relations presents a particular problem for Marxism. In volume 1 of the Diplomatic Dictionary published in 1960, the efforts of bourgeois scholars to construct a science of international relations or international politics were derided as 'artificial and unfounded'. An understanding of the subject required a combination of history, economics, international and domestic law (Gromyko *et al.* (1960, vol. 1: 458).

7. The need for area specialists and international relations theorists was recognized while Khrushchev was in office. It took time, however, for institutes to be established and specialists to emerge. There are a number of interesting Western studies of the development of political science and international relations in the Soviet Union. See, for example, Powell and Shoup (1970), Theen (1971), Zimmerman (1971), Goormaghtigh (1974), Lynch (1984).

8. There are signs that Gorbachev intends changing the system, having recognized the extent to which it stifles initiative and responsibility. His call for *glasnost'* (openness) certainly seemed to be a demand that past mistakes be recognized and admitted. Moreover, the kind of economic discussions which took place in his first year as General

Secretary suggested radical changes in the status and nature of theory. Whether he will succeed in changing something that seems to have become part of Soviet political culture remains to be seen.

9.   There are other views about the extent to which democratic centralism still reigns in Soviet theory. Hough (1980), for example, maintains that published views can no longer be assumed to represent official doctrine. They may be an attempt to criticize that doctrine, or to draw attention to phenomena or interpretations that have been neglected. They may also represent propagandistic statements to a mass domestic or foreign audience. Hough may be correct in some instances. Propagandistic aims, however, can quickly be detected from the type of journal or the size of the edition of a book in which the view appears. If the intention is criticism of official doctrine or the rein-statement of neglected theory, a refutation will almost certainly be published quite quickly unless the view has official support.

10.   To mention just three contemporary theorists who hold positions in the Central Committee apparatus and who will be quoted frequently in this work, Brutents and Ul'yanovsky are both deputy heads in the Third World section of the Central Committee International Department, while Shakhnazarov was deputy head of the department responsible for liaison with foreign Communist parties, and has been promoted by Gorbachev to first deputy head.

11.   For an interesting synthesis of the international relations theory of Marx, Engels and Lenin, see Kubálková and Cruickshank (1980, 1985). It is ironic (given the usually sensitive Soviet response to views that are considered anti-Soviet) that although these authors are critical of Soviet theory and policy, they have been favourably quoted by Soviet theorists because they recognize that there *is* a Soviet theory. See, for example, Petrenko and Popov (1981: 8–9). For a critique of Kubálková and Cruickshank, see Halliday (1987).

12.   The implication, of course, is that selection by Soviet theorists has sometimes served the purpose of finding evidence to support current theory, while ignoring evidence which refutes it. In the course of making this study the author has been particularly aware of the danger that selection can turn into selectivity designed to serve preconceived ideas. Every effort has been made to avoid this temptation. But the author agrees with the Soviet view of the inherent partisanship of scholarship and therefore understands that the endeavour has probably only been partly successful.

2 Relations Between Socialists and Capitalists I: Peaceful Coexistence Under Lenin and Stalin

The frequent insistence by Soviet political leaders and international theorists after 1956 that peaceful coexistence was one of the two Leninist principles which had always underpinned Soviet foreign policy (the other was proletarian internationalism, which will be discussed in Chapters 6 and 7) may appear to be no more than an example of the constant need to legitimize present Soviet policies by finding doctrinal support from the Marxist-Leninist classics. The invocation of Lenin was certainly intended to reinforce the orthodoxy of both the theory and practice of peaceful coexistence, but it is a fact that the term was used by Lenin (although he preferred the Russian word, *sozhitel'stvo*, cohabitation, to the word currently used for coexistence, *sosushchestvovanie*). It was used as well by Trotsky (1917: 163, 165 and 326). [1] However, to call this early use of the phrase 'theory' is, perhaps, to elevate it beyond the context in which Lenin coined the expression. In fact, Stalin also often maintained that Soviet foreign policy was based on the principle of peaceful coexistence, but once the process of de-Stalinization had begun, his use of the term was ignored by Soviet writers on Soviet international theory. In other words, contemporary Soviet theorists are factually correct in claiming that Soviet foreign *policy* has always been based on peaceful coexistence, but whether that policy has always been based on a *theory* of amity between socialists and capitalists is arguable.

If peaceful coexistence is defined as competition between socialist and capitalist states stopping short of military confrontation, from October 1917 onwards this has certainly been the aim of successive Soviet leaders. With the exception of the fourteen-nation intervention in the Civil War, the Polish War, the Winter War and the terrible experience of the Great Patriotic War, Soviet theorists can justly maintain that they have been reasonably successful in implementing the principle in their relations with capitalist states. It is also the case that peaceful coexistence has been a consistent theme in Soviet writing about foreign policy. But contemporary Soviet scholars claim more than continuity of theory and policy. They imply that the content of peaceful coexistence has remained constant and that the only change has been in historical circumstance, which, in turn, has required different ways of implementing the theory. Examining Lenin's brief references to the principle and comparing them with later versions of the theory suggests, however, that both the intent and the content have changed more radically than post-Stalin leaders and theorists have cared to admit.

In terms of the history of Soviet foreign policy peaceful coexistence became a necessity as soon as the Revolution had occurred, although it was not until the Civil War was over that the Bolshevik leadership had the opportunity to practise it. It entailed business-like relations with the capitalist world which would enable the Russian economy to be rebuilt. After Lenin's death it was adopted by Stalin and was an essential element in his doctrine of socialism in one country. Although it retained its business-like connotation, it gradually came to be envisaged as a long-term strategy. In the 1930s, when collective security seemed to be the only way that fascism could be halted, peaceful coexistence was even more important as a means of convincing the capitalist countries that the Soviet Union was a worthwhile ally. The attempt to negotiate with Britain and France failed, but the theory turned out to be a useful way of explaining the pact with Nazi Germany. Throughout the Cold War which followed the victory over Germany in the Second World War, the Soviet leadership continued to claim that their foreign policy was based upon peaceful coexistence.

Thus the concept of peaceful coexistence was well established before Khrushchev promoted it to one of the main principles of Soviet foreign policy. In this chapter the origin and development of the term is examined by considering, first, Lenin's use of it and then Stalin's. The third part of the chapter deals with the status of peaceful coexistence during the Cold War. By the time Stalin died, it was beginning to be clear that the concept presented certain theoretical difficulties which would need to be resolved if capitalists were to believe in its sincerity and socialists were to retain faith in Soviet support for international revolution.

PEACEFUL COEXISTENCE IN MARXISM AND LENINISM

Its is beyond the capabilities of even the most astute Soviet specialists to find much doctrinal support for the theory or practice of peaceful coexistence in the works of Marx and Engels (Trush 1977: 32–3). The best that can be done is to attribute to Marx and Engels the prevision that a temporary simultaneous existence of states with two opposing social systems would be possible (Petrenko and Popov 1981: 114–15). But there is considerable evidence that both Marx and Engels thought that the Revolution would occur ' "all at once" and simultaneously' (Marx and Engels 1965: 47) and therefore the question of peaceful coexistence did not arise in their work (see the commentary by Kubálková and Cruickshank 1985: 36–7).

It was Lenin who really turned the idea of the simultaneous existence of different kinds of states into theory in his development of the view that he shared with Trotsky that one of the features of monopoly capitalism was its uneven development (Lenin 1915c: 339–43; see Trotsky 1906, in Trotsky 1962: 161–254). This meant that a socialist revolution would not necessarily be international, but would begin at the weakest link of the capitalist chain and only then spread to the rest of the capitalist world. It followed that until the revolution spread, socialism and capitalism would exist simultaneously (Lenin 1916e: 77–93). But Lenin did not then lay particular emphasis on this intervening stage, since he did not expect it to be prolonged. The first revolution would act as the spark for the rest, and the success of the first would depend upon this (see Ch. 6 for a more detailed discussion of his argument). It was only after the October Revolution that he seriously contemplated the consequences of the absence of immediate revolution elsewhere. Peaceful coexistence became the tactical means by which the Soviet state could survive until the international revolution occurred. The length of time for which it was thought it would endure increased as the prospect of other revolutions diminished.

Since most of Lenin's theoretical work was written before the Revolution, and before he seriously considered the possibility or necessity of peaceful coexistence, there is very little in his major works which can be related to the concept. Later Soviet writers are correct in attributing the use of the term to him, but their insistence that it was one of his important theories is rather exaggerated. Nor can it be considered part of a well thought out and elaborated programme of socialist foreign policy. Indeed, Chicherin maintained that 'before the October revolution no attempt was ever made to work out a programme of the foreign policy of a socialist state in the midst of capitalist states' (Chicherin 1961: 276). He also pointed out that Lenin's contribution to Bolshevik foreign policy after the Revolution was made on an *ad hoc* basis, since the speed and intensity of events made the thorough, time-consuming labour of constructing and writing theory impossible. Thus, much of the coherence that there is in Lenin's theoretical pronouncements after the Revolution has been imposed by his successors.[2] A consummate politician, Lenin was unafraid of changing his mind, adapting or even reversing theory if it advanced his cause. And his cause after the Revolution was pre-eminently the survival of the Bolshevik state. It was to ensure this survival that he advanced the idea of peaceful coexistence.

Lenin saw peaceful coexistence essentially in instrumental terms, first in relation to offering concessions to capitalist firms and then to reintegrating Soviet Russia into the international economic system. The announcement and practice of peaceful coexistence would reassure the capitalist world that Bolshevik Russia was essentially peaceable. Thus war would be prevented and the urgent task of reconstructing the Russian economy could proceed. The idea was predicated on Lenin's conviction that imperialists were, above all, businessmen, more interested in profit than in ideology. Russia required a 'breathing space' (the need for a breathing space or *peredyshka* was a universal theme after the Revolution), and peaceful coexistence was how it was to be achieved. His first mention in 1919 of 'the coexistence side by side of socialist and capitalist states' was made in connection with the need to attract foreign technical aid by granting concessions to foreign firms (Lenin 1919e: 39). This set the context in which he was always to use the phrase—the urgent necessity for economic reconstruction. Although peaceful coexistence came to mean rather more than this in the post-Stalin period, it has always retained this economic aspect. Lenin thought that granting concessions to exploit Russia's natural wealth would attract foreign capitalists to invest in the economic future of socialism. Although there were risks involved in using foreign capital, the benefits outweighed any danger. It was not just that Soviet Russia would gain materially by being able to keep a proportion of the production. More importantly, there would be an opportunity to learn both techniques and technology.[3]

The idea that coexistence shifts the inevitable conflict between socialist and capitalist states away from military confrontation to the economic and ideological spheres (a point that is particularly emphasized in modern Soviet explanations of peaceful coexistence) has always been integral to the Soviet definition of the term. Lenin was quick to point out that trade relations did not mean that 'the capitalist wolf would lie down with the socialist lamb' (Lenin 1920f: 452). But it seemed logical that it would be more difficult for capitalist states to go to war with Russia once they had taken up concessions. Thus there were both economic and political arguments in favour of granting them. For the offer to be successful, it had to be preceded by peaceful coexistence, but once accepted, concessions would themselves serve to consolidate peaceful coexistence. Lenin stressed that this did not denote an absence of conflict between socialism and capitalism. The inevitable conflict would merely be transposed to a new sphere, or, in Lenin's words, 'the *war of guns* and tanks yields place to economic warfare' (Lenin 1920f: 459).

Lenin's theme was soon taken up by his fellow Bolsheviks. The treaty signed with Estonia in 1920 was described as 'a dress rehearsal for our agreement with the Entente, our first experience in breaking the blockade and our first experiment in peaceful coexistence with bourgeois states' (Chicherin 1961: 135). Chicherin seemed to be more realistic about the duration of peaceful coexistence than Lenin. Since it was as essential to the capitalist world as it was to Soviet Russia, it would be a prolonged relationship (Chicherin 1961: 145). Lenin was less sure that the 'highly unstable equilibrium' could last, but he was certain that Soviet Russia had to 'make the greatest concessions and sacrifices in order to preserve the peace' (Lenin 1921a: 148–9).

By 1921 the Civil War had ended and the economic system of War Communism had proved a failure. The Kronstadt uprising was the result of this failure. It was put down and a recurrence was averted at the price of the New Economic Policy (NEP) (see Carr 1966, vol. 2, for the introduction of NEP). Peaceful coexistence was an essential ingredient of NEP, since economic development would depend on foreign capital, or, as Lenin phrased it, concessions would be a way of 'directing the development of capitalism into the channels of state capitalism' (Lenin 1921d: 345). But concessions were not enough—Russia had to be reintegrated into the international economic system. This was as important to the capitalist world as it was to the Bolshevik government. The Soviet delegation arrived at the Genoa Conference in 1922 imbued with the confidence instilled by Lenin: they were merchants and the result of their business-like behaviour would be trade on advantageous and politically suitable terms (Lenin 1922a: 212–26). Chicherin (leader of the Soviet delegation) announced at the first session:

'. . . the Russian delegation recognizes that in the present period of history, which permits the parallel existence of the old social order and of the new . . . economic collaboration between the states representing these two systems of property is imperatively necessary for the general economic reconstruction'.

(Chicherin 1922, in Degras, 1951, vol. 1: 298)

Although Lenin also used the term 'peaceful coexistence' to describe ideal political relations—maintaining, for example, that the League of Nations was marked by an absence of anything like peaceful coexistence and that without Russian participation in the settlement of the Middle East question there would remain no grounds for peaceful coexistence (Lenin 1922b: 383–9)—it was primarily in the economic context that he used the term. Moreover, since he never modified his view about the inevitability of war, it remained a tactic aimed at staving off war.

Lenin's successors both broadened the range of relations to which peaceful coexistence applied and gradually extended it from a tactic to a longer-term strategy and then to an abiding principle of Soviet foreign policy. However, since an even older principle has always been the peaceful nature of socialist foreign policy which implies peaceful coexistence on the part of the socialist states, the elevation has had more to do with the expected response from the capitalist world than with any change in Soviet behaviour. In other words, Soviet theorists and policy-makers maintain that the foreign policy of their country has always been based on peaceful coexistence. What has changed is the reaction of capitalist governments to the principle.

STALIN AND PEACEFUL COEXISTENCE BEFORE THE WAR

Stalin won the first round in the struggle for the leadership after Lenin's illness and death by opposing the slogan 'socialism in one country' to Trotsky's theory of permanent revolution. After the 1905 revolution, Trotsky had argued that there would be a permanent state of revolutionary development between the democratic revolution in Russia and the socialist reconstruction of society. He also maintained that socialist reconstruction required constant internal struggle. The domestic revolution would, therefore, be permanent. Finally, he believed that the success of the Russian Revolution depended upon revolution in the advanced countries of Europe. The international dimension of the revolution would thus also be permanent (Trotsky 1962: 8–9). In 1924 Stalin resurrected Trotsky's 1905 theory to attack it in 'Foundations of Leninism' (Stalin 1924a: 1–85). According to Stalin, Trotsky had not understood the important role of the peasantry in the Russian Revolution, and he had underestimated the strength and capacity of the Russian proletariat to lead the peasantry (Stalin 1924a: 24–5). Furthermore, the uneven and spasmodic development of capitalism meant not only that revolution could occur in individual countries, but that the victorious proletariat could and should begin building a socialist society (although the complete and final victory of socialism would require a victorious revolution in several countries). The Russian Revolution was to be regarded, therefore, 'not as a self-sufficient entity but as an aid, as a means of hastening the victory of the proletariat in other countries' (Stalin 1924a: 28).

Skilfully using quotes from Lenin to legitimize his argument, Stalin thus stood the previously expected relationship between the Russian and world revolutions on its head. Far from the former requiring the latter, the former would aid the latter. And it would be able to do so more effectively if, instead of being expected to 'vegetate in its own contradictions and rot away while waiting for the world revolution' (Stalin, 1924c: 93), the Russian Revolution established and consolidated socialism in one country. The building of socialism in one country required the survival of that country in a world of capitalist states. In other words, it was predicated on a period of peaceful coexistence.

Stalin adopted the instrumental sense of Lenin's use of the term peaceful coexistence, often using it in tandem with the phrase 'business-like relations' (see, for example, his political report to the Fourteenth Party Congress 1925a: 294–5). He also, at least to begin with, saw it essentially as a temporary phenomenon, the product of a 'temporary equilibrium of forces', although he pointed out that the expected brief *peredyshka* had become 'a whole period of respite' (Stalin 1925a: 267–8). But each time the international situation deteriorated, he depicted peaceful coexistence as a fragile state of affairs. In 1927, for example, at the height of the war scare,[4] Stalin warned that:

Whereas a year or two ago it was possible and necessary to speak of a period of a certain equilibrium and 'peaceful coexistence' between the USSR and the capitalist countries, to-day we have every reason for asserting that *the period of 'peaceful coexistence' is receding into the past*, giving place to a period of imperialist assaults and preparation for intervention against the USSR.

(Stalin 1927b: 295)

Stalin's depiction of peaceful coexistence as a tactic comes across very clearly in this speech. The intention was said to be to take account of intra-imperialist contradictions and postpone war by 'buying off' the capitalists—the longer war could be warded off, the better would be the Soviet position when it finally occurred (Stalin 1927b: 296). By 1929 the advantages of stretching out the breathing space won at Brest included not only the opportunity to build up the Soviet economy, but also, according to one Soviet theorist, time for Western Communist Parties to bring the working class together and for the national revolutionary movement in the East to develop ('Vneshnyaya politika SSSR bez Lenina', 1929). The origins of peaceful coexistence were firmly attributed to Lenin, and it was said to apply particularly to economic relations.

The idea that peaceful coexistence shifts the capitalist–socialist conflict to non-military spheres was emphasized in the theses adopted at the Sixth Congress of the Communist International (Comintern) in 1928. Great stress was given to the inevitability of war, but the Soviet peace policy was said to be essential to protect the international revolution and allow socialism to be constructed. It did not imply that the Soviet Union had become reconciled to capitalism. On the contrary, it was another, more favourable form of the struggle against capitalism (Eudin and Slusser 1966, vol. 1: 138–9). Both the idea that conflict persists despite peaceful coexistence and the depiction of peaceful coexistence as a particular form of the class struggle were to become important elements of the theory under Khrushchev and Brezhnev. But neither element suited the kind of peaceful coexistence promoted during the Soviet search for collective security in the 1930s.

Despite the hard line taken by Stalin in 1927 and the ultra-revolutionary policy adopted by the Comintern in 1928 at its Sixth Congress, peaceful coexistence soon began to be envisaged as a state of affairs that would last 'until the moment when history carries out its task' (Eudin and Slusser 1967, vol. 2: 437). What is more, it was accorded central importance in Soviet foreign policy. Although the contradictions between the Soviet Union and its capitalist encirclement were said to represent the basic antagonism of the world, 'the problem of the peaceful coexistence of these two systems is the main pivot around which are grouped all the cardinal problems of international politics' (Eudin and Slusser 1967, vol. 2: 437). The Rapallo Treaty (the article which is cited here commemorated the treaty, signed between Germany and Russia in 1922) offered a model of how relations could be established between countries with opposing socio-political systems, but with common economic and foreign-policy interests.

Once the dangers of Nazism had become apparent to the Soviet leadership, the call for peaceful coexistence began to be used in the campaign to establish a collective-security agreement in Europe. As an instrument in this campaign it had perforce to apply to more than the economic relations between different systems of ownership. Thus in his maiden speech at the League of Nations in 1934, Litvinov gave the relationship between the many nations forming the Soviet Union as the best example of peaceful coexistence and went on to point out that the invitation to join the League represented a victory of the principle at the international level. The Soviet Union had always believed that some form of association between states with different social and political systems was possible, 'so long as there is no mutual hostility and if it is for the attainment of common aims' (Litvinov 134: 92). He defined the political conditions necessary for successful peaceful coexistence as 'reciprocal non-interference in the domestic affairs of the states . . .; and secondly, the existence of common aims' (Litvinov 1934: 92–3).

By the mid-1930s the penalties for disagreeing with Stalin were already too harsh for any real difference of interpretation to be noticeable amongst the leadership. None the less, a difference in emphasis can be detected in comparing Litvinov's and even Molotov's views on peaceful coexistence with those of Stalin. Stalin tended to emphasize that Soviet foreign policy aimed at preserving peace and strengthening trade relations (see, for example, his report to the Seventeenth Congress of the CPSU, Stalin 1934: 224–43). He did not use the term 'peaceful coexistence' in his reports to either the Seventeenth or Eighteenth Congresses of the CPSU. Instead he laid great stress on 'business relations' (Stalin 1934: 242; 1939: 345–6). Litvinov, on the other hand, consistently used the term 'peaceful coexistence' to describe Soviet foreign policy: 'Our collaboration with other countries and our participation in the League of Nations are based on the principle of the peaceful coexistence of two systems—the socialist and the capitalist' (Degras 1953, vol. 3: 220). In 1935, without making any attempt to explain it, Molotov pointed to the apparent contradiction between a policy of peaceful coexistence and the inevitable conflict between the two systems:

In the complex international system there is at one and the same time rivalry and collaboration between two opposite social systems. It may be objected that such a statement is self-contradictory, but it corresponds with the actual state of affairs. Rivalry, or, if you wish, a struggle is proceeding; but at the same time, and in ever newer forms, collaboration is developing between the USSR and various capitalist countries.

(Degras 1953, vol. 3: 107).

The recognition that there is any contradiction between peaceful coexistence and conflict was rare enough to be noteworthy. The 'ever-newer' forms of collaboration mentioned by Molotov included trade relations and cooperation to maintain peace. By 1939 the forms of collaboration between socialism and capitalism had been extended to include the Nazi–Soviet Non-Aggression Pact, a pact which, according to Molotov, 'since it meets the interests of the USSR . . . is in accord with our principle of peaceful coexistence' (Degras 1953, vol. 3: 368). In contravention of the principle and of the Pact, Nazi Germany attacked Soviet Russia in June 1941. Peaceful coexistence had given way to the inevitable war so long predicted, yet so unexpected when it occurred.

PEACEFUL COEXISTENCE AND THE COLD WAR

There are two striking features in Soviet writing about international relations after the war. The first is the extreme sycophancy with which Stalin was treated by senior and junior colleagues, as well as by scholars. The second feature is that the Cold War did not seem to diminish the frequency with which peaceful coexistence was proclaimed. Moreover, it acquired a broader, more permanent meaning long before Khrushchev gave the term prominence, and certainly before the belief in inevitable war was jettisoned. Although its meaning continued to include the fostering of trade relations, it became more closely related to Soviet encouragement of the peace movement than to the 'business-like relations' that Stalin had stressed before the war.

Sycophancy was not, of course, confined to the field of international relations. None the less, when one looks at the work of specialists like Korovin, for example, whose writings on international law and relations span a long period before the Second World War, the Cold War and the post-Stalin era, it seems inconceivable that a man of his stature would voluntarily (much less seriously) have larded his prose with meaningless, redundant phrases of which the following (it comes directly after a number of pages in which Stalin's every mention of peaceful coexistence is recorded in great detail) is only one of the innumerable examples:

Basing himself on the teaching of Lenin and Stalin about the possibility of peaceful coexistence and co-operation of the two systems—capitalist and socialist—Comrade Molotov has formulated the principles of peaceful coexistence at the present stage. Guided by the statement of the great leader of all progressive mankind, Stalin, who confirmed that he certainly believed in the possibility of friendly and prolonged cooperation between the Soviet Union and the Western democracies, despite the existence of ideological disagreements, and also believed in 'friendly competition' between the two systems, Comrade Molotov indicated that 'this must be a type of international co-operation which would unite in the interests of peace and security the efforts of states having dissimilar social and political systems'.

(Korovin 1951: 572–3).

As the personality cult became increasingly ubiquitous in the period after the war, so more and more credit was given to Stalin for various aspects of Marxist-Leninist thought. Stalin himself pronounced on a variety of subjects, but he was acclaimed as the intellectual expert and co-founder, with Lenin, of *every* aspect of doctrine or policy,[5] including the philosophy and policy of peaceful coexistence. One writer, for example, maintained that 'As the genius who continued the great ideas of Marx and Lenin, Comrade Stalin, to his great credit, developed the teaching about the possibility of the coexistence of two social systems and their cooperation' (Lazarev 1949: 12). Whether Stalin's references to the possibility of coexistence constituted a theoretical development is debatable. His post-war formulation was not very different from what he had said about peaceful coexistence in the 1920s and 1930s. He did point out that it took two to coexist peacefully—the possibility of cooperation and the will to cooperate were by no means identical. Both existed in the Soviet Union, but the desire was often missing in the capitalist countries, and this was why peaceful coexistence sometimes failed (Stalin 1947: 75–92). In the last couple of years of his life he scarcely mentioned peaceful coexistence,[6] emphasizing instead the peaceful nature of Soviet foreign policy and the effect of the peace movement on reducing the inevitability of some wars (see, for example, Stalin 1952a, 1952b). But this is not to imply that Stalin ceased to favour or believe in the policy—if that had been the case, it is extremely unlikely that anyone else would have dared to continue writing about it with enthusiasm.

Despite the hostile and implacable rhetoric of the early Cold War period typified by Zhdanov's speech at the founding of the Communist Information Bureau or Cominform (Zhdanov 1947: 2), Soviet commitment to peaceful coexistence continued to be articulated regularly. Parallel to the statements about the division of the world into two camps, the increasingly dangerous encirclement of the socialist camp and the aggressive nature of imperialism, every public speech on Soviet foreign policy contained some reference to the fact that peaceful coexistence was, and always had been, a cardinal principle of socialist foreign policy.

There was, however, a subtle change in the way the preconditions for peaceful coexistence were explained after the Second World War. Lenin had believed that the economic advantages of coexistence would outweigh any ideological objections on the part of the capitalists. In other words, the bourgeois states would choose coexistence because it was good for business. The Cold War explanation of its origins concentrated more on the way it had been forced upon capitalism by its own impotence on the one hand, and by the strengthening of socialism on the other. In particular, it was made possible by intra-imperialist conflict, the conflict between the imperialist states and the colonies, the growth of the revolutionary movement within capitalist countries with a concomitant rise in popular sympathy for the Soviet Union, all of which weakened the capitalist camp. This weakness and the strength and might of the Soviet proletariat, its success in building socialism and the organized force of the Soviet army made it necessary for the capitalist camp to accept peaceful coexistence (Lazarev 1949: 12). Fear of Soviet power, rather than business interests, was now thought to motivate peaceful coexistence. This has become an increasingly prominent aspect of the theory.

Another change from the way in which Lenin had envisaged the period of cooperation was in the length of time for which it was thought it would last. Lenin had expressed doubt on the matter, and while Chicherin had envisaged a longer period, it was still essentially considered to be a 'respite' or 'breathing space' in the inevitable conflict between socialism and capitalism. Lenin's doubts were forgotten in the post-war attribution of the idea. Malenkov maintained that coexistence was 'inevitable for a long period of time' (Malenkov 1947:3) and both Lenin and Stalin were said always to have believed in prolonged cooperation:

The great leaders of the Soviet Union, Lenin and Stalin, have often firmly asserted that the Soviet Union proceeds from the fact that the peaceful coexistence of the two systems, socialism and capitalism, is inevitable for a prolonged period of time.

(Korovin 1951: 566)

Particular attention began to be paid to the reciprocal aspects of peaceful cooperation. Korovin quoted both Zhdanov (1947) and Malenkov (1947), for example, when they separately, but using identical words, insisted in 1947 that coexistence could only be based upon observation of the principle of reciprocity and the fulfilment of obligations which have been undertaken (Korovin 1951: 572). Molotov preferred the word cooperation to coexistence. He called for peaceful competition, which would enable individual states to fulfil their inherent potential and enjoy 'closer and more all-embracing mutual co-operation with one another' (Molotov 1949: 263). Cooperation did not require identical systems, merely 'respect for the system which the nation has approved' (Korovin 1951: 25).

While stressing reciprocity, the idea which had been shelved during the search for collective security in the 1930s, namely that conflict shifts to other spheres, began to be emphasized again. The competitive aspects of peaceful coexistence were welcome because they would demonstrate the superiority of the socialist economic system: 'We are sure that in conditions of the peaceful coexistence of the two systems and in conditions of peaceful competition, the socialist economic system must be victorious' (Seleznev 1951: 31).

By the time Malenkov presented the main report at the Nineteenth Congress of the CPSU in 1952, many of the elements of peaceful coexistence later to be stressed by Khrushchev were included in his explanation of what it implied. Malenkov attributed the policy to Stalin, and there can be no doubt that Stalin approved of the contents of Malenkov's speech. He declared that the Soviet Union was desirous of developing international cooperation, particularly with the United States, Britain, France and the other bourgeois nations. The Soviet commitment to peace and security was based on the premise that:

The peaceful coexistence of capitalism and communism and co-operation are quite possible, given a mutual desire to co-operate, readiness to carry out commitments undertaken and observance of the principle of equality and noninterference in the internal affairs of other states. The Soviet Union has always stood for and now stands for the development of trade and co-operation with other countries, irrespective of differences in social systems. The Party will continue to pursue this policy on the basis of mutual advantage.

(Malenkov 1952: 105)

Malenkov returned to an economic explanation of why peaceful coexistence would be a rational policy for bourgeois states to follow. Instead of needing to produce more and more arms, capitalist industry would be kept busy by the expansion of trade with the socialist countries. The economy of underdeveloped countries would also be assisted by peaceful coexistence, he maintained, although he did not enlarge on how this would occur. Malenkov also saw peaceful coexistence in terms of peaceful economic competition, a competition which would prove the superiority of the socialist system.

Malenkov's exposition disclosed the essential contradiction which had always been present in peaceful coexistence, both in its Leninist, more limited, instrumental variant and, even more so, in the later broader interpretation. While it is clearly the case that peace provides the most favourable conditions for building socialism, it must also delay international revolution. If war exposes and aggravates the endemic conflict within bourgeois society, speeding up the disintegration which eventually causes the collapse of capitalism (see Ch. 8), it is only logical to suppose that peace must delay this process which promotes the speedier establishment of socialism. In other words, peace not only provides favourable conditions for building socialism. It also prolongs the conditions under which capitalism can consolidate itself. And if Malenkov was right in saying that peaceful coexistence is good for the capitalist economy, allowing for full employment without the need to expand the arms industry, then it must also prevent the economic crises which, according to Marxism-Leninism, hasten the moment when revolution becomes inevitable.

CONCLUSION

It is clear that peaceful coexistence was a much articulated theme of Soviet foreign policy long before it received prominence as part of Khrushchev's new doctrinal package announced at the Twentieth Party Congress in 1956. Indeed, between 1953 and 1956 it was as much the platform of his rivals for leadership as it was his. Given the prevalent fear that the imperialist countries might take advantage of Stalin's death to launch an attack on the Soviet Union, it is perhaps not surprising that Malenkov gave the assurance in his oration at Stalin's funeral that the Soviet Union's foreign policy was 'based on the Lenin-Stalin premise of the possibility of prolonged coexistence and peaceful competition of two different systems' (Malenkov 1953a: 249). Later, when that fear (and the fear of Beria) must already have been allayed, he repeated the assurance, adding that there was no objective reason for conflict between the Soviet Union and the United States— both their national and trade interests, as well as international security would be ensured by normal relations between them (Malenkov 1953b: 3–12). Since it has always been an unambiguous tenet of Marxism-Leninism that there is every objective reason for conflict between capitalism and socialism (even if it became transposed to the economic sphere under peaceful coexistence), it can be argued that his analysis was as revisionist as anything produced later by Khrushchev.

That the new version of peaceful coexistence was intended to involve more than just the absence of war and expansion of trade relations soon became clear. While international economic links were said to be an objective economic need of all countries, determined by the international division of labour, political and cultural cooperation was also envisaged. Successful cooperation was said to require strict observation of the norms of international law, particularly respect for sovereignty and non-interference in the internal affairs of other states (Selektor 1955: 38–40). This was a far more extensive application of peaceful coexistence than had occurred previously. And it was to bring to the fore some of the theoretical problems inherent in the concept.

In fact, ever since the term had first been used, it had contained a potential clash of security and revolutionary interests. In the Stalin era little attempt was made to explore the relationship between it and international revolution, or to explain the contradiction between peaceful coexistence and the equally firmly held belief in inevitable conflict between the two systems. After Stalin's death, however, considerable efforts were made to show that peaceful coexistence, like the peaceful nature of Soviet foreign policy, was in the interests of the international working class. In 1955, for example, one scholar explained the relationship of peaceful coexistence to revolution in the following way:

> it is their devotion to proletarian internationalism which makes Soviet leaders follow a policy of peace. The successful building of communism in the Soviet Union is the fundamental contribution made by the Soviet Union to liberating other countries from the yoke of capitalism. The more successful the Soviet Union is in building communism, the more it will inspire the peoples of the capitalist, colonial and dependent countries. So, by building communism and struggling for peace to do it in, the CPSU and the Soviet state fulfils its international duty to the working class and all workers.
> (Selektor 1955: 38)

As we shall see in the next chapter, the need to rationalize the apparent contradictions became particularly urgent once the Chinese had begun to dispute the idea that peaceful coexistence was good for revolution. But it is difficult not to conclude with the Chinese that although peaceful coexistence may be in the *security* interests of the international working class, it can hardly be in its revolutionary interests if it serves to delay the revolution. In the early years of Soviet power it may have seemed rational to make international revolution subservient to Soviet state security (that is, reasonable to all except the left-wing revolutionaries who, in Lenin's term, were suffering from an 'infantile disorder'), at least until the Soviet Union was strong enough to defend itself. After the war, and particularly before any Soviet leaders admitted that nuclear weapons made the risks of war unacceptable and the survival of either revolution or reaction unlikely, the argument that peaceful coexistence served the interests of the revolution became far weaker. As will become evident when the Sino-Soviet dispute is discussed in Chapter 7, once the authority of Stalin could no longer be used to affirm the correctness of the teaching, the argument that international revolution required peaceful coexistence did not convince the Chinese, even when the potential destructiveness of nuclear weapons was admitted. The intellectual effort which Soviet scholars put into refuting the idea that there was any contradiction between the interests of the Soviet Union and the future of international revolution and the theoretical development of the concept of peaceful coexistence which resulted from it, forms the subject of the next chapter.

NOTES

1. Western scholars sometimes seem to imply that it is significant that Lenin used the word *sozhitel'stvo* and not *sosushchestvovanie* (see, for example, Kubálková and Cruickshank 1980: 106–7). In fact, the only significance is probably that the former word means cohabitation and is usually used for more intimate personal relationships than were ever intended by the term 'peaceful coexistence'. Egorov denies that there is any difference between the terms (Egorov 1971: 119–21). He also denies emphatically that Trotsky coined the term or the policy. For a discussion of the origins of the term, see Griffiths (1964).

2. This is not, of course, unique to Soviet scholars. A not dissimilar process can be observed in Western scholars who wish to discredit Soviet theory, particularly as it relates to peace and peaceful coexistence. They tend to search out contradictions in Lenin and to use them to prove that Soviet leaders cannot be sincere, or cannot mean what they proclaim. Kolakowski, for example, quotes Lenin's view in

1920 that 'while capitalism and socialism live side by side they cannot live in peace' to prove that he did not really believe in peaceful coexistence (Kolakowski 1978, vol. 2: 497). See Egorov (1971) for examples to which Soviet scholars particularly object. The temptation to select extracts to prove one's thesis is almost irresistible, as this author is all too well aware (see Ch. 1, n.12).

3. Lenin constantly urged his fellow Bolsheviks to learn from the bourgeoisie. Those Soviet *mezhdunarodniki* who have pressed for the adoption of 'Western' methodology in the study of international relations have quoted him on this topic to lend respectability to their plea for a more sociological approach to the subject. See, for example, Ermolenko (1977: 62).

4. It is debatable whether Stalin really expected war in 1927. But it is certain that he used the war scare as one of the reasons for the forced pace of the First Five-Year Plan which was adopted soon afterwards. But at the same time as the warnings about imminent war were being voiced, an interesting aspect of economic peaceful coexistence emerged in an effort to protect the Soviet economy from the harmful consequences of any future economic sanctions and from the growing protectionism of the times. The Soviet Union made the first of a number of proposals for an economic non-aggression pact to an International Economic Conference in Geneva in 1927 ('Vneshnyaya politika SSSR bez Lenina' 1929: 163). The call was repeated in 1931 in a draft protocol submitted by the Soviet delegation to the Commission of Enquiry on European Union (Degras 1952, vol. 2: 499–500), and again in 1933. An essential element of the draft proposal was acceptance of the principle of 'the peaceful coexistence of all nations irrespective of their social, political and economic systems' (Eudin and Slusser 1967, vol. 2: 533). These calls for economic non-aggression bear a close resemblance to Gorbachev's proposals in his political report to the Twenty-Seventh Congress (Gorbachev 1986).

5. An active industry of the time consisted of combing Stalin's *Works* as the successive volumes appeared, to find references to various subjects. Articles would then be written on 'J. V. Stalin on . . .' whatever subject had been researched (see, for example, Lazarev 1951, who wrote on 'J. V. Stalin about Non-interference in the Internal Affairs of a State and the Concept of Intervention' or Zadorozhny 1951 on 'Questions of International Law in the Thirteenth Volume of the *Works* of J. V. Stalin'). Another aspect of this endeavour involved interpreting the significance of Stalin's pronouncements on a particular subject for other fields of study (see Kechek''yan 1952 and Kozhevnikov 1951 on the significance of the work of J. V. Stalin on Marxism and the question of linguistics for the history of political studies and international law, respectively.

6. Korovin, for example, listed every mention by Stalin of peaceful coexistence. He cited interviews given by Stalin in 1946, 1947, 1948 and 1949, and then suddenly returned to a 1936 quote. Since he quoted things that Zhdanov, Malenkov and Molotov had said on the subject after 1949, it was not that his account did not go beyond that year (Korovin 1951: 569–72).

3 Relations Between Socialists and Capitalists II: Peaceful Coexistence from Khrushchev to Brezhnev

Khrushchev's announcement at the Twentieth Congress of the Communist Party of the Soviet Union in 1956 that Soviet foreign policy was based on the principle of peaceful coexistence with states of different socialist systems had a profound effect on Soviet foreign relations, but not at first with the states to which the principle pertained. The Chinese leadership interpreted it as one of the many examples of the diminution of Soviet revolutionary fervour and proof that Khrushchev was not a fitting leader of the international communist movement.

As far as the statesmen to whom it was primarily addressed were concerned, peaceful coexistence was generally believed to be no more than a new tactic in the Soviet plot to mislead and disarm the West. One could speculate that a swifter and more positive response from the Western leaders to whom the new policy was directed might have averted some of the later events which were seen as proof positive that nothing had changed. But Khrushchev's victory in the post-Stalin leadership struggle coincided with Eisenhower's election as American president, the implacably anti-Soviet state secretaryship of John Foster Dulles and the replacement of the policy of containment by the rhetoric of 'roll-back'. The prevailing mood amongst Western decision-makers was not conducive to détente.

Khrushchev himself was ambivalent about the priorities of Soviet policy. He was intent on projecting Soviet influence, as well as improving East–West relations. Moreover, he had to convince the Chinese that he had not lost interest in international revolution. Not surprisingly, his foreign policy often seemed erratic. Soviet intervention to suppress the Hungarian uprising, the Berlin crises of 1958–61 and the Cuban Missile crisis all seemed to confirm to Western policy-makers that peaceful coexistence did not imply anything new in Soviet international politics. None the less, Khrushchev and his successors continued to insist that Soviet foreign policy towards capitalist states was and always had been based on peaceful coexistence.

As we have seen in Chapter 2, the claim that Soviet policy towards capitalist states had always been based on the principle of coexistence is not as far-fetched as it was thought to be when Cold War passions were high. No previous leader, however, had used the term quite as insistently as Khrushchev did, and it was taken up widely by writers on Soviet foreign policy. For that reason peaceful coexistence is pre-eminently associated with Soviet foreign policy in the period after 1956. But even when Khrushchev fell from power and his name disappeared from Soviet writing on foreign policy, peaceful coexistence retained its currency. In fact, although it was Khrushchev who promoted the concept to what some theorists called the 'general line of Soviet foreign policy', his success in promoting it was less impressive than that of Brezhnev. The high point came in the early 1970s, when a period of détente in Soviet–European and Soviet–American relations was crowned with summit meetings, the SALT accords and the Helsinki Agreement on Security and Cooperation in Europe.

By the time the latter was signed, however, détente had already begun to decline. The West perceived Soviet arms procurements and policy in the Third World to be infringements of peaceful coexistence. Soviet policy-makers, on the other hand, maintained that détente was being undermined by a Western (particularly American) leadership which could not accept a new, reduced role in world affairs. Despite disappointment in the fruits of détente, Soviet policy towards states with a different social structure is still said to be based on the principles of peaceful coexistence.

As far as the development of the concept is concerned, peaceful coexistence expanded in meaning after Stalin's death, from simple business-like relations to something that was said to be more than just peace or the absence of war. It was no longer a tactic or even a strategy, but had become, with proletarian internationalism, the principle on which Soviet foreign policy was based. On the one hand, it implied co-operation, non-interference in domestic affairs and mutual respect for sovereignty, territorial integrity and independence. On the other hand, while excluding military confrontation, it included economic competition and ideological struggle. It was said to be a particular manifestation of the class struggle and to be consonant with the furthering of international revolution. These claims and the theoretical problems they have caused form the subject of this chapter.

It will become clear that the concept of peaceful coexistence did not trouble Soviet theorists much until it was elevated to one of the twin pillars on which Soviet foreign policy was based. Once it was expanded beyond the simple idea of the absence of war and the encouragement of international economic relations, however, it became apparent that there were contradictions between peaceful coexistence (which defined state relations) and proletarian internationalism (which defined class relations) that were extremely difficult to reconcile. There were also inconsistencies in the different goals peaceful coexistence was intended to pursue and the kind of world it was to promote. These contradictions would, perhaps, have remained less pronounced, or at least less open to public scrutiny (although they would not have disappeared) if it had not been for the Chinese objections to the theory. In response to these objections, Soviet scholars expended a great deal of effort on showing that peaceful coexistence was consonant with international revolution and that the Soviet Union could be both the standard bearer of peace and a force for radical change within other societies. Their efforts have not been entirely successful. The revolutionary aspects of the theory have remained unpersuasive and it is, therefore, difficult not to conclude that peaceful coexistence is a coherent theory of interstate relations, but an unconvincing one for positing the spread of socialism.

KHRUSHCHEV'S PEACEFUL COEXISTENCE

The 20th Party Congress

Khrushchev by no means claimed originality when he listed the steadfast pursuit of the Leninist policy of peaceful co-existence first amongst the tasks confronting Soviet foreign policy in his report to the Twentieth Party Congress (Khrushchev 1956a: 38). On the contrary, he too insisted that peaceful coexistence had always been the general line of Soviet foreign policy and that it was neither a policy of expediency nor a question of tactics, but a fundamental principle. But he explained the options in a far more stark way than they had ever before been described:

there are only two ways: either peaceful coexistence or the most destructive war in history. There is no third way.

(Khrushchev 1956a: 37)

For a while after the enunciation of the Pancha Shila,[1] many Soviet theoretical exegeses of peaceful coexistence concentrated on the five principles, the democratic foundations of international relations which, while not far-reaching enough to encompass entirely socialist international policy, certainly formed part of the principles that guided that policy (Korovin 1956: 51). The principles were respect for territorial integrity and sovereignty; non-aggression; non-interference in internal affairs; equality and mutual benefit; and, finally, peaceful coexistence, which, it was said, both summarized the other four principles and had a more active element, entailing all-round cooperation to strengthen peace and improve living conditions (Korovin 1956: 47–8).[2] Some Soviet theorists were particularly eager to demonstrate the international legal aspects of the five principles. They were said to represent, by their nature, the essence of international customary law, the starting point for defining rules of a more particular type. This meant that even if they were not incorporated into specific treaties, they were still valid, since 'the embodiment of a custom in a treaty is merely a case of its formal confirmation' (Durdenevsky 1956: 616–7).[3]

The niceties of showing that the five principles already existed in international law and that therefore peaceful coexistence applied to all international relations whether or not it was explicitly recognized as valid by individual countries soon, however, had to give way to more pressing needs. If peaceful coexistence was to remain credible, it had to be proved that the intervention in Hungary had not contravened its principles. Not long afterwards it became necessary to demonstrate that the pursuit of peaceful coexistence with capitalist states did not diminish Soviet revolutionary zeal or international responsibility.

The response to doctrinal objections

Whereas in 1956 the placing of bases on foreign territory 'with or without forced consent' was defined as a violation of the principle of respect for territorial integrity and sovereignty (Korovin 1956: 47),[4] a distinction began to be made between actions taken 'by invitation' and others, at least in relation to socialist countries. The problem was that although peaceful coexistence referred to socialist–capitalist relations rather than to relations among socialist countries, socialist internationalism, on which socialist—socialist relations were based, was said to subsume the 'general democratic principles' which constituted peaceful coexistence (see Ch. 7). But it also included the duty of offering fraternal aid and cooperation, and these latter elements could (and were) used to explain the intervention in Hungary in 1956 (see for example, Ponomarev 1960: 650–1). None the less, care was taken to explain that Soviet actions had not infringed any of the principles of peaceful coexistence:

It should be emphasized that giving help to a friendly government who asks for it against an attack by armed bands . . . is not interference. As the recent Hungarian events showed, such aid serves the purpose of defending international peace and security.

(Krylov and Durdenevsky 1957: 12)

The Chinese objections to peaceful coexistence probably took a while to surface. But in the aftermath of Hungary there was an urgent need to re-establish cohesion within the international movement. A meeting of representatives of Communist and Workers' Parties was held in 1957, where the correctness of the main points of the new doctrine announced at the Twentieth Party Congress was confirmed (the other issues discussed at the 1957 conference will be dealt with in Ch. 7). The main content of the epoch was the transition from capitalism to socialism. World development was determined by the competition between the two systems, a competition in which socialism would demonstrate its superiority. Renewed faith was expressed in the principles of and need for peaceful coexistence', and all the signatories of the 1957 Declaration, including the Chinese, regarded the struggle for peace as their foremost task. They agreed that:

the Leninist principle of peaceful coexistence of the two systems . . . is the firm foundation of the foreign policy of the socialist countries and the reliable foundation of peace and friendship among the peoples. The five principles advanced jointly by the Chinese People's Republic and the Republic of India and the program adopted by the Bandung conference of African and Asian countries correspond to the interests of peaceful co-existence.

('Declaration of the Conference of Communist
and Workers' Parties' ['Declaration'] 1957: 4)

Although the Chinese signed the 1957 declaration, they were not really convinced that peaceful coexistence represented anything more than selling out to capitalism. A further meeting was held in 1960 and this time the object was to reconcile the Chinese leadership. It had become necessary, therefore, to be more explicit about the advantages of peaceful coexistence for the future of socialism. For one thing, socialist foreign policy was said to rest on 'the firm foundation of the Leninist principle of peaceful coexistence and economic competition between the socialist and capitalist countries' ('Statement of the Meeting of Representatives of the Communist and Workers' Parties' [Statement'], 1960: 7). For another, it was clearly restated that the choices were peaceful coexistence or destructive war. But it was also affirmed that 'peaceful coexistence of states does not imply renunciation of the class struggle'. On the contrary, it provided favourable opportunities for the development of the class struggle in the capitalist countries and the national liberation movement ('Statement' 1960: 8).

This explanation clearly did not resolve all the problems caused by peaceful coexistence. Soviet theorists spent the next few years arguing against three separate kinds of opposition to it or to the Soviet interpretation of the term. At one extreme were the bourgeois opponents who falsified history to prove that Soviet theory had never been, and could not be, based on peaceful coexistence. Equally misguided were the revisionists who believed that peaceful coexistence applied not only to relations between opposing systems but also to inter-socialist relations. At the other extreme, dogmatists denied that there was any need for peaceful coexistence and misinterpreted its effects on revolution. In reply to the bourgeois opponents, detailed historical evidence was produced to prove Lenin's devotion to peaceful coexistence (see, for example, Gromyko 1962, Ch. VII; Zorin *et al.* 1963; Trukhanovsky 1963). The revisionists were merely acting as apologists for (and playing into the hands of) the imperialists by not recognizing that socialist international relations went beyond peaceful coexistence (Gromyko 1962: 71). Dogmatists (it was not explicitly stated who they were until after the Sino-Soviet dispute became public in 1963) also armed the imperialist opponents of peaceful coexistence, since they affirmed that peaceful coexistence could never be more than a temporary truce (Gromyko 1962: 72).

Khrushchev himself insisted that peace and peaceful coexistence were not one and the same thing. Peaceful coexistence was more than the absence of war, or an unstable truce between wars. It was based on the mutual renunciation of war as a means of settling international disputes (Khrushchev 1961b: 49).[5] But Soviet theorists did not rest with accusing dogmatists of the treachery of providing ammunition for the imperialist opponents of peaceful coexistence. Instead they began to demonstrate the revolutionary nature of peaceful coexistence, emphasizing in particular that it did not denote the end of class struggle, that it augured well for the spread of socialism and that it implied both economic competition and ideological vigilance.

Peaceful coexistence was said to be 'a specific form of the class struggle between socialism and capitalism' (Nikitin 1959: 339) which did not mean that there was conciliation between the two systems or that antagonisms between them disappeared (Gromyko 1962: 102–3). In fact, peaceful coexistence could not and would not affect any antagonisms which arose from the objective processes of historical development. As far as the historically determined conflict between the working class and the bourgeoisie in particular countries was concerned, it would continue, whether or not there was peaceful coexistence. But peaceful coexistence made it more likely that the means of waging it, and therefore of accomplishing the transition to socialism, would be peaceful (Gromkyo 1962: 98–9). Nor did peaceful coexistence decrease intra-imperialist contradictions. On the contrary, it served to aggravate them since they could no longer be temporarily resolved at the expense of the socialist countries. So the struggle would be turned inwards at the very time that the imperialist camp was, in any case, becoming smaller. The Soviet Union was not, however, in favour of these contradictions being resolved by force, since this would draw the working masses into the horror of war. In any case, there was a danger that an inter-imperialist war would escalate into world nuclear war (Gromyko 1962: 104).

The way in which Soviet scholars explained the role of peaceful coexistence in the international class struggle was particularly convoluted. On the one hand, it was said to be a specific form of the class struggle. On the other hand, peaceful coexistence was an *international* form of the class struggle which manifested itself through inter-state relations, but which also had profoundly beneficial effects on the domestic class struggle within capitalist states. It limited and paralysed imperialist aggression, and it aided the domestic class struggle in three other ways: first, by supporting it against imperialist reaction and, second, by allowing the Soviet Union to demonstrate proletarian solidarity by putting forward a peaceful foreign policy. Finally, by enabling socialism to be constructed successfully, it gave the proletariat a powerful weapon in the class struggle: the demonstration of the superiority of socialism. This was proof that the bases of Soviet foreign policy 'fully answers the class needs of the proletariat, answers to its vital interests and to the vital interests of all Workers' (Gromyko 1962: 98).

As far as the national liberation struggle was concerned, proletarian internationalism rather than peaceful coexistence operated in the relationship between the socialist countries and the colonial countries. As a result, the Soviet Union would continue to support their struggle for independence.

This would not contradict the principles of peaceful coexistence. None the less, peaceful coexistence would itself have very positive effects on the national liberation struggle, since it involved supporting disarmament, and without arms, the colonizers would not be able to use force to suppress the colonial peoples (Gromyko 1962: 111–14).

It was simpler to explain how the peaceful competition to which conflict between the social systems had been transposed would positively influence the spread of socialism. Socialism would win the economic competition and this would demonstrate its advantages. But the purpose of the competition was to benefit humankind:

The proposed competition serves honourable aims: which system guarantees the best conditions for people's lives, who produces more peaceful industrial and agricultural goods, builds more houses, guarantees better conditions for science and culture, for the flowering of the human personality?

(Korionov and Yakovlev 1961: 110–11)

More over, the competition was not one in which the stronger side aimed to crush the weaker or to exploit it or extract profits from it. On the contrary, 'this competition presupposes an expansion of cooperation between the two social systems and cultural links between them' (Korionov and Yakovlev 1961: 111).

Contrary to what Malenkov had suggested several years previously, expanding economic links would not save capitalist countries from economic crises (Gromyko 1962: 111). The inevitable crises would continue to take place, and meanwhile the clear advantages of socialism would ensure the victory of the socialist mode of production (Ponomarev 1960: 665). Although cultural links were envisaged, Soviet theorists increasingly emphasized that peaceful coexistence did not extend to ideology. On the contrary, a tense struggle was developing in the ideological field (Ponomarev 1960: 665). Any attempts by bourgeois politicians to impose peaceful coexistence in the sphere of ideas was described as 'direct ideological subversion aimed at spiritually and ideologically disarming the builders of socialism and communism' (Sovetov 1964: 8).

In Suslov's public announcement of the Sino-Soviet dispute, it became clear who the dogmatists were in relation to peaceful coexistence. Suslov listed the Chinese objections to it in his exposition of the ideological disagreements between the fraternal parties (for their other objections, see Ch. 7). The Chinese, Suslov said, did not understand the imperative of peaceful coexistence which resulted from the urgent need to avoid thermonuclear war. Moreover, they discredited the idea of peaceful economic competition between the two systems (Suslov 1963: 7–11). It is not inconceivable that the desire to impress upon the Chinese that the Soviet Union, too, was unafraid of the American 'paper tiger' had some influence on the decision to place missiles in Cuba in 1962. In the event, the Cuban missile crisis failed to convince the Chinese of the resoluteness of Soviet policy. It also served to discredit Khrushchev's avowal of peaceful coexistence (although the aftermath produced measures like the institution of the hotline and the signing of a limited Test Ban Treaty). Finally, it left Khrushchev with very little time to achieve the improvement in capitalist–socialist relations for which he had sacrificed the solidarity of the international communist movement.[6]

PEACEFUL COEXISTENCE AND DÉTENTE UNDER BREZHNEV

The hallmark of Brezhnev's foreign policy, particularly in the early years, was caution. There was little immediate change in Soviet policy towards the other socialist countries, and relations with the capitalist West were not immediately affected by Khrushchev's dismissal. But to begin with there was a definite change in the tone of foreign-policy pronouncements. While it continued to be maintained that Soviet foreign policy towards states with a different social system was based on the principles of peaceful coexistence, Brezhnev used the term far less abundantly and with considerably less enthusiasm than Khrushchev had.[7] He was perhaps even more verbally belligerent in his criticism of Western, particularly American, international politics (see, for example, his report to the Twenty-Third Congress of the CPSU in 1966, Brezhnev 1966: 36–67). He also had less predilection for theorizing, and his speeches tended to be concerned with events rather than the developments of theory.

On the other hand, Brezhnev pursued the policy of peaceful coexistence with a great deal more success than Khrushchev, and he enshrined the term in the new 1977 Soviet Constitution (*Constitution of the Union of Soviet Socialist Republics* 1985: 23). By the beginning of the 1970s, once relations with the West began to bear fruit, he extolled the advantages of a cooperative relationship with the capitalist countries, particularly the United States, as frequently as Khrushchev had done, preferring, however, to use the term détente rather than peaceful coexistence. Theorists, too, began to write about the 'process' of détente and the 'principle' of peaceful coexistence (see, for example, Trofimenko 1975: 3).[8]

The 1970s were, both in the real world and in Soviet theory, the highpoint of détente. Soviet writing on international relations, like Brezhnev's speeches, was filled with the universal benefits it brought. By the end of the decade, however, Brezhnev and his theorists were forced to consider why it was failing. The causes were seen to be entirely imperialist, since Soviet policy was said to be steadfast in upholding the principles of peaceful coexistence. Brezhnev's report to the Twenty-Sixth Party Congress in 1981 (Brezhnev 1981: 27–41) indicated his disappointment. He scarcely mentioned peaceful coexistence, concentrating instead on a catalogue of American infringements. If it is true, as many Western Sovietologists believed, that Brezhnev, like Nixon, wanted to be known to posterity as the man who had made détente, he must, towards the end of his life, have feared failure.

Although Brezhnev himself did not devote much time to international relations theory, the *mezhdunarodniki* (the academic international relations specialists) continued to analyse various aspects of peaceful coexistence. In countless articles and books, peaceful coexistence was defined, its successes listed (in terms of arms treaties like the Non-proliferation Treaty of 1968, mutually advantageous economic agreements and Soviet proposals for disarmament, collective-security agreements and nuclear-free zones), and then it was affirmed that the class struggle would not only continue but would benefit from détente (see Zagladin 1973: 179–83 for an authoritative example of an almost universal set of themes). Amongst the subjects that were investigated, many theorists considered the question of why peaceful coexistence had become possible.

Peaceful coexistence as a consequence of the changing correlation of forces

Soviet and socialist commonwealth statements about imperialism had for some time been drawing a distinction between reactionary forces and the realistic politicians who recognized the need for peaceful coexistence (see, for example, 'Tasks at the Present Stage of the Struggle against Imperialism and United Action of the Communist and Workers' Parties and All Anti-Imperialist Forces' 1969: 29). The successes of détente were thought to show that a new realism on the part of Western politicians had prevailed (Arbatov 1973: 264–5). The way in which the new realism was explained is an interesting illustration of an increasing reliance on the concept of power in Soviet international relations theory.

It will be remembered that Lenin had suggested that peaceful coexistence could succeed because it would appeal to the desire for profit which motivated the capitalist class. It was not that he thought that the bourgeoisie had changed its nature, merely that the promise of economic benefits would prevail over ideological antipathy. Modern theorists continued to believe that there were inherent mutual economic advantages in détente. But the profit motive was no longer used to explain why capitalist–socialist relations had improved, despite the implacable hostility and ineluctable aggression which was thought to underlie the foreign policy of imperialist states. What had made détente possible was a combination of factors of which the most important was the change in the correlation of forces in favour of socialism. Imperialist states had been coerced into peaceful coexistence by Soviet power. Although power is not entirely synonymous with military strength in Soviet theory,[9] even before détente had really taken off in the early 1970s, many theorists described the reasons for the new possibilities of peaceful coexistence primarily in terms of Soviet defence potential. It was said, for example, that:

Soviet successes in science, technology and industry, which resulted in the development of the most modern means of defence, restrained the imperialist politicians from turning the Cold War into a hot one, and compelled the bourgeois world to accept peaceful coexistence or at least coexistence with the Soviet Union and other socialist countries.

(Trukhanovsky 1968: 59)

Soviet theorists have frequently used words like 'compulsion' and 'imposition' to describe the acceptance of peaceful coexistence by the West (see, for example, Novopashin 1978: 166; Sanakoyev and Kapchenko 1977: 113). Some have also recognized a subjective change in Western thinking. Shifts within the imperialist camp, and particularly the decline in American authority in relation to other bourgeois states, have also been said to have prompted the acceptance of peaceful coexistence (Sanakoyev and Kapchenko 1973: 78–9). Almost all Soviet theorists, however, attributed the change above all to the new correlation of forces in the world. The following quotation expresses the general Soviet scholarly consensus: 'It was only when they had lost their military superiority that the ruling circles of capitalist countries began to understand the inevitability of peaceful coexistence' (Shakhnazarov 1984: 22).[10]

Peaceful coexistence and the class struggle

It can be assumed that the successes of détente took some of the sting from Chinese accusations that peaceful coexistence demonstrated Soviet revisionism. In any case, it was clear in the 1970s from Chinese foreign policy itself that the Chinese leadership no longer considered peaceful coexistence with capitalism inconceivable or incompatible with furthering the international revolution.[11] The theoretical problems of demonstrating that détente and the international revolution were consonant none the less continued to preoccupy Soviet scholars. However vital peaceful coexistence was said to be, it was still considered by some theorists to be less significant in foreign policy than proletarian internationalism, the other pillar of Soviet foreign policy (Trukhanovsky 1966: 59).[12]

It was not that Soviet theorists openly admitted that there might be any contradiction between the two principles. Indeed, peaceful coexistence was still said to facilitate proletarian internationalism precisely because it preserved peace and provided the external political conditions necessary for building socialism and communism (Trukhanovsky 1968: 60). But it must have been clear that this simple assertion did not really deal with the fundamental problem that had always been inherent in peaceful coexistence. Which of the two principles, for example, explained Soviet relations with the working class in capitalist countries, if inter-state relations were based on peaceful coexistence? That this presented a conundrum is perhaps indicated by the frequency with which recourse was had to the linguistic formula that 'The principle of peaceful coexistence is inapplicable to the relations between oppressor and oppressed, between colonizers and the victims of the colonial yoke' (Brezhnev 1966: 63). From both a theoretical and a practical point of view, this covered the seeming contradiction between peaceful coexistence and the national liberation struggle. Peaceful coexistence did not apply to national liberation movements. It therefore neither contradicted the right of oppressed peoples to fight for liberation by whatever means necessary, including arms ('Tasks at the Present Stage of the Struggle against Imperialism and United Action of the Communist and Workers' Parties and All Anti-Imperialist Forces' 1969: 35) nor interfered with the duty of giving socialist aid to nations struggling for national liberation (Sanakoyev and Kapchenko 1973: 87–8). This particular interpretation of the limits of peaceful coexistence had been upheld consistently ever since it had become a prominently acclaimed principle of Soviet foreign policy in 1956. The problem was that the Western response to such aid was first 'linkage' and then withdrawal from détente.[13] But the relationship of the socialist countries to the class struggle within capitalist states presented a far more complex theoretical problem.

As we have seen, Soviet theorists and policy-makers have constantly reiterated that peaceful coexistence is a form of class struggle. But one of the cardinal principles of peaceful coexistence is non-interference in the domestic affairs of other states. It was evident that Soviet theorists and political leaders did not only intend this to mean military intervention, since they frequently used non-military examples to illustrate the way in which imperialist states contravened the principle. Foreign aid, for example, had long been given as an example of unacceptable American interference (Korovin 1956: 46–7). In other words, whether intervention took a peaceful or a non-peaceful form, it was still interference and it was considered by Soviet writers to contravene one of the fundamental principles of peaceful coexistence.

On the face of it, the belief that intervention contravened peaceful coexistence was as applicable to interference by the international communist movement in the domestic class struggle as it was to American interference in, say, Soviet emigration policy. But if it *was* equally applicable, it was difficult to explain how peaceful coexistence could be seen to aid the class struggle. One of the forms the aid had been said to take was support for local progressive forces against imperialist reaction (Gromyko 1962: 98). Another was aid to the national liberation movement (Zorin *et al.* 1963: 32). Within the socialist commonwealth the problem of theoretical coherence had been resolved by differentiating between 'invited' and imposed interference. This did not necessarily convince the opponents of the Soviet Union. It also led to practical problems when no credible leader could be found on the spot to do the 'inviting' (as happened, for example, in Afghanistan at the end of 1979 before Babrak Karmal's return). Soviet scholars, however, seemed satisfied with their explanation that the principle had not been infringed. It did not, however, deal with the problem of aiding the class struggle within capitalist states while pursuing peaceful coexistence and honouring the principle of non-interference. For interference not to infringe peaceful coexistence (and international law) any 'invitation' would have to come from the legitimate government.

While the argument continued to be voiced that peaceful coexistence included the principle of non-interference, it also remained a repeated tenet that peaceful coexistence did *not* extend to internal processes of class struggle. Relations with bourgeois states were based on principles of peaceful coexistence, whereas relations with the working class of those states were based on proletarian internationalism (Trukhanovsky 1968: 56). This was one way in which the 'dialectical relationship' between the two principles, which was said to characterize socialist foreign policy, was expressed (Sanakoyev and Kapchenko 1973: 76). But the theoretical and practical difficulties of basing relations with the governments of capitalist states on one principle, when relations with the majority of its citizens were based on a different principle, were not really tackled by Soviet scholars. Nor was it admitted (or perhaps even perceived) that aid which was an integral part of the definition of proletarian internationalism would contravene an equally inherent aspect of the definition of peaceful coexistence. No recourse to a real or fictitious invitation (as in the case of intervention in socialist countries) could obviate this particular contradiction. As a result, it was never really clear what was entailed in proletarian internationalism when it was applied to the working class of capitalist states.

In fact, Soviet theorists have either been vague about the relationship of socialism to the domestic class struggle in the countries with which the Soviet Union enjoys cooperative relations, or they have referred to the dialectic of peaceful coexistence, without being specific about what this means. The principles of peaceful coexistence and proletarian internationalism have been said, for example, each to be relatively independent and to have their own sphere of application. At the same time, the two are in a relationship of dialectical interdependence (Butenko 1975: 311). But what the nature of the dialectical relationship was in this case was not made explicit. To obscure the meaning even more, peaceful coexistence was *itself* said to be dialectical. Many authors have used the term to describe the simultaneous workings of cooperation and struggle (Trukhanovsky 1968: 60, for example), or the twofold nature of peaceful coexistence: 'a definite system of international relations' and, at the same time, 'a special form of class struggle in the international arena', the two making a unity because 'both struggle and cooperation proceed in peaceful forms and are conducted by peaceful means' (Menzhinsky, 1969: 45). A slightly different explanation denied that there was a combination of peaceful coexistence and struggle because that would imply that the struggle was supplementary. In fact, 'struggle expresses the essence of relations of peaceful coexistence' (Butenko 1975: 306n). A third variation of the term, 'complicated dialectics', was used to describe the fact that:

In their efforts to avert a nuclear war and to develop economic, scientific and technical ties, countries with different social systems are, at the same time, pursuing for [*sic*] different class goals in the foreign policy.

(Kortunov 1979: 85)

In the case of the socialist countries, the class goals were the creation of favourable conditions for communist construction and the development of the world revolutionary process. The capitalist states, on the other hand, hoped to protect bourgeois society, retard social progress and further their own class interests (Kortunov 1979: 85–6). All these explanations still concentrated on inter-state relations, however, without explaining how the dialectic affected the relationship between the socialist states and the inevitable class struggle within capitalist society.

Soviet scholars seemed not to have advanced much on this subject from the thinking of the early 1960s. Imperialist governments were warned, for example, that they could not expect any guarantee of 'class peace' in return for recognizing the principle of peaceful coexistence. It was not that the Soviet Union would interfere in their domestic affairs, but just that the class struggle was an ineluctable and objective law governing the development of society and nothing could abolish it (Trukhanovsky 1966: 57). In the 1970s it became fashionable to use the term 'social and political status quo' to explain what it was that would inevitably change despite the excellent inter-governmental relations between socialist and capitalist states. Détente and peaceful coexistence.

in no way mean the maintenance of the political and social status quo in the various countries, but on the contrary create the optimum conditions for the development of the struggle of the working class and all democratic forces.

('Statement of Conference of the Communist and Workers' Parties of Europe' 1976: 25)

When it came to explaining how the optimum conditions for the class struggle were to be brought about, the explanations were not very different from those that had been given in the pre-détente days. One influential theorist predicted that the class struggle and the struggle to avert war would merge. Moreover, the world revolutionary process would gain in strength and unity from the struggle for peace, since the masses would gain political consciousness from it and lead the struggle for democratic and social rights within the capitalist countries (Zagladin 1973: 184–7). Another scholar pointed out that the contradictions between the two social systems would not cause a revolutionary situation within the capitalist system directly, since this was only one of the many conditions required for a successful struggle of the proletariat against the bourgeoisie. Whether the class conflicts within capitalist states which peaceful coexistence were said to exacerbate would be resolved by peaceful or non-peaceful means was left open. What was certain was that 'revolutionary class force' would be required, but this could either be peaceful or non-peaceful, depending on the amount of resistance offered by the ruling class (Butenko 1975: 306). But all theorists continued to insist that revolution could and would not be exported (see, for example, Kortunov 1979: 87).

The only course of action which the socialist states seemed determined to undertake in support of the international class struggle and international revolution was to continue the war of ideas, but even here they were not very explicit about the form this would take.

Peaceful coexistence and the ideological struggle

Although it had always been said that peaceful coexistence did not affect the war of ideas, there seemed to be a new urgency in the Soviet insistence in the 1970s that the ideological struggle would continue despite détente. On the one hand, it was a reaction to the schools of thought fashionable amongst Western sociologists and political scientists that ideology would cease to be important in post-industrial society or that a convergence was taking place between socialism and capitalism. These ideas were anathema to Soviet political scientists and a great deal of energy was expended in refuting them.[14] On the other hand, it was also partly a response both to suggestions that détente is incompatible with ideological struggle and to those parts of the Final Act of the European Conference on Security and Cooperation which promised greater exchange of information and cultural interchange. Western hopes that this would bring about a relaxation in censorship in Eastern Europe, and ideological change there, were quite open. Soviet determination that ideological contamination would not be permitted was equally overt.

This does not imply that the firmly stated views that 'on ideological questions there can be no compromises' (Trukhanovsky 1968: 60) were merely reactive and defensive responses. The Soviet belief in the efficacy and necessity of propaganda is even older than the October Revolution and, as we have seen, peaceful coexistence had never been intended to embrace ideas. On the contrary, the better détente worked, the more important the ideological struggle was believed to be. Arbatov, for example, maintained that the very existence of two systems made it inevitable that the ideological struggle would continue until the progressive system was victorious (Arbatov 1973: 274–6). He pointed out that the demand that communist and socialist parties abandon the ideological struggle was itself the expression of an ideology, or of 'ideological subversion' (Arbatov 1973: 279). This was the geneally accepted view. A call to halt the ideological struggle was, at best, an attempt at peaceful penetration of the socialist countries (Sanakoyev and Kapchenko 1973: 89–90). At worst it reflected a desire to achieve unilateral ideological disarmament of the socialist countries (Kortunov 1979: 89–91). In either case, 'Marxist-Leninists resolutely act against the idea of the possibility of a peaceful coexistence of the bourgeois and socialist ideologies and against compromise in the ideological field' (Milovidov 1977: 217).

It also became generally accepted terminology to talk of the war of ideas or the ideological struggle when it was being conducted by socialists and of psychological warfare when it was being waged by capitalists (see, for example, Mshvenieradze 1985, Ch. 3). This terminological distinction was itself, perhaps, part of the war of ideas. However, Soviet theorists have been far less explicit about the intentions and effects of the socialist campaign in the war of ideas than they have been about Western intentions. They have also not been very specific about the forms the socialist side of the struggle takes. There have been regular calls for ideological vigilance, but they are hardly new (in fact, the jamming of foreign radio broadcasts to the Soviet Union decreased briefly after the Helsinki Final Act was signed). The Soviet Union spends a great deal of money and effort on publishing and broadcasting information for foreign dissemination, but this too is part of a long-standing programme. In short, it is not at all clear that the increased anxiety about the ideological struggle has produced any innovatory techniques or means of using the war of ideas to serve the class struggle or international revolution.

The decline of détente

Brezhnev's preference from the mid-1970s onwards for the term 'détente' rather than peaceful coexistence neither meant that the two were entirely synonymous nor that the latter term fell out of favour. Peaceful coexistence retained its meaning as one of the principles of Soviet foreign policy, while détente was used to denote both a process and an existing or desired situation of reduced tension, in particular military tension. To begin with, the term 'détente' was usually used in combination with peaceful coexistence (but far less frequently). Brezhnev seemed to avoid both, speaking instead of the struggle for peace, and the peace-loving policy of the Soviet Union (Brezhnev 1966: 36–130). It was only at the Twenty-Fifth Party Congress in 1976, when he seemed to be most optimistic about the international situation (although the strains in détente must already then have been felt), that he began to use 'détente' more frequently and often without the accompanying peaceful coexistence.[15] The term then began to be used by other speakers in preference to peaceful coexistence in public speeches and announcements about foreign policy (see, for example, 'Statement of Conference of the Communist and Workers' Parties of Europe' 1976). It was then, too, that theorists began to favour the term.[16]

Ironically, this coincided with Brezhnev's publicly expressed doubts about the commitment of the West to détente in his speech to the conference of European Communist and Workers' Parties in 1976 (Brezhnev 1976b). Although it had always been conventional wisdom to express reservations about capitalist intentions, and warnings about the inescapable aggression of imperialism, from 1970 onwards the underlying tone had been optimistic. After 1976 the prevailing mood became increasingly gloomy and pessimistic and this gradually began to be reflected in theoretical works. In 1975, for example, the failure to achieve most-favoured nation status in the United States (except at the price of concessions on emigration which the Soviet leadership was not willing to pay) was explained as the unfortunate effect of 'influential forces in the United States' who were trying to 'hinder the onward march of the process of détente' (Trofi-menko 1975: 11). By 1980 it was not only influential forces that were blamed, but the general characteristic of the American leadership, which wished 'to use détente to strengthen the world position of imperialism, particularly American imperialism'. The American ruling elite had inten-tionally aggravated the international situation at the begin-ning of the 1980s (Usachev 1980: 208–9).

Any serious attempt by Soviet scholars to analyse the reasons for the increasingly tense international atmosphere was rendered impossible, however, by the imperative of ascribing all blame for the deterioration in détente to the capitalist states. The point is not whether this was necessarily incorrect. But the *a priori* assumption that the capitalist states were solely to blame and the inability to consider the possi-bility, say, that Soviet actions might have prompted Western perceptions that were deleterious to détente, precluded serious analysis. This problem is not unique to the theory of peaceful coexistence and détente. It points to one of the weakest aspects of Soviet international relations theory in general, and one of the major reasons why it is difficult to agree with Soviet writers and policy-makers who claim scien-tific status for their policy.

CONCLUSION

To summarize the evolution of the concept of peaceful coexis-tence, it was implied by Lenin's theory of the uneven develop-ment of capitalism, but it is debatable whether the sense in which Lenin used the term after the revolution can be called theory. The survival and economic recovery of the Bolshevik state required a breathing space which would be achieved by peaceful coexistence. But Lenin saw it essentially as a short-term tactic, predicated on the belief that the capitalists' profit motive would be strong enough to overcome their ideological antipathy. Stalin adopted the term and extended the period for which it would be operative: socialism in one country required a lengthy period of peaceful coexistence. In the context of the need for collective security to contain fascism in the 1930s, peaceful coexistence was a useful way of indicating the reliability of the Soviet Union as an ally. Moreover, it was sufficiently flexible both to explain the Nazi–Soviet Pact in 1939 when negotiations with Britain and France broke down, and cooperation with those countries and the United States after the attack by Germany on the Soviet Union in 1941.

Peaceful coexistence remained an active ingredient of Soviet international relations theory during the Cold War. It was no longer said to be motivated by the search for profit on the part of the capitalists, however, but to be due to the power of the socialist system. Most of the elements of the theory which are usually attributed to Khrushchev can, in fact, be traced to the period before Stalin's death. It acquired particular prominence, however, when Khrushchev revised the theory of Soviet foreign policy at the Twentieth Party Congress of the CPSU in 1956. The Chinese rejected peaceful coexistence as revisionist, a sign that the Soviet Union was no longer committed to international revolution. Soviet theorists began exploring the relationship of peaceful coexistence to proletarian internationalism, the class and ideological struggle. They did not, however, succeed in resolving the theoretical difficulties which had arisen.

Brezhnev was less enthusiastic about the term than Khrushchev, but his policy of peaceful coexistence was very successful at first. The problems faced by Soviet scholars were very similar, however, to those which had always arisen from the theory of peaceful coexistence. It was easy to explain why peaceful coexistence was good for the socialist states which already existed. It was far more difficult to prove that it would promote other socialist revolutions.

By the beginning of the 1980s a vast number of books and articles had been written about the theory of peaceful coexistence. Many prominent and competent international relations theorists had turned their minds to explaining its aetiology and history, the reasons for its successes and failures, its effects on other aspects of Soviet theory and policy, its likely duration and its probable outcomes. And yet, in a very real sense, the theory was not much better developed than it had been when it was first used to mean something more extensive and more permanent than good international economic relations. To some extent the limitations which prevent Soviet theorists from questioning Soviet foreign-policy behaviour are responsible for retarding the development of theory. But the paradoxical nature of the concept of peaceful coexistence and the extent to which it is inherently incompatible with other aspects of Soviet theory are even more to blame.

At one level the theory of peaceful coexistence can be seen as a mirror image of containment theory. Its successes are attributed to the firm rebuff and resistance which has been offered to imperialist aggression. In other words, it is claimed to contain imperialism, rather like containment was intended to prevent the advance of communism. It presupposes similar psychological sources of imperialist conduct to those identified by Kennan in Soviet behaviour in the article which heralded containment (Kennan 1947). Like containment, it does not suggest exporting its own system beyond its borders. None the less, and again like containment, there is an underlying hope and expectation that change will take place. In the case of containment it was to be democratic change, whereas with peaceful coexistence it is to be progressive change (which is also called democratic by Soviet theorists). In both cases the emphasis is on firmness of intent and the known ability to respond, rather than the overt use of force. The theoretical difficulties for Soviet *mezhdunarodniki* came from the requirement that peaceful coexistence should both contain imperialism and promote a more active advance of socialism than can be attained by the waiting-and-hoping implied by containment. The practical difficulty for Soviet policy-makers was that many of their Western counterparts perceived peaceful coexistence as a holding operation in Europe while revolution and the destruction of imperialism proceeded elsewhere.

The problem has been exacerbated by the unavoidable knowledge that, contrary to all the optimistic predictions from 1917 onwards, the socialist world has not taken the lead in the sphere of material production, 'the determining sphere of social activity' (Butenko 1975: 308). In other words, the spread of socialism by force of example is less likely because the example has become less successful. Yet all Soviet theorists insist that peaceful coexistence does not mean the maintenance of the political and social status quo. Peaceful coexistence is thus expected to produce two seemingly mutually exclusive conditions: it must both provide the necessary peaceful environment for building socialism and communism in the existing socialist countries, and it must promote the circumstances which encourage a change in the political and social status quo. No theorist has managed to find a synthesis for the apparently inescapable contradictions of these two demands.

In Soviet theory in general there has been a turn from the voluntarism of pre-revolutionary Leninism to a more Marxist determinism, and this is clearly reflected in the theory of peaceful coexistence. The insistence that revolution cannot be exported and that history itself will bring about change is evidence of this. None the less, Soviet scholars often maintain (and it is difficult to argue with them) that capitalists are unlikely to give up their privileges voluntarily. Moreover, whether or not social change takes place peacefully depends not on those who want change, but on those who have to give up their class privileges. They will resist forcibly, according to Soviet theory, unless the forces against them are so obviously overwhelming that struggle is hopeless. But one of the advantages of peaceful coexistence is said to be its ability to create the kind of atmosphere in which 'democratic and social rights' can be attained (Zagladin 1973: 184–7). If this is the case, it is difficult to see how it can also produce the kind of polarization and tension that is likely to precede the profound change in the political and social status quo envisaged by Soviet theorists. Similarly, if trade and economic cooperation are mutually advantageous, they must preclude, or at least postpone, the economic crises which are endemic to capitalism and which aggravate class conflict, thus hastening the socialist revolution. For these reasons, peaceful coexistence seems unlikely to have the effects claimed for it by Soviet *mezhdunarodniki*.

There is another striking paradox in the Soviet theory of peaceful coexistence. It is said to benefit the international class struggle and to promote progressive change. But Soviet theorists are equally adamant that imperialist governments are implacably hostile to this kind of change. Moreover, their foreign policy, like all foreign policy, is designed to defend their class interests. This raises the question of why capitalist governments should consent at all to a form of international relations which is destined to undermine and then finally destroy their power. The explanation usually offered, as we have seen, is that they are reluctant partners in a relationship of peaceful coexistence which has been imposed upon them by the superior moral and military force of socialism. Yet peaceful coexistence, according to Khrushchev and all his successors without exception, is more than just the absence of war. It includes mutual understanding, trust and active co-operation. In other words, what is required from capitalist governments is the voluntary surrender of the class interests their foreign and domestic policies are designed to defend. If class struggle is sincerely believed to be 'the essence' of peaceful coexistence (Butenko 1975: 306n), Soviet theorists should wonder less that détente has powerful opponents in the West. In fact, the class-struggle aspect of peaceful coexistence is so unconvincing that the insistence that peaceful coexistence promotes the spread of socialism seems merely to be an act of theoretical cap-doffing to an outdated tenet which cannot be explicitly abandoned.

The Soviet desire for relations between different social and economic systems based on the principles of peaceful coexistence is long-standing. There is every reason to suppose that it is sincere. The intention of this argument is not to impugn the Soviet desire for peace, but to cast doubt on the logic of aspects of the theory. Not even the most dialectical of reasoning seems able to reconcile the various elements of the theory to make it internally consistent.

NOTES

1. In June 1954 five principles (Pancha Shila) of relations were accepted by India and China (Daniels 1984 vol. 2: 217–18). This formulation of peaceful coexistence was greeted with much enthusiasm in the Soviet Union (see *Pravda*, 29 June and 1 July 1954). It was supported by a declaration of the Supreme Soviet in February 1955 and it immediately became the basis for much of the Soviet writing on peaceful coexis-

tence. It was also adopted by the Bandung Conference as the basis of Afro-Asian international relations. For the Soviet response to Pancha Shila, see Krylov and Durdenevsky (1957: 5). For a Western view that despite the use of the term by Soviet theorists and policy-makers before 1956, it was Khrushchev who was the founder and creator of the current Soviet concept, see Marantz (1982).

2. Later it was denied that the socialist meaning of the term 'peaceful coexistence' was identical to the five principles. The content of these five traditional democratic principles had been enriched by socialist ideas. Through socialist pressure, for example, non-aggression had acquired international recognition. In a rather radical assertion, one author claimed that the principle of non-aggression now applied not only to interference in the domestic affairs of sovereign states, but also to the affairs of peoples and nations struggling for the right to self-determination (Butenko 1975: 309–10). But non-interference and non-intervention have had a chequered career in Soviet legal thinking. Korovin (1926) distinguished between 'reactionary' and 'progressive' intervention. Korovin (1951), after quoting Stalin at length on the subject, criticized his own previous 'unscientific' distinction, and insisted that interference is always an infringement of sovereignty and never progressive. Soviet declaratory practice has retained the later definition, while Soviet policy clearly continues to make the distinction.

3. For other examples of discussions of the international legal aspects of peaceful coexistence, see Tunkin (1956), Krylov and Durdenevsky (1957) and Gromyko (1962, Ch. VI).

4. In this particular article Korovin seemed to violate the spirit, if not the letter, of the very peaceful coexistence with the United States which he, Khrushchev, and every other spokesman on Soviet foreign policy were promoting. His examples to illustrate infringements of the principles were based on US transgressions: US bases on foreign territory 'with or without forced consent' violated the principle of respect for territorial integrity and sovereignty; the Anglo-American practice of 'fostering restrictive aggressive military blocs' and dictating policy 'from positions of strength' violated non-aggression; Marshall Aid and other kinds of US aid violated the principle of non-interference; while the 'open-door' and 'equal opportunities' policies so favoured by American diplomacy violated the principle of equality and mutual benefit, since they were based on deep-seated inequality (Korovin 1956: 46–7). The point is not whether Korovin's diagnosis was correct or not, but that his tone and examples were hardly consonant with a desire for relations based on cooperation with his chief villain.

5. Kubálková and Cruickshank maintain that Khrushchev stressed the peaceful content of peaceful coexistence to make it sound like a policy which aimed at preserving the status quo, instead of what it really was, a 'strategy for world revolution' (1980: 166). As we shall see, Khrushchev and the theorists who wrote about peaceful coexistence stressed that it corresponded to the norms of international law. But they also placed far more emphasis on ideological and economic competition

than had previously been customary. It is difficult to agree, therefore, that the peaceful content was stressed more than under Stalin. Indeed, given that Khrushchev frequently adopted an abrasive tone and that his foreign-policy decisions were erratic, peaceful coexistence often seemed a more belligerent policy between 1956 and 1964 than it did before or after.

6.   Although it is generally accepted that the Cuban missile fiasco played no small part in Khrushchev's dismissal two years later, Soviet theorists never reproach him in print for the crisis or see it as a contravention of peaceful coexistence on the part of the Soviet Union. The Cuban missile crisis has always been interpreted as the fault of American imperialism, and the standard phrase for describing Khrushchev's response to Kennedy's demand is that it 'combined principled firmness with tactical flexibility', although Khrushchev is not mentioned by name. See, for example, Lebedev (1982: 133), Stepanova (1982: 85). For a detailed Soviet account of the crisis (in which Khrushchev's name is never mentioned), see the chapter by Anatoly A. Gromyko in Zhurkin and Primakov (1972: 70–95).

7.   This does not imply that Brezhnev did not insist that Soviet foreign policy was peaceable. He merely used the term 'peaceful coexistence' sparingly, in the early years often preferring 'peaceful cooperation'. In his Central Committee report to the Twenty-Third Congress, for example, he mentioned the term four times. At the 1969 Conference of European Communist and Workers' Parties and in his 50th anniversary speech in 1967, he used it once only in each (Brezhnev 1973: 36–130). But the new doctrine announced at the Twentieth Party Congress (and, as Soviet writers put it, reaffirmed at the Twenty-First and Twenty-Second Party Congresses as well as in the international statements of 1957 and 1960) was by no means repudiated. Fulsome tribute continued to be paid to it, although it was no longer credited to Khrushchev. See Egorov (1971, *passim*) and, for a more recent tribute, Petrenko and Popov (1981: 155). One Western scholar, Marantz (1982: 234) believes that it was precisely because Khrushchev's colleagues believed that he had over-emphasized the term that it was downgraded after his dismissal.

8.   It was not a question of linguistic convenience. The term 'détente' is no less cumbersome in Russian than 'peaceful coexistence'. The Russian term for peaceful coexistence is *mirnoe sosushchestvovanie*, whereas détente is *razryadka napryazhennosti*, relaxation of tension (sometimes shortened to *razryadka*).

9.   The change in the correlation of forces in favour of socialism is considered to be due partly to the increase in the number of socialist states, partly to the growth of peace-loving and progressive forces in the capitalist world, and partly to the economic and military power of the Soviet Union and the socialist world. See Chapter 9 for a detailed discussion of Soviet definitions of power and the correlation of forces.

10. For other examples of theorists attributing the success of peaceful coexistence to Soviet power, see Lebedev (1976: 41), Mshvenieradze (1981: 109), Petrenko and Popov (1981: 167).

11. This is not to imply that the thaw in Sino-Western relations pleased the Soviet Union. Indeed, few international changes have caused them more anxiety. There is, moreover, reason to identify the improvement in Sino-American relations as an important motive for Soviet–American détente. Nor did the change in Chinese policy towards the West moderate Soviet objections to the earlier opposition to peaceful coexistence. Two prominent theorists explained the sequence of events as follows: until the early 1960s the Chinese had approved of peaceful coexistence. They then began to attack it as a betrayal of the revolution, demanding confrontation with the capitalist states. Their plans failed and after the Cultural Revolution they suddenly changed foreign-policy tactics and began to use peaceful coexistence in their own interests. Although the sincerity of the new tactics were considered doubtful, these theorists welcomed the change (Sanakoyev and Kapchenko 1973: 91–2). After the thaw in Sino-American relations, Soviet spokesmen (Arbatov 1973: 256, for example), went on claiming that the attitude towards relations between capitalist and socialist states was 'one of the principal issues between Leninism and opportunism'. The Chinese leadership, together with Trotskyists and the extreme left, represented the opportunists who propounded revolutionary war, contradicting the basic tenet of Marxism-Leninism that socialist revolution could not be imposed on people by force (Arbatov 1973: 257–9).

12. Egorov criticized a thesis which he maintained had been current at one stage (and which he attributed in particular to Soviet international lawyers like Tunkin and Federov, although he implied that there were other offenders) that peaceful coexistence was the general line of Soviet foreign policy. He called this 'a voluntaristic interpretation of the basic principles of the foreign policy of the USSR' (Egorov 1971: 160). It contradicted the theoretical basis and practice of Soviet foreign policy. Peaceful coexistence was only one line of Soviet foreign policy and concerned only relations with states with different social systems. In distinguishing between these two kinds of relationship, Egorov did not deviate from the accepted categories. But he seemed rather innovative in describing relations with newly independent countries as 'relations based on the principle of peaceful coexistence which may develop into relations based on the principles of proletarian internationalism' (Egorov 1971: 161). Other scholars have always implied or stated that the relations between socialist states and the ex-colonies are based on proletarian internationalism. See, for example, Butenko (1975: 311).

13. Western and Soviet differences of opinion about the relationship of Soviet aid to the national liberation movement and peaceful coexistence was a major reason for the breakdown in détente from the middle of the 1970s. The Western interpretation of peaceful coexistence has never included the Soviet right to extend military aid to the Third World. When the initial Western response of 'linkage' was ineffective and Soviet aid began to include Cuban troops and Soviet logistic support, détente quickly began to crumble.

14. See, for example, the first chapter in Egorov (1971) or Shakhnazarov (1984: *passim*). A number of books have been written on the ideological struggle and détente, for example, Arbatov (1973), Lebedev, Dracheva and Knyazhinsky (1981), Gantman (1981), Sanakoyev and Kapchenko (1981). It is interesting that the Soviet response to Reagan's ideological rhetoric has been a warning that the ideological struggle can get out of hand. After Reagan's 'evil empire' speech, for example, a Soviet theorist, Zamoshkin's spoke at Chatham House calling for a decrease in the ideological struggle. This call has been repeated by Gorbachev. See Light (1987) for the decline in ideology in Gorbachev's foreign-policy statements.

15. Although Brezhnev seemed to avoid the term 'peaceful coexistence', at this stage his verbal preferences were not yet immediately reflected in the terms chosen by *mezhdunarodniki* or other political leaders (the speed and frequency with which the top leader's words are exactly echoed may well be a way of measuring the extent of the personality cult!). In his report to the Twenty-Fourth Party Congress in 1971, when détente was already well established, he only used the term three times. His optimistic report to the Twenty-Fifth Congress in 1976 contained thirteen references to détente and only six to peaceful coexistence. One of the latter references was an offer to normalize relations with China 'in accordance with the principles of peaceful coexistence (CPSU 1976: 14). This signified a major theoretical departure. Until then it had been firmly maintained that peaceful coexistence only applied to relations between states with different social systems. Inter-socialist relations were founded on proletarian and socialist internationalism. No theoretical justification was given for the suggestion that two different types of relations could be operative within one group of states (or for the other possible implication—that the Soviet model was changing from a triangular to a quadrilateral model of the world). In fact, the offer had been made as early as 1972 (Brezhnev 1973: 434) and had been quoted by some international theorists (see, for example, Sanakoyev and Kapchenko 1973: 92). Kubálková and Cruickshank (1978: 191–8) maintain that the 1972 offer was low-key and that it only became significant in 1976.

16. For sample of the many books and articles with détente in the title rather than peaceful coexistence, see Usachev (1980), Gantman (1981), Mshvenieradze (1981), Deborin *et al.* (1982).

4 Incorporating the Third World I:
Socialism and Colonialism

As with all foreign policy, Soviet relations with less-developed countries (LDCs) and with the national-liberation movement are justified by reference to Marxist-Leninist theory. When relations with the Third World were revived after the Second World War, Lenin's theory seemed uncannily accurate. The disintegration of the colonial system after the Second World War was thought to prove the accuracy of his predictions about the fate of imperialism (Gromyko and Ponomarev 1981, vol. 2: 17–18). Similarly, the establishment of socialist and socialist-oriented states in Asia, and later in Africa and Latin America, seemed to prove the contention of both Marx and Lenin that in certain circumstances the capitalist phase of development can be avoided. There seemed to be no reason why other aspects of Marxist-Leninist theory would not prove equally useful. In fact, it can be argued that decolonization disproved as much of Lenin's theory of imperialism as it proved. In the vast majority of cases independence was granted rather than won through force of arms. Their colonies had become so expensive that far from weakening the metropolitan countries, they were strengthened by losing them. With regard to socialism in the colonies and ex-colonies, too, the theory has not been entirely reliable. The capitalist phase may have been skipped by some countries, but this has by no means proved invariable. Nor has the establishment of socialism proved quite as simple as Lenin seemed to suggest. In other words, although none of the original theories have been repudiated explicitly, it has become necessary to develop others to explain why outcomes other than those predicted by

Marx and, more particularly, by Lenin have occurred. That body of theory forms the subject of the next chapter. But an appreciation of how the theory has developed requires an outline of what the original theory was and how it was interpreted in the early days of decolonization. This chapter aims to provide that outline.

It begins with a brief examination of what Marx and Engels wrote about the colonies. There is a very direct link between their views and those of Lenin, although Soviet theorists pay more attention to what Lenin wrote. The colonies figured more in their journalism than in their political theory, but they drew attention to the potential advantages to socialism of colonial revolution. Whether they continued believing in a unique 'Asian' mode of production has become a contentious subject amongst students of and believers in Marxism. It is a term that was used by the Third Communist International (Comintern), although modern Soviet theorists believe that Marx had discarded the concept by the 1870s. It is uncontentious, however, that Marx and Engels prefigured Lenin's view that under certain conditions some underdeveloped countries would be able to proceed to socialism without going through the capitalist stage of development.

The second part of the chapter examines Lenin's view of the colonies and semi-colonies in two sections: his pre-revolutionary views and his attitudes after the revolution, particularly his contribution to the debates in and the policy adopted by the Comintern. This is followed by a consideration of Stalin's contribution to Soviet theory. Since the main thrust of the policy of both the Soviet state and the Comintern in the colonies and semi-colonies was directed towards China in the 1920s, and it was Stalin who personally controlled Soviet and Comintern Chinese policy, the first part of this section contains an account of Stalin's China theory and the policy which it produced. The second section describes the changes in Soviet attitudes towards the colonies and the first ex-colonies in the aftermath of the Second World War. It will be seen that although Soviet theory became very radical, a more moderate view began to prevail before Stalin's death. In other words, the origin of the theory and the policy launched by Khrushchev can be traced back to the period before Stalin's death.

MARX, ENGELS AND THE COLONIES

Soviet theorists pay relatively little attention to what Marx and Engels wrote about the colonies. There are two related reasons for this. First, although Marx and Engels were acutely aware and highly critical of the evil effects of colonialism, in their writing about the colonies they often displayed the patronizing values of Victorian Europeans. This attitude, as Avineri points out (Avineri 1969: 13), is a source of embarassment to orthodox communists. Second, their theory of the Asiatic mode of development forms part of that writing, and this particular concept has been rejected by Soviet theorists.[1] It is, however, relatively easy to trace the connections between their views and Lenin's on colonialism and the effects of colonial revolutions on metropolitan countries. Moreover, the idea of an alliance between the peasantry and the proletariat, pre-eminently credited to Lenin, is prefigured by Marx and so is the possibility of skipping the capitalist stage of development. In other words, both Lenin's theories about the East and his views on the prerequisites of revolution in Russia can be traced back to Marx.

Much of what Marx and Engels wrote about colonialism took the form of newspaper articles analysing current events. Their criticism of its deleterious effects seems remarkably modern and acute. They understood, for example, that traditional ways of life were undermined by colonialism. They deeply disapproved of the opium trade and they defended the 'unethical' means used by the Chinese in fighting the Opium Wars (Marx 1951b).[2] But at the same time they were unambiguous in their belief that colonialism was a positive and necessary phenomenon. It was a progressive force and the external agent without which the colonial peoples would not be able to advance from their traditional, stagnant way of life. No matter how mercenary their motives, the colonizers imparted civilization to the backward peoples of Asia and Africa who lived in a state of 'Asiatic barbarity'. There seems little doubt that both Marx and Engels believed that Western civilization was superior to 'the jealousy, the intrigues, the ignorance, the cupidity and corruption of the Orientals', or the 'rotting semi-civilization' represented by China (Engels, in Marx 1951b:45). Despite the nastiness and Slavonic filth of

Russian rule, it was a civilizing force for the Bashkirs and Tartars of the Black and Caspian Seas and Central Asia (Engels to Marx, in Marx 1969: 447). Marx called the conquest of Algeria 'an important and fortunate fact for the progress of civilization' (Marx 1969: 47). As far as India was concerned, Britain had given it political unity, a native army, a free press, private land ownership and had encouraged the emergence of an educated class capable of governing (Marx 1951a: 67–8). More important than the motives behind colonialism was the question:

[Could] mankind fulfil its destiny without a fundamental revolution in the social state of Asia? If not, whatever may have been the crimes of England, she was the unconscious tool of history in bringing about that revolution.

(Marx 1951a: 29)

The low esteem in which Marx and Engels held the colonial peoples was, perhaps, typical for Europeans of the nineteenth century. But it fitted with their poor opinion of the peasantry, since the Asian society they described contained only despots and peasants. Marx felt what one modern Western scholar has called 'the conventional disgust of an urban intellectual for the backward and stagnant provinces' (Mann 1983: 16–17).

But whatever contempt Marx and Engels may have felt for peasants, they did not rule out temporary alliances between them and the urban proletariat under the leadership of the proletariat (Marx and Engels 1850a: 106–17). In fact, they understood that peasant participation was essential to the proletarian revolution in peasant countries. It would provide 'that chorus without which [the proletarian revolution's] solo song becomes a swan song in all peasant countries' (Marx 1851: 340). This legitimized Lenin's later arguments for a worker–peasant alliance in Russia. But as far as the colonies were concerned, there was no proletariat with which the peasants could ally themselves. Indeed, there were no recognizable class divisions.

Oriental society and the Asiatic mode of production

It was the absence of recognizable class divisions which made Marx and Engels call the Oriental way of life stagnant. Social classes, and the antagonism which developed between them, were the prerequisites for the historical pattern of change which they had discerned in Europe (progressing from primitive communism to slave-owning, feudal and capitalist society). They could not detect any internal mechanism for change in Oriental society. This was why colonialism, for all its evils, was beneficial. Without the impact of an external force like colonialism, there was no prospect of change and development. At times Marx seemed to depict the mode of production in India as first in a developing sequence and therefore part of a universal historical development: 'In broad outlines Asiatic, ancient, feudal and modern bourgeois methods of production can be designated as progressive epochs in the economic formation of society' (Marx 1859: 383). Later, however, both Marx and Engels wrote about the Asiatic form of production as something static and unchanging and therefore substantially different from European modes of production with their inherent imperative for change. What distinguished Asian society was the absence of private property, caused mainly by 'the climate, taken in connection with the nature of the soil, especially with the great stretches of desert' (Engels to Marx, in Marx 1969: 452). In such climatic conditions, agriculture was impossible without irrigation on a scale which could not be undertaken privately. It had to be provided by a central government. A supplementary feature of Asian life which contributed to its stagnation was the extent to which society was atomized: 'the whole empire, not counting the few larger towns, was divided into *villages*, each of which possessed a completely separate organisation and formed a little world in itself' (Marx 1969: 455). Because these self-sufficient villages were cut off from one another, they remained traditional and conservative. There was very little commerce between them and, consequently, no development of a bourgeoisie. As a result of this atomization and the central economic role of the state, it tended to be despotic.

Since, to Marx, history meant change and he could detect no motor for change in Asiatic society, he maintained that it had no history, or 'at least no known history' (Marx 1951a: 67). A consequence of this description of the Asiatic mode of production as something which stood outside of history was that Marx's claim to have discovered universal laws of history was undermined. If much of the world outside Europe lived under this particular mode of production, then the historical progress from feudalism to capitalism and then socialism was inevitable only in Europe (unless, of course, colonialism transferred capitalism to the colonies; but even then the agent of change would not be the inevitable internal dialectic of the conflict between material productive forces and existing relations of production, but an outside force). Marx himself later claimed only to have written an 'historical sketch of the genesis of capitalism in Western Europe . . . [not] an historico-philosophic theory of the general path of development prescribed by fate to all nations, whatever the historical circumstances in which they find themselves' (Marx 1877: 293). His modern Soviet successors have preferred to ignore the Asiatic mode of production and retain the claim that Marxism is a universal theory.[3]

The possibility of omitting a stage of development
Neither Marx nor Engels seemed to envisage that development would be possible for countries with an Asiatic mode of production without going through the capitalist stage. If progress was to occur at all, it would be via the transfer of capitalism. But they did not consider what would happen after capitalism had been introduced from without.[4] However, whereas there was no suggestion that capitalism was a stage that could be skipped by the colonial countries, a number of years later they implied that Russia could skip the capitalist stage. Marx decried developments in Russia after the emancipation of the serfs. Russia would 'lose the finest chance ever offered by history to a people and undergo all the fatal vicissitudes of the capitalist regime', instead of proceeding from village communities 'by developing the historical conditions specifically her own' (Marx 1877: 292). The Russian peasant community could be the mainspring of Russia's social regeneration if hostile influences were eliminated and spontaneous development occurred (Marx 1881: 319–20). While Engels ridiculed the idea that Russian peasants were socialist by instinct or that Russia had the material foundations for socialism, he too thought that Russia could avoid capitalism if a proletarian socialist revolution took place in the West (Engels, cited in Mann 1983: 29). It is possible, of course, that

he would by then have come to the same conclusion about the colonial countries of Asia or Africa, but they had ceased to be a focus of his attention. In any case, his views about Russia, reiterated later by Lenin, served as a useful basis for later theories of post-independence colonial development.[5]

The relationship between colonial and metropolitan revolutions

One of the results of colonialism was the rise of nationalism in the colonial countries. As we shall see in Chapter 6, Marx and Engels only supported nationalism in Europe when they considered that it would further the aims of revolution.[6] But even in those cases, they saw it essentially as an auxiliary force in bringing about a democratic or socialist revolution in the metropolis.

Similarly, the nationalism engendered by colonialism should be supported not for its own sake but because it would bring about colonial revolutions which, in turn, would bring about revolution in the metropolitan countries. It was particularly in connection with Ireland that the power of colonial revolution to bring about revolution in England seemed obvious. Indeed, Marx believed that 'the decisive blow against the English ruling classes . . . cannot be delivered *in England* but *only in Ireland*' (Marx 1870: 221. It was therefore particularly important to 'make the English workers realize that *for them* the *national emancipation of Ireland* is . . . *the first condition of their own social emancipation*' (Marx 1870: 223). The duty of socialists to support colonial liberation movements became an important part of Lenin's theory of the East.

Marx and Engels were ambivalent, however, about the relationship between the colonial and metropolitan revolutions. At first Marx thought that revolution abroad would provoke revolution in Europe but would not itself be successful until after the metropolitan revolution. He said of the Chinese struggle for example:

it may safely be augured that the Chinese revolution will throw the spark into the overloaded mine of the present industrial system and cause the explosion of the long-prepared general crisis, which, spreading abroad, will be closely followed by political revolutions on the Continent.

(Marx 1951b: 7)

At other times, he seemed to imply that the success of a colonial revolution, at least in terms of improving local conditions, did not necessarily depend upon revolution in the metropolis. With regard to India he seemed to think that either variant was possible:

The Indians will not reap the fruits of the new elements of society scattered among them . . . till in Great Britain itself the now ruling classes shall have been supplanted by the industrial proletariat, or till the Hindus themselves shall have grown strong enough to throw off the English yoke altogether.
(Marx 1951a: 71)

What remained unclear was the form these 'fruits' would take. Indeed, however necessary they believed capitalism was to colonial development, their analyses of its effects in Europe were filled with descriptions of the awful social conditions it caused. If the history of European industrialization was to be repeated in the colonies, there was little ground for optimism. Marx's fear that Russia would fall victim to the 'fatal vicissitudes' of capitalism indicates that whatever the final benefits in terms of becoming ripe for a socialist revolution, he thought that capitalism itself had little to recommend it. But neither he or Engels dwelt on colonial or post-colonial developments. Engels maintained that only idle hypotheses could be advanced about the various social and political phases through which the colonies would pass before arriving at socialist organization (Marx and Engels 1975: 331).[7]

What Marx and Engels wrote about the colonies did not, in any sense, form a complete theory. Moreover, their interest was less in the colonies *per se* than in the potential effect of events in the colonies on the metropolitan countries. As a result they paid little attention to developments within colonial societies. None the less, a number of their views were reflected in the writings of subsequent Marxists, most particularly (in terms of the subject-matter of this thesis at least) in Lenin's theory.

LENIN AND THE REVOLUTION IN THE EAST

Lenin's best-known writing on colonialism was contained in his pre-revolutionary 'Imperialism: The Highest Stage of Capitalism' (Lenin 1916d: 185–304) and in his post-revolutionary draft theses for the Second Congress of the Comintern (Lenin 1920c: 252–9). But the complex Bolshevik teaching on nationalism and self-determination referred as much to the colonies as to the Russian Empire. Moreover, both the theory of uneven development and the analysis of why revolution would begin in Russia could equally apply to the colonies.[8] These theories were and are often referred to by later theorists in their discussion of independence movements and post-colonial developments (see, for example, Butenko 1975: 370; Trush 1977: 164–5). In fact, Lenin's writings turned out to be inadequate for explaining developments in the colonial and post-colonial world when de-colonization began after the Second World War for much the same reason that those of his predecessors fell short. Like Marx and Engels, Lenin was primarily interested in the effects of colonial revolution on the metropolitan countries. As a result, he paid little attention to the situation within the colonies, the means by which independence could be hastened or likely developments after independence.

Although colonialism was the subject-matter of 'Imperialism' and was not irrelevant to other pre-revolutionary theoretical issues, the East really only became a live political issue after the October Revolution. By then the Bolshevik attitude to the colonies was an issue in their relations with other countries too. The British government, for example, was very anxious about the influence of Bolshevism on the British colonies, particularly India. The price of a commercial agreement with Britain in 1921 was the promise not to proselytize in the British colonies. Lenin did not change his ideas about the East very radically after the Revolution, but it is convenient to begin by looking at his pre-revolutionary writings, before turning to the situation after 1917, particularly in the Comintern.

Pre-revolutionary theory
The class structure of the colonies

Despite Lenin's rather poor opinion of the peasantry as a class, he astutely developed an agrarian policy for Russia that would ensure peasant support for the Bolshevik Party. Unlike Engels, he did not believe that the Russian peasant commune could serve to prevent Russia from going through a capitalist stage of development. He argued that the Russian system of farming sustained feudal relationships in the countryside (Lenin 1914a: 375–7). But he understood that although socialism would require a more advanced method of farming, in a country like Russia, where the peasantry formed 80 per cent of the population, neither the bourgeois democratic nor the socialist revolutions could succeed without peasant support. The only way to get that support was to offer the peasants the land that they wanted. In 1905 he supported the seizure of the land by the peasants, and in 1917 he used their demand for (and spontaneous confiscation of) land to enlist their support for the Bolsheviks by adding land to the Bolshevik call for 'bread, peace and freedom'. None the less, he believed that the peasants were petty bourgeois by nature and his opinion of them was not much better than that of Marx and Engels.[9]

Curiously, although Lenin must have understood that the proportion of peasants in the colonial population was even higher than in Russia, he sometimes seemed to misunderstand the nature of the colonial class structure. He implied that colonialism was creating a vast proletariat in the colonies. In 1908, for example, he maintained that:

the age-old plunder of India by the British and the contemporary struggle of all these 'advanced' Europeans against Persian and Indian democracy, will *steel* millions, tens of millions of proletarians in Asia to wage a struggle against their oppressors. . . . The class-conscious European worker now has comrades in Asia, and their number will grow by leaps and bounds.
(Lenin 1908: 22)

Colonialism not only turned the colonial peasantry into a proletariat very quickly, but also spoilt the European proletariat, infecting it with 'colonial chauvinism' (Lenin 1907: 18). The reason for this was that it was no longer the labour of the European proletariat which maintained society but the labour of 'the practically enslaved natives in the colonies'. The upper

strata of the metropolitan working class had thus been corrupted. Privileged sections had been created which were
detached from the broad masses of the proletariat and prone
to opportunism (Lenin 1916d: 281). What Lenin meant by
opportunism was that the European proletariat was often in
favour of colonialism and therefore did not support colonial
independence movements.

There was also a difference between the colonial bourgeoisie and the metropolitan middle class. When Europe was
feudal, the bourgeoisie had been a progressive class. Now,
however, it was 'decayed'. The colonial bourgeoisie, on the
other hand, was still revolutionary, 'capable of championing
sincere, militant, consistent democracy ... still capable of
supporting an historically progressive cause' (Lenin 1912: 47).
The principal social support of the Asian bourgeoisie in its
democratic struggle was the peasant. No matter how progressive the colonial bourgeoisie, however, Lenin recognized (in
contrast to his optimism regarding the growing size of the
colonial proletariat) that it was still small. In 1916 he maintained that bourgeois-democratic movements had hardly
begun or still had a long way to go in the East (Lenin 1916g:
151). European socialists should demand the immediate liberation of the colonies and

render determined support to the more revolutionary elements in the
bourgeois-democratic movements for national liberation in these countries
and assist their uprising—or revolutionary war, in the event of one—*against*
the imperialist powers that oppress them.

(Lenin 1916g: 151–2)

The possibility of omitting a stage of development
In his writing before the Russian Revolution, Lenin explicitly
denied that capitalism could be prevented or avoided, describing the Chinese view that this was possible as reactionary
(Lenin 1912: 47–9). In any case, capitalism had already begun
in the colonies. The main difference between capitalism and
monopoly capitalism was that the former exported goods,
whereas monopoly capitalism exported capital. And the
result of exporting capital was to 'greatly accelerate the development of capitalism in those countries to which it was
exported' (Lenin 1916d: 243). Thus the East had already
embarked on the capitalist path, on the 'struggle for the ideals

which the West has already worked out for itself' (Lenin 1912: 47). Lenin clearly agreed with Marx that capitalism was progressive, at least in relation to the system of economic relations it replaced in the colonies. Later, as we shall see, he changed his mind about whether capitalism was an essential phase of development.

Apart from viewing the construction of capitalism within the colonies as an inevitable consequence of colonialism, Lenin paid little attention to economic, social or political developments within the colonies. 'Imperialism', for example, contained a description of how imperialism had occurred: first, production became concentrated in monopolies; second, bank capital and industrial capital merged to form a financial oligarchy; third, capital was exported; fourth, international monopolist combines were formed; and fifth, the whole world was divided up territorially amongst the largest capitalist powers (Lenin 1916d: 266–7). It also contained a polemical argument against Kautsky, whose definition in 1914 and 1915 (Kautsky 1970) of a phase of 'ultra-imperialism' (in which the partition of the world would be stabilized and the risk of war eliminated) Lenin was intent on refuting, and an explanation of why imperialism necessarily entailed war. But it did not contain an analysis of the social and economic structure of the colonies, of the consequences for them of the development of capitalism or of the results of the inevitable struggle for national emancipation which accompanied imperialism. He implied that the collapse of imperialism would precede colonial independence. Colonial liberation could occur under capitalism, but 'only by way of exception or at the cost of a series of revolts and revolutions both in the colonies and the metropolitan countries' (Lenin 1916c: 338). He did not consider what would happen if the exceptions proved more numerous than the rule (as they did after the Second World War) or how further development within the colonies would occur after liberation. He realized, however, that there would be a problem, since the colonies could not be extricated from dependence on European finance capital: 'The colonies have no capital of *their own*, or none to speak of, and under finance capital no colony can obtain any except on terms of political submission' (Lenin 1916c: 338). The absence of capital and, therefore, the difficulty in following traditional Marxist stages of development may have been why Lenin later postulated that capitalism could, under certain conditions, be skipped.

The relationship between colonial and metropolitan revolutions

As we have seen, Marx had argued that colonial revolution would provoke European revolution (although he did not think that the colonial revolution would necessarily be successful without a European revolution). Lenin, on the other hand, sometimes seemed to visualize simultaneous revolutions. The revolution in Europe would occur in 'an epoch in which are combined civil war by the proletariat against the bourgeoisie in the advanced countries and a *whole* series of democratic and revolutionary movements . . . in the underdeveloped, backward and oppressed nations' (Lenin 1916a: 60). To imagine that social revolution was '*conceivable* without revolts by small nations in the colonies and in Europe' was to '*repudiate social revolution*' (Lenin 1916c: 355). At the same time, no matter how essential colonial revolutions were, Lenin was adamant (he was arguing against the Polish social-democrats at the time) that uprisings by small European nations were infinitely more valuable to the success of socialist revolution than any number of more intense rebellions in remote colonies (Lenin 1916c: 357). It is clear that it was socialist revolution rather than colonial liberation that was his prime concern. European socialist revolutions became even more important to him after the October Revolution.

Post-revolutionary theory

Lenin's belief in the right of the nations belonging to the Tsarist Empire to secession was eroded by the Civil War (see Ch. 6).[10] However, the right of the colonies to self-determination continued to be upheld. But the imminent expectation of revolution in Europe meant that the Bolsheviks' main attention was directed towards Europe, not the East.[11] None the less, the relationship between revolution in the East and European revolution remained a subject of debate. Trotsky and Zinoviev both maintained that national liberation in the East was contingent upon successful European socialist revolution, while others, sometimes including Lenin and, as we shall see, most particularly Stalin, claimed that European socialist revolution could not succeed without the aid of colonial revolution.[12] Self-determination for the colonies became a more important issue as European revolution became less credible. The 'East' acquired a new importance in Bolshevik theory and practice, most particularly at the Second Congress of the Comintern in 1920, but it was an importance that waxed and waned, depending on how imminent European revolution seemed.[13]

Which forces should be supported: Lenin vs Roy

The Second Congress set out to formulate a policy for the Comintern on the national and colonial question. There were four key issues: how important the East was; why it was important; which groups of people should be supported; and the need for European parties to pay more attention to the colonial question. The only issue on which there was complete agreement was the last (although little substantive was done to translate words into deeds). A commission was established to discuss two sets of theses, one drafted by N. M. Roy, the Indian delegate, who expressed the 'Eastern' opinion, the other by Lenin, embodying a more 'Western' view.

On the first issue, Roy was certain that the Comintern should devote its major attention to the East. Lenin agreed that the East had been neglected, but he did not think that the Comintern effort in Europe should be diverted. On the question of why the East was important, Roy asserted that the European revolution was dependent upon the Asian, while Lenin merely maintained that revolution in the colonies would facilitate revolution in Europe and help to save Soviet Russia. The argument about which forces should be supported in the colonies was the most important, since it was to have long-term consequences for colonial socialists. Roy argued that the transfer of capitalism to the colonies would soon produce an alignment of forces that resembled that of the West. The national bourgeoisie would become richer, coalesce with the feudal classes and compromise with Western imperialism against the proletariat and the peasantry. The anti-imperialist struggle, therefore, would be led not by the bourgeoisie but by the proletariat and peasantry. The Comintern ought urgently to create communist organizations of

workers and peasants rather than support the unreliable
national bourgeoisie (Eudin and North 1957: 65–7). This view
contrasted with Lenin's belief that the revolution in the East
should be based on the bourgeois nationalism which had been
awakened in the colonies as a result of the war (Lenin 1919a:
230–41). In his draft theses Lenin argued that bourgeois-
democratic and peasant movements should be assisted in
more backward states and nations. Socialists should form
alliances with them, while preserving their independence by
refusing to fuse completely (Lenin 1920c: 252–9). The debate
which ensued, the subsequent vote and the way it was interpreted were to have a profound effect on both Comintern and
Soviet policy (in so far as the two were separable) towards the
national-liberation movement for many years.[14]

Both sets of theses appear to have enjoyed considerable
support. As a result, they were amended slightly (Lenin's so
that the term 'bourgeois democratic' was replaced with
'national revolutionary', which excluded reformist movements likely to collaborate with imperialists against revolutionary movements) and both were adopted, even though
Lenin's theses called for support of the struggle of all Eastern
nations against Western imperialism, while Roy's insisted
upon the hopelessness of such a policy and the need to support
socialists. In the years after the Congress, Roy's theses fell
into abeyance and Lenin's view prevailed, although it reflected, in the words of one Western historian:

[A] child-like conviction that your adversary will not understand your
intentions, though you express them quite openly, that he will continue to
co-operate with you as long as *you* want it and allow himself to be
overthrown when it suits *you*.

(Borkenau 1962: 292–3)[15]

There were three reasons why Lenin's view prevailed: first,
it was very similar to the Bolshevik policy which had worked
so well in achieving a successful revolution in Russia. Both
Bolsheviks and other Comintern members were inclined to
believe that it would work equally well elsewhere. Second,
Bolshevik and Comintern policy rapidly grew less radical after
the Second Comintern Congress. Lenin's theses, rather than
Roy's, corresponded to the new line of compromise which
seemed essential and which Lenin prescribed in 'Left-Wing

Communism: An Infantile Disorder' (Lenin 1920a: 17–118).[16]
Third, although the revolution in the East was said to be vital,
Soviet and the Comintern's interest remained focused on
Europe. Successful colonial independence movements
would, it was thought, weaken the European countries and
make the socialist revolution more likely. And independence
movements were far more likely to be successful if they were
led by the national bourgeoisie (or the national revolutionaries, which amounted to the same thing) and not by nascent
or weak communist organizations.

The possibility of omitting a stage of development
It was at the Second Comintern Congress that Lenin changed
his mind about the necessity for colonies to go through a
capitalist phase of economic development. He now argued, as
Marx had argued about Russia, that:

> If the victorious revolutionary proletariat conducts systematic propaganda
> among [the backward nations] and the Soviet governments come to their aid
> with all the means at their disposal—in that event it will be mistaken to
> assume that the backward peoples must inevitably go through the capitalist
> stage of development.
>
> (Lenin 1920d: 270)

In the years that followed the Second Comintern Congress
the growing interest in the East was reflected in a number of
developments. Two congresses were specifically devoted to
the East: in September 1920 a Congress of Toilers of the East
took place in Baku, and in January 1922 a Congress of Toilers
of the Far East took place in Moscow and Leningrad. In
addition, the Red International of Labour Unions (Profin-
tern) and the Peasant International (Krestintern) were
formed in 1921 and 1923 respectively. A Communist University of Toilers of the East was set up, and Comintern agents
made contact with Asian revolutionary movements.[17] This
activity, however, had very little impact on the course of
revolution in the East, except in Outer Mongolia, where a
Mongolian People's government was set up in 1921 with
Soviet aid. The Soviet Union agreed to keep troops in the
country for as long as required (Degras 1951, vol. 1: 252–3).
Mongolia was organized as a Soviet but not a socialist
republic. It was never incorporated into the Soviet Union, but

it relied heavily on Soviet aid (see Carr 1972, vol. 3: 833–902 for an account of the early post-revolutionary developments in Mongolia).

There was very little discussion about colonial affairs at the Third Comintern Congress in 1921. By 1922, however, and the Fourth Comintern Congress, reviving conservatism in the West made the Eastern national revolution an increasingly desirable goal. Lenin took little part in the discussion, except to urge moderation. Once again a compromise resolution was adopted: collaboration with the bourgeoisie would continue for as long as it supported social and agrarian reform. Refusal by socialists to enter into alliance with national revolutionary movements (called opportunism) and remaining aloof from class struggle in the name of national unity were equally criticized. However, within the alliance, socialists should continue preserving an independent identity. Their tasks were dual: to fight for radical solutions of the problems of the bourgeois-democratic revolution and to organize the workers and peasants for class struggle (Degras 1960, vol. 1: 383–93).

In Lenin's last published article he expressed a renewed faith in the East. Since Russia, India, China and so on constituted a gigantic majority of the world's population, and since this majority had rapidly been drawn into the struggle for emancipation in the past few years, there could not be 'the slightest doubt what the final outcome will be . . . the complete victory of socialism is fully and absolutely assured' (Lenin 1923a: 318). Once again, however, it was disappointment in the absence of revolution in Europe rather than a belief in the intrinsic importance of the colonial world which prompted this turn to the East.

Considering Lenin's work as a whole, and the very small amount of it that was devoted to colonialism, it is clear that modern Soviet theorists exaggerate his part in shaping Soviet theory and policy towards the Third World. As McLane points out, the only systematic consideration he gave to the subject was in 1920, and even then his formulation was vague, often irrelevant and frequently a source of misunderstanding and confusion (McLane 1966: 75–6). His real contribution lay in directing the Comintern's attention to the world beyond Europe. None the less, modern theorists quote him constantly, particularly in relation to the need to support bour-

geois independence movements and the possibility of skipping the capitalist phase of development. But after his death
both Bolshevik and the Comintern Eastern policy and theory
more and more reflected Stalin's views. In fact, as Commissar
for Nationalities from October 1917 onwards, Stalin's views
had carried weight even before Lenin's illness and death. It
was in relation to China that his theory and his policy were
most clearly demonstrated.

STALIN AND THE COLONIAL QUESTION

Although Stalin's views on the national question had long
been considered authoritative, he did not hold any important
positions in the Comintern.[18] Since two of his rivals for power,
Trotsky and Zinoviev, were prominent in the Comintern and
could count on considerable support, he tended, until his
position had been secured, to bypass it. He had, however,
linked the national question to developments in the colonies
even before the revolution, pointing out that the Bolshevik
policy towards the national minorities in Russia should be
combined with support for revolutionary movements against
imperialism. This would create 'a rear for the vanguard of the
socialist revolution' and build a bridge between West and East
(Stalin 1917: 67).

The images of the October Revolution as a 'bridge' and the
colonial revolution as the 'rear' remained amongst Stalin's
favourite themes after the Revolution. He warned, for example, against forgetting the East because it represented the
' "inexhaustible" reserve and "most reliable" rear of world
imperialism' (Stalin 1918a: 359). He maintained that the
October Revolution had transposed the national question
into the more general question of colonial emancipation, thus
erecting 'a bridge between the socialist West and the enslaved
East' (Stalin 1918b: 76). He also insisted that the successful
resolution of the Russian national problem (by which he
meant overcoming the two deviations of Great Russian
chauvinism and local nationalism, and materially aiding the
backward border peoples of Russia to develop a socialist
economy without passing through the stage of industrial
capitalism) was vital for the domestic well-being of the

October Revolution. It would also be of international significance, providing an example that would stir up and revo-
lutionize 'the far imperialist rear—the colonial and semi-
colonial countries of the East—and thereby hasten the fall of
capitalism' (Stalin 1923: 148). Although, to use Boersner's
categories (see n. 6), Stalin was rather more 'Eastern' in his
view of the importance of colonial revolution, in the long run
he saw no prospect for either successful emancipation without
the overthrow of capitalism, or for lasting proletarian victory
without colonial emancipation. In other words, he had a far
more interdependent view of the relationship between the
two revolutions than either Roy or Lenin:

the victory of the world proletarian revolution may be regarded as assured
only if the proletariat is able to combine its own revolutionary struggle with
the movement for the emancipation of the toiling masses of the non-
sovereign nations and the colonies against the power of the imperialists, and
for a dictatorship of the proletariat.   (Stalin 1921: 115)

Stalin's interest in the East became more pronounced as the
climate in Europe became less revolutionary. Once the Bolsheviks had failed at Warsaw in 1921 and in Hungary and
Germany, they realized that the European revolutionary
movement was slowing down (Stalin 1923: 147–8). But the
revolutionary possibilities in the colonial liberation movement were not yet exhausted and they could be 'utilized for
the purpose of overthrowing imperialism' (Stalin 1924a: 52).
China became the focus of attention because it was there that
both Nationalist (Kuomintang) and Communist Parties (the
Chinese Communist Party, CCP, was established in 1921)
existed and had been persuaded to form an alliance. Moreover, the Soviet government had signed an agreement to aid
the Kuomintang.[19] It was for these reasons, first, that Soviet
government policy towards China was more important than
the Comintern policy (until the two became indistinguishable
after Stalin had attained supreme power) and, second, that
Soviet policy was pre-eminently Stalin's policy and thus
served as one of the issues in the Stalin–Trotsky dispute.[20]

Stalin and the Comintern
Which forces should be supported?
Although Stalin did not work through it at first, the

Comintern did not entirely ignore the national and colonial question. The Fifth Congress in 1924 was preoccupied with the failure of the uprising in Germany in 1923 and the 'Russian question' (i.e. the opposition within the Russian Communist Party), but there was a debate between Roy and Manuilsky on colonial affairs. Roy urged prudence in the matter of alliance with the national bourgeoisie, pointing to Lenin's agreement at the Second Congress that support should be given to revolutionary and not to reformist parties. Building up reliable local communist parties should be the most important task. In dismissing Roy's objection, Manuilsky gave an intimation of future trends, in particular the way in which Stalin would become co-legitimator of all policy and the Comintern would express the interests of the Soviet state rather than those of the international revolution. First, he linked Stalin's name with Lenin's as the source of revolutionary theory and co-architect of the theses adopted by the Second Congress. Second, he implied that Asian nationalism was more useful to Soviet foreign policy than proletarian or peasant movements (because it harassed Russia's European enemies). Asian communists should therefore collaborate with or even, if necessary, organize petty-bourgeois parties (for a discussion of the debate, see Carr 1972, vol. 3: 89–91, 632–5). A few years later Stalin was to explain that the Comintern support for the Kuomintang in 1926 and 1927 had been correct because it enfeebled and undermined imperialism, 'thus facilitating the development of the hearth and home of the world revolution, the USSR' (Stalin, 1927d: 237).

The debate between Roy and Manuilsky, like the previous debate between Roy and Lenin, was an argument between Eastern and Western viewpoints. Roy, while overestimating the size of the colonial proletariat, was promoting the socialist future of the colonies, whereas Manuilsky was primarily interested in encouraging those colonial developments that would weaken capitalism in the metropolitan countries, and thus encourage revolution in Europe. The extent to which Manuilsky reflected Stalin's view may be seen by Stalin's evaluation of the national movements in Afghanistan and Egypt:

The struggle which the Emir of Afghanistan is waging for the independence of his country is objectively a *revolutionary* struggle, despite the monarchist views of the Emir and his entourage, for it weakens, disintegrates and undermines imperialism . . . For the same reason, the struggle which the Egyptian merchants and bourgeois intellectuals are waging for the independence of their country is objectively *revolutionary* despite the bourgeois origin and bourgeois calling of the leaders of the Egyptian national movement and despite the fact that they are opposed to socialism . . . the national movement of the oppressed countries should be judged . . . from the point of view of the actual results in the sum total of the struggle against imperialism.

(Stalin 1924b: 194)

Stalin, however, was eclectic about which national movements should be supported and when. Where they came into conflict with the interests of the development of the proletarian movement, support was 'entirely out of the question' (Stalin 1924b: 52). He distinguished between three kinds of colonies. In those in which there was no proletariat the task of Communists was to create a united national front against imperialism. In countries like Egypt or China, in which there was a small proletariat and the bourgeoisie had already split into revolutionary and compromising parties, Communists should form a revolutionary bloc of workers and petty bourgeoisie (he gave the Kuomintang as an example of this kind of bloc), while retaining leadership of the revolutionary party and freedom of agitation and propaganda. Finally, in countries like India, where the compromising section of the bourgeoisie had already come to an agreement with imperialism, the proletariat should systematically be made ready to become hegemonic in the liberation movement (Stalin 1925b: 216–18). The situation in China gave him the opportunity to try out his theories.

Stalin and the Chinese Revolution, 1924–7

There is general agreement amongst Western scholars that Stalin's China policy was spectacularly unsuccessful. McLane, for example, maintains that:

Stalin's single full-fledged venture in Asia, marred by misjudgments and a Byzantine devotion to intrigue, was a disaster from which recovery was possible only in the avoidance of similar ventures in the future.

(McLane 1966: 483)

It is certainly true that the Chinese Communist Party paid heavily for following his advice. Moreover, it was in relation to China that the Comintern most obviously became first a forum for his struggle against Trotsky and then his mouth-piece. International revolution was replaced by defence of socialism in one country (in other words, the security of the Soviet state) as the first priority. Whether colonial revolution was ever really of primary importance to either Stalin or the Comintern is debatable. From its inception colonial represen-tatives often complained that insufficient attention was paid to revolution in the East. But it was only in 1935 that it became apparent that there could be serious conflict between Soviet security and colonial revolution.

Stalin's 'venture' in China can be divided into three phases: from 1924 to April 1927 he insisted that the Chinese Revo-lution was a 'bourgeois revolution of an anti-imperialist type' and that therefore an alliance between the Kuomintang and the CCP was required (Stalin 1927e: 196), even after Chiang Kai-shek (who had succeeded Sun Yat-sen as leader of the Kuomintang) began restricting the CCP. The climax of this phase was Chiang Kai-shek's attack on the communists of Shanghai who, on orders from Moscow, had hidden their arms. Stalin maintained that his and the Comintern's position had been 'absolutely correct' (Stalin 1927e: 196) and that the CCP was at fault. The national bourgeoisie, Stalin admitted, had deserted the Chinese Revolution, but the compensation was that the Revolution had entered a higher phase of development.

The second phase in 1927 was, according to Stalin, 'a gigantic agrarian revolution' (Stalin 1927e: 198). The correct policy for the Chinese communists was to continue their alliance with the left wing of the Kuomintang, impelling it leftwards to 'transform it into the core of a revolutionary-democratic dictatorship of the proletariat and peasantry' (Stalin 1927e: 203). Stalin would not at this stage consider the establishment of soviets in China because that would have meant rushing ahead and becoming divorced from the masses (Stalin 1927a: 245). He maintained that the Chinese Revo-lution had suffered a temporary defeat and only when a new upsurge had become a fact would it be appropriate to set up soviets (Stalin 1927e: 217). But he agreed that the CCP should

sponsor agrarian reform. The second phase ended in July
when the left Kuomintang expelled the communists, arresting
some and killing others. Once again the CCP was blamed and
told to change its leadership.

During both first and second phases of the Chinese Revolution Stalin was, in fact, applying the principles Lenin had set
out at the Second Comintern Congress. But he went on
insisting on alliance with the Kuomintang, even when it
became obvious that collaboration was little more than a
fiction and immensely dangerous to the Chinese communists.
The problem may have been that he was a captive of his own
theory (i.e. that the correct tactics for the bourgeois-
democratic stage of the Revolution was alliance with
nationalist forces). But a more important reason may have
been his domestic power struggle against Trotsky and the left
opposition, who were proposing a more radical (and probably
more suitable) policy. Admitting that he was wrong and
changing tactics to adopt their policy would have resulted in
loss of prestige, perhaps even enabling Trotsky to gain ascen-
dancy. It was probably only at the end of 1927, when he had
defeated the left and was about to turn against his own right
wing, that he could afford to change policy. Unfortunately, it
was too late and the victims once again were the Chinese
communists.

In the third phase of Stalin's venture in China, from August
to December 1927, he ordered the new CCP leadership to
'make use of the experience of the Russian October Revolution' and organize armed defence against the counter-
revolutionary forces of the bourgeoisie (Degras 1960, vol. 2:
410). Soviets should now be established. The CCP duly
undertook a series of armed uprisings, all of which failed. In
December 1927 a commune was set up in Canton. It lasted a
brief few days, before being defeated in a devastating battle in
which thousands of communists were killed. As a result the
CCP lost what little remaining influence it had in the cities,
becoming what one Western historian has called 'an organization of intellectuals leading peasants' (Borkenau 1962:
323).

This time, too, Stalin insisted that the fault lay with shortcomings in the CCP, including 'insufficient preparatory
work', 'inadequate knowledge of what was happening in

Canton' and 'weakness of the political mobilization of the masses' (Degras 1960, vol. 2: 437–40, quotes on p.439). But he minimized the significance of the failure. At the Fifteenth Congress of the CPSU(b) he enunciated his new theory of colonial revolution, which was to form the basis of Soviet analysis of the East for the next few years:

Great popular revolutions never achieve final victory in the first round of their battles. They grow and gain strength in the course of flows and ebbs. That has been so everywhere, including Russia. So it will be in China.
(Stalin 1927g: 290)

And so it *was* in China, but whether the strength of the CCP and its eventual victory owed anything to Stalin is debatable. The dismal failure in 1927, however, led to a reappraisal of the general Comintern line, in the colonies as well as in Europe.

The new crisis of imperialism
A new radical programme was adopted by the Sixth Comintern Congress in September 1928, based on the new revolutionary crisis of imperialism detected by Stalin. Part of the programme analysed the situation in the colonies. The immediate problems for colonial and semi-colonial countries with rudimentary industry and a predominant Asiatic mode of production (the term was still in use) were to struggle against feudalism and pre-capitalist forms of exploitation, to bring about agrarian revolution and to struggle against imperialism and for national independence. The transition to proletarian dictatorship would require a series of preparatory phases and the transformation of the bourgeois-democratic into a socialist revolution. Successful socialist construction would only be possible with the help of countries where the proletarian dictatorship had already been established. In even more backward countries which did not have a bourgeoisie, national liberation was the central task. Victorious national uprisings could lead the way to socialism, bypassing the capitalist stage if sufficient aid was given by the countries with a proletarian dictatorship (i.e. the Soviet Union) and by the international proletarian movement generally.

The rather contradictory implication to be drawn from this analysis was that *more developed* colonial and semi-colonial countries would take *longer* to travel through the intermediate preparatory phases to socialism than the entirely underdeveloped countries (Degras 1960, vol. 2: 506–7). Certain minimum prerequisites had to exist in more developed countries: 'a certain level of industrial development, of trade union organization and a strong communist party' (Degras 1960, vol. 2: 537), while the undeveloped countries would be able to omit an entire stage of economic development. Aid from the victorious proletarian dictatorship would thus, on the one hand, enable backward colonies to embark on a 'non-capitalist path of development' immediately and, on the other, transform the bourgeois-democratic revolution in more advanced countries rather more gradually into proletarian socialist revolution (Degras 1960, vol. 2: 533; see McKenzie 1964: 83).

The programme listed eight special tasks for the communist parties of colonial countries: the overthrow of foreign imperialism, feudalism and landlord bureaucracy; the establishment of a democratic dictatorship of the proletariat and peasantry on the basis of soviets; national independence and political unification; cancellation of state debts; nationalization of large foreign imperialist enterprises; expropriation of large landowners, church and monastery estates and the nationalization of land; introduction of an eight-hour day; establishment of a revolutionary workers' and peasants' army (Degras 1960, vol. 2: 505–8).[21] New theses on the revolutionary movements in the colonial and semi-colonial countries were adopted, spelling out in greater detail the strategy and tactics that should be adopted by communists. The lessons learnt in China were reflected in the warning to communists that 'an incorrect appraisal of the national-reformist tendency of the bourgeoisie . . . may give rise to serious errors in the strategy and tactics' (Degras 1960, vol. 2: 526–48, quote on p.538). Moreover, although the theses began by stating that Lenin's 1920 theses were still valid, the 1928 version vindicated Roy to some extent (Roy, however, was expelled from the Comintern in 1929) by insisting that building up and developing communist parties had become an urgent task (Degras 1960, vol. 2: 542). In China the immediate practical task was to prepare for and carry through armed insurrection to complete the bourgeois-democratic revolution by destroying the power of the Kuomintang and the militarists and to establish a Soviet regime (Degras 1960, vol. 2: 543–4). Within a few years, however, alliance with the Kuomintang once again became the order of the day.

Decreasing interest in the East

From 1928 onwards the Communist International increasingly reflected Soviet state policy and decreasingly concerned itself with colonial revolution. The fact that there were conflicts between Soviet state interests and the interests of international and colonial revolution was perhaps indicated by the absence of a Comintern Congress between 1928 and 1935. It also demonstrated the decline in the importance of the Comintern. The official line remained that the colonial East was entering a new stage of revolutionary upsurge (Safarov 1930a: 69), but there was little Soviet or Comintern engagement in colonial affairs. Although Chinese rural soviets began to be identified as a symbol of the revolutionary movement there, the transition of the Chinese Revolution to a socialist phase was increasingly postponed to the distant future.[22] In his report to the Seventeenth Congress of the CPSU(b) (Stalin 1934: 470–538), Stalin did not mention the colonies. The Seventh (and last) Comintern Congress was held in 1935. The purpose was to create a platform for announcing the new Soviet and Comintern line—popular fronts against fascism. In the colonies the popular front was to take the form of an anti-imperialist united front. But it was here that the seriousness of the contradiction between Soviet state interests and the interests of colonial revolution was demonstrated in stark reality. It was one thing to call for an anti-imperialist united front in China, where the imperialist enemy, Japan, was also the enemy of the Soviet Union. But the imperialist enemies against whom the national revolutionaries in other colonies were to unite were the very Western powers with which Stalin sought to join forces against Germany.[23] Despite the apparently revolutionary formula 'anti-imperialist united front', a choice had to be made by the Soviet leadership. In the East it was made against colonial movements.

After 1935 Soviet diplomatic efforts were taken up with the Spanish Civil War and, increasingly urgently, with attempts to construct a collective-security agreement against Nazi

Germany. It was only after fascism had been defeated that the Soviet Union turned back to the East. But the Comintern had been disbanded in 1943 and Soviet leaders and scholars took some time to recognize the significance of post-war colonial independence movements.

Colonialism and the Cold War

The popular front policy, suspended when the Stalin–Hitler Pact was signed in 1939, was resumed when Germany attacked the Soviet Union in June 1941. It applied as much to the colonies and semi-colonies as to Europe. Chiang Kai-shek, for example, was called the leader of the Chinese people and a symbol of Chinese unity, while the demand for Indian independence was said to be untimely (Lemin 1942: 76–84). Soviet interest in the colonies only revived after the Yalta conference in February 1945. But even then it took eighteen months for a policy towards China to be formulated and even longer towards other colonies. In the immediate aftermath of the war Soviet leaders were preoccupied with dealing with the economic consequences of the war, with post-war Europe and the almost immediate outbreak of the Cold War. Stalin seemed to expect to continue the popular-front policy. He advised against proceeding with the civil war in China and suggested a continuation of the alliance between the CCP and the Kuomintang. The Soviet government had signed a Pact of Friendship and Alliance with China in August 1945 and although the Red Army allowed the CCP to liberate some areas after the Japanese surrender, very little public attention was paid to the CCP until the middle of 1946.[24]

When the change occurred, Soviet leaders and theorists became far more radical in their approach to international relations in general and far more aware of the revolutionary potential of colonial uprisings and unrest. But once again it was not really independence *per se* that was valued. The colonies and ex-colonies were seen as instruments in the Cold War struggle. One Western study of the Soviet Union and South-East Asia found, for example, that:

The Soviet attitude toward national liberation in any given instance was . . . determined not by Communist strength in the movement seeking it or by the imminence of independence but by the irritation the national liberation movement, Communist or non-Communist, was capable of producing in the metropolitan.

(McLane 1966: 346–7)

It is usually implied in Western literature that Soviet policy remained radical until Khrushchev came to power. It would be a mistake, however, to credit Khrushchev with being the sole instigator of a more moderate attitude towards the colonial world. While it is true that Soviet theory became far more radical in 1947, a careful reading of what Soviet leaders were saying and Soviet theorists were writing at the beginning of the 1950s makes it clear that Stalin was planning a change in policy before he died.

When the change in attitude towards the Chinese Revolution became public in 1946, it began to be reflected in commentaries on other colonial matters. But theory and policy really only emerged in the reaction to Varga's theory about the stabilization of capitalism. In the first version of his book, Varga (1946) suggested that the relationship had changed between many colonies and metropolitan countries. The colonies were no longer necessarily in debt to the metropoles. This would change their political relations. The obvious upsurge in anti-imperialist movements had been caused by a strengthening of the native bourgeoisie and proletariat, the military training received during the war and the consequent availability of colonial troops to participate in the independence struggle. Varga seemed to think that it was possible that the colonies could evolve towards independence (Varga 1946, 219–26). In refuting these evolutionary ideas, Soviet theory suddenly became far more radical, resembling the 1928 Comintern programme and theses, and moving away from moderate popular-front class alliances.[25]

Colonialism in the two-camp world
Most Western scholars see Zhdanov's speech at the Cominform founding meeting as the first public indication of a new hard line in Soviet theory and policy. Zhdanov divided the world into two camps, the imperialist, anti-democratic camp and the anti-fascist camp. The latter consisted of the Soviet

Union, the new democracies of Eastern Europe, and countries like Romania, Hungary and Finland, which had broken with imperialism. Indonesia and Vietnam were associated with it, and Egypt and Syria were sympathetic to it. It was also backed by labour and democratic movements, by communist parties and by the fighters for national liberation in the colonies and dependencies (Zhdanov 1947a: 2).[26] The antifascist camp was thus both geographic, or (to use the terminology adopted in Kubálková and Cruickshank 1980) 'horizontal', in that it included groups of states, and class-based, or 'vertical', including some groups which, in a purely horizontal division, would perforce have belonged to the opposing camp. One interesting aspect of Zhdanov's speech in light of subsequent Soviet interpretations of the causes of successful national-liberation movements was that he did not give any particular credit to the Soviet Union except in so far as it had been responsible for the defeat of fascism. The war *had* resulted in a change in the correlation of forces, but it was the war rather than the correlation of forces which had led to changes in the colonial system:

World War II aggravated the crisis of the colonial system, as expressed in the rise of a powerful movement for national liberation in the colonies and dependencies. This has placed the rear of the capitalist system in jeopardy. The peoples of the colonies no longer wish to live in the old way. The ruling classes of the metroplitan countries can no longer govern on the old lines. Attempts to crush the national liberation movements by military force now increasingly encounter armed resistance on the part of the colonial peoples and lead to protracted colonial wars.

(Zhdanov 1947a: 2)

It was commonly accepted then that the increased activity of the colonial anti-imperialist movements was a natural phenomenon and not due to the 'hands of Moscow'. None the less, the Bolshevik Revolution, in particular the way it had dealt with the development of the backward peoples of the Tsarist Empire, and aided Mongolia to complete its bourgeois-democratic revolution and acquire 'the necessary prerequisites for further progressive development', was often offered as a model to the colonies (see, for example, Zhukov 1946: 43). This was not a new suggestion; Stalin had been making the same analogy since 1918.

Varga's view of the colonies had already begun to be refuted by the time that Zhdanov made his speech. The possibility of a peaceful transition to independence was precluded, since the economic prerequisites were lacking (Vasil'eva 1947: 64). Moreover, cooperation with the national bourgeoisie was no longer considered acceptable. To begin with, no attempt was made to distinguish between various kinds of bourgeoisie—since it was willing to compromise with imperialists it was, as a whole, anti-national (Zhukov 1947a: 6). A little later, however, alliance with the petty bourgeoisie and middle sectors was authorized, although communists were to constitute the main force of the anti-imperialist struggle (Zhukov 1947c: 55). Whether or not that struggle needed to be an armed struggle was unclear, but there was no ambiguity about neutralism. The theory of a 'third force' between communism and imperialism was 'an imperialist device to slander the USSR by placing it on the same level with American imperialism' (Zhukov 1947c: 63; see Ch. 8 below).

By 1949 three changes were evident in the Soviet interpretation of the situation in the colonial world. First, the successes of the national-liberation movement were now said to be due to the change in the correlation of class forces, which in turn was the result of an increase in the power of the Soviet Union (Zhukov 1949: 56). Second, the condemnation of the nationalist bourgeoisie for being reformist became even stronger (Maslennikov 1949: 62–75). Nehru, who until 1947 had been considered sympathetic to the democratic camp, was now called an 'imperialist lackey' (Zhukov 1949: 59). At the same time, the political weight and power of the colonial proletariat tended to be overrated:

. . .*the working class is the admitted hegemon in the colonial revolution and the communist party, directly or through wider mass organizations, leads the national liberation movement.*

(Zhukov 1949: 55)

The third change marked an attempt to explain how the transition to socialism would take place in the ex-colonies. It was envisaged that the transition would be similar to that taking place in the People's Democracies of Eastern Europe (and the ex-colonies were called 'the new People's Democracies of the East'), but that 'the transition to the solution of socialist tasks may prove more protracted' than in the People's Democracies which had not been colonies (Zhukov 1949: 60). The first of these changes (attributing colonial revolution to Soviet power), was to remain standard practice in future Soviet theory. The latter two changes, however (the explanation of the class structure in the colonies and ex-colonies and of the way in which the transition to socialism would take place), signalled theoretical problems which, together with the question of the economic structure of the underdeveloped countries, would continue to preoccupy Soviet theorists in the post-Stalin era.

Despite the evident radicalization of Soviet attitudes towards the colonies, theorists had already begun to search for alternative ways of advancing Soviet influence. There was some delay before the search was reflected in Soviet theory and practice, however, partly because of the impetus provided by the success of the Chinese Revolution in 1949 and, more particularly, because of the outbreak of the Korean War in 1950. For a while the Chinese model was extolled for all colonial revolutions. Colonialism could only be overcome by proletarian revolution and the overthrow of imperialism. Although a broad revolutionary movement was required, it should be led by the working class and its vanguard, the Communist Party (Potekhin 1950: 24–7). But it soon became clear that not all Soviet theorists believed that China could serve as a universal model.

Theoretical diversification

At a conference held at the Oriental Studies Institute in November 1951 on the character and attributes of the system of People's Democracies in the Orient (the countries so termed were China, Mongolia, Vietnam and Korea), a number of opposing views were expressed. Zhukov, the most prominent of the participating scholars, maintained that although the Chinese Revolution was extremely significant, it should not be regarded as a 'stereotype' since many countries did not possess revolutionary armies ('Discussion of the Character and Effect of People's Democracy in the Orient', 1952: 3). Two of the discussants disagreed: similar conditions applied in other countries of the Orient, including India, and the events in Burma, Vietnam, Korea, Malaya and the Phillipines were examples of the role of revolutionary armies ('Discussion of the Character and Effect of People's Democracy in the Orient' 1952: 6). They did not, however, succeed in changing Zhukov's mind, from which it can be assumed that this particular theoretical proposition had been settled: China was no longer to be considered a universal model and armed revolution was not everywhere applicable.

The relevance of the Chinese experience was not the only controversial subject discussed at this conference, however, and the other subjects were less easy to settle. In essence, an agenda was set of theoretical issues which were to remain problematical for many years to come. The participants considered which features the People's Democracies in the Orient shared with the European People's Democracies and which were specific. They also discussed the thorny problem of creating a people's democratic system in countries which lacked a proletariat (e.g. Mongolia), whether India and China had or could embark on a path of non-capitalist development, the definition of the non-capitalist path, and how the transition of the people's democratic revolution to the socialist revolution would take place ('Discussion of the Character and Effect of People's Democracy in the Orient' 1952: 4–7). In summing up the discussion Zhukov insisted that China had already embarked upon the path of non-capitalist development. Given the low level of industrialization, it was, however, too soon to speak of building socialism in Mongolia. He pointed out that Mongolia had neither a proletariat nor a national bourgeoisie, but that none the less its people's democratic regime did not differ qualitatively from those of other countries of Asia:

In regard to Mongolia . . . the constant, disinterested assistance and the ideological-political support of the USSR ensured the necessary proletarian leadership for the Mongolian people's regime. . . . By virtue of this . . . the people's revolutionary regime . . . performed the functions of a revolutionary democratic dictatorship of the proletariat and peasantry.

> (Discussion of the Character and Effect of
> People's Democracy in the Orient 1952: 7).

He was neither specific about the kind or amount of assistance, nor did he explain how assistance and ideological-political support could ensure proletarian leadership in the absence of a proletariat. The published report ended by indicating the need for 'a scientific elaboration' of the problems ('Discussion of the Character and Effect of People's Democracy in the Orient' 1952: 43). And the problems which required scientific elaboration were basically those noted above as future perennial conundrums for Soviet theorists: the social-class structure of developing countries, the transition to socialism and the economic structure of developing countries.

CONCLUSION

It is clear that while only a small proportion of Marx's writing related to the colonies, a considerable amount of Lenin's work both before and after the Revolution was relevant to the subject. The colonies also formed an important but controversial part of Stalin's theory and revolutionary activity in the 1920s. It is also evident that the initial dichotomous and polarized view of the world presented by Soviet theorists in the early years of the Cold War had already been modified before Stalin's death. Distinctions were drawn between various colonies and ex-colonies and a theoretical agenda was set. It retrospect, some of Khrushchev's innovations in 1956 seem less original when the discussions about the colonies before Stalin's death are considered.

It would be incorrect to suppose that the colonial world greatly preoccupied Soviet theorists and policy-makers at that time, however. Malenkov's Central Committee report to the Nineteenth Congress of the CPSU in 1952 indicated that the LDCs constituted a rather unimportant part of the Soviet world view (Malenkov 1952: 99–124). He spoke of the upsurge in the colonial independence movements after the war (mentioning, in particular, Vietnam, Burma, Malaya, the Philippines, Indonesia, India, Iran and Egypt) and the decline in the economies of the colonial and dependent countries as a result of prolonged oppression. He also gave a fairly detailed and optimistic report on the economic development of China, Korea and Mongolia. In listing the Party's tasks in the sphere of foreign policy, however, he included China, Mongolia and

Korea with the People's Democracies with whom relations of inviolable friendship were to be strengthened, but made no reference to national-liberation movements (Malenkov 1952: 106). Thus, while the change in Soviet attitudes towards the newly independent countries cannot be attributed entirely to Khrushchev, it is certainly true that he moved them to a more central position in Soviet foreign policy. Moreover, it was Khrushchev who turned the study of the theoretical problems into a safe occupation. Resolving the problems proved to be more difficult, however, and some of the attempts to do so form the subject of the next chapter.

NOTES

1. Avineri maintains that the Asiatic mode of development led Marx inexorably to the position of 'having to endorse European colonial expansion as a brutal but necessary step toward the victory of socialism' (Avineri 1969: 13). Orthodox communists reject this view (see, for example, Nikiforov 1975 for a refutation of the Asiatic mode of production and, in particular, of the theories of Karl Wittfogel (1957) and his application of the concept to the Soviet Union. Nikiforov's criticism of Wittfogel is analysed in Gellner 1978). For a modern analysis of imperialism that is close to Marx's interpretation, see Warren (1980). Avineri also points out that Marx disapproved of imperialism and distinguished between the motives behind colonialism and its historical significance. His analysis of colonialism was far more sophisticated than Lenin's. He understood, for example, something that Lenin did not: that the costs of colonialism far outweighed the financial benefit obtained and that, as a result, the metropolitan working class was the net loser (Avineri 1969: 18–22).
2. Although the collection *Marx on China* bears only Marx's name, one of the articles, 'Persia–China', was written by Engels.
3. Kolakowski 1978, vol. 1: 349–51) believes that the Asiatic model was excluded from the Soviet view of history because, apart from denying the thesis that productive forces have the primary role in history, it contradicted the view of the uniformity of human evolution and thus detracted from the universality of Marxism. For an analysis of the disappearance of the concept and its partial re-emergence, see Hough (1986: 38–54). Nikiforov (1975) has argued forcefully that Marx himself rejected the Asiatic mode of production in 1877. It is interesting that Petrenko and Petrov (1981), for example, devote a chapter to the international relations theory of Marx and Engels but do not refer to any of the writings on the colonies.
4. Avineri (1969: 22–4) puts this down to Marx's reluctance to predict

when there were several intervening stages between the present stage and the universal trend towards a new form of society. But it is probably also a reflection of his preoccupation with Europe and the fact that his interest in the colonies primarily concerned its effects on Europe.

5. More importantly, they legitimized a revolution in Russia as long as a socialist revolution was imminent elsewhere in Europe.

6. Boersner (1982: 1–58) calls their attitude to nationalism 'relativist and dialectical' (by which he means that they supported nationalism only where they saw it as an objective carrier of historical progress). He distinguishes between a Western (Proudhon and Marx before 1867) and an Eastern view of nationalism (Marx after 1867 and Lenin) in Marxism. The former was impatient of nationalism and wanted to press on with realizing socialism. The latter was conscious of the national problem and believed that national demands had to be satisfied before socialism could come about.

7. Engels maintained that colonies with European populations could become independent immediately after the socialist revolution, while those inhabited by a native population would need to be taken over by the proletariat and led towards independence (Marx and Engels, 1975: 331).

8. For further discussion of these theories, see Chapter 6. In one sense they applied even better to the colonies than to Russia: the necessary but uncertain condition guaranteeing the success of the Russian Revolution was revolution in the rest of Europe. The colonies, on the other hand, did not have the uncertainty. They would be able to rely for aid on the socialist state already in existence. It was this aid, for example, which was said to have allowed the Mongolian People's Republic to embark upon a non-capitalist path of development (Trush 1977: 177).

9. For a detailed analysis of his attitude to the peasantry and its role in the revolution, see Mann (1983).

10. Stalin (writing in *Pravda* in November 1918) claimed that the bourgeois-democratic movements amongst the oppressed nationalities in Russia had proved themselves incapable of meeting the demands of the toiling masses. After the October Revolution they had become reactionary and counter-revolutionary. Stalin meant that they continued to opt for secession, whereas the workers would choose, if they could, to remain linked to the Soviet state (Stalin 1918b: 68–77).

11. It should be noted, however, that an appeal was issued to 'All Muslim Toilers of Russia and the East' soon after the Revolution. Russian Moslems were assured that their beliefs and usages, their national and cultural institutions were henceforth free and inviolable, while those of the East were urged to overthrow the imperialist robbers and enslavers of their countries (Degras 1951, vol. 1: 16).

12. For a discussion of the various viewpoints, see McLane (1966: 8–12).

13. The Comintern had been established the previous year, in 1919. Little attention was paid to the East at its First Congress, and very few Eastern delegates attended it. Its manifesto (written by Trotsky) maintained that liberation in the colonies was unthinkable without the

liberation of the working class in the metropolitan countries. It included an appeal to 'Colonial slaves of Africa and Asia! The hour of
proletarian dictatorship in Europe will also be the hour of your liberation' (Degras 1956, vol. 1: 38–47, quote on p. 43). Boersner (1982: 66)
points out that this was a Western-orientated view of the colonial
question. (See n. 6 above for the distinction between Western and
Eastern views of the national and colonial question.)

14.   The debate and its effects are discussed in McLane (1966: 12–24) and
in Boersner (1982: 80–93). See also Carr 1966, vol. 3, ch. 26).

15.   Borkenau (1962: 293–4) vividly conveys just how incompatible the two
sets of theses were. The Turkish delegates to the Congress (and to the
Congress of the Toilers of the East in Baku) did not enjoy popular
support in Turkey. They were stoned as they passed through Turkish
villages on their return. They were finally arrested, tortured and
thrown out to sea. The Comintern had to choose between supporting
them or enjoying relations with the government of Kemal. It chose
Kemal (in other words, Lenin's theses, rather than Roy's) and gave
little support to the Turkish Communist Party.

16.   In discussing the reasons why Lenin's theses prevailed, Carr (1966,
vol. 3: 258–61) points out that cooperation with bourgeois movements
was thought to be a short-term expedient, since it was still hoped that
proletarian revolution would occur shortly in Europe. Moreover,
existing national movements were thought to be almost entirely
dependent upon Moscow, which meant that Moscow could decide the
terms on which support should be given. It was only when the theses
were applied over a long period and national governments were
sufficiently strong to lay down their own conditions for alliance that
difficulties emerged. Borkenau, on the other hand, indicates that
problems arose immediately (see n. 15 above).

17.   The proceedings of the two conferences were recorded in *Pervyi s"ezd
narodov Vostoka; stenograficheskii otchet* (Moscow, 1921) and *Pervyi
s"ezd revolyutsionnykh organizatsii Dal'nego Vostoka; sbornik*
(Petrograd 1922). Both Congresses were dominated by Comintern
spokesmen and although the atmosphere is said to have been very
revolutionary, neither Congress achieved very much and neither was
followed by further meetings (see Boersner 1982: 98–9 and McLane
1966: 25–6). The Communist University of the Toilers of the East
drew students not only from the East beyond Russia. In 1925 Stalin
said that there were representatives from fifty nationalities and ethnic
groups, one group of which came from the Soviet East and the other
from colonial and dependent countries. The former were trained to
become competent cadres to minister to the needs of the Soviet
Eastern republics, while the latter were to minister to the revolutionary needs of the colonies (Stalin 1925b: 205–6).

18.   Stalin's only theoretical work before the revolution was 'Marxism and
the National Question', written in Vienna under Lenin's tutelage at
the end of 1912 and published in 1913 (Stalin 1913: 3–61). In it he set
out the Bolshevik support for national self-determination as well as
the arguments against the Austrian Social-Democratic programme for

national autonomy and the Jewish Bund's proposal for a federal party (see Ch. 6 below for further discussion of Stalin's attitudes towards nationalism).

19. The Kuomintang–CCP alliance was urged upon the CCP by Maring, *acting on behalf of the Comintern*, in 1922. But in January 1923 an agreement was made between Sun Yat-sen, leader of the Kuomintang, and Joffe, *representing the Soviet Commissariat for Foreign Affairs* (*Narkomindel*) on Soviet–Kuomintang collaboration (Rubinstein 1966: 100–1). In the autumn of 1923 Borodin was sent to Canton as Sun Yat-sen's adviser. But he *represented the Russian Communist Party*, not the Comintern or Narkomindel. Thus *Narkomindel*, the CPSU(b) and the Comintern were all separately involved in China. Ironically, of the three, the Comintern was most peripherally involved (see North 1953).

20. The issues over which Stalin and Trotsky fell out can be summarized as: permanent revolution and socialism in one country (see Ch. 2); NEP and the need for industrialization; Party democracy and the growth of the bureaucracy; and Comintern policy (in respect particularly of Germany and China). For a succinct summary, see Fitzpatrick (1982, Ch. 4). Borkenau (1962) argues that Stalin firmly followed Lenin's precepts. Moreover, Trotsky agreed initially with the policy followed in China and changed his mind only in 1926, at the height of his dispute with Stalin. Thus, 'Trotsky, in shouting about treason, simply accuses the unsatisfactory reality of the system which he has himself helped to create' (Borkenau 1962: 306, 316–18, quote on p. 318). Soviet theorists, even at the height of de-Stalinization, have never criticized Stalin's Chinese policy. The authoritative *Istoriya vneshnei politiki SSSR* (edited by Gromyko and Ponomarev in numerous editions) omits Soviet–CCP relations and all the events of the late 1920s, mentioning only the establishment of relations with Sun Yat-sen in 1923. For an account of the early years of the Chinese Revolution and the Soviet role, see Brandt (1958).

21. The programme went on to use the terms which have become associated with Mao Tse-tung rather than with the Comintern (or with Bukharin, who, ironically considering that it was a radical programme which contained an attack on the right, drafted the programme). Colonial and national liberation revolutions were important aspects of the conquest of power by the working class. In the transition period colonies were important 'because they represent the village on a world scale *vis-à-vis* the industrial countries, which represent the town in the context of the world economy' (Degras 1960, vol. 2: 508).

22. McLane (1958) believes that the last identifiable instance of Soviet intervention in the affairs of the CCP was in January 1931. In part this was due to the reduced role the Comintern played after 1930 as an instrument of Soviet foreign policy and to the physical inacessibility of the scattered Soviet districts in China. But most importantly it was due to the threat from Japan, which caused the Soviet government to curtail support for revolutionary movements and to re-establish relations (broken off at the end of 1927) with the Kuomintang in 1932.

23. The dilemma was apparent even when the imperialist enemy was not one of the countries with which the Soviet Union hoped to negotiate a collective security agreement. The Italian invasion of Abyssinia, for example, was clearly identified by Molotov in 1936 as an imperialist war to extend Italy's colonial possessions (Degras 1953, vol. 3: 156). Litvinov reacted sharply against it in the League of Nations (Degras 1953, vol. 3: 139–41). But he also reassured the Italian ambassador in Moscow that the Soviet Union was 'inspired by an unchanging desire to maintain and develop the best relations' with Italy (Degras 1953, vol. 3: 149).

24. Djilas (1969: 141) claims that Stalin admitted that he had been wrong to urge the Chinese Communists to reach a *modus vivendi* with Chiang Kai-shek. McLane (1966: 254–60) suggests that the reason Stalin changed his mind about supporting the CCP in the Chinese Civil War was probably that there were signs that the United States was considering giving greater aid to the Nationalists. Roy Medvedev, by contrast, maintains that the reason why Stalin urged the CCP to compromise with the Kuomintang was fear that American intervention would lead to defeat of the CCP and the occupation of China by the United States (Medvedev 1986a: 18–20). Medvedev and Djilas also both believe that even then Stalin felt disquiet about a new Communist great power.

25. Varga was publicly criticized for his views about the effect of the Second World War on the capitalist economies, in particular his contention that these economies were increasingly able to withstand crises. See 'O nedostatkakh i zadachakh nauchno-issledovatel'skoi raboty v oblasti ekonomike' (1948) for the speeches at the meeting at which he and his colleagues were criticized. He was forced to change his book but his troubles persisted. He was dismissed from his positions and his institute and journal were closed down. He was rehabilitated after Stalin's death. His institute was reopened and he republished his views on the capitalist economies in 1964. One of his colleagues, Trainin, died soon after the furore, and although he was given a long and respectful obituary, his 'mistakes' were listed in detail ('Pamyati Akademikia Bol'shevika' 1949: 1–6). For accounts of the Varga dispute and the doctrinal changes in 1948–9, see Skilling (1951a: 16–33; 1951b: 131–49), Lynch (1984: 32–44) and Hough (1986: 106–14).

26. In fact, the two-camp metaphor used by Zhdanov had been used by Lenin (1923a: 317) and by Stalin. In pressing for the formation of the Soviet Union in 1922, for example, Stalin had said that 'the states of the world have split into two camps: the camp of socialism and the camp of capitalism. (Stalin 1922: 127). A little later he used the same image to distinguish between the camp of colonizing nations and the camp of oppressed and exploited colonial peoples (Stalin 1924a: 54).

5 Incorporating the Third World II: Relations with National-Liberation Movements and Less-Developed Countries

No single aspect of policy, not even arms acquisitions and dispositions, contributed more to the decline of détente in the 1970s than Soviet activity in the Third World. It was believed by some in the West that under cover of détente the Soviet leadership had adopted an unprecedented, forward policy and was making incursions into areas traditionally considered at least neutral, if not firmly within the Western sphere of influence. It was not, of course, that Soviet diplomatic relations with the less-developed countries (LDCs) were unprecedented. Nor did Soviet arms sales to LDCs represent a departure. What was thought to herald a new, dangerous Soviet activism was the role played by Cuban troops (with Soviet logistic support) in Angola in 1975 and in Ethiopia in 1977. The climax was the direct intervention of Soviet troops in Afghanistan in 1979. This was variously interpreted as an extension of the Brezhnev doctrine outside Europe, a push towards the oil-rich countries of the Persian Gulf, the building of a *cordon sanitaire* against infection by Muslim fundamentalism, or even another step towards the realization of the ultimate Soviet dream: world revolution.

In fact, Soviet Third World policy has arguably been rather less successful than these interpretations have suggested. To mention just a few examples, since active relations with the ex-colonies were launched in the mid-1950s the Soviet leadership has lost as an ally the strongest LDC, China; it has also lost prestige in the international communist movement by continuing relations with regimes that have suppressed local Communist Parties (the best and most dramatic example is

Egypt); it has been the victim of post-independence coups and regime changes (e.g. in Ghana and Mali); it has backed two historical rivals (Somalia and Ethiopia) and been forced to abandon one (Somalia), thereby losing valuable naval bases; it has supported the loser in an independence movement coalition (in Zimbabwe) and thereafter experienced difficulty in establishing relations with the winner; and it has favoured cruel, crude and unreliable leaders (e.g. the Amins of both Uganda and Afghanistan, and Gadaffy) and it has felt forced to intervene in Afghanistan in an attempt to establish a more acceptable and malleable leader.

On the positive side of the balance, the Soviet Union enjoys diplomatic and economic relations with a large number of Third World countries (between ninety and 100, depending on the definition of a Third World country, see Gromyko *et al.* 1984: 314–24); it can frequently rely on their support in the United Nations; and the number of states which are considered socialist-oriented has grown to about fifteen.

But the political, economic and social development of the LDCs has not entirely conformed to the expectations of earlier Soviet theorists and policy-makers. This chapter considers some of the attempts that have been made to understand why and to explain the structure of society in the LDCs. The background to the discussion is the doctrine enunciated by Khrushchev at the Twentieth Party Congress in 1956.

In his report to the Congress Khrushchev declared that wars between socialism and capitalism were no longer inevitable and that relations between states with different social structures should be based on peaceful coexistence. But he also abandoned Stalin's dichotomous division of the world, and introduced a third zone of peace, neither socialist nor capitalist, which could draw on the achievements of the socialist bloc and receive aid 'free of any political or military obligations' (Khrushchev 1956a: 29–38, quote on p. 34). It has been suggested that Khrushchev's other famous revision, the possibility of a peaceful transition to socialism, commonly thought to have been intended to woo Yugoslavia back into the Soviet bloc, may also have been directed towards allaying the fears of the governments of the former colonies that local communist parties were potential sources of civil war (D. Dallin 1962: 325). Khrushchev was firm, however, that no matter what form the transition to socialism took, 'an absolute and decisive requirement is political leadership of the working class, headed by its vanguard' (Khrushchev 1956a: 38). Like Malenkov in 1952, he made no mention of the national-liberation movement in listing the foreign-policy tasks of the CPSU (it appeared regularly from the Twenty-Second Party Congress Report onwards), but he did list India, Burma, Afghanistan, Egypt, Syria and other countries standing for peace amongst those with which bonds of friendship and cooperation were to be strengthened.

In fact, policy had predated theory. In 1955 Khrushchev and Bulganin had made a much publicized tour of India, Burma and Afghanistan, and in July 1955 an arms deal had been concluded between Egypt and Czechoslovakia. The Soviet leaders were less interested in encouraging national liberation in the colonies which had not yet reached independence than in establishing good relations with those that had. And since the governments in power were usually nationalist and were often unwilling to cooperate with (or sometimes even tolerate) local communist parties, this created certain theoretical and practical difficulties. One Western theorist has pointed out that:

'The Soviet leaders . . . expected that new chances for the Communists of the new states would be gradually created by their diplomacy, as a long-term by-product of growing Soviet and Soviet bloc influence.'

(Lowenthal 1977: 187)

But Khrushchev's problem in launching a successful and more outgoing state policy which, at the same time, did not contradict the revolutionary imperative of aiding the national-liberation movement lay partly in the dearth of specialized knowledge in the Soviet Union about foreign countries or about international relations. This affected both theory and practice. Many speakers at the Twentieth Party Congress decried the state of the social sciences in the Soviet Union, urging, amongst other things, research in the area of international relations. The outcome of the criticism was the reopening of the Institute of World Economy and International Relations (closed as a result of the Varga controversy; see Ch. 4, n. 25), Varga's rehabilitation, a change in the editorial board of the journal *Sovetskoe vostokovedenie* (Soviet Eastern Studies), the establishment of a number of new institutes and the gradual emergence of a new generation of *mezhdunarodniki*.[1]

Of course, the study of international relations remained firmly within the framework of Marxism-Leninism, but it became a more flexible system of ideas, particularly in relation to the LDCs. There has been no lack of Soviet theory about the Third World since 1956 and, apart from a few eternal verities which have been generally accepted by all scholars, a number of issues have failed to produce a consensus. When Khrushchev fell from power his Third World policy was high on the list of mistakes for which he was blamed. But although his policies were repudiated, the doctrine he had enunciated at the Twentieth Party Congress was retained more or less intact and it has continued to form the parameters within which discussion takes place. Even after Khrushchev's name had been expunged from the literature, credit continued to be given to the correctness of his reports to the Twentieth, Twenty-First and Twenty-Second Congresses of the CPSU and to the development of theory in the declarations published after the 1957 and 1960 international meetings of Communist Parties, as well as to the subsequent statements by Brezhnev (see, for example, Brutents 1977, vol. 1: 106).

Although the range of topics concerning LDCs which have been considered legitimate spheres of enquiry by *mezhdunarodniki* has increased, amongst the theoretical problems which have preoccupied them have been those which were noted above in Chapter 4 which they had inherited unresolved from the past. Soviet theorists have continued trying to find an appropriate categorization of the social classes in underdeveloped and developing countries. They have searched for an adequate explanation of how the transition to socialism takes place in non-industrialized countries and they have tried to analyse the economic structure of the LDCs and how non-capitalist economic systems can be established.

These three theoretical problems are, of course, very closely interrelated: as we have seen in previous chapters, the bourgeois-democratic revolution which would introduce bourgeois reforms could, according to Marxist-Leninist theory, either be led by the proletariat or by the bourgeoisie. But the socialist revolution would certainly be carried out by the proletariat and its vanguard party. Having taken over the bourgeois state and the means of production, the proletariat, under the guidance of its vanguard party, would introduce a dictatorship of the proletariat (or of the proletariat and the peasantry) and proceed to socialize the economy. It was envisaged that the socialist revolution should ideally take place in countries with industrialized economies, but Lenin had posited that it was possible for certain underdeveloped countries to proceed to socialism without ever going through a capitalist phase of development. The condition which was thought to make this possible was aid from those countries which were already socialist (and industrialized). The early Soviet model of de-colonization (i.e. the development of the peripheral areas of the Tsarist Empire) had involved industrializing those regions. But it had also required a transfer of resources from the already socialist centre to create the necessary facilities to educate and train local people to enable them to participate in modernization.

This model presented several complex problems when applied to the LDCs. First, a working class had to be identified, and if there was no working class, another group or class which could carry out the bourgeois-democratic and socialist revolutions. Second, the interim period between independence and socialism had to be described. What was the nature of the non-capitalist path of development and what distinguished it from capitalist development? How would the transition to socialism take place? In the absence of a proletariat and a vanguard party, could a socialist consciousness be inculcated in the indigenous masses? And what kind of aid was required from the existing socialist states? What if they proved unable to provide the kind of aid that had made it possible for the Russian underdeveloped areas to skip the capitalist stage of development? Finally, although it was agreed that non-capitalist development was the prelude to the socialist stage of development, was it certain that it ensured economic development and industrialization and that it invariably led to socialism? These were not, of course, the only problems that were studied by Soviet theorists, but it could be argued that they proved to be the most intractable. The rest of this chapter will examine the attempts to answer them.

CLASSES IN THE LDCs: THE EVOLUTION OF THE SOVIET VIEW, 1956–82

It has always been difficult to apply Marxist-Leninist class categories, developed essentially on the basis of European empirical data of the nineteenth century, to the Third World, where tribe, caste, race and religion have often been far more prominent than class. The difficulty has been compounded, first, by the desire to identify a proletariat which could take the lead in the transition to socialism and, second, by the fact that many Third World countries are governed by military regimes, which may or may not be progressive, but which do not fit well into a Marxist-Leninist class analysis. The recognition of the revolutionary propensities of the national bourgeoisie before and the petty bourgeoisie after independence has not really resolved the difficulty, since LDCs often lack not only a proletariat but also a bourgeoisie. Because of these difficulties, a working class, a peasantry and a bourgeoisie have continued to be identified in the LDCs but at the same time Soviet scholars have recognized that these divisions are insufficient to describe societies often vastly different from European societies and from one another. The result has been the identification of a number of sub-groups, part of which form the 'revolutionary democrats', who undertake many of the tasks traditionally carried out by the proletariat.

The working class

Despite the recognition that 'in the vast majority of developing countries there is no large and influential proletariat' (Deborin and Manusevich 1965: 37) and that often 'the population is still divided into tribes and the process of forming a nation has not been completed' (Ponomarev 1961: 41–2), the tendency to overestimate the role and political power of the working class has been difficult to eliminate from Soviet theory about the Third World. The 1961 Party Programme maintained that an alliance between the working class and peasantry was the fundamental condition for a successful struggle to achieve democratic change and achieve economic and social progress ('Programme of the Communist Party of the Soviet Union' 1961: 11). It was difficult, therefore, to envisage democratic change and progress without a working class. As a result, theorists recognized that the working class was small, but still expected it to be a strong revolutionary vanguard. One prominent scholar, for example, described its small size (Brutents 1965b: 35–6), but none the less claimed that it could achieve considerable influence or even lead the national liberation revolution (Brutents 1965a: 18). A second, equally prominent scholar recognized that:

in conditions where nationalist, religious and other traditional forms of ideology are widely disseminated or even predominate, where tribal, patri-archal and caste vestiges exert great influence . . . . Marxist-Leninist teaching cannot be completely accepted by the broad masses in a short historical time.

(Ul'yanovsky 1972: 421)

But he claimed that the working class was growing in an unprecedented way in terms of numbers, organization and political organization and that it was the most active cham-pion of national and social liberation (Ul'yanovsky 1972: 417–18).

When it became obvious that the working class in most Third World countries was neither developing rapidly nor necessarily becoming revolutionary, this optimism gradually dwindled. It was explained that the emerging working class had not lost its bonds with the countryside, and this:

quite naturally tended to slow down the development of class conscious-ness, and made the proletariat susceptible to the petty-bourgeois ideology, hampering their escape from the grip of nationalistic attitudes, and caste, religious and—in many African and some Asian countries—tribal survivals.

(Brutents 1977, vol. 1: 80)

Other scholars began to believe that the small numerical size of the working class and its low level of culture made it difficult for it to become the leading force in the anti-imperia-list struggle (Zagladin 1973: 294–7). This was why the social content of the national liberation revolution had not become socialist (Butenko 1975: 396). But the absence of a large working class was not thought to prevent development along the non-capitalist path. Other classes and groups were identified to lead the newly liberated countries in their development.

The peasantry

It was quite clear that the largest and most exploited class in the LDCs was the peasantry (Grigoryan 1966: 52), and Soviet theorists were optimistic that exploitation had turned it into a revolutionary class. The landless peasants and agricultural workers, in particular, were thought to play an active role in the national-liberation movement (Tyagunenko 1967: 10). Moreover, independence was all too often followed by deteriorating social and economic conditions, and this served to activate the peasant movement, turning it into a powerful (though vacillating and rather unreliable) political force (Ul'yanovsky 1972: 418). Soviet theorists were unclear whether the peasantry formed part of the petty bourgeoisie. One theorist declared that:

> The 'Third World', not excluding the most developed of the economically underdeveloped countries (e.g. India) . . . is, in an economic, political, social and moral sense, an ocean of petty bourgeois-dom.
>
> (Ul'yanovsky 1972: 546)

He estimated that this 'ocean' constituted between 80 and 90 per cent of the population and he must therefore have included the peasantry in his calculation. Other theorists have been quite explicit that the peasantry are the most numerous and the most important part of the petty bourgeoisie (Levkovsky 1970: 111).

As in Russia after the October Revolution, the peasantry was seen to be the natural ally of the working class in the anti-imperialist struggle. Indeed, it was recognized that where the national-liberation movement was large, this was almost always because of the participation of the peasantry; that where it used armed struggle to achieve independence, the violence often took the form of 'a particular kind of "peasant war" '. The peasantry, in fact, 'provided the backbone' of the national-liberation movement (Brutents 1977, vol. 1: 91). But Soviet theorists envisaged an even more revolutionary role for the peasantry in the LDCs than had eventually been considered possible in Russia (where the alliance between the working class and the peasantry was broken violently and permanently during the enforced collectivization of agriculture). In the developing countries peasants could become 'the nub of the revolutionary process' (Zagladin 1973: 107), but they had to understand that 'in practical terms their aims can only be achieved in alliance with the working class and under its direction' (Zagladin 1973: 303). The reason for this was that although the peasantry provided 'the social basis and the mass army of the national-liberation movement', it did not act within it 'as an independent class force' (Brutents 1977, vol. 1: 91–2). Thus the working class had to be the senior partner in the alliance. This did not, of course, deal with the problem of who would direct the alliance in the absence of a working class.

The bourgeoisie

Neither the working class nor the peasantry have given as much theoretical trouble to Soviet theorists as the colonial and ex-colonial bourgeoisie. It was the first class to receive serious analysis after Khrushchev's encouragement of the social sciences. A seminar, in which some Third World Marxists participated, was held in 1959 on the role of the bourgeoisie, and this marked the end of the condemnation of bourgeois reformism which had been common since the end of the 1940s ('The National Bourgeoisie and the Liberation Movement' 1959a, 1959b). In 1959 it was decided that on the whole the bourgeoisie remained a positive force in the national liberation struggle. But no matter how revolutionary it was at the time of independence, the working class had to be promoted to a leading position if political and economic independence were to be retained ('The National Bourgeoisie' 1959b: 79). After independence the national bourgeoisie would reveal its conventional bourgeois traits:

The policy of the national bourgeoisie is contradictory. It participates in the struggle against colonialism and tries to weaken the control of foreign monopolies over the national economy but at the same time it supports relations with the imperialist powers and makes possible the further inflow of its capital. While trying to restrain and weaken feudalism, [it] . . . makes concessions to the landowners, supporting an alliance with them against the democratic forces. It finds the development of a national industry and the nationalization of foreign capital advantageous . . . supports industrialization and is prepared for the state sector to be expanded. But [its] leadership . . . intends conducting this whole policy on the basis of capitalist methods . . . . Exhorting the people to cooperate in fulfilling the tasks of economic development, at the same time it strengthens the bureaucratic apparatus, refuses to extend democracy or to take measures to improve the condition of the people.

(Ponomarev 1961: 42)

The question about whether the bourgeoisie was hesitant and indecisive, or revolutionary and inclined to support profound social change and progressive development (Grigoryan 1966: 23–4), was thus resolved by deciding that it changed from being anti-imperialist and anti-feudalist before independence to being a 'vacillating and double-minded force' afterwards (Zagladin 1973: 314).

But over the years some Soviet theorists had begun to realize that it was not just the working class which was lacking in many LDCs. It was often difficult to identify a group which could really be called a bourgeois class (see, for example, Avakov and Stepanov 1963: 46–54: Kiva 1975: 113–14; Tarabin 1975: 58). The reason for its absence was simple: capitalist production had been imported into the colonies and very often foreign bourgeois groups had settled there as well. As a result a local national bourgeoisie had often been economically unnecessary. This also explained why, in so far as it existed, it tended to be poorly organized, have little political experience, lack initiative and be rather inert (Brutents 1977, vol. 1:93–8). These negative features did not prevent it from participating in the national-liberation movement, but meant that it rarely acted as the leading force. To explain why this was not invariably the case and why therefore it was difficult to define the nature of the national bourgeoisie, a 'dialectical assessment' was required: there *was* a fundamental contradiction between the national bourgeoisie and imperialism, but how this contradiction expressed itself depended, first, upon how acute the antagonism was between the bourgeoisie and the local working class; second, upon the particular stage of the national liberation struggle; third, upon international factors; and fourth, upon the presence within the bourgeoisie of sections with different economic interests (Brutents 1977, vol. 1: 106).

Since the national bourgeoisie was unreliable, Soviet theorists began to look to the petty bourgeoisie and the non-proletarian and semi-proletarian middle sections for the revolutionary motive force in Third World society.

The intermediate strata and the revolutionary democrats

It was evident that with or without a sizeable working class or a revolutionary bourgeoisie, many countries had changed, and some had expressed an intention to develop along the non-capitalist path. The class to which Soviet scholars turned for an explanation was the petty bourgeoisie, 'the most numerous and, to a certain extent, the most important class at given stages of evolution of the majority of states in the Third World' (Levkovsky 1970: 106). Nowhere else had the petty bourgeoisie been considered progressive. In the Third World, however, it had developed in a unique way, quite unlike its development in European industrialized countries. Moreover, it did not act on its own, but formed an alliance with other strata in society.

The term that was commonly used to denote the groups which governed those liberated colonies that had chosen the non-capitalist path of development (e.g. Algeria, Burma, Tanzania, etc.) was 'revolutionary democrats', necessarily an alliance of various groups, since:

The unique feature of the social conditions in most liberated countries is the fact that none of the social classes is sufficiently developed to govern the social, economic and political processes without a reliable alliance with all the anti-imperialist forces. The attempt by one class, social stratum or group to gain the monopoly of political power usually destroys political stability.
(Ul'yanovsky 1972: 423–4)

It was relatively easy to explain the political predispositions of the revolutionary democrats. They were opponents of capitalism, supporters of socialism and patriots who identified with the working class and with scientific socialism (Grigoryan 1966: 45–6). Their policies closely resembled socialist policies and they relied upon the support of the world socialist system and the international communist and workers' movement (Tyagunenko 1967: 13). Marxist-Leninist parties were encouraged to form alliances with the revolutionary-democratic parties, since this would speed up the world revolutionary process (Ul'yanovsky 1972: 433–4).

The class composition of the revolutionary democrats was

more difficult to explain, however, and a variety of definitions have been offered. The problem arose partly because of the enormous differences between the revolutionary democrats of various countries which made it difficult to generalize (Brutents 1977, vol. 2: 14). The generic term that gained acceptance to encompass this conglomerate of elements was the 'intermediate' or 'transitional' 'section' or 'stratum' (*promezhutochny* or *sredny sloi*). Defined as a combination of petty bourgeois, non-proletarian and semi-proletarian elements, together with the civilian and military intelligentsia, civil servants, small traders, artisans and handicraftsmen, the most radical section of this large group formed the revolutionary democrats (Mirsky 1976: 42). Some theorists used the term with a certain diffidence, recognizing that it was 'vulnerable, especially in the strict economic sense', given its '*ad hoc* nature' (Brutents 1977, vol. 1: 107). But it was not so much the name, or the *ad hoc* nature of the group that was interesting, as the explanation of how it had formed and why it did not behave like an ordinary petty bourgeoisie.

The intermediate stratum was said by Soviet theorists to arise because normal or classical capitalism had never become consolidated in the underdeveloped countries: before independence capitalism was imported, and afterwards the extent of underdevelopment meant that economic needs were too great to be satisfied by private capital. As a result, the state played a uniquely important role in post-independence society. Only the state could mobilize the resources necessary for creating a strong economy with its own national industry (Mirsky 1976: 42). The consequence was that the petty bourgeoisie, led by the intelligentsia, developed not under the influence of the big bourgeoisie but under the aegis of the state. It thus became a far more independent class than its European counterpart, and it was this independence which enabled it to choose a non-capitalist path of development (Mirsky 1979: 139–40). In most colonial and semi-colonial countries, the intermediate sections had led the national-liberation movement. Brutents (1977, vol. 1: 123) calculated that this had been the case in forty out of seventy countries. However, choosing the non-capitalist path was not thought to be inevitable or irreversible. It was not excluded that the transitional stratum could develop pro-bourgeois tendencies and opt instead for capitalist development (Brutents 1977, vol. 1: 115). Nor was it impossible that countries could change course, as had happened in Ghana, Egypt, Mali and Somalia (Ul'yanovsky 1979: 116). Perhaps the most novel aspect of the way in which the intermediate stratum was described was the implication that it could develop a class consciousness independent of its class origins. The international proletariat was thought to provide the necessary consciousness, and this explained how the transition to socialism could take place in the absence of a working class.

The concept of the intermediate stratum enabled Soviet theorists to incorporate military regimes in their class analysis. There has always been a fear in the Soviet Union that if the military have too much power or popularity, 'Bonapartism' will follow.[2] But just as the Third World petty bourgeoisie have been considered progressive, so there has been considerable tolerance towards Third World military regimes (e.g. in Iraq, Congo, Benin, Ethiopia and Peru). The intelligentsia in general, including the military intelligentsia, has been thought to be the leading element of the intermediate stratum and consequently active in the revolutionary-democratic party. The army, or that part of it that formed the military intelligentsia, could therefore 'become an important progressive factor in the political struggle for further development of the national-democratic revolution' (Solodovnikov 1973: 47). Perhaps more importantly, it was recognized that the army was often the strongest national institution, with concomitant opportunities to influence local developments: since the political structures of developing states were often embryonic, political parties were non-existent or amorphous and there was a low level of political consciousness, the army has often been the only authoritative institution (Brutents 1977, vol. 1: 246–8). If it was led by a progressive military intelligentsia it could be the source of progressive change.

Despite this theoretical tolerance, the assessment of the role of the military in the struggle for independence and the way in which post-independence military regimes have been regarded have largely depended upon the political stance adopted by post-independence military governments and the attitude of particular regimes towards the Soviet Union. But even when relations have been good and military regimes have enjoyed Soviet support, there has been considerable pressure on them to form vanguard parties and include civilians in the government. It has been suggested, for example, that:

In some countries . . . the army is regarded as the best organised social force. And sometimes this is offered as a reason for the establishment of military governments. In actual fact a revolutionary-democratic party . . . is not only the advanced, but also the best organised detachment of the alliance of all progressive forces.

(Chirkin and Yudin 1978: 79)[3]

This brief discussion indicates some of the confusions and difficulties encountered by Soviet scholars in trying to interpret Third World society in Marxist-Leninist terms. As early as 1963 Mirsky entitled an article on the LDCs 'Creative Marxism and the Problems of National-Liberation Revolutions' (Mirsky 1963: 63–8). The creativity that has been required to apply Marxist class categories to a variety of societies, many of which are actually pre-class, has led to lively discussion and sometimes to disagreement in print (see, for example, Butenko 1975: 370–1n), a relatively rare phenomenon in Soviet theoretical literature. In the last few years there has been general agreement about one thing: there is still considerable empirical and theoretical work to be done on post-independence Third World societies, whether the path followed by the regime is capitalist or non-capitalist (see, for example, Gudymenko and Starostin 1981).

THE TRANSITION TO SOCIALISM

Defining which classes or strata were revolutionary in the LDCs was part of the larger problem of explaining how the transition to socialism could take place in conditions so different from those envisaged by Marx or Lenin, and what was required in the transitional period. At first Soviet theorists found it relatively easy to define the necessary form of government for managing the transition from independence to socialism. The emergence of a proletariat and its vanguard party was, it was thought, essential if the transition was to take place. It seemed equally clear that aid from the socialist system was indispensable to the transition. But certitude gradually gave way to doubt with the realization that the transition was far less simple than envisaged at first and with the increasing reluctance of the Soviet leadership to accept the economic commitment of promoting the transition.

The government of the newly independent countries

The belief that the ex-colonies would follow a similar, but rather slower, path to the one on which the European people's democracies had embarked after the Second World War (Zhukov 1949: 60) was modified at the end of the 1950s. The term 'people's democracy' of the East was replaced by 'national democracy', defined at the 1960 Moscow Conference of Eighty-One Communist and Workers' Parties as:

a state which consistently upholds its political and economic independence, fights against imperialism and its military blocs, against military bases on its territory; . . . fights against the new forms of colonialism and the penetration of imperialist capital; . . . rejects dictatorial and despotic methods of government; . . . in which the people are ensured broad democratic rights and freedoms (freedom of speech, press, assembly, demonstrations, establishment of political parties and social organizations), the opportunity to work for the enactment of an agrarian reform and other domestic and social changes and for participation in shaping government policy.

('Statement of the Meeting of Representatives of the
Communist and Workers' Parties' 1960: 11)

Political power in the national democracies was thought to be held by a combination of progressive patriotic forces. But it was expected that as the masses became increasingly disenchanted with their bourgeois leaders, the influence of the proletariat would grow (Arzumanyan 1961: 12). This was considered essential 'to clear the way for the ultimate advance towards socialism' (Khrushchev 1961a: 20). Communists had been amongst the most active of the forces struggling for independence, and the fact that communist parties were still forced to remain underground in many liberated countries was decried (Ponomarev 1961: 45).[4] Although it was accepted that some ex-colonies would develop along capitalist lines, it was thought probable that once the tasks of national liberation had been completed, a class struggle would develop between the working class and the national bourgeoisie for leadership of the united front (Kim 1962: 5).

The immediately important tasks of the national-demo-cratic state were land reform, the restriction of foreign mono-polies and the elimination of imperialist domination, parti-cularly if the intention was to follow a non-capitalist path of development. Economic independence would be achieved by creating a state sector which would 'concentrate efforts on developing the most important branches of the economy, increase the speed of development and . . . prepare the material basis for the gradual transition to a non-capitalist path of development' (Ponomarev 1961: 44; see Clarkson 1978 for a detailed analysis of the political economy of the state sector). National democracy was *not* socialism, it was emphasized, but 'a transitional stage on the path to socialism' (Arzumanyan 1961: 12). There was general agreement with Lenin's thesis, however, that with the help of the working class of the advanced countries, the LDCs could reach socialism without going through a capitalist phase. Ponomarev, for example, pointed to the example of the peoples of the Caucasus and Central Asia, who had 'arrived at socialism from feudalism and tribal relationships', as well as to Mongolia and Vietnam, which had developed along the non-capitalist path (Ponomarev 1961: 48). It was even suggested that pre-feudal societies would be able to skip both feudalism and capitalism (Brutents 1965b: 27–8). Marxist-Leninist ideas were thought to be increasingly popular. The proof was the growing number of leaders who had announced that they had chosen a socialist path of development. Although their version of socialism had little in common with scientific socialism, the historical significance of using socialist slogans was enormous (Brutents 1965a: 19–20). Another feature which was thought to make it likely that the ex-colonies would choose socialism was said to be attractiveness of the model of rapid development offered by the Soviet Union and the other socialist states (Brutents 1965b: 28).

When the term 'national democracy' was first used, it seemed that Soviet theorists envisaged a rather short passage from national democracy to the non-capitalist road of devel-opment and then a transition to socialism. However, it soon became clear that the tasks were so complex that there would have to be a lengthy transition period. Attaining political independence was only the beginning of the struggle. Far more difficult and far more important was achieving economic liberation (Dvorzhak 1965: 5). Apart from removing foreign and large national monopolies and introducing agrarian reform, all feudal and pre-feudal relations had to be removed from economic, social and cultural life. Education had to be extended, the standard of living improved, and society had to be democratized (Brutents 1965a: 23). Moreover, foreign aid could only be a supplementary means of achieving these goals. It was more important to mobilize internal resources (Dvorzhak 1965: 19–20). While the state sector continued to be thought essential, some Soviet theorists began to advise against hasty nationalization, suggesting that a balance had to be found between public and private sectors (Zagladin 1973: 287–8). The distinctions between capitalist and non-capitalist developing states (previously defined as the creation of a strong industrial state sector, a decrease in the private capitalist sector and the introduction of planning) became far less obvious. More importantly, the early certainty that

there are no countries which, owing to their economic backwardness or any other internal reason, cannot take the path of socialist revolution. With the aid of socialist states, these countries too have the opportunity of beginning their movement towards socialism.

(Kuusinen 1961: 605)

was replaced by the belief that extreme social and economic backwardness could be a serious obstacle to non-capitalist development (Brutents 1972b: 115–16). It explained why the progress was frequently so slow.

The term 'non-capitalist development' had consistently been used to describe those states in which the revolutionary democrats were instituting progressive policies. In the late 1960s the term 'socialist-oriented state' began to be used as a synonym (see, for example, Brezhnev 1969: 162) and it soon gained predominance.[5] Socialist-oriented states were defined as countries which, though not yet socialist, had rejected capitalism and were led by revolutionary national-democratic parties which were introducing radical social changes which would hasten their transition to socialism (Ul'yanovsky 1979: 115).[6] Good relations and organic links (Primakov 1981: 7) were enjoyed with the socialist system, but socialist-oriented countries had not been able to end their dependence on world capitalism (Ul'yanovsky 1979: 117). Although the difficulties facing them were by no means underestimated (e.g. the need to destroy archaic political institutions inherited from the past, the difficulty of nation-building; see Mel'nikov 1981: 123), Soviet theorists began occasionally to be rather critical of the way in which they were tackled.

The criticism took the form, first, of a disapproval of locally grown socialism which had nothing in common with real socialism (Sanakoyev and Kapchenko 1977: 194). Second, undemocratic practices like excessive presidential power, the retention of a one-party system (which, unless it *was* a Marxist-Leninist party, or at least a vanguard party, by definition precluded the formation of Marxist-Leninist parties), a weak mass political party and the tendency towards bureaucratization and corruption were criticized (Brutents 1972b: 121–6). Third, some socialist-oriented states were said to have 'got stuck' at the stage of state capitalism. As a result, capitalist productive relations were developing, particularly in agriculture, trade and the service industries. Progress towards socialism required a class mobility which was absent (except in Cuba, Vietnam, Angola, Ethiopia and Mozambique, where the beginnings of socialist development could be detected) (Maidanik and Mirsky 1981: 25–6). Although there were tangible shortcomings which caused this criticism, there were two other underlying reasons: the chronic economic backwardness of the LDCs seemed to be increasing rather than becoming less prominent, and there was a growing belief that without a vanguard party, progress towards socialism would be impossible.

The need for a vanguard party

As we have seen, Soviet theorists have maintained that the revolutionary democrats had predominated in the national-liberation movement. Their success in the independence struggle had depended on forming popular, mass parties. Only in this way had they been able to unify the various tribal, religious, caste and national elements within the LDCs (Tyagunenko 1967: 17). The question arose whether, since the working class was developing only slowly and did not have its own vanguard party, the revolutionary-democratic parties would be able to launch their countries onto the path of non-capitalist development or even the socialist path. To use a favourite Soviet phrase, 'life itself' had posed the question. Many one-party nationalist regimes which had banned their communist parties were, none the less, considered progressive. The only way to explain their progressiveness seemed to be to deny the need for proletarian vanguard parties. Moreover, the expected rapid enlargement of the proletariat had not been realized. One theorist captured the essence of the conundrum:

If the working people of an economically underdeveloped country . . . had to wait for the possibility of forming a national proletarian dictatorship to begin the transition to socialist development, it would mean that capitalism would have to be developed rapidly, so that a working class might be created . . . and subsequently, a Marxist-Leninist party might be formed on this basis.

(Ul'yanovsky 1966: 114)

Some theorists adopted a rather traditional view: large, mass parties could certainly lead the struggle for independence and promote national unity, but social and political transformation required vanguard parties governed by the theory of scientific socialism (Tyagunenko 1967: 17). Other theorists became rather more innovative. The reason for the transition to a non-capitalist path of development was not the class conflict that was normally expected to presage a socialist revolution, but the example of existing socialism. The transition would occur before the social differentiation and class polarization which accompanied the development of capitalism. It would also occur before the proletariat developed into a class for itself and organized a leading, Marxist-Leninist party. But this need not delay the transition to a non-capitalist path of development (Grigoryan 1966: 45). The revolutionary democrats, together with the world socialist system, could fulfil the necessary functions (Brutents 1965b: 29).

To begin with, there was little to distinguish revolutionary democrats from Marxist-Leninists in Soviet descriptions. Like communists, they repudiated capitalism, nationalized foreign and large domestic capitalist enterprises, introduced agrarian reforms and sided with the socialist states on important international issues (Ul'yanovsky 1966: 112). They identified with the working class and were attracted by the principles and

concepts of scientific socialism. The only discernible difference between revolutionary democrats and Marxist-
Leninists seemed to be in class origin. Indigenous communists
had been instructed to form united fronts with them (Grigoryan 1966: 45–6) and to act as the friends and assistants of
national leaders (Ul'yanovsky 1966: 113). On the face of it
there seemed no reason why they should not establish non-
capitalist development and even proceed to lay the foundations for socialism—the boundary between the two was, in
any case, extremely vague. Lenin was invoked to explain why
communist parties did not need to be formed in countries
where there was no proletariat and why mass national-revolu-
tionary parties were more suitable. It was only when the
building of socialism became the immediate aim that the mass
party needed to evolve into a communist party (Primakov
1981: 5). But the disillusion described above both with the
performance of the revolutionary democrats and with the
dismal economic situation of the Third World, as well as the
recognition of the danger of relying on the policy of a single
charismatic revolutionary democrat led other theorists to
reaffirm the need for a vanguard party. The revolutionary
democrats, because of their heterogeneity and petty-bourgeois character, could not but be inconsistent and contradictory (Brutents 1977, vol. 2: 24–5).

The most acute problem seemed to be assuring that revolutionary-democratic parties did not revert to pro-capitalist
policies, as had happened in Ghana, Mali, Egypt and
Somalia. It was one thing to introduce non-capitalist socio-
economic policies but another to retain them. What was
required for progressive socio-political development was the
establishment of strong, democratic government organs, the
proper training of cadres, a strong army, close ties between
party, state and the masses, an economic programme to
improve domestic conditions, close links with the socialist
countries and, above all, the creation of a vanguard party
(Ponomarev 1980: 42). The key variable in making non-
capitalist development irreversible was to strengthen the
socialist nature of the superstructure, and the precondition
for achieving that was strengthening the leading force of the
regime—the vanguard party (Maidanik and Mirsky 1981: 26).
But one of the reasons why the creation of a vanguard party

seemed so pressing may have been that the role of the socialist system in the development of the LDCs was being reassessed.

The role of the Soviet Union and the international socialist system

The success of the national-liberation movement had, since the end of the 1940s, been attributed to the October Revolution, the victory of the Soviet Union in the Second World War and the subsequent change in the correlation of forces, which protected the LDCs from imperialist aggression. But the role that was first intended for the socialist system, in particular the Soviet Union, went much further than this. Lenin's theory that the capitalist stage of development could be avoided was predicated on a world in which socialism already existed in some countries. There was no question of skipping the capitalist stage without aid. The model for jumping a stage which was constantly evoked, that of the Russian border lands and of Mongolia, involved substantial aid from Moscow. The implication in offering it as a model was that similar aid would be given to the LDCs. Since Soviet relations with the peoples of the Third World were said to be based on proletarian internationalism (Sanakoyev and Kapchenko 1977: 118), and a key element of this principle was fraternal cooperation and mutual aid (see Ch. 7 below), there was all the more reason for the LDCs to expect that they could rely on socialist aid for their economic development.

But it was not just a question of financial aid. There were other functions which, according to Soviet scholars, could be fulfilled by the socialist system. It was thought, in particular, that it could replace the proletariat in the LDCs, acting as 'a powerful proletarian vanguard and as an ally of the peasant and semi-proletarian masses as well as of all the transitional strata in the former colonies and semi-colonies' (Grigoryan 1966: 36). It was clear what this meant in terms of foreign policy: helping the revolutionary democrats in the struggle against any attempt to export counter-revolution, giving them diplomatic and, if necessary, military support against imperialist attacks and against any attempt to reverse the social transformations which had taken place (Brutents 1965b: 29). It also meant serving as an example and a model (Ul'yanovsky 1966: 111–12). Non-capitalist development was said to be a new historical phenomenon precisely because of its ability to rely on socialism. It was

'a special form for a number of countries to progress towards socialism without direct guidance from the working class but with reliance on the socialist countries and in alliance with the international workers' and communist movement'.

(Zagladin 1973: 287)

In fact, what was implied was not just financial, diplomatic and military aid. The socialist system would provide the proletarian consciousness which would make possible the transition to socialism. As one theorist expressed it, the socialist system was not just an external prerequisite or secondary factor, 'it influences significant aspects of the national-democratic revolution, the forms and prospects of its development' (Butenko 1975: 377). But how this transfer of consciousness would take place remained a mystery.

As far as financial aid was concerned, there was a change from the ostentatious, prestige aid projects initiated by Khrushchev to the more cautious approach of his successors, who dispensed aid rather less liberally and with an eye to economic returns for the Soviet Union.[7] Although Khrushchev's aid policies had been unpopular, some theorists thought them correct. Two scholars, for example, pleaded that economic, technical and cultural aid would be more useful to the liberated states than mere military, political and diplomatic support, pointing out that 'you cannot go far on revolutionary phrases and anti-imperialist slogans alone' (Etinger and Melikyan 1964: 26–7).

Soviet theorists have reacted rather angrily to accusations that Soviet aid has been meagre and have made considerable efforts to prove it superior to capitalist aid. What made it superior, they said, was that it was directed towards local development, not given in the interests of the donor. It was granted to LDCs irrespective of the kind of regime and always on the basis of 'equality and mutual advantage, respect for national integrity and sovereignty' (Dvorzhak 1965: 50). However, socialist-oriented states were offered more aid and better terms.[8] Socialist aid was also said to have important indirect effects. For one thing, the mere existence of the socialist bloc had changed the correlation of forces and therefore made it safe for underdeveloped countries to accept capitalist aid without risking neo-colonial exploitation (Tyagunenko 1967: 16). For another, imperialist states were forced to offer better aid and trade terms to LDCs, since they were competing with socialist states (Butenko 1975: 381–93). What upset Soviet theorists even more than aspersions about socialist aid, however, were attempts to include them in the effort to close the North–South gap.

It was not that Soviet leaders and scholars did not support the New International Economic Order (NIEO). They had long been pressing for the establishment of just and equal international economic relations. But they objected strenuously to attempts by First or Third World leaders to lay the same responsibility on socialist states to compensate for economic backwardness as that which rightly should be born by the capitalist states. In response to the demands made in 1976 at the UNCTAD and Colombo conferences to the socialist countries to improve their terms of trade, strong exception was taken to this attempt to

involve the socialist world in a scheme to divide countries into rich and poor and, in this way, to put socialist countries on a par with imperialist countries as far as the historical responsibility for the economic backwardness of the developing countries is concerned and for the consequences of the colonial yoke and the neocolonial exploitation of these countries.
(*Pravda*, 5 October 1976, quoted in Sanakoyev and Kapchenko 1977: 170)[9]

Apart from resenting the financial implications of what was termed 'the so-called principle of automatically transferring a fixed proportion of national income' (Ul'rikh 1981: 58), the idea of a North–South divide was anathema to Soviet theorists, who took it for granted that class divisions mattered more than geography. The issue, they insisted, could not be reduced 'simply to distinctions between "rich North" and "poor South" ' (Brezhnev 1981: 21, and afterwards almost invariably quoted by theorists). From the Soviet point of view, the monopoly capitalist countries were historically responsible for underdevelopment and therefore it was up to them to provide the cure. They could not therefore understand on what grounds the Third World based its expectations (Chekhutov 1981: 55).

The call for a NIEO coincided with two things which probably in part accounted for the response (although the Soviet Union had long been accused of generally being 'first to criticize, last to pay' (quoted by Gati 1980: 242) when it came to multilateral aid). On the one hand, the growth rate of the Soviet economy was declining. This meant that even if the political will had been there to cooperate in the NIEO and to provide sufficient aid to ensure the rapid development of the socialist-oriented states and the transition to socialism, the economic means were unavailable. On the other hand, Soviet theorists had, in any case, begun to understand the enormous and intractable difficulties of profound underdevelopment. It is to the way in which the underdeveloped economies were analysed that we now briefly turn.

THE ECONOMY OF UNDERDEVELOPMENT

Soviet theorists had at first been optimistic about the prospects for Third World development, particularly in the noncapitalist countries. They had also proposed a model of development which roughly mirrored Soviet modernization in the 1920s: expropriation of foreign and large local capitalist enterprises, nationalization of the commanding heights of the economy, the development of the state sector, rapid industrialization, particularly of heavy industry, the encouragement of voluntary agricultural cooperatives, and education and training to produce qualified cadres.

As we have seen, to begin with it was assumed that this programme would be attainable by any ex-colony, no matter how poor. Two modifications to the original model gradually became apparent: first, it was recognized that a certain minimum level of economic development was required for noncapitalist development (Brutents 1972b: 115–16) and, second, it was accepted that whether capitalist or non-capitalist, LDCs were and would remain in the world capitalist economic system (Primakov 1981: 7). The monoculture of their economies, their low levels of productivity and the positions still occupied by foreign monopolies contributed to keeping them dependent on developed capitalist states. For all of them the problem of economic growth was the most important political and social task (Butenko 1975: 388). It was also recognized that the economic situation of many LDCs had deteriorated after the attainment of political independence and that the gap between the economic levels of the developed and developing world had increased. Even in countries where there was rapid economic growth, the growth would need to double if the gap was to begin to decrease (Shakhnazarov 1984: 200).

Some theorists began to try to find the cause of this dismal state of affairs, turning, in particular, to Leninist theory for explanations. Amongst the approaches that emerged, two were particularly interesting. The first was based on a little-quoted phenomenon noted by Lenin in pre- and immediately post-revolutionary Russia: the multidimensional nature of social and economic structures (see, for example, Lenin 1921b: 329–65 and the discussion in Hough 1986). This concept offered a means of explaining the socio-economic situation in the developing countries.

Within most of the newly independent countries there existed not just one, but a number of different socio-economic structures, that is 'vastly different social types of economic management' (Levkovsky 1970: 9). The result was *mnogouk-ladnost'*, multidimensionality, an interlacing of old and new forms of production and management and a unique multi-structured economic system, quite different from the pre-industrial systems of Europe and North America (Medovoi and Yashkin 1975: 106).[10] Capitalist economic forms had been imported during the colonial period and had been grafted onto some old forms of production, while replacing others. This explained the complex class structure of the ex-colonies which deviated from orthodox Marxist models, the transitional nature of the society and the difficulty these countries had in 'taking off' into economic development. It also explained why the state played such a vital role in the LDCs. Its function was not only to lead the country out of dependence, but also to regulate between forms or layers, mediating contradictions within and between them (Medovoi and Yashkin 1975: 107–11). In the Soviet Union:

Victory of socialism in the USSR signified the elimination of *mnogouklad-nost'*, the establishment of total supremacy of social ownership in state and cooperative collective farms and the creation of a unified, planned socialist economic system.   (Blishchenko 1970: 66)

Development in the LDCs thus required overcoming the phenomenon of multidimensionality and evening out the various structures.

The second application of Leninist theory to underdevelopment concerned a rather better known but not unrelated concept—the theory of uneven development. It had frequently been used to explain why revolutions could take place in non-industrial countries, but it was now applied to Third World economic development, both before and after the achievement of independence. On the one hand, it explained the enormous disparities between Third World countries (particularly evident since the oil crisis in the mid-1970s) and the increasing gap between developed and underdeveloped countries. On the other hand, it could also be reflected within countries, where uneven development meant that in some respects they were more ready for revolution than in others. The fact that the material prerequisites for the new society had not been created in the course of pre-revolutionary development, for example, indicated uneven development of the economic and social aspects. This could give rise to serious contradictions in the countries of socialist orientation. The contradictions, in turn, explained why progressive social transformations were often delayed or even reversed: the necessary material base was lacking. Sometimes the transformations were introduced despite the absence of the necessary base. This damaged or undermined the economy. Uneven development could also manifest itself in a weak ruling party which failed to activate the masses to defend the progressive socio-economic transformations which had already taken place (Primakov 1980b: 28–47).

While neither of these applications of Leninist theory offered a cure for underdevelopment (or a complete explanation of why it persisted), they were interesting examples of new attempts to make better use of empirical data, to stress specific features of diverse regions or countries and to move away from vague generalization and dogmatic formulation (for other aspects of Soviet development theory, see Clarkson 1978 and Valkenier, 1983: 73–108). In so far as the proponents of either approach suggested the means of overcoming under-development, they stressed the importance of internal eco-nomic efforts and the need for time. On the one hand, political solutions were no longer considered a means of over-coming backwardness. Moreover, Third World leaders were advised to adopt less, rather than more, radical economic policies and to recognize that their economies were firmly tied into the world capitalist market. On the other hand, the idea that socialist aid would be used to enable developing countries to skip the capitalist phase of development and progress to socialism had been abandoned. It had explicitly become ac-cepted that the transition to socialism would be prolonged. Implicitly, this also meant that it would be a far more complex process than had been envisaged by Lenin.

CONCLUSION

Although the final sections of this chapter have touched only briefly on some of the investigations done by Soviet theorists in relation to the LDCs, it is evident that this is one of the richest fields of the Soviet study of international relations. It is diverse, it contains more overt debate and argument than other fields of international relations theory, there is more use of empirical data and theorists have been unusually innova-tive. Many of the more contentious theoretical issues have yet to be resolved, and it is a field of study that is still evolving. While it is often the case in other branches of theory that there are outstanding issues that have not yet been settled, it is rare to find the admission that this is so. In the study of the Third World, on the other hand, one frequently finds the implicit recognition that experience has not always confirmed theory and that the course of history has differed from that envisaged by Marx, Engels and Lenin and from the early optimistic expectations of theorists, first after the October Revolution and then after the Second World War. The consequence is, perhaps, that Soviet Third World theory is less consistent and less coherent than other branches of international relations theory. It is certainly far less easy to encapsulate in a brief description. But it is also more interesting.

The admission that history has not always followed the expected course has not, however, been accompanied by a refutation or even a critique of those aspects of Marxist-Leninist theory which have been proved inaccurate or wrong. As with all foreign policy, Soviet leaders and scholars maintain that Soviet relations with the LDCs are based on Marxist-Leninist theory. Lenin's theory seemed uncannily accurate when Soviet relations with the Third World were revived after the Second World War. The disintegration of the colonial system after the Second World War was thought to prove the accuracy of his predictions about the peoples of the East. Similarly, the establishment of socialist and socialist-oriented states in Asia, and later in Latin America and Africa, seemed to prove the contention of both Marx and Lenin that in certain circumstances the capitalist phase of development can be avoided. There seemed to be no reason why other aspects of Marxist-Leninist theory would not prove equally useful. In fact, however, it could be argued that neither of those theories was accurate, and that adhering to Lenin's Second Comintern Congress theses, rather than to Roy's, has sometimes had negative consequences for the spread of socialism.

As far as the theory of imperialism was concerned, it is true that Lenin predicted de-colonization. But he expected it to take place as the result of a series of inter-imperialist and national-liberation wars which would weaken the imperialist powers. In fact, negotiated de-colonization was as frequent as independence resulting from a liberation war. The Second World War had weakened the colonial powers, but it can be argued that they were strengthened by granting independence to colonies that had become too expensive to maintain. Moreover, by the time that de-colonization took place, the arch-capitalist power was the United States (in fact, Lenin realized as early as 1919 that this had become the case; see, for example, Lenin 1919a: 235; and Soviet theorists have called it that ever since then). Far from being weakened by de-colonization, the United States, it could be argued, gained enormously in political and economic influence. Just as Lenin wrote 'Imperialism' to update Marx by taking account of new developments, it has been necessary to update Lenin. But this has proved to be a more delicate task than that faced by Lenin in 1916. As we have seen, the one theorist who tried to do so, Varga, found himself without an institute and forced to recant. And although both he and his work were rehabilitated after Stalin's death, the result has been the coexistence of two theories (not always peaceful), rather than the strengthening or the replacement of the classical theory.

The thesis that underdeveloped countries would be able to skip the capitalist phase of development has proved true for some underdeveloped countries, but it is no longer considered invariable. The resulting system (in Cuba, Vietnam, Laos or Korea, for example, which are said to have already reached socialism) is clearly not always what was envisaged in terms of industrialization and prosperity. To some extent, therefore, the original theory has been adapted. The limiting circumstance to avoiding capitalism is now said to be a certain minimum level of development. But there seems to be no precise definition of what that level is and no self-evident reason why it should not be defined. Economic typologies of developing countries have been constructed (see, for example, *Tipolgiya nesotsialisticheskikh stran* 1976). If some Third World states are recognized to be non-capitalist, others socialist-oriented and still others already socialist, it should be possible to say what the economic criteria are for passing from each of these stages to the next, and what the minimum take-off criteria are for becoming non-capitalist. Furthermore, the fate of countries below the minimum level is not specified: will they remain stagnant, will they have to pass through capitalism, or if sufficient aid was to be made available, could they embark upon non-capitalist development? Or could it be that the criteria are not just economic?

This last question ties up with the old problem of which forces to support in the drive for national liberation. Lenin's theses at the Second Comintern Congress have always been considered valid and bourgeois-democratic movements have continued to enjoy Soviet support. The result has sometimes been embarrassment for the Soviet leadership when the movements have come to power and repressed indigenous communist parties. But the concomitant lack of support for local socialists and communists may also have served to keep them weak, thereby making it even more difficult for a vanguard party to be formed before or after independence to ensure the transition, first to non-capitalist development and then to socialism. Whether this is one of the reasons why the transition has often proved difficult to effect is a question that has not been tackled by Soviet theorists, perhaps because if it *is* the reason, Roy may well have turned out to be correct rather than Lenin. And yet in terms of providing a guide to Soviet policy and ensuring its success, the need for theoretical clarity on this issue is vital.

There are other reasons, however, why adapting classical theory has been difficult. For one thing, the classical theory does not really address the intractable problems of under-development or the rapid regime change which has been a feature of post-independence government. Nor can it easily be adapted to explain phenomena like the Iranian Revolution, which caused considerable conceptual confusion, some theorists interpreting it optimistically in terms of progressive social development (e.g. Kim 1980), others recognizing that it contained an equal potential for retrogressive change (e.g. Primakov 1980a). (In fact, Iran is recognized as being anti-imperialist, but Soviet–Iranian relations have been worse since the Revolution than before).[11] It does not allow for the possibility of war between two socialist-oriented states (e.g. Vietnam and Kampuchea) or between two underdeveloped states (e.g. Iran and Iraq). For another, Soviet–Third World relations are said to be an example of a new type of inter-national relations, combining the principles of peaceful coexistence with the principles of proletarian internationalism (Butenko 1975: 403–13). In other words, they are a combi-nation of state relations and class relations, or of 'horizontal' and 'vertical' relations. In so far as they are class relations they are based 'on the Leninist teaching that the national-libera-tion movement is an integral part of the world revolutionary process' (Novopashin 1978: 134). And in so far as they are state relations, they are based on the principles of inter-national law which include the principles of peaceful co-existence. The problem arises when these two aspects contradict one another (there is a similar problem in relations with capitalist states, as we have seen, and an identical one in relations with socialist states, which will be discussed in Chapter 7). In other words, when good state relations require the neglect of a movement that would, if it attained power, probably be more sympathetic to socialism, or conversely, when proletarian international support for national-liberation movements results in poor inter-governmental relations or adversely affects East–West détente, there is a dilemma. Soviet theory does not deal with it, although it had become evident very early in Soviet history. Soviet practice has often resolved it in favour of good state relations and at the expense of the national-liberation movement, or at least of the local socialists.

In those aspects of Soviet theory which are less directly based on the classical writing, there seem to be surprising gaps. Concern that the effect of aid might be to increase the relative advantages of the already advantaged, doubts about the efficacy of industrial models as a solution to Third World underdevelopment, worry about the effects of the disintegration of traditional societies, the rising birth rate, the depletion of natural resources and the effects of pollution are common in a variety of Western and Third World theories. These concerns are rarely voiced in Soviet theory or are treated with optimism. Western demographers who calculate that the world will run out of food resources are accused of being Malthusians (Shakhnazarov 1984: 123). The gap between rich and poor, Soviet theorists maintain, will remain until a new social order reigns throughout the world, but mankind's technical expertise and the scientific and technical revolution are sufficient to resolve resource scarcity in the short term (Shakhnazarov 1984: 135–8). Works like *The Limits to Growth* (Meadows 1972) and the Brandt Report (Brandt Commision 1980) are either 'somewhat sensational' (Shakhnazarov 1984: 124) or harmful because they promote an atmosphere of panic and the expectation of imminent disaster (Khvoinik 1980: 49). Despite the doubts expressed by recent theorists, the Soviet remedy for underdevelopment remains effective industrialization and the gradual introduction of socialism. What Soviet theorists fail to explain, however, is how these remedies will solve endemic Third World problems which, they increasingly admit, are far from being identical to those faced by the Soviet Union in the 1920s. The problems of modernization are simply not perceived as acutely in the Soviet Union as they are in the West and, more importantly, in the South. In other words, there seems to be no coherent theory of *socialist* development which sets out how the problems which accompany *any* development will be avoided. Second World theorists are no closer than First or Third World theorists in solving the problems of underdevelopment.

NOTES

1. The East had not suffered the same neglect as other area studies and social sciences under Stalin (although categorizing all the colonies as 'the East' denoted a certain lack of geographic discrimination). To some extent this proved to be a disadvantage afterwards, since Orientalists continued criticizing the 'bourgeois regimes' of newly independent countries even after Khrushchev had launched his new, active policy. As a result, a number of people were dismissed. When the first edition of *Sovetskoe vostokovedenie* under its new editorial board appeared in 1956 (four months late), various people in Eastern studies were accused of sectarianism and dogmatism ('XX s"ezd kommunisticheskoi partii Sovetskogo Soyuza i zadachi izucheniya sovremennogo Vostoka' 1956: 3–12). Zimmerman (1971: 36) tied the personnel changes to the struggle within the CPSU between Molotov and Khrushchev . The Twentieth Party Congress speeches urging research (those by Mikoyan, Suslov and Shepilov are particularly relevant) are translated in Gruliow (1957). Rozman (1985) has argued that some of the recent, interesting work done by Orientalists, particularly on China, is intended as a surrogate for the study of Soviet history and Stalinism. There are a number of interesting studies on the international relations and area-studies institutions and their effect on Soviet policy. See, for example, Remnek (1975), Eran (1979), Saivetz (1982) and Malcolm (1984), and see also the authors cited in Chapter 1, n. 7, above.
2. Throughout Soviet history generals and military leaders have been removed as soon as they became too popular or too powerful. The first position that Trotsky lost during his dispute with Stalin, for example, was that of Commissar for War. Zhukov was demoted first by Stalin and then by Khrushchev.
3. Military regimes in capitalist developing states have been particularly ferociously criticized. One theorist, for example, explained that the moving force in the capitalist developing world was the 'surrogate' of the national bourgeoisie 'in the form of the "bureaucratic", parasitic, neocomprador bourgeoisie or militarist neo-bonapartist dictatorships' (Maidanik and Mirsky 1981: 24–5). The considerable differences in the views held by the Soviet military and by civilians on the role of the military in the Third World have been documented by Katz (1982). See also Saivetz (in Duncan, 1980: 135–51) and Hosmer and Wolfe

(1983). The absence of a mass party in Ethiopia was the cause of considerable criticism of Menghistu (see, for example, Primakov's remarks about the weakness of the ruling party in some countries and the need to involve the masses, Primakov 1980b: 42–3). Menghistu finally formed the Workers' Party of Ethiopia, which held its First Congress in September 1984 (Staar 1985: 92, 97).

4. In 1959 at the Twenty-First Extraordinary Congress of the CPSU Khrushchev spoke out against anti-communist campaigns, mentioning the United Arab Republic by name (Khrushchev 1959b). At the Twenty-Second Congress in 1961 he again objected to the anti-communist policy of some national democracies (Khrushchev 1961b: 47) but Soviet state policy did not change as a result of the repressions. Egypt remained the recipient of the largest amount of military and economic aid until 1965 (when it fell to second place) even though Nasser would not legalize the Egyptian Communist Party. See Heldman (1981: 48–9) and Saivetz (1982: 126–33).

5. One Western theorist calls the concept of non-capitalist development 'a teleological model, a programmatic statement of how to get from a traditional to a Soviet-type society' (Saivetz 1982: 15). The introduction of the term 'socialist-orientation' was a way of getting round the gap between the proclaimed goals of many LDCs and the reality of their successes and failures (Saivetz 1982: 296–97). It also represented a shift from prescription to a more analytical theory (Saivetz 1982: 297–90). According to another Western theorist, changes in the late Brezhnev period reflected both a greater sophistication in scholarly and policy-oriented discourse and a general lowering of expectation regarding Soviet influence in the Third World and the revolutionary potential of Third World countries (Bialer 1980: 271). For an analysis of the further lowering of expectations, see Valkenier (1986).

6. In 1979 non-capitalist LDCs were classified as follows:

    1. *Long-established socialist-oriented states:* Algeria, Burma, Guinea, the People's Democratic Republic of Yemen, the Congo, Syria and Tanzania.
    2. *Recently established socialist-oriented states:* Angola, Madagascar, Mozambique, Ethiopia 'and others'. Afghanistan was then said to have just joined this group.
    3. *States which had avoided capitalism and already reached Socialism:* Vietnam, Korea, Laos, and Cuba.

    The last group had been led by people's democratic governments, while the government of the LDC socialist-oriented states were revolutionary national-democratic, undergoing a similar development to Mongolia. Ghana, Mali and Egypt were classified as having reverted to capitalism, as had Somalia (Ul'yanovsky 1979: 116–17). According to the papers captured in Grenada, the New Jewel Movement found its acceptance as a fraternal Marxist-Leninist party 'maddeningly slow'. Its representative in Moscow explained that this was because the Soviet authorities had burnt their fingers giving support to the wrong groups, for example in Egypt, Somalia, Ghana and Peru (US Department of State and Department of Defence 1984: 26/3).

Grenada was accepted as being 'at the national-democratic anti-imperialist stage of socialist orientation' (US Department of State and Department of Defence 1984: 26/2). Jacobs, the New Jewel representative, added ruefully: 'they regard Grenada as a small distant country and they are only prepared to make commitments to the extent of their ability to fulfil, and if necessary, defend their commitment' (US Department of State and Department of Defence 1984: 26/2). In fact, the New Jewel Movement was considered a petty-bourgeois vanguard party, inferior to a Marxist-Leninist party (Irkhin 1982: 58).

7. See Heldman (1981) for an analysis of Khrushchev's aid policies and Valkenier (1983: 1–36) for the changes which have occurred in aid policies from 1955 to the end of 1982.

8. Chekutov maintained that more credits are offered to states with socialist orientation. But according to his figures, 40 per cent of credits granted in the mid-1970s went to the contiguous states of India, Iran, Pakistan and Turkey, none of which are considered socialist-oriented (Chekhutov 1981: 54). He criticized Western assertions that the volume of socialist aid is inferior to that from capitalists on the grounds that Western economists do not correlate volume of aid with the export of goods or with the per capita income of donor country. If the volume is so correlated, the socialist commonwealth will be seen to donate double the volume of capitalist aid (Chekhutov 1981: 58–9). In fact, most Western scholars maintain that the Soviet global aid effort is insignificant compared to Western aid (see Donaldson 1981, for example).

9. For an account of the Soviet contribution to the NIEO debate, see Donaldson (1981: 358–83), Gati (1980: 241–70) and Valkenier (1983: 109–46).

10. As Valkenier (1983: 105, n. 24) explains, the word *uklad* in the term *mnogoukladnost'* almost defies translation. It means the various types of productive relations which make up the economy. The types usually coalesce into feudal, capitalist or socialist formations. In undeveloped economies coalescence has not yet taken place because a number of types of productive relations exist. Hough (1986: 55) translates the word *uklad* into 'substructure'. He describes the emergence of the concept and the controversy it produced, particularly as used by Levkovsky, who 'explicitly emphasized . . . that a society without a dominant class could not have a government that was subordinated to a dominant class' (Hough 1986: 59).

11. Following Brezhnev's formulation at the Twenty-Sixth Party Congress (Brezhnev 1981: 17), the revolution in Iran was defined as 'social and national in content', with both anti-imperialist and conservative features. The situation in Iran confirmed that Islam can both be the cause of liberation struggle (as in Iran) and be used by reactionary forces in the service of counter-revolution (as in Afghanistan). In Iran, however, 'the Islamic ideology is used by one and the same social and political forces as the basis of both anti-imperialist and anti-democratic slogans and actions, to confirm the false thesis of "a special Islamic way" opposed to both West and East, that is opposed to both capitalism and socialism' (Maidanik and Mirsky 1981: see 18–19).

6 Relations Among Socialists I:
Nationalism and Internationalism

The principle which has always been said to underpin the relations between members of the international workers' movement is proletarian internationalism. It is still ranked as one of the two pillars on which Soviet foreign policy is based (the other, as we have seen, is peaceful coexistence). After the Second World War, when socialism moved beyond the borders of one country to become the dominant system in a region, proletarian internationalism became the basis of inter-state relations. In its inter-state form, it began to be called socialist internationalism.

The modern concept of socialist internationalism, like proletarian internationalism, is said to stem from the work of Marx, Engels and Lenin on relations between socialists. This presents a theoretical problem, however, in that neither Marx nor Engels conceived of relations between socialist *states*. Their use of the term 'internationalism' referred essentially to relations within a class. On the one hand, the socialist revolution would be international and it would lead to the disappearance of national differences. There would therefore be no need for foreign policy. And on the other hand, the state would wither away after the revolution and there could therefore be no inter-*state* relations. Lenin, however, believed that national differences would remain for some time. Moreover, he insisted that socialists should support the right of nations to self-determination. He also extended the period during which a state would be necessary and therefore available to engage in international relations. But Lenin, too, used proletarian internationalism primarily to refer to relations within the

the working class or between socialist parties.

Stalin further postponed the disappearance of both national differences and the state. He also maintained that socialism could be built in one or several countries. Once it was postulated that socialism could occur in one or more country and that the state would be retained in each, theoretically there could be inter-state relations between them. After the Second World War the theoretical possibility became a reality. It became necessary both to relate the internal changes in the countries of Eastern Europe (and in North Korea, North Vietnam and China) to the Soviet model and to explain the form relations between them should take. In the case of their domestic developments it proved relatively easy to adapt aspects of Leninist theory. It was far more difficult, however, to conceive of foreign relations which both encompassed the normal features of inter-state relations, and also included the principle of proletarian internationalism, which by then had come to mean putting Soviet state interests first.

The purpose of this chapter is to trace the development of Soviet theory from the belief that the state would wither away to the beginning of a theory of relations between socialist states. It begins with a brief look at the concepts of nationalism and internationalism in the writings of Marx and Engels before turning to three aspects of Lenin's theory which are considered relevant to relations between socialists. In the third section of the chapter, Stalin's theory of nationalism is considered. Finally, the gradual extension of proletarian internationalism to relations between states is traced by examining the establishment of the socialist camp after the war and the depiction under Stalin of developments within and relations between what became known as the People's Democracies. This sets the scene for Chapter 7, in which the development of a theory about a new type of international relations will be examined.

NATIONALISM AND INTERNATIONALISM IN MARX AND ENGELS

Since Marx and Engels expected an international revolution, they paid little attention to the external relations of the future socialist world. Although later Soviet scholars (e.g. Lebedev 1982: 23) have mocked Trotsky's much-quoted dictum when he became Commissar for Foreign Affairs in 1917 that he would publish the secret Tsarist treaties and then 'shut up shop', Trotsky was being true to the same Marxist theory which is now invoked by Soviet scholars and policy-makers in support of greater integration within the Soviet bloc (see Ch. 7). Marx believed that class similarities were more important than national differences. He observed that capitalism was creating interdependence and that national antagonisms were disappearing. This process would, he thought, be speeded up by the victory of the proletariat. In the 'Communist Manifesto' he claimed that:

> In proportion as the exploitation of one individual by another is put an end to, the exploitation of one nation by another will also be put an end to. In proportion as the antagonism between classes within the nation vanishes, the hostility of one nation to another will come to an end.
>
> (Marx and Engels 1848: 51)

It was the duty of communists 'to point out and bring to the front the common interests of the entire proletariat, independently of all nationality' (Marx and Engels 1848: 46). Workers of all countries were exhorted to unite in a common struggle, a struggle which Marx believed would lead to a revolution throughout the 'civilized world'.

If Marx and Engels had thought about a socialist foreign policy, they would not have expected it to be the function of traditional state institutions. They believed that the state was the instrument through which the ruling class protected its interests and that 'political power . . . is merely the organized power of one class for oppressing another' (Marx and Engels 1848: 54). Once the proletariat had seized power, it would establish its own dictatorship for the transition period from socialism to communism (Marx 1875: 32–3). When classes and class antagonisms finally disappeared, there would be no further need for a state. Engels later elaborated this idea:

> As soon as there is no longer any social class to be held in subjection . . . a special repressive force, or state, is no longer necessary. The first act by virtue of which the state really constitutes itself the representative of the whole of society—taking possession of the means of production in the name

of society—this is, at the same time, its last independent act . . . the government of persons is replaced by the administration of things, and by the conduct of processes of production. The state is not 'abolished', it *dies out*.

(Engels 1877: 150–1)

However, neither Marx nor Engels underestimated the force of nationalism. They believed that claims to self-determination should be supported if they furthered the aims of socialist revolution, or resulted in the formation of large and powerful units. But the claims of 'petty states' deserved no encouragement (Engels, in Marx and Engels 1980: 170). Thus Polish independence was considered both viable and a blow against the Tsarist autocracy, whereas the nationalist aspirations of other Slav nations were no more than a manifestation of a Pan-Slavism that would serve the Russian Tsar (Engels, in Marx and Engels 1980: 140, and see the discussion in Herod 1976: 6–38). Marx and Engels saw the establishment of the nation as a bourgeois phenomenon (Marx and Engels 1848: 38) and their support of nationalism was thus conditional on its usefulness to socialism.

LENIN, NATIONALISM AND THE STATE

Three aspects of Leninist theory are particularly relevant to relations within the socialist system. The first, Lenin's theory of uneven development, explained how a socialist revolution could occur in countries which had not yet reached the stage of advanced capitalism and why, therefore, national differences would be retained even after the revolution. The second aspect, Lenin's complicated theory of national self-determination and its relationship to the internationalism in which he, like Marx and Engels, very firmly believed, is pertinent to the complex balance between national and international interests within the socialist system. The way in which Lenin's original ideas were applied during the Civil War demonstrated the vulnerability of this theory in the face of a threat to the survival of the state.

The third relevant aspect of Lenin's theory explains why inter-state relations are required at all within the socialist world, given the Marxist belief that 'the working men have no country', that national differences would diminish, and that the nation-state would disappear when the state withered away. In writing about the development of society after the Revolution, Lenin prolonged the dictatorship of the proletariat and postponed the withering away of the state, thereby postponing almost indefinitely other features which Marx, Engels and he himself had predicted would be characteristic of socialism and communism.

Even more useful to subsequent theorists in justifying policies which, to the outside observer, seem more concerned with Soviet state interests than with the ideals of internationalism are the many, often contradictory, statements Lenin made on these issues after the October Revolution, when he was preoccupied with the future survival of the Soviet republic rather than with international theory.

Uneven development and the Revolution

As early as 1897 (Lenin 1897), but more particularly after the 1905 Russian Revolution (Lenin 1905), Lenin was concerned to explain how a socialist revolution could take place in a country as poorly developed as Russia, where neither advanced capitalism nor bourgeois democracy existed. The experience of 1905 made it obvious that the Russian bourgeoisie was unlikely to take power and even less likely to keep it.[1] The bourgeois-democratic revolution would therefore have to be made by the Russian proletariat, in alliance with the peasantry in a 'revolutionary-democratic dictatorship' of the proletariat and the peasantry (Lenin 1905: 56).[2]

There was no question, at this stage of Lenin's thinking, of bypassing the capitalist stage of development. Once bourgeois democracy had been instituted and capitalist development had accelerated, the proletariat would need to abandon the peasantry. The socialist revolution would be accomplished by an alliance of the proletariat and 'the mass of the semi-proletarian elements of the population' (Lenin 1905: 100). That there would be a gap between the two revolutions was clear, but Lenin was ambiguous about its length. Although he argued against Trotsky's theory of permanent revolution (see Ch. 2 above), their ideas were very similar, and by April 1917 he was advocating that the Bolsheviks should proceed directly to the socialist revolution (Lenin

1917h: 55–92). In later years Lenin's theory of a single, two-phase revolution was used to explain how socialism had been established in some of the People's Democracies (see, for example, Sobolev 1951; Figurnov 1954). It was also used, as we have seen in Chapters 4 and 5, to explain colonial revolution.

In 1917 Lenin was convinced that the success of a socialist revolution depended both upon the cooperation of the Russian peasantry and upon the support of a European socialist revolution (see, for example, Lenin 1917c). It was not until 1921 that he gave up immediate hope for a European revolution and tried to ensure the cooperation of the Russian peasantry by introducing the New Economic Policy. By the time the countries of Central and South-East Europe became socialist after the Second World War, the relationship that Lenin had initially envisaged between the European revolution and the Russian revolution had been stood on its head: the Russian revolution had made the European revolution possible and fidelity to the Soviet Union was required to ensure the survival of both.

Lenin observed that capitalism had developed unevenly throughout the world (Lenin 1916a: 60). This was natural since 'there never has been and never could be harmonious or proportionate development in the world of capitalism' (Lenin 1919d: 308). It was, therefore, unlikely that social revolution would be the result of the united action of the proletarians of all countries simultaneously (Lenin 1916a: 58–9). A more probable scenario was that revolution would occur first in a less developed country on the periphery, where the weakest link of capitalism was to be found, for example in Russia.

But Lenin stressed that it was easier for the Russians 'to *begin* the great proletarian revolution' than 'to *continue* it and carry it to final victory' (Lenin 1919d: 310). The final successful establishment of socialism would require that the revolution spread from Russia to the more advanced capitalist countries. Since this meant that revolution would take place in countries at varying stages of development, the forms it would take, and the subsequent changes brought about by the dictatorship of the proletariat, were bound to differ. In writing about the socialist commonwealth since the war and the national differences which have occurred in the establishment of socialism, most Soviet theorists cite Lenin's view that:

All nations will arrive at socialism—this is inevitable, but all will do so in not exactly the same way, each will contribute something of its own to some form of democracy, to some variety of the dictatorship of the proletariat, to the varying rate of socialist transformations in the different aspects of social life.

(Lenin 1916a: 69–70)

None the less, Lenin believed that certain aspects of the Russian Revolution were universally applicable. For one thing, he was convinced that successful revolutionary parties had to be modelled on the Bolshevik Party. For another, he saw the dictatorship of the proletariat as an essential element in establishing socialism:

the transition from capitalism to communism is certainly bound to yield a tremendous abundance and variety of political forms . . . but the essence will inevitably be the same: *the dictatorship of the proletariat.*

(Lenin 1917g: 413)

In 1948 the people's democracies were proclaimed to be new types of the dictatorship of the proletariat which conformed to Lenin's theory.

Proletarian internationalism and national self-determination

On the question of national self-determination, Lenin developed a complex view which he reiterated constantly in debate with those Marxists who eschewed nationalism as a bourgeois and therefore retrograde phenomenon. It was precisely because it was a bourgeois phenomenon that nationalism should be supported. Supporting the right of nations to self-determination would give socialists 'the strength to accomplish the socialist revolution and overthrow the bourgeoisie' (Lenin 1916c: 336). But although it was the duty of socialists in *oppressor* states to struggle against the enforced retention of oppressed nations within the boundaries of other states, socialists in the *oppressed* nations should, with equal force, insist on their right to unite with the workers of the oppressor nation (Lenin 1916g: 147–8). To support the freedom to secede was not to encourage separatism, Lenin insisted, and to confuse the two was a foolish 'as accusing those who advocate freedom of divorce of encouraging the destruction of family ties' (Lenin 1914b: 422).'

Lenin believed that a transitional period of complete emancipation would eliminate national friction and mistrust (Lenin 1916g: 147). Once hostility between nations had disappeared, the process of 'drawing together' (*sblizhenie*) and 'fusion' (*sliyanie*) could begin, a process 'that will be completed when the state *withers away*' (Lenin 1916c: 325). The length of time fusion would take thus depended upon how long it would take for the state to wither away. The end point that Lenin evisaged in his theory of national self-determination was 'complete equality, the closest association and the eventual *amalgamation* of all nations' (Lenin 1916c: 346). No coercion was to be involved in the fusion, however, and none would be required: it was expected that the workers would gravitate irresistibly towards union. But by 1920 Lenin was already admitting that amalgamation would take a little longer than previously envisaged, since national and state distinctions would 'continue to exist for a very long time to come, even after the dictatorship of the proletariat has been established on a world-wide scale' (Lenin 1920a: 92).

Whatever the rights of nations, individual socialists were certainly expected to be above bourgeois nationalism and to oppose it. Lenin claimed that bourgeois nationalism and proletarian internationalism were 'two irreconcilably hostile slogans' (Lenin 1913: 26). For individual socialists the claims to self-determination could never supersede the claims of internationalism. To be an internationalist meant placing the interests of all nations above those of one's own nation (Lenin 1916c: 347). In the First World War this implied following a policy of national defeatism. In the aftermath of that war and the establishment of the Third Communist International on strict democratic-centralist principles, it meant subordinating national revolutionary interests to the line laid down by the Executive Committee of the Communist International. Thus, as Carr points out (Carr 1966, vol. 1: 430), Lenin, like Marx and Engels, never gave absolute validity to the right to self-determination:

While recognizing equality and equal rights to a national state [the proletariat] values above all . . . the alliance of the proletarians of all nations, and assesses any national demand, any national separation, *from the angle* of the workers' class struggle.

(Lenin, 1914b: 411)

By 1918 the Civil War had begun and the incompatibility of national self-determination and 'the workers' class struggle' was strikingly obvious. Immediately after the Revolution, the Bolsheviks had proclaimed the right of nations within the Tsarist Empire to self-determination up to and including secession. The independence of Poland, Finland and the Baltic states was accepted (in the case of the latter two, not particularly gladly), but Ukrainian self-determination threatened the existence of the new Soviet state, first, because of the Ukraine's economic importance to Russia and second, because this was where the Civil War began.[3] In 1919 Lenin insisted that an international workers' brotherhood was required to vanquish international capital. He still preferred a voluntary union, but if the Ukrainian workers and peasants chose independence, the question to be decided was not secession but the kind of federal ties necessary to bind the Ukraine to Russia (Lenin 1919b: 291–7).

By the time the immediate danger of the Civil War was over, it seemed to be accepted that the secession of the borderlands would threaten the economic viability and security of Soviet Russia. Although Lenin strongly objected to the manner in which Stalin and Orzhonikidze foisted Bolshevism and a Transcaucasian Republic on Georgia, he understood that a solution was required which endorsed the right to self-determination without threatening the security of Soviet Russia.

The compromise was embodied in the first Constitution of the Union of Soviet Socialist Republics adopted in 1924, which was federal in form, but centralist in content (to paraphrase Stalin's explanation of national culture under the dictatorship of the proletariat—'a culture *socialist* in content and national in form', Stalin 1930: 260). The constituent republics were granted the theoretical right to secede, but the institutions of government were hierarchical and highly centralized and very few (primarily cultural and educational) functions were relegated to the republican level (the text of the Constitution is given in Unger 1981: 58–76). The theory of national self-determination and voluntary union had fallen victim to Soviet state interests. When voluntary union failed to materialize, constitutional lip-service was paid to national self-determination and unity was imposed in the name of the interests of the Revolution. The precedent was set for the future fate of national self-determination. Where secession from the socialist system was seen to threaten the security of that system, the right to secession would be considered invalid.

The proletarian state

A strict interpretation of Marx's and Engels' theory led some Bolsheviks to expect the state to be abolished. But the adoption of a new constitution in 1924 suggested that there was very little sign of the state withering away. Lenin had indicated even before the October Revolution that the transitional period of the dictatorship of the proletariat would last longer than Marx and Engels had seemed to imply. The immediate task of the proletariat after the Revolution was to destroy the bourgeois state. But this did not mean that post-revolutionary society would be able to do without any form of state:

> During the *transition* from capitalism to communism, suppression is *still* necessary; but in this case it is the suppression of the minority of exploiters by the majority of exploited. A special instrument . . . is necessary, but this is now a transitional State.
>
> (Lenin 1917g: 463)

Lenin believed that the bourgeois state would be destroyed, but that when they used the phrase 'wither away', Marx and Engels were referring to the gradual, elemental disappearance of the proletarian state which is 'so constituted that it begins to wither away immediately, and cannot but wither away' (Lenin 1917g: 402). This would come about by replacing the operations of the bourgeois state bureaucracy with the functions of 'foremen and accountants' who would be revocable and modestly paid. The result would be the gradual decay of all bureaucracy (Lenin 1917g: 426). But the final stage of the process could and would not be reached before communism had been attained:

The state will be able to wither away completely when society adopts the rule: 'From each according to his ability; to each according to his needs'; that is, when people . . . will voluntarily work *according to their abilities*.

(Lenin 1917g: 469)

Lenin's optimism that the withering away of the proletarian state would begin immediately did not survive the chaos of the early post-revolutionary period. By 1918 he maintained that 'at present we certainly uphold the state' (Lenin 1918b: 147), and from then until the end of the Civil War he was concerned with strengthening the state. Although by the end of his life he was worried about the excessive bureaucracy in both Party and state institutions, he understood that he had miscalculated the speed with which transformation would come about. He also recognized that a state was essential to the dealings of Soviet Russia with other countries.

Since Lenin continued to believe that it was merely a matter of time before the European Revolution took place, the question of whether it would be sufficient for communism to arrive in Russian society for the state to disappear, or whether international communism was required, did not really arise until Stalin posited the possibility of building socialism in one country. And by that time it was obvious that 'the economic foundation of the withering away of the state' (as one of the chapters of Lenin's 'State and Revolution' was called) was far from being attained. As the dictatorship of the proletariat increasingly became the dictatorship of the Party and then of Stalin, the state certainly 'withered away', but the process and the end product bore little resemblance to what Marx, Engels or Lenin had envisaged.

STALINISM AND INTERNATIONALISM

In a damning dismissal of Stalin's theoretical pretensions, the Polish expatriate philosopher Kolakowski maintains that Marxism-Leninism under Stalin consisted only of Stalin's own doctrine of the day, plus the quotations he selected from the works of Marx, Lenin and Engels. The twists and turns in the policies of the Comintern, for example, had nothing to do with ideology and doctrine, and 'any ideological grounds adduced to defend them were invented for the purpose and have no bearing on the history of ideology' (Kolakowski 1978, vol. 3: 3–9, quote on p.8). Lowenthal, on the other hand, believes that Stalin reconciled three inherent contradictions in Leninism: the fiction of democracy and the fact of the dictatorship; the palpable continued existence of the state; and the probable conflict between Soviet state interests and the interests of world revolution (Lowenthal 1964: 39–45). These views, on the surface irreconcilable, are actually two sides of the same coin. What Stalin did was to adapt Leninism first to the needs of a Soviet state ideology, and then to his own requirements. He could, perhaps, be accused of being a revisionist, but in that respect he was following an example already set by Lenin.

Stalin and nationalism before the Second World War

Stalin's theoretical career had begun under Lenin's tutelage: the Bolshevik theory of self-determination before the war was based on the work he wrote in Vienna in 1913 (Stalin 1913). It can be argued, moreover, that there was little that he added to the *theory* of proletarian internationalism that would have seemed alien to Lenin. Lenin did, however, object to the way Stalin put his theory into practice.

Although Lenin realized soon after the October Revolution that unity (even if it could not be obtained voluntarily) was a higher priority than the fulfilment of the national aspirations of the peoples living in the borderlands of the old Tsarist Empire, he resented the tactics and manner Stalin used to impose unity and Bolshevism on Georgia. None the less, Stalin can hardly be accused of deviating from Bolshevik Party policy in respect of national self-determination at this stage. The Party as a whole seemed to be agreed that survival required a unitary state. Stalin invoked Marx's disapproval of southern Slav nationalism in support of his contention that not every national movement was deserving of the proletariat's support. Where the national movements came into conflict with the interests of the development of a proletarian movement (and by implication this was the case in the Russian borderlands), support was, according to Stalin, 'out of the question' (Stalin 1924b: 193).

But the formation of a unitary Soviet state did not necessarily imply the extinction of the nations that were subsumed within that state. Indeed, the view that national differences would disappear rapidly became categorized as a 'creeping' Great Russian chauvinist deviation (Stalin 1930: 256). In defence of a variety of national cultures and languages within the Soviet Union, Stalin quoted Lenin's view that national and state differences would continue for a long time even after the establishment of the dictatorship of the proletariat on a world scale (Stalin 1930: 257). Although Stalin's actual treatment of the national minorities bore little resemblance to his theoretical claims, the Soviet theoretical model of dealing with the national question was consistently proposed to the new regimes of the multinational states of Eastern Europe after the Second World War.[4] What was to become more problematical was whether it should also be the model for relations between East European states and the Soviet Union.

As far as relations between Communist Parties were concerned, it was Lenin who imposed the twenty-one conditions on the constituent Parties of the Third Communist International, which internationalized democratic centralism and effectively turned proletarian internationalism into loyal adherence to the policies decided by the Russian-dominated Comintern Executive Committee (ECCI) (the conditions can be found in Degras 1956, vol. 1: 166–72). But there is general agreement that Lenin sincerely believed that the Russian model of Party organization was an assured way to international revolution and that he did not intend the Comintern to become an institution for promoting Soviet state policy (see, for example, Borkenau 1962: 191; Kolakowski 1978, vol. 3: 105–9). Stalin, however, turned the Comintern first into an instrument in the factional fighting in the Russian Communist Party and then, once he was the undisputed victor of the power struggle, an auxiliary of Soviet *raison d'état*.

Stalin's interpretation of the meaning of the term 'proletarian internationalism' was unambiguous:

An internationalist is one who is ready to defend the USSR without reservation, without wavering, unconditionally; for the USSR is the base of the world revolutionary movement, and this revolutionary movement cannot be defended and promoted unless the USSR is defended.

(Stalin 1927d: 53–4)

Thus Soviet state interests were declared to be the supreme interests of international communism and of the world proletarians who should 'pledge their lives to the defence of the Soviet Union' (Degras 1960, vol. 2: 409). According to the 1928 Programme of the Comintern, when socialism existed in only one country, that country was 'fatherland' of the proletariat (Degras 1960, vol. 2: 512). As Seton-Watson pointed out, logically this meant that all workers owed their allegiance to the Soviet Union and acting against it was tantamount to treason (Seton-Watson 1961: 403). It also meant that the member Parties of the Comintern followed Stalin's line, whether or not it was in the interests of their own revolutionary struggle. And, as we have seen in Chapter 4 in connection with China, when the policy failed, blame invariably fell not on Stalin or on the line but on the individual Party, which would then be forced to purge its membership.

One of the inherent contradictions of Leninism—the dilemma of possible conflict between Soviet state interests and the interests of world revolution—was thus resolved by Stalin in favour of the Soviet state. In later years, after socialism had spread to other countries and there was more than one 'fatherland', the question of whether the interests of the new socialist states should continue to be subordinated to the needs of the Soviet union became an insoluble theoretical and practical problem.

During the purges Stalin resolved another inherent contradiction in Leninism: the fact that far from withering away, the state, or at least that part of it that dealt with state security, was ever more ubiquitous. He declared that the class struggle intensifies as socialism advances, thus explaining why there was a continued need for an ever-stronger state (Stalin 1937: 213). In 1939 he answered his own rhetorical question: will the state remain in the period of communism? 'Yes, it will, unless the capitalist encirclement is liquidated, and unless the danger of foreign military attack has been eliminated' (Stalin 1939: 387). Stalin had thus shifted from the position he had held in his argument against Trotsky in 1924, when he had maintained that the building of socialism could begin but not be completed in one country (see Ch. 2 above). He now envisaged communism in one country, but it was to be a communism in which the state remained intact. This raised two theoretical questions: first, if other countries embarked on the road to socialism, would they also retain the state? And second, what form would relations take between socialist states? After 1945 both questions required urgent answers.

The People's Democracies

The development of a theory about the countries of Eastern Europe liberated by the Red Army was closely related to the establishment and consolidation of Soviet influence in that area. Although Stalin seems to have been sure at the Yalta and Potsdam conferences that Eastern Europe would remain under Soviet domination, he does not seem to have had a clear blueprint about what this implied for the political systems of those countries. In practice, it was only in 1948 that a political and economic pattern emerged which strongly resembled the Soviet political and economic model. It was then too, that theoretical conformity and consistency were required from Soviet theorists and the East European regimes.

Until 1948 Soviet theorists seemed to be searching for a definition to explain the political and economic structures of the countries of Eastern Europe and their relations to one another and to the Soviet Union. Some, like Varga, called Yugoslavia, Bulgaria, Poland, Czechoslovakia and Albania (it took longer for Hungary and East Germany to be described in this way) 'democracies of a new type'.[5] Varga explained that the ruling classes in these countries had been discredited during the war because they had cooperated with the Nazis. As a result, the remnants of feudalism had been eliminated at the end of the war and land had been distributed to landless and poor peasants (Varga 1947: 3–6). This had ensured an alliance between town and country and support for the new regimes from the peasantry.[6] Although private property still existed, foreign capital had been eliminated and the commanding heights of industry had been nationalized. Moreover, economic planning had been introduced and the socialist sector dominated the economy (Moshetov and Lesakov 1947: 41–50). But the 'democracies of a new type' were neither socialist nor capitalist: they were transitional states with a mixed economy, in which socialist economic changes had yet to be reflected in the superstructure.[7] Thus various forms of government existed, ranging from coalition parliamentary democracies (a form considered compatible with the political rule of the workers), to Soviet-type regimes (Varga 1947: 13). In all cases the state and coercive apparatus served the interests of urban and rural workers rather than those of the monopoly bourgeoisie (Varga 1947: 3–6). In these unique transitional systems the contradictions between the material productive forces of society (i.e. the type of machinery and labour) and productive relations (i.e. who owned the means of production) would diminish as the socialist sector was extended, but fierce class struggles were to be expected.

Other theorists preferred the term 'democracies of a special type'. Trainin, for example, saw Spain in 1936–8 as the precursor of the states of Eastern Europe. The Spanish Communist Party had participated in a coalition Republican government which had introduced agrarian reforms and nationalized industry, transport and the banks. Trainin believed that the urgent tasks confronting the East European regimes consisted of combating fascism and struggling against imperialism, rather than moving further towards socialism (Trainin 1947a: 1–13).

By 1948 a third term, 'people's democracy', was becoming standardized, although it had not yet acquired authoritative definition. Greater emphasis was placed on the leading role of the Communist Parties. The unification of Communist and Socialist Parties into United Workers' Parties was lauded, particularly if the socialists agreed to 'break completely with their opportunist past and . . . there is full recognition and undeviating fulfilment of all programmatic, tactical and organizational proposals of Marxism-Leninism' (Burdzhalov 1948: 44). The idea that national peculiarities could imply various routes to socialism was emphatically denied:

Of course, one must take the unique into account in the transition of a country to socialism . . . . But this does not cancel the general laws of development. The assertion that every country goes towards socialism in its own original way, that as many countries as there are, so many paths are there to socialism cannot be accepted as correct . . . . The general laws of the transition from capitalism to socialism revealed by Marx and Engels, proven and made concrete and developed by Lenin and Stalin on the basis of the experience of the Bolshevik party and the Soviet state are obligatory for all countries.

(Burdzhalov 1948: 51)

There were two separate issues at stake. The first was whether the countries of Eastern Europe would proceed towards socialism at all. The danger that they might revert to capitalism became apparent in the amount of interest they showed in the Marshall Plan. The second issue was whether, if they did become socialist, they would adopt the Soviet model or whether various forms of national communism would develop. The danger that diverse forms of national communism might form arose, first, from the absence of a unifying international organization to impose a line (the Comintern had been disbanded in 1943).[8] A second reason for diversity was the latitude allowed to the Eastern European states before 1948 and the fact that many East European leaders had spent the war years cut off from Moscow, acquiring independent views and popular support in the process. The extent of the latter danger became manifest as the quarrel between Stalin and Tito developed, but their dispute merely highlighted divergencies which already existed.

The possibility of defection from the Soviet zone of influence was averted by the imposition of Communist Party rule throughout Eastern Europe in 1948. The danger of uncontrollable forms of national communism (and possible rivals to Stalin as the leader of the world communist movement) caused the establishment of the Communist Information Agency (Cominform) and the expulsion of Yugoslavia from the bloc. The Cominform was intended as a forum for exchanging information and an agent for spreading a uniform policy and theory, via its journal, *For a Lasting Peace, for a People's Democracy*. Although it had been correct to disband the Comintern because mass parties could not be directed from a single centre, there was now said to be a new need for 'mutual consultation and voluntary co-ordination of action' (Zhdanov 1947a: 4). In fact, both the organization and its journal soon became devoted almost entirely to criticizing Tito and the various deposed leaders accused of Titoism.[9] But by then there was little danger of unacceptable theoretical innovations gaining currency. The expansion of socialism in one country into socialism in one bloc had been accompanied by the extension of Stalinism into Eastern Europe.

Soon after the publication of Burdzhalov's article, Trainin and Varga were taken to task for their 'vulgar distortion of Marxist-Leninist teaching about the leading role of the working class' (Farberov 1949: 5).[10] They had failed to show that the People's Democracies were in a transition period from capitalism to socialism and had ignored one of the salient features of the proletarian revolution, namely 'that socialism gains victory first in the political realm, and only then, on this basis, in the economic and cultural realms' (Farberov 1949: 5).[11] The difference between what Varga and Trainin had written and the new theory concerned emphasis and timing rather than substance. The people's democratic regimes were now considered to be a particular form of the dictatorship of the proletariat made possible by the leading role of the Communist Parties within those political systems and the existence of Soviet power (Farberov 1949: 30).[12] The reorganization of coalition governments to establish Communist Party hegemony had enabled the development and consolidation of this kind of dictatorship of the proletariat (Farberov 1949: 26). Although the class struggle would intensify as socialism approached, the disenfranchisement of the old exploiting classes was not required. This was an obvious departure from the Soviet model, where a one-party state had been instituted in 1918 and the former bourgeoisie had remained disenfranchised until 1936. It was asserted that:

Experience has proved that people's democratic regimes may fulfil the functions of the dictatorship of the proletariat even if there are several parties, but on the definite condition that the leading and directing force of the state is the vanguard of the working class—the communist party.

(Sobolev 1951: 30)

But this was not in itself sufficient to explain why the People's Democracies could depart from the Soviet model in this respect, particularly since the universality of the Soviet experience was constantly stressed and the Soviet model of collectivization and industrialization was considered the essential route from merely embarking on the path to socialism to becoming countries which had constructed socialism (Korovin 1951: 382). Clearly, what was more to the point was the extent to which the people's democratic regimes owed their existence to the Soviet Union: it was the Soviet army which had liberated them and which, Soviet theorists maintained, prevented Anglo-American intervention in their affairs. The Soviet Union also gave them moral and political support, economic aid and the rich experience of its own social transformation (Sobolev 1951: 27).

Although the implication might seem to be that revolution had been exported to Eastern Europe, this suggestion was emphatically denied. The revolution in Eastern Europe had neither been artificially propagated nor was it the result of coercive intervention. It had been a revolution based on a broad front under the leadership of the working class, at the head of which stood the Communist Party, and this was why it had not been violent in spite of the acute class struggle (Figurnov 1954: 133).

There was a slight disagreement about the nature of the Eastern European revolution. One theorist believed that single-phase 'revolutions of a socialist type' had taken place (Mankovsky 1949a: 7). Others offered a more Leninist interpretation, detecting two phases: the first, agrarian, anti-feudal and anti-imperialist stage had fulfilled the tasks of the bourgeois-democratic revolution under the leadership of a dictatorship of the working class and the peasantry. The second phase had laid the foundations of socialism under the dictatorship of the working class alone (Sobolev 1951: 26–30). The second formulation, which remained the accepted explanation even after Stalin's death (see, for example, Figurnov 1954: 125–6), was virtually indistinguishable from Varga's interpretation of the historical development of Eastern Europe. The point at which the first phase passed over to the second was marked by the institution of a one-party system, something which was said to have been necessitated by the clearly counter-revolutionary intentions of the bourgeois parties (Figurnov 1954: 127–8).[13]

Although all the theorists who wrote about the People's Democracies before and after 1948 until Stalin's death stressed that cooperation and friendship with the Soviet Union was the *sine qua non* of their present well-being and future success, they were essentially discussing traditional inter-state relations.[14] The relations between the Soviet Union and the People's Democracies were already claimed to be of a new type (Generalov 1950: 17), on the grounds that their political and economic relations were based on full equality, mutual advantage and respect for sovereignty (Malenkov 1952: 106). But these features were not really different from those on which relations of peaceful coexistence with capitalist states were based. What was said to make inter-socialist relations different was the similarity between these countries:

The treaties of the USSR and the countries of the People's Democracies are a new type of international co-operation based on the common character of the political and socio-economic structures of these countries.

(Korovin 1951: 145)

Moreover, while bourgeois states tended to ignore the norms of international law when it suited them, they were always observed in the relations between the Soviet Union and the People's Democracies. Stalin also claimed that no capitalist country could have given such effective, cheap and technically competent economic assistance to the People's Democracies, directed towards promoting economic progress (Stalin 1952a: 468).

The term 'proletarian internationalism' was used in discussing the People's Democracies, but at this stage the concept was not considered relevant to relations between states. Instead, it was used to illustrate how national discrepancies and potential conflicts had been overcome within the Soviet Union. It was recommended as a model for dealing with ethnic problems within the People's Democracies (Farberov 1949: Ch. 1). Dimitrov had insisted that the workers needed to be educated to understand proletarian internationalism, so that they would become aware of the importance of a firm, united front of the People's Democracies and the Soviet Union and of the leading role of the Bolshevik Party (Dimitrov 1949: 3). But before Stalin's death Soviet theorists rarely mentioned proletarian internationalism as the organizing principle in the relations between the People's Democracies or between them and the Soviet Union.[15]

CONCLUSION

Thus, by the time Stalin died, a theoretical explanation of the economic and political structures of the East European countries had been formulated. The theoretical arguments about whether the new socialist state of Eastern Europe and Asia were 'democracies of a new type' or 'people's democracies' were, in essence, arguments about the distribution of political power. Varga's term, 'democracy of a new type', had implied power-sharing through coalition government until the economic bases of these societies had become socialist (Varga 1947: 3–14). Only then would the political superstructure become socialist. But once the countries were declared people's democracies, and once people's democracies were defined as a particular form of the dictatorship of the proletariat (Farberov 1949: 30), it was clear that in theory as well as in practice the Communist Parties were no longer to share political power. Socialism was to begin in the superstructure and spread from there to the economic base, and this could only be achieved through the establishment of the hegemony of the Communist Parties (Farberov 1949: 2, 26).

The question of who the actors were in inter-socialist relations had also been resolved. In fact, by then the withering away of the state had ceased to be an issue in Soviet theory. As long as capitalist states existed, socialist countries would require states and those states would engage in relations both with capitalist countries and with one another. But it was already clear that if relations among socialist states were depicted as identical to those between capitalist states, the claim that they were a new type of relations would seem rather flimsy. As long as Stalin was alive, however, there was little need (and little scope) for theoretical development. It was only when de-Stalinization was in the process of taking place and when dissent within the bloc became a serious problem that Soviet theorists began to consider the need for a theory of relations among socialist states. The evolution of that theory forms the subject of the next chapter.

NOTES

1. The 1905 revolution was entirely spontaneous. Urban discontent and rural rebellion combined to force the Tsar to institute some democratic reforms. The bourgeoisie played little part in the revolution and in subsequent years, as the Tsar gradually whittled away the reforms, they showed no inclination to oppose him.

2. E. H. Carr pointed out that this particular dilemma was not unique to Russia: 'Once bourgeois democracy was recognized as a stepping stone to socialism, it could be brought about only by those who believed also in socialism . . . . The trouble was not that conditions in Russia were not yet ripe for the western revolutionary drama; it was that the drama had been played out in the west, and could no longer be re-acted elsewhere' (Carr 1966, vol. 1: 54). Since Western history and experience is accessible to the East, there is no reason for this insight to be restricted to Europe. This was not something which the Bolsheviks understood very well, or else Lenin's view would not have prevailed over N. M. Roy's regarding the proper policy for the Comintern in the colonies. It is even clearer that Stalin did not understand it. As we have seen, he expected Chiang Kai Shek to allow himself to be used and discarded. See Ch. 4 for Stalin's policy in China and Ch. 5 for the theory and practice of Third World policy.

3. Ironically, the Bolshevik regime was actually saved by Ukrainian nationalism. For one thing the White Armies were intent on restoring both the monarchy and the Empire and thus found little support amongst the Ukrainian nationalists. For another, when the Polish armies invaded the Ukraine in 1920, the nationalists remembered that they disliked the Poles even more than the Russians. The Bolsheviks were less fortunate with Polish nationalism. They expected Polish workers to practice proletarian internationalism when the Red Army extended the war into Poland and were dismayed to find that the Polish workers defended Poland rather than fighting for the international revolution.

4. Carr (1966, vol. 1: 395–400) gives a brief account of the incorporation of Georgia into a Transcaucasian Republic and its bolshevization. Stalin's treatment of the national minorities in the USSR, both in terms of Russification and, more particularly, during and after the Second World War, was an example of the very Great Russian chauvinism he deplored and bore little relation to the Marxist or Marxist-Leninist theory of national self-determination.

5. See Skilling (1951a, 1951b), and Brzezinski (1967, vol. 1), who points out that local East European communists provided the impetus for the conceptual development which took place at this time. It was Tito who coined the term 'people's democracy' and it was Dimitrov who first gave it public definition in a widely quoted speech (Dimitrov 1949: 3–4).

6. Varga also said that the mistake of turning the expropriated land into state farms had been avoided. This probably contributed to the wrath

he aroused in Stalin. Although Tito was criticized before 1948 for collectivizing too fast, after 1948 the 'socialist transformation of the countryside' was insisted upon in all the People's Democracies.

7. Varga used the term *mnogoukladnyi* for mixed economy, a term which, as we have seen in Chapter 5, was used later to explain the social and economic structure of the Third World.

8. One Soviet theorist maintained that the Cominform had been disbanded to put an end to German propaganda about Soviet interference in the domestic affairs of other states (Lazarev 1949: 5).

9. The Comintern was set up in September 1947. Its headquarters were scheduled to be in Belgrade, but were shifted to Bucharest when Yugoslavia was expelled from the organization. The members consisted of the ruling Communist Parties (with the exception of Albania) and the French and Italian Communist Parties. Stalin and Tito fell out over a number of issues, but the underlying cause was whether Soviet interests still had precedence now that there was more than one socialist state. For a detailed account of the Cominform's activities in the Stalin–Tito dispute, see Ulam (1952). Seton-Watson (1961: 313–14) argues that the Cominform was intended to counteract the Marshall Plan.

10. As we have seen, Varga was already under attack for the views he had expressed in his book on the effect of the Second World War on the capitalist economies (Varga 1946; see Ch. 3 in this volume, n. 25). The doctrinal changes in 1948–9 are analysed by Skilling (1951a: 16–33; 1951b: 131–49).

11. The effect of the superstructure on the base was given even more authoritative expression by Stalin: 'No sooner does it arise than it becomes an exceedingly active force, actively assisting the base to take shape and consolidate itself, and doing everything it can to help the new system finish off and eliminate the old base and the old classes' (Stalin 1950: 408).

12. In 1949 Farberov applied the term to the countries of Central and South-East Europe, as well as to Mongolia and North Korea. By 1951 some theorists were also including China in the category.

13. Farberov was rather disingenuous in the way he described the formation of one-party states: 'In the struggle for the development of popular democracy, the unity of the working class became stronger. The joining of the Communist and Social-Democratic parties in a single party was an expression of the strong political, ideological and organizational unity for the working class. A pre-condition for their unification was the expelling of the right-wing reactionary elements from the Social-Democratic parties' (Farberov 1948: 33).

14. One theorist, countering Yugoslavia's claim to non-alignment, maintained that any slackening in the friendship between the Soviet Union and the People's Democracies would threaten the very basis of their existence. And an attempt to leave the socialist camp to become a 'third force' or 'bridge' between the two blocs was merely a cover for entering the other bloc (Galkin 1953: 17).

15. See, for example, Farberov's discussion of the foreign policy of the

People's Democracies (Faberov 1949: 89–97). Brzezinski pointed out how seldom Stalin spoke about the People's Democracies (Brzezinski 1967: 158). In 'The Economic Problems of Socialism' for example, Stalin mentioned them only in connection with the deepening crisis of capitalism (Stalin 1952a: 445–81).

7 Relations Among Socialists II: From Proletarian to Socialist Internationalism

Under Stalin unity was imposed on the People's Democracies. It had been feasible for Tito to leave the bloc because he enjoyed enormous popular support and there was no Soviet army in Yugoslavia to enforce Soviet leadership. But Soviet army divisions were present in the other People's Democracies (with the exception of Czechoslovakia), and in any case, once the 'Titoists' had been eradicated, it was unlikely that the leaders who replaced them would either want to, or be able to, rely on popular support to develop their own brands of national communism. But Khrushchev was determined to dissociate himself from Stalinism, and once de-Stalinization was set in train, a new means of cohesion had to be found for the bloc. Khrushchev hoped that coerced unity could be replaced by cohesion based on voluntary international solidarity. The term that was used to denote that solidarity was 'proletarian internationalism'.

The nature of the relations within the socialist regional system have changed over the years. Moreover, it is not just the states of Central and South-East Europe which proclaim themselves socialist. There are outposts of the socialist system in the Caribbean and South-East Asia. There are a number of intermediate, 'socialist-oriented' states around the world. And there are also outcasts from the system, which either do not have any relations at all, or which have (or have had) predominantly hostile contact with the Soviet Union. The disputes with states which have, either temporarily or permanently, become pariahs have, to a considerable extent, been conducted through the medium of doctrine. In the process, the theory on which proletarian internationalism is said to be based has been made more explicit and the term has been adapted to include principles normally associated with ordinary inter-state relations. In its new form, proletarian internationalism is called 'socialist internationalism'. Soviet theorists maintain that because the relations between members of the world socialist system are based on socialist internationalism, they are qualitatively different from those which pertain within the capitalist system or between socialist and capitalist states. They are international relations of a new type. This chapter investigates that claim.

It begins by examining the tension between proletarian internationalism and the separate national interests within the socialist system. The first climax of that tension was the intervention by Soviet troops in Hungary in 1956. The Soviet attempt to impose unity and to deal with the phenomena of revisionism (in other words, Yugoslavia) and dogmatism (or China) is analysed in the second part of the chapter. Efforts to promote cohesion through integration accompanied the arguments about revisionism and dogmatism. They were not wholly successful, since they prompted the Romanian leadership to take an unexpectedly independent stand. The third section of the chapter considers, first, some of the theoretical arguments offered by Soviet theorists in favour of an international socialist division of labour and, second, the theoretical implications of the Brezhnev doctrine and the events in Czechoslovakia in 1968 and in Poland in 1980. The chapter concludes by pointing out some of the theoretical difficulties of the concept of socialist internationalism and the claim that it represents a new type of international relations.

PROLETARIAN INTERNATIONALISM

The elevation of proletarian internationalism to a fundamentally new type of international relations and the organizing principle for relations between socialist states began with Khrushchev's attempts to woo Yugoslavia back into the bloc and, paradoxically, reached new heights when his efforts failed and the dangers of revisionism (in other words, divisive forms of national communism which threatened the leading role of the Soviet Union) endangered the cohesion of the bloc.[1] Thus, when the term first began to be widely used after Stalin's death, it implied more room to manoeuvre and a greater equality within the bloc. After 1957 it reverted to meaning recognition of Soviet leadership.

Khrushchev used the concept of proletarian internationalism to prove to Tito that it would be safe for Yugoslavia to return to the socialist camp. What he offered in return was a partial admission that Tito had been wronged in 1948 (Beria was blamed, but Tito was expected to take part of the responsibility) and the recognition that there was more than one possible road to socialism. Although this was patently true, by admitting the fact Khrushchev legitimized the revolutions in both Yugoslavia and China. As a result, the Soviet Union lost the monopoly of being the first and uniquely valid Marxist-Leninist revolution. The implications of the loss did not, however, become apparent immediately. But it was soon evident that the offer did not have the intended effect. Tito was happy to reinstate good diplomatic and economic relations, but he rejected the overtures to enter into close Party association even after the Cominform, the symbol and instrument of Yugoslavia's excommunication, was disbanded in April 1956. Moreover, as Lowenthal demonstrates, it gradually became obvious that Tito had ambitions to end the satellite status of the other People's Democracies (Lowenthal 1964, Ch. 4).

The term 'proletarian internationalism' began to be used to define relations between all socialists immediately after Stalin's death, but support for the Soviet Union was still considered a measure of reliability:

The attitude towards the Soviet Union of the workers of other countries is a touchstone of their loyalty to the interests of their own nations and their ability to combine national and international tasks.

(Azizyan 1953: 7)

There was some recognition, however, that national needs and interests were important:

To realize consistently a policy of proletarian, socialist internationalism, correct account must be taken of the unique national features in any given country . . . . A correct understanding of the particular national features and a creative application of Marxist-Leninist national policy in accordance with these features makes it possible for communists to unite all toilers.

(Azizyan 1953: 6)

But a clash between national and international interests was unthinkable. Proletarian internationalism and socialist patriotism were two sides of the same coin ('Svyaz' teorii s praktikoi i partiinaya propaganda' 1955: 7). Moreover, as Khrushchev proceeded with his plans to change the basis of intra-bloc relations, international interests began to be construed in terms of support for the socialist bloc as a whole rather than for the Soviet Union alone:

One cannot be a genuine internationalist without being a defender and supporter of the socialist camp, since it is on the existence of that camp, on its power, that the success of all toiling mankind depends.

(Titarenko 1955: 103)

The world socialist system, it was said, had reached a new stage of relations. This new stage included fraternal friendship and trust based on proletarian internationalism on the one hand, and genuine equality, respect for national independence, cooperation and mutual aid on the other. The two together were the essence of socialist internationalism ('Velikaya sila Leninskikh idei internatsionalizma' 1955: 7–8). Thus socialist internationalism subsumed both Party relations based on proletarian internationalism and state relations based on the norms of international law. It was the former aspect which proved unpalatable to Tito.

The first obvious changes in relations within the socialist camp after Stalin's death were economic. The economic ties between the Soviet Union and the People's Democracies began to be remodelled in the wake of riots in East Germany in 1953. The joint-stock companies which had enabled the Soviet Union to cream profits from Eastern Europe were abolished. A certain degree of economic liberalization was encouraged within each country at the same time. The way in which these changes were depicted in Soviet writing was particularly interesting.

Economic relations between members of the world socialist system were said to reflect both friendship and mutual aid. But the joint companies were not denigrated: they were said to have been a useful means of transferring technical documentation and training specialists. That aim having been fulfilled, they would now revert entirely to the People's Democracies. As far as agriculture was concerned, it continued to be maintained that the socialist transformation of the peasant economy was essential if agriculture was to keep pace with rapid industrial development. But there was now said to be no need to nationalize land. The cooperative movement would grow despite the private ownership of land (Chistyakov 1954: 135–7). This method of changing tack not only without repudiating past policy, but while insisting that it had been correct at the time is perhaps the most typical feature of change in both Soviet doctrine and policy.[2]

The departure from the Soviet economic model was reinforced by a call to abandon autarky: national economic plans should henceforth be coordinated with a view to establishing a socialist division of labour which would enable specialization and economic development based on national resources and domestic demand as well as the needs of the whole socialist market (Chistyakov 1954: 47–50). This was the first of the calls for greater economic integration which was to become one of the means by which successive Soviet political leaders and theorists would try to promote intra-bloc cohesion. As we shall see, the pressure to integrate soon became a divisive issue, regarded with suspicion particularly by the less industrialized East European states.

The new basis of relations between socialist states was given authoritative public confirmation at the Twentieth Congress of the Communist Party of the Soviet Union in February 1956. In his report on domestic and foreign affairs, Khrushchev quoted Lenin in support of his view that:

It is quite probable that the forms of transition to socialism will become more and more varied; moreover, achieving these forms need not be associated with civil war under all circumstances . . . [I]n the European people's democracies . . . things went without civil war . . . . In all forms of transition to socialism, an absolute and decisive requirement is political leadership of the working class, headed by its vanguard.

(Khrushchev 1956a: 38)

But Khrushchev also made a secret speech at the Congress on the cult of Stalin (Khrushchev 1956b: 172–88). Whatever his motives were in revealing some of Stalin's crimes, he cannot have intended the effect his revelations produced. There was a profound loss of faith in Marxism-Leninism and in the CPSU as the accomplice (and victim) of Stalinism which reverberated throughout the international communist movement. In making the secret speech, Khrushchev thus lost for himself and for the CPSU much of the moral authority which had previously been accorded unquestioningly to the Soviet Party and its leader. The loss of moral authority was exacerbated by Khrushchev's recognition in his public speech (Khrushchev 1956a: 37–8) that there were a variety of ways of reaching socialism. By legitimizing the Yugoslav and Chinese roads to socialism (as well as allowing for the possibility of parliamentary paths), he lost for the CPSU its previous authority of possessing the first and the uniquely valid historical experience. Once the Soviet road to socialism was no longer the only route, there was no reason for the CPSU to be the unquestioned and unquestionable leading Party. Khrushchev's hopes of replacing despotic authority with legitimacy were dashed. Overt force was used to reimpose unity in 1956 and the efforts after 1956 to promote cohesion without resorting to coercion have suffered repeated setbacks. Moreover, Khrushchev's ambition to reintegrate Yugoslavia in the bloc failed and his attempts to do so initiated the dispute which finally led to China leaving it.

The repression by Soviet troops of the revolution in Hungary later in 1956 made it clear that there were limits to the separate roads which would be permitted and that the boundaries did not extend to a multi-party system with a proclaimed neutral foreign policy. But there was at first an unprecedented public admission that the socialist states had legitimate grounds for grievance.[3] An apology for the blood shed in repressing the uprising was published in *Pravda* on 31 October 1956. The article recognized that there had been mistakes in Soviet relations with the East European socialist countries. Soviet economic advisers would be withdrawn and the stationing of Soviet troops under the terms of the Warsaw Pact would be discussed with member governments. According to the article, Hungarian demands had been legitimate to begin with, but reactionary forces had gained control in Hungary and this was why intervention had been necessary

(Gruliow 1957: 230–1).

Within a very few days the line had changed and the role of the Soviet army had been reinterpreted: the new Hungarian government had invited Soviet aid to suppress a counter-revolutionary uprising instigated by anti-socialist reactionary forces abetted by the imperialist powers (Farberov 1957). In a keynote speech on the anniversary of the October Revolution, Suslov stressed the immutable laws and common features of socialist revolution.[4] Although he recognized certain national differences (the forms, methods and rate of reaching socialism would differ; each country would make a contribution to the theory and practice of socialism by analysing national conditions and working out the best forms and methods of struggle), the overwhelming message was the need for unity in a hostile external environment (Suslov 1956).

In the following years practical politics and scholarly activity were concerned with finding the optimal mix of the seemingly mutually exclusive elements which were said to characterize relations within the socialist system—national diversity and international unity. Although Yugoslavia's revisionism seemed to provoke the theoretical debate, with hindsight it became clear that what was at issue was whether China or the Soviet Union would predominate in the socialist system.

UNITY RESTORED AND LOST

From November 1956 to November 1957 great efforts were made to reunite the bloc by repairing the damage which had resulted from the intervention in Hungary and by persuading Tito to modify his revisionist stand. The Chinese played a major role in these efforts, which culminated in a meeting of representatives of the Communist and Workers' Parties of the Socialist Countries in Moscow after the fortieth anniversary celebrations of the October Revolution.[5]

Khrushchev intended that the meeting should produce the nucleus of a new international organization and recognition of the leading role of the Soviet Union. In fact, it resulted in compromise: a modified formula was adopted to describe

Soviet status, both national differences and universal general laws were recognized, no permanent organization was formed, although it was agreed to publish a journal, *Problems of Peace and Socialism* (later called *World Marxist Review* in the English-language version). The meeting condemned revisionism and, as a result, the Yugoslav representative (Tito did not attend the meeting) refused to sign the declaration issued by the meeting. Thus the November meeting marked the rejection of the Yugoslav road to socialism and an attempt to define the parameters of diversity.[6] The 'Declaration of the Conference of Representatives of Communist and Workers' Parties of Socialist Countries' ['Declaration' 1957] served as an authoritative statement on the state of the world, the laws of socialist development and the principles of relations between socialist states for the next decade.

According to the declaration, the general laws of socialist development included the leadership of the working class (itself led by a Marxist-Leninist party) in bringing about the revolution and establishing some form of dictatorship of the proletariat; the necessity of an alliance with the peasantry and other strata of society; the establishment of public ownership of property and the gradual socialist reorganization of agriculture; economic planning aimed at building socialism and communism and raising the standard of living; a cultural and ideological revolution and the establishment of a socialist intelligentsia; the elimination of national oppression and the institution of equal national rights; the defence of socialism and solidarity with the working class of other countries. But these laws were said to be manifested everywhere alongside a great variety of historically formed national features and traditions to which due regard should be given ('Declaration' 1957: 5).[7] Relations between socialist states and between Communist Parties were said to rest on the principles of Marxism-Leninism and proletarian internationalism:

The socialist countries base their relations on the principles of complete equality, respect for territorial integrity and state independence and sovereignty, and non-interference in one another's affairs . . . Fraternal mutual aid is an integral part of these relations. The principle of socialist internationalism finds effective expression in this aid.

('Declaration' 1957: 4)

But it was incumbent upon socialist states (and compatible with their vital interests) to support the Soviet Union, 'the first and mightiest socialist power' ('Declaration' 1957: 4).

The declaration listed two deviations which threatened socialism: revisionism and dogmatism. The former represented the main danger, though each Party should decide for itself which was the greater danger at any given moment. This was the declaration of a new ideological war against Tito in which the Chinese played a rather more vociferous role than the Russians. Until the Sino-Soviet dispute became irreparable, the watchword for the bloc was unity and its main enemy was said to be revisionism.[8]

Revisionism

Revisionism, of course, meant revising the teachings of Marx and Lenin. But since Marx had revised himself, Lenin had revised Marx and both Stalin and Khrushchev had called for creative Marxism-Leninism, not every revision was castigated as revisionism. In the 1957 declaration revisionists were accused of declaring Marxism outmoded, killing its revolutionary spirit, denying the historical necessity for proletarian revolution and the dictatorship of the proletariat, repudiating the leading role of Marxist-Leninist parties, rejecting the principles of proletarian internationalism and democratic centralism and turning the Party from a militant revolutionary organization into a debating society ('Declaration', 1957: 5–6 and quoted in numerous articles and books thereafter). Revisionists were also accused of promoting the idea of national communism, an invention of imperial reaction which encroached upon the unity of the world socialist system (Kuusinen 1961: 773–4).

Although Yugoslavia was the obvious and usually explicit target of these criticisms, they had two other, more covert purposes: first, to convince the Chinese of the renewed revolutionary militancy of the CPSU and, second, to discourage the revisionist tendencies which had become manifest in the course of 1956–7 within the rest of Eastern Europe, particularly Poland. One of the ways in which Soviet theorists expressed revolutionary militancy was by modifying Khrushchev's formulation of non-violent revolution. The necessity for violence in certain circumstances was recognized, particularly if the ruling classes offered resistance ('Declaration' 1957: 6). The warning to potential revisionists in Eastern Europe took the form of an emphasis on the universality of the Soviet experience. As far as Yugoslavia was concerned, by refusing to sign the 1957 declaration Tito had, it was said, ignored the goodwill of the CPSU and other Marxist parties who were trying to normalize relations on the basis of Marxist-Leninist principles. The Yugoslav 'apostasy' was confirmed by the programme adopted by the League of Communists of Yugoslavia in 1958, which 'all the Communist and Workers' Parties of the world qualified . . . as revisionist' (Ponomarev 1960: 700–1). The programme proclaimed, amongst other unacceptable formulations, that proletarian internationalism could no longer be defined in terms of attitude to the Soviet Union. It should signify mutual respect and non-interference amongst all socialist forces.[9]

In fact, mutual respect and non-interference were amongst the principles that Soviet theorists and policy-makers claimed to follow in their relations with other socialist states. As we have seen in Chapter 3, it was explicitly denied that the activities of the Soviet troops in 1956 constituted interference in Hungary's domestic affairs. The fraternal aid had been 'a worthy example of fulfilment of international duty and of proletarian solidarity' (Kuusinen 1961: 773). The other principles which governed relations between socialist states continued to be defined as fraternal friendship, mutual aid under conditions of full equality, respect for territorial integrity, state independence and sovereignty (Deborin 1958: 16). It was recognized that the call for unity might seem to contradict these principles, but most theorists insisted that unity, in fact, guaranteed both independence and sovereignty (Korovin 1958b: 24–9).

There was a related discussion in the late 1950s and early 1960s about the relationship of national interests to bloc interests. Most writers denied that any clash between the two could occur. The struggle for national interests, freedom and independence could only take place on the basis of fraternal cooperation with other socialist states and solidarity with the international workers' movement (Ponomarev 1958: 212). As long as national interests were 'correctly understood', it was said, there would be harmony between national and bloc interests (Vinogradov 1959: 85). One writer was adamant that:

Given correct policies by the Communist Parties, which presuppose the combination of the principles of socialist internationalism and national interests, there can be no conflicts or aggravation of the mutual relations between socialist states.

(Tolkunov 1961: 24)

But a rather more realistic warning was given: the call for unity and the establishment of socialism would not make national differences disappear automatically. Conflict between socialist countries was, therefore, quite possible. But it would be non-antagonistic conflict, temporary and untypical, and therefore easy to deal with (Mitin 1961: 20–1).

Despite the status of the Soviet Union as 'the first and mightiest socialist power' ('Declaration' 1957: 4), Soviet theorists insisted that the members of the socialist camp were equal. The CPSU merely set an example, it did not claim a special leading role and there were 'no hegemons, no satellites, no superior and subordinate parties' in the socialist camp (Kuusinen 1961: 775–6). None the less, it was increasingly emphasized that the Soviet experience in building socialism was of international importance and that it had therefore been natural that proletarian internationalism had been expressed as support for the Soviet state after the October Revolution. From the Soviet side, proletarian internationalism was said to be reflected in support for the international workers' movement (Ponomarev 1958: 212). The Soviet Union was already implementing the 'developed building of communist society'. The other countries of the socialist camp were only 'laying the foundations of socialism', although a few had already reached the state of building 'a developed socialist society' (Tolkunov 1961: 15). As if to stress the equality of bloc members it was said that the different stages of development would not affect the transition from socialism to communism—all socialist states would enter communist society at more or less the same time (Kuusinen 1961: 850–2).[10]

Although a dictionary of political terms published in 1958 (Ponomarev 1958) did not even list 'socialist internationalism', the term began to be used widely to express the special nature of relations in the 'socialist commonwealth', another term which rapidly gained currency to emphasize equality within the bloc. Previously, socialist internationalism had been used as a synonym for proletarian internationalism. Now a distinction began to be made. Proletarian internationalism was defined as:

in the first place, the scientifically confirmed ideology of the community of interests of the working classes of all countries and nations. Secondly, it is the feeling of solidarity of the working people of all countries, of the brotherhood of the working people. Thirdly, it is a definite form taken by the relations between the national detachments of the working class. These relations are based on unity and concerted action, mutual aid and support. The special characteristic of these relations is that they are built on a *voluntary* basis, on the realisation that such relations correspond to the fundamental interests of the workers of all countries.

(Kuusinen 1961: 375)

Socialist internationalism signified rather more than proletarian internationalism: it involved not only general principles like equality and respect for sovereignty, but also 'a *voluntary* union of efforts in the struggle for the victory of socialism, fraternal mutual aid and support' (Tolkunov 1961: 20; my emphasis). In other words, it subsumed the international legal principles which governed the relations between *all* states, irrespective of their social structure, and 'fraternal co-operation, *mutual* aid and *sincere mutual* support . . . on the basis of proletarian internationalism' (Ponomarev 1960: 637; my emphasis). The problem, of course, was that the first part of the equation, that is respect for sovereignty and equality, could only be claimed as long as the mutuality and voluntary nature of the second half were genuinely sincere.

In general, while equality, sovereignty and territorial integrity were extolled, emphasis continued to be placed on the need for unity (reflecting the growing dispute with China rather than the struggle against revisionism, although this was not yet clear). Unity was said to be required for similar reasons to those that had prompted the formation of the Soviet Union: the need for the combined defence of socialist achievements and the struggle against imperialism (Tolkunov 1961: 20). In what now seems remarkably like a forerunner both of the Brezhnev Doctrine and the explanation of why intervention in Afghanistan had been necessary, the warning was issued that: 'Every Marxist party, every socialist state is responsible not only for the fate of socialism in its country, not only for its fate within the commonwealth, but also for the fate of socialism throughout the world' (Tolkunov 1961: 25).

What made the unity of the socialist commonwealth different from imperialist unity (which was based on exploitation and coercion) was, first, its voluntary nature and, second, the fact that the drawing together of equal peoples was an objective tendency of development (Kuusinen 1961: 766). It was said to be reflected in bilateral friendship treaties as well as in the multilateral Council for Mutual Economic Aid (CMEA) and the Warsaw Treaty Organization (WTO). But more importantly, there was held to be a fundamental perception of a common identity which did not require permanent institutional embodiment. While not implying uniformity and allowing for diversity in details, local peculiarities and methods of approach, this led to a situation in which:

> While remaining politically and organisationally independent, the Communist Parties *voluntarily, by mutual agreement*, proceeding from the unity of their views on the international problems of the working class, unite their action, jointly elaborate, if necessary, a unified line of conduct, and act as a unified international force.
>
> (Kuusinen 1961: 437–8)

In fact, by the time these words were published in 1961, the socialist commonwealth had ceased to talk or act with one voice and dogmatism had replaced revisionism as the main doctrinal heresy.

Dogmatism

A meeting of Communist Parties was held after the November anniversary celebrations in 1960 to try to conciliate the increasingly divergent Soviet and Chinese world views.[11] Although unanimity was eventually achieved in the declaration issued after the meeting ('Statement of the Meeting of Representatives of the Communist and Workers' Parties' ['Statement'] 1960), the price was a compromise formulation which broke down almost immediately, first in the respective public stands taken in the Soviet–Albanian quarrel and later in the increasingly bitter polemical exchange between the CPSU and the Chinese Communist Party (CCP), which finally caused a schism in the world communist movement.

The first sign of estrangement had occurred more than two years previously, when Mao launched China's Great Leap Forward and announced that the people's communes were the first step on what he initially envisaged as a short journey to communism.[12] This implied that China would reach communism before the Soviet Union. It might also offer a more relevant and attractive model to underdeveloped countries. Thus the leadership position of the Soviet Union, based both on possessing a universal model of development and on alone having completed the construction of socialism and embarked on building communism, was twice threatened. The Soviet response was to announce its own programme for the transition to communism (Khrushchev 1959b: 41–72). Although Mao had backed down by that time (as much because the 'leap' proved impossible as to conciliate Khrushchev), Soviet writers continued proclaiming that:

The transition to communism is inconceivable without an abundance of the material and spiritual good things of life . . . . What is involved is in fact a new gigantic advance in the development of the productive forces.
                                                                    (Kuusinen 1961: 795–6)

The next contentious issue between Mao and Khrushchev arose out of Khrushchev's pursuit of peaceful coexistence with the United States in 1959. In practical terms, a rapprochement between the Soviet Union and the United States would isolate China. Moreover, the withdrawal of the offer of nuclear aid, together with Khrushchev's promotion of a test-ban treaty, exacerbated Mao's sense of isolation. In doctrinal terms, this particular issue was reflected in Chinese criticism of Khrushchev's reformulation of the theory of the inevitability of war. In 1956 Khrushchev had announced that war was no longer inevitable (Khrushchev 1956a: 37; see Ch. 8 below). Probably to placate Mao, he soon modified his view to stress that even if world war could be averted, the danger of war would continue, since the nature of imperialism had not changed. Moreover, just wars of national liberation remained inevitable. The Chinese also wanted Khrushchev to modify his views that peaceful roads to socialism were more likely than revolutionary violence. By adopting an increasingly militant tone in relation both to the possibility of violent revolution and to the continuing danger of war, Soviet theorists demonstrated a willingness to compromise for the sake of unity. The debate died down as preparations began for the 1960 Moscow conference.[13]

At first the Moscow declaration seemed a victory for the Soviet view. But in fact it embodied the compromises which Soviet theorists had already made, and it combined Soviet and Chinese views in a rather incoherent way. It would clearly not be able to serve as a universal programme for very long. According to the statement, the growth in power and influence of the world socialist system, the disintegration of the colonial system and the intensification of class struggle and decline in the capitalist system were the most important features of the present epoch. A new stage had been reached in the development of the world socialist system.[14] Since the Soviet Union was the first country in history to be constructing communism, it served as 'the most striking example and the most powerful bulwark for the peoples of the world' ('Statement' 1960: 4). The people's revolution in China had contributed to the change in the balance of world forces and it exerted enormous influence, particularly on the peoples of Asia, Africa and Latin America.

The 1957 formulation of the correct mix of specifically national and universal features was repeated. Progress in the socialist countries was the result of 'a proper application of the general objective laws governing socialist construction, with due regard to the historical peculiarities of each country and to the interests of the entire socialist system' ('Statement' 1960: 5). On the other hand, undue emphasis should not be placed on the role of national peculiarities. What was required was a proper combination of the principles of socialist internationalism and socialist patriotism. The warning against nationalism was rather more pointed than in the 1957 declaration. The socialist camp was a social, economic and political community of free and sovereign peoples with equal rights. National antagonisms were diminishing within the camp since there were no objective reasons for contradictions and conflicts: the interests of the socialist system as a whole and national interests were harmoniously combined. But manifestations of nationalism and national narrow-mindedness did not disappear automatically. The inculcation of a spirit of internationalism was required.

The 1960 statement was adamant that war was no longer fatally inevitable and insistent on the need for peaceful coexistence. War could and should be prevented and this made negotiation and disarmament extremely important. Peaceful coexistence and economic competition would reveal the advantages of socialism and enable the spread of socialism. But while the only correct and reasonable principle of international relations was peaceful coexistence, vigilance was required: the danger of war still persisted and would persist as long as imperialism existed. Moreover, colonial peoples might still require armed struggle to win independence. Revolution could not be exported, but the export of counter-revolution would be resisted. Marxist-Leninist parties would seek to achieve socialism by peaceful means, but 'the possibility of non-peaceful transition should be borne in mind' because experience had shown that the ruling classes never relinquish power voluntarily ('Statement' 1960: 14).

The declaration proclaimed the need to continue the struggle against revisionism, but gave a more specific warning than the 1957 declaration of the dangers of dogmatism and sectarianism:

Dogmatism and sectarianism . . . rob revolutionary parties of the ability to develop Marxism-Leninism through scientific analysis and apply it creatively according to the specific conditions. They isolate Communists . . . doom them to the passive expectation of Leftist, adventurist actions in the revolutionary struggle.

('Statement' 1960: 15)

As in 1957, the international situation was said to require consolidation of the world communist movement. Communist and Workers' Parties were independent and equal, but they were responsible not only to the working people of their own country but also to the international working-class and communist movement. The meeting was reported to have agreed unanimously that the CPSU remained the universally recognized vanguard of the world communist movement and that its experience in building socialism was of fundamental significance for the whole movement.

Throughout the previous year the Chinese had been

lobbying for support within the international movement (laying themselves open later to the charge of fractionalism, an activity which had been outlawed since the Tenth Congress of the Russian Communist Party adopted a decree on unity in 1921). Their one unflinching ally was Albania, and the Albanians began to attack revisionism loudly and often.[15] Soviet writers, in turn, sharpened their definition of dogmatism and sectarianism:

Sectarianism is based on a dogmatic attitude to various theoretical propositions and formulas, as though they offered a solution for all possible problems of political life. Instead of studying actual life, dogmatists proceed from a scheme, and if the facts do not fit into the scheme, they ignore the facts. Dogmatism means losing touch with reality, and, if the Party does not fight dogmatism, it becomes a sect out of touch with life . . . . The essence of sectarianism consists in isolation from the masses, the failure to take advantages of the available opportunities for revolutionary work and an effort to evade the vital issues raised by life itself.

(Kuusinen 1961: 433–4)

It became vital to demonstrate the cost of siding with China, so that the East European Parties would not follow suit. In 1960 a pro-Khrushchev faction was eliminated in Tirana, and the Albanians continued to attack revisionism, restating Chinese positions in the process. When Soviet warnings had no effect, Khrushchev first suspended economic aid and withdrew Soviet personnel from Albania and then launched an unexpected public attack on Hoxha at the Twenty-Second Congress of the CPSU. The Albanian leaders, Khrushchev said, had begun to depart from the commonly agreed line, and in the interests of their people and the cause of building socialism in Albania, 'they should renounce their mistaken views and return to the path of unity and close cooperation . . . with the whole international Communist movement' (Khrushchev 1961b: 70). The Chinese withdrew from the Congress in protest. Shortly afterwards the Soviet Union broke off diplomatic relations with Albania. Subsequently, an attack by the Albanians on Khrushchev was reprinted in China. A verbal war of attrition ensued in which the Chinese attacked Yugoslav revisionism, while the Soviet leaders attacked Albanian sectarianism. The Sino-Soviet dispute continued by proxy in this way until all pretence at unity was abandoned in March 1963 and letters from each Central Committee to the other were published admitting that there were serious difficulties.[16]

After the Sino-Soviet dispute had finally become public, Suslov summarized the ideological differences between the two Parties in a long article in *Pravda* in April 1963. First, he accused the Chinese of discrediting the idea of peaceful co-existence and economic competition, a competition that would be won by the socialist world, making socialism more attractive to the rest of the world. Second, the CCP had attempted to shake the foundations of the socialist common-wealth, curtailing ties and discrediting CMEA. The CPSU, on the other hand, believed that it was vital to develop political and economic ties and to consolidate cultural, scientific and technical cooperation. Third, it was clear that thermonuclear war had to be prevented and war averted and that disarma-ment was an important step in this direction. But the Chinese underestimated the danger of nuclear war. They called the nuclear bomb a 'paper tiger' and believed that those who fought for peace hindered revolution. Fourth, the Chinese misunderstood the present epoch. The rise of the world system of socialism had brought about profound changes. The most important characteristic of the current epoch was not, as the Chinese maintained, the national-liberation struggle, but the struggle between socialism and capitalism. That struggle required peaceful coexistence and economic competition. Fifth, the Chinese believed that revolution could be exported and that it necessarily needed to be violent. The CPSU, on the other hand, maintained that revolution could not be exported and that the transition to socialism could be peaceful or non-peaceful, depending on the concrete historical situation. In either case it was essential that it should be followed by the establishment of a dictatorship of the proletariat. Finally, armed uprisings would be supported by the CPSU, but they were not always timely. The CCP failed to recognize this and recommended armed struggle at all times. It seemed clear that the CCP was trying to split the international communist movement (Suslov 1963: 5–16).

Western analysts of the Sino-Soviet dispute have found more doctrinal differences than those listed by Suslov and it is, of course, natural that as the dispute hardened and as each state followed independent policies, so the theoretical diffe-rences multiplied and broadened.[17] But it was also the case that once the rift had occurred, the two sides became increa-singly polarized, each perceiving the other's theoretical state-ments and behaviour as inimical to the true faith in a process not unlike the deeds and beliefs attributed by conformists to heretics and witches in medieval times. There were also strong non-ideological aspects to the quarrel, which arose in part from historical differences relating both to Tsarist and Soviet times, and in part from the very different positions each state occupied in the world. Soon the conflicts of interest became paramount and the 'non-antagonistic' conflict between socialist states turned into a bitter border war.

Although Khrushchev's revisionism (as the Chinese and Albanians now openly called it) had turned Soviet theory into a more flexible instrument for describing the real world, it turned out to be insufficiently pliable to deal with a dispute between two socialist powers. According to the theory, it was non-antagonistic, but it was extremely acrimonious. The Soviet leadership began by taking refuge in the assertion that the Chinese leadership had fallen victim to petty-bourgeois nationalism. Later, particularly after the armed conflict in 1969 and the very real panic caused by the Sino-Western rapprochment, China ceased to be considered socialist:

Peking's foreign policy is based on anti-Sovietism, hostility to the socialist commonwealth and alliance with the reactionary, imperialist states and thus has nothing in common with a class approach or with internationalism, in other words, it is not a socialist foreign policy.

(Petrenko and Popov 1981: 11).[18]

Whatever functions were served by recourse to doctrine in the mutual name-calling that characterized the Sino-Soviet dispute in the middle and late 1960s, the serious and scholarly development of Marxist-Leninist theory of international rela-tions was not amongst them. But by this time doctrine had ceased to play an important role in the dispute. For the future role of the Soviet Union in the socialist commonwealth perhaps more ominous than the lack of theoretical develop-ment was the fact that Khrushchev's attempt to use 'conciliar' (the term is Lowenthal's) methods to retain unity had failed spectacularly. It proved impossible to rally sufficient support to excommunicate the Chinese in the ritualistic way that the Cominform had denounced Tito. The CPSU had the support of most of the East European countries, but it no longer had the authority to insist that the whole international movement publicly follow the Soviet line. Democratic centralism had ceased to operate effectively in the communist movement. Consequently, it became increasingly difficult to formulate and impose a general line, as the Romanian leadership was soon to prove. But any hope that this made unrestricted pluralism possible in the theory and practice of socialism within the bloc was destroyed by the intervention in Czechoslovakia in 1968.

COHESION THROUGH INTEGRATION

Even after Khrushchev fell from power and his name became taboo, Soviet theorists continued to quote with approval the 1957 and 1960 declarations and the reports to the Twentieth, Twenty-First and Twenty-Second Congresses (although without reference to the date at which communism would be attained) and their contribution to Soviet international relations theory. The new collective leadership soon clamped down domestically on the cultural thaw which had been condoned intermittently since the mid-1950s, but there was little change in policy towards the other socialist countries. Economic reform was permitted, and Khrushchev's promotion of economic integration was continued. The attempt to extend integration within the CMEA produced the next public demonstration of dissension within the socialist commonwealth. It also provoked theoretical work on the international socialist division of labour.

The international socialist division of labour
Despite its name, the Council for Mutual Economic Aid, established in 1949, had little to do with mutual aid and less with the promotion of integration within the socialist system in the first decade of its existence. Each East European regime strove to develop a heavy industry, to bring about a 'socialist transformation of agriculture' (in other words, collectivized agriculture) and to achieve economic autarky. In economic

terms the result was a failure to develop a raw material and power base consonant with the developing industry, so that there were tremendous disproportions in economic development and increasing dependence on the Soviet Union for industrial raw materials. Economic planning became chaotic as the disparity between planned production targets and volume of available raw materials increased (for the early history of CMEA, see Kaser 1965). In social terms the result was a decline in the value of real wages, a fall in the standard of living and increasing popular discontent, as Brown points out (Brown 1966: 75–9). The first signs of dissension after Stalin's death were riots in East Germany caused by economic discontent. The Soviet leadership responded by turning the joint companies over to the national governments, withdrawing economic advisers, offering loans and credits and encouraging more realistic planning. Khrushchev, however, quite soon began to think of more radical economic reform and, in particular, integration. But economic nationalism proved to be even more difficult than political nationalism to eradicate, particularly amongst the less industrialized countries of Eastern Europe.

Economic nationalism was not the only factor inhibiting integration, however. Neither the political, nor the economic structures of CMEA members were conducive to integration. Pricing policies, for example, tended to be arbitrary and would need to be standardized. The economic systems would need to become more flexible and responsive. The free movement of labour across CMEA borders would be required. The extent and depth of the problems and the fierceness of the opposition gradually became apparent. But meanwhile Soviet theorists had begun to promote the advantages of integration.

Early supporters of the socialist international division of labour maintained that it would lead to faster growth. They explained that each country could concentrate on those branches of industry for which it was best suited and less-developed countries would be able to catch up with the rest, so that all could arrive at communism at more or less the same time (Fedoseyev and Pomelov 1959).[19] The model that was suggested was that of Soviet economic development in the period of the first five-year plans: the economic integration of the various constituent republics then had encouraged the economic development of all the republics and under-developed areas had caught up with the more advanced (Sergeev 1964). The influential *History of the Communist Party of the Soviet Union* maintained that the 'gradually shaping' international division of labour amongst the socialist countries was part and parcel of the socialist world economy: it involved coordination of economic plans and specialization and coordination of production, based on comradely co-operation and mutual assistance (Ponomarev 1960: 640). An equally authoritative textbook contended that there was no need for autarky in the world socialist economy because the international division of labour avoided parallelism and waste of resources. It was inexpedient to build up a full range of industries in each socialist country. International specialization and cooperation in production should instead be extended (Kuusinen 1961: 776–81). The kind of warped one-sided growth which was a feature of capitalist integration would not occur. As a result of planned, proportional development and the ideology of Marxism-Leninism, 'no country in the socialist camp, however small, is threatened with the danger of being turned into an agrarian raw-material appendage of a stronger and economically more developed state' (Kuusinen 1961: 781).

In the early 1960s almost every article about intra-bloc relations called for coordination of national economic plans, the socialist international division of labour, coordination and specialization of production. Until then, Soviet theorists had insisted that a socialist division of labour would not infringe sovereignty. CMEA was an international agency which would aid the sovereign socialist states 'jointly and on a voluntary basis' and prepare proposals for the socialist international division of labour. But it was 'by no means . . . a supra-state agency with authority to intervene in the affairs of sovereign states' (Kuusinen 1961: 780). When supra-national planning began to be proposed, opposition within some socialist countries became public.

In 1962 an agreement 'On the basic principles of the socialist division of labour' was adopted by a meeting of representatives of CMEA members and incorporated into the CMEA Charter.[20] A Soviet theorist, perhaps unwittingly, made it clear how difficult it was proving to institute coordination when he praised the agreement not only for its political significance, but for its international legal significance: member countries would henceforth be obliged to be guided by the agreement in their economic relations (Morozov 1963: 79–80). In fact, the first round had already been lost. In June 1962 Khrushchev proposed the establishment of a supranational planning authority and an investment plan for the exploitation of raw materials. The economically developed socialist states which had supported the initial scheme balked at the possible loss of national sovereignty. The less-developed countries which had opposed integration from the start felt extremely threatened that they would remain 'raw-material appendages'.

The Romanian leadership which had just embarked on a very ambitious five-year plan felt particularly vulnerable. In March 1963 the Romanian Central Committee denounced the idea of the international socialist division of labour and invoked the principles that had so often been vaunted by Soviet theorists and political leaders: Romania would base its cooperation with the other socialist countries on the principles of national sovereignty and independence, equality of rights, fraternal aid and mutual interest (for an account of the stand taken by Romania, see Fejtö 1974: 157–64).

In the face of the Romanian veto, the scheme was shelved but not abandoned. However, it was partly to prevent the kind of cohesion that would make it possible for the scheme to be imposed on socialist states that Romania began playing a neutral role in the Sino-Soviet dispute. Soon Romania had achieved a unique position in the socialist commonwealth, daring an independence no other country could risk, playing political loyalty off against economic concessions and *vice versa* and ensuring that full economic integration would remain a goal of the international socialist economic system rather than an achievement.[21]

After Khrushchev fell from power plans for the international socialist division of labour were revived quite strenuously, but with little more success. Soviet economists interpreted the general international division of labour as an objective historical process. The *socialist* division of labour, a new form, was also a manifestation of historical processes. It was an objective, historical natural law of the economic development of the world socialist system, based on the commonality of new, socialist productive relations and arising on the basis of objective economic laws.

(Sergeev 1964: 85)

Unlike the integration of capitalist economies, the socialist division of labour would eliminate inequality and allow under-developed countries to catch up with the more advanced. Disappointment in the rate of progress was, however, reflected in the complaint that:

For all the undoubted achievements in this sphere, the current level of specialization of production . . . does not answer the demands of the growing scientific and technical revolution and the greatest possible increase in labour productivity.

(Bogomolov 1967: 17)

Agreement was finally reached in 1971 on a new Comprehensive Programme for the Further Deepening and Perfecting of Cooperation and Development of Socialist Economic Integration of Member Countries of CMEA (Council for Mutual Economic Aid 1971). While undoubtedly extending the process of integration and promoting the coordination of economic plans, the programme also insisted on the voluntary nature of participation and the absence of any supra-national bodies.[22]

Summing up the detailed theoretical work on socialist integration which accompanied the two-year process of drafting an acceptable programme, one Soviet theorist drew attention to the fact that socialist countries were involved in the international socialist division of labour to varying degrees (Dudinsky 1976: 259). Soviet economists, he said, had concluded that socialist and capitalist integration differed fundamentally in substance, method of implementation and in the socio-economic consequences of the process. Integration was clearly a vital factor for the future development of the world socialist system, but the concept of supra-nationalism had been rejected because it was based on coercion. The most important characteristic of socialist economic integration was its harmonious combination of the national interests of member countries with the common interests of the common-wealth as a whole (Dudinsky 1976: 262–3). This combination

helped to encourage 'the optimal inclusion of national industries in the international socialist division of labour and [to]
create the prerequisites for an ever deeper and more stable
specialization of production' (Dudinsky 1976: 263). Economic integration was said to be vital for the efficient func-
tioning of the socialist military alliance. The WTO was held to
be an extraordinary alliance which did not represent 'a
mechanical sum of national defence measures', but 'the qualitatively higher degree of relations which is inherent in the
system of socialist states' (Milovidov 1977: 144). But this
'higher degree' required the kind of economic integration
which would allow for cooperative manufacture and specialization.

The objections to integration in 1976 were clearly little
different from those that had been expressed in 1962, and they
reflected a general tension within the socialist commonwealth. Although there has been progress since then in some
fields of specialization and joint projects have been launched,
Romania has continued to be the stumbling-block. Ceausescu
has successfully withstood intermittent but strong pressure to
conform to plans for specialization and coordination and,
from early on, increased Romania's economic ties with the
West. Soviet theorists have recognized the problems.
Dudinsky, for example, concluded, more in sorrow than with
impatience:

Inherent in the process of integration is a particularly characteristic contradiction—that is the contradiction between the need for the uninterrupted
deepening of the international division of labour and specialization of
production and cooperation on an international basis and the complex
economic, social and political-economic factors which . . . restrict the participation of one or another country in the international process and place
certain limits on such participation. Overcoming this contradiction is an
extraordinary complex matter.

(Dudinsky 1976: 270)

Rakowska-Harmstone (1976) has pointed to the central
paradox in the policy of East European economic integration:
it has become economically burdensome but politically desirable to the Soviet leadership. For the East Europeans, on the
other hand, it has become economically desirable, but it
represents a political burden and dependence that most East

European leaders would prefer to avoid.

The Brezhnev Doctrine and after

Ceausescu's independent stand and the economic reforms which transformed Hungary were, it seemed, symptoms of a new liberalization signalling *carte blanche* for the development of national communism. But there were limits to the diversity which could be tolerated, and 'socialism with a human face' in Czechoslovakia evidently transgressed the bounds. Revisionism once again became the main danger. The combined forces of the WTO (minus Romania) intervened to impose conformity on Czechoslovakia on the night of 21 August 1968.[23] In the aftermath an explicit (but by no means new and not very well-defined) announcement was made of what the bounds were.

Western observers called the new announcement the Brezhnev Doctrine. In an article published in *Pravda* a month after the intervention, the international interests of the socialist commonwealth were proclaimed to take precedence over the individual national interests of the constituent states. It was not only the right, but the *duty* of socialist states to come to the defence of socialism whenever it was threatened (Kovalev 1968, in Remington 1969: 412–16). In effect, national self-determination had again been declared invalid for socialist states. In fact, Brezhnev had been unambiguous about the Soviet position before the intervention took place, maintaining that 'we cannot and never will be indifferent to the fate of socialist construction in other countries' (Brezhnev, *Pravda*, 4 July 1968). But a year later he denied that sovereignty was limited within the socialist commonwealth:

Bourgeois propaganda goes out of its way to malign the principles of the independence, sovereignty and equality of the national contingencies of the working class and the communist movement. That is the purpose for which imperialist propagandists have fabricated and put into circulation the notorious theory of 'limited sovereignty'.

(Brezhnev 1969: 175)

There are strong grounds for doubting the sincerity of Brezhnev's protest, but the fact that he felt called upon to make it at an international meeting of Communist and

Workers' Parties indicates the unease with which the international movement had reacted to the intervention.

In retrospect it was not really surprising that the Soviet leadership had been worried by the events in Czechoslovakia. It was not only concern for the security of the bloc which had been aroused (and there is no reason to doubt that the concern was genuine and that it was considered necessary to station Soviet troops in Czechoslovakia, even though there had been no overt threat to leave the WTO). The demands voiced in Czechoslovakia for the abolition of censorship could spread, and several countries within the socialist commonwealth were already experiencing difficulties with recalcitrant dissidents. Moreover, it was not at all clear that the Czech Party retained its leading role—from the outside it looked remarkably as if the Party was being led. The publication of the draft Party statutes on 10 August 1968 served to aggravate this fear since the new rules explicitly abolished the principle of democratic centralism (see Press Group of Soviet Journalists 1968: 38 for Soviet condemnation of this attempt to 'legalize factionalism').

One Western analyst calls the reason for the intervention (and the third limitation to be placed on diversity within the bloc after loyalty to the alliance and single-party rule) 'loss of control' (Lowenthal 1982: 277). What was perhaps surprising was first, that the decision to intervene seemed to be taken with great difficulty, as Dawisha (1980) demonstrates; second, that it was not only (and perhaps not unanimously) the decision of the Soviet Politburo; and third, that Ceausescu disassociated Romania from the decision and publicly criticized the intervention with impunity, though not without considerable risk. The Czech events seemed to signal a new state of affairs in the socialist commonwealth, and the Brezhnev Doctrine was only one of the symptoms.

The assumption is often made in the West that the Brezhnev Doctrine implied a new hard line policy on the part of the Soviet leadership. In fact, Soviet *domestic* policy had become less liberal as soon as Khrushchev fell from power. Moreover, it had been implicit from the end of the war onwards that the loss of one of the states forming a buffer between the Soviet Union and Western Europe would not be tolerated. The invasion of Hungary in 1956 had confirmed that this was the case. And in terms of articulated theory, both after 1956 and in the 1960 declaration, there were, as we have seen, explicit statements about the responsibility of socialist states not only for the fate of socialism in their own country, but also for the movement as a whole, or for socialism internationally. What the Brezhnev Doctrine did was to reiterate the warning forcefully, in an attempt to explain the intervention *ex post facto*. It also made it clear that there were still limits beyond which socialist states could not go. But what it did not do was to define those limits. The other justification for the intervention offered by Soviet writers at the time and later (an imminent counter-revolutionary attack aided and abetted by imperialism; see, for example, Gromkyo and Ponomarev 1981, vol. 2: 345–6) served only to make it even more difficult to deduce where the bounds of diversity were.

In the aftermath of the crisis there was an international meeting of Communist and Workers' Parties in June 1969, attended by seventy-eight parties and characterized by unusually frank discussion and outspoken criticism of the intervention (see the account in Fejtö 1974: 480–2). A long statement (the 1957 declaration was only five pages long, the 1960 and 1969 declarations were fifteen pages each) was issued after the conference on the state of the world and the current accepted interpretation of it ('Tasks at the Present Stage of the Struggle Against Imperialism and United Action of the Communist and Workers' Parties and All Anti-Imperialist Forces' ['Tasks'] 1969: 25–39).

Most of the statement was taken up with a continent-by-continent analysis of the sharpening historic struggle between socialism and imperialism. But it stated firmly and unambiguously in a short separate paragraph that 'the defence of socialism is an internationalist duty of Communists' ('Tasks' 1969: 31). It also stressed the need for cohesion. However, some of the forcefulness was immediately dispelled: amongst the principles of international relations between socialist states, the formula 'non-interference in each other's internal affairs' was affirmed equally unambiguously. Moreover, there was explicit recognition of difficulties in the development of the world socialist system. Divergences could arise because of differences in the level of economic development, in social structure, in international position or because of national distinctions. These differences could and should 'be settled on the basis of proletarian internationalism, through comradely discussion and voluntary fraternal co-operation' ('Tasks' 1969: 31). The declaration carried a mildly worded warning about the danger of both 'Right- and Left-opportunist distortions of theory and policy', as well as of revisionism, dogmatism and left-sectarian adventurism. But there was no mention of either China or Czechoslovakia.

The 'comradely discussions' mentioned in the document were one of the ways in which ideological conformity was maintained within the socialist commonwealth after 1968. Annual meetings of East European Party first secretaries and the CPSU, as well as individual visits by bloc leaders to the Crimea, became an institution, during which problems were aired and views reconciled (Petrenko and Popov 1981: 248). Attempts were also made to increase the role of Eastern European countries in the international organizations of the socialist commonwealth (see Brown 1975 for an account of these efforts). Meetings of the Political Consultative Committee of the WTO became more regular. Soviet theorists paid increasing attention to the value of coordinating the foreign policies of the socialist states (see, for example, Sanakoyev 1972: 403–4). The establishment of a committee of WTO foreign ministers was said to be particularly useful for this purpose (Brezhnev 1981: 8). In one sense at least the events immediately preceding the Czechoslovak intervention must have comforted the Soviet leadership—the Polish and East German support for intervention implied that ideological conformity was no longer the sole concern of the Soviet leadership, but was a shared value. In the aftermath of the intervention Soviet efforts were directed towards ensuring that it remained a shared value. The official Czechoslovak and East German responses to events in Poland in 1980 suggested that it had.

The evident contradiction in the 1969 declaration between non-interference and the higher socialist duty to defend socialism was reflected in the Friendship Treaties between the Soviet Union and the East European socialist states, most of which came up for renewal in the 1970s. The common defence of socialist achievements was a feature of the Soviet–Czech treaty of 1970 ('Treaty of Friendship, Co-operation and

Mutual Aid between the USSR and the Socialist Republic of Czechoslovakia' 1970: 30–1) and the Soviet–East German treaty ('Treaty of Friendship, Co-operation and Mutual Aid between the USSR and the German Democratic Republic' 1975: 12–13). It recurred in other bloc agreements, including the 1977 Soviet Constitution (*Constitution of the Union of Soviet Socialist Republics* 1985). But it was not mentioned in the Soviet–Romanian Friendship treaty ('Treaty of Friendship, Co-operation and Mutual Aid between the USSR and the Socialist Republic of Rumania' 1970: 242–5). That this signified that Romania would not accept the formulation, rather than a change of heart in the Soviet leadership, seemed to be confirmed by the definition of sovereignty which was conventionally offered:

> Sovereignty of a socialist state imples not only the right to independence, but also responsibility to the community of fraternal countries, the international communist and working class movement for the destiny of socialism.
>
> (Grechko 1977: 321)

In theoretical terms, the contradiction between national sovereignty and socialist internationalism was expressed in warnings about the danger of nationalism to internationalist unity. Nationalism, it was pointed out, 'disappears from the minds of people more slowly than other survivals of capitalism and produces more relapses' (Sanakoyev 1972: 122). It was a particularly dangerous phenomenon when it surfaced in socialist countries. It led inevitably to disunity within Communist Parties and between socialist states (Zagladin 1973: 450–8). The antidote offered by Soviet theorists and policymakers was the extension of the principles which were said to govern inter-national relations within the USSR to relations between socialist states. In part this was merely a reiteration that proletarian internationalism applied to relations between socialist states. But it was also a call for closer political and cultural ties to accompany the economic integration which continued to be promoted. Closer ties would lead the socialist states from a condition of 'drawing together' (*sblizheniye*) to the final communist aim of *sliyaniye* or fusion (Katushev 1973: 17–31, and see the discussion in Rakowska-Harmstone 1976). These terms had previously been used by Lenin (as we have seen in Ch. 6), and they were also used to characterize relations between nations within the Soviet Union (see, for example, 'Programme of the Communist Party of the Soviet Union' 1961).

The idea that socialist internationalism undermined national sovereignty was rejected firmly as a ploy by 'imperialist ideologists . . . to undermine the co-operation of fraternal socialist countries' (Sanakoyev 1972: 404). Socialist internationalism did not run counter to the principles of sovereignty, non-interference, equality and the right of nations to self-determination' (Sanakoyev 1972: 269). But while stressing the principle of equality, Soviet theorists also drew attention to the special vanguard role played by the Soviet Union and the CPSU within the system (see, for example, Sanakoyev 1972: 129). The contradictions between sovereignty and internationalism and between equality and the leading role of the CPSU were clearly not really closer to being resolved. The negative response to the phenomenon of Eurocommunism indicated that diversity among non-ruling Parties was no more welcome than diversity within the socialist commonwealth (see Whetten 1984 for the various manifestations of Eurocommunism).

Twelve years after the intervention in Czechoslovakia, a similar set of changes in Poland—loss of Party control, emergent pluralism, the collapse of the principles and practice of democratic centralism, the breakdown of censorship, with the added dimension of what seemed to be a revolution from below—led inexorably to a re-establishment of authority, this time in the form of martial law (for the events preceding martial law, see Sanford 1984). The explanation offered in Soviet literature was that extremist forces within Solidarity, together with the Committee for Social Defence/Committee for Defence of the Workers, were planning a coup for 17 December 1981 (Alekseeva, Babak and Kokeev 1982: 87).

Most Western commentators assumed that martial law was Soviet inspired (see, for example, Lowenthal 1982; Sanford 1984). But the prolonged impotence of those who objected to the Polish reforms and the form the clamp-down took were unexpected. Moreover, there was considerable evidence of indecision about the best way to deal with an appalling economic situation and a grass-roots popular movement (see

Anderson 1982, for some of the evidence). Prior to the declaration of martial law the situation in Poland was explained by Soviet theorists as the result of 'mistakes and miscalculations' in internal policy and subversion on the part of imperialism which combined to create an ideal environment for anti-socialist elements within Poland (Zagladin 1981: 17). But Soviet theorists seemed reluctant to explore the nature of Solidarity and the implications of its mass appeal. The fear was voiced that the Polish United Workers' Party had irretrievably lost its leading role, and events in Poland were said to confirm how important it was for Communist Parties to remain in close touch with the masses and to fight against bureaucratism and voluntarism (Brezhnev 1981: 13). Soviet theorists echoed Brezhnev in warning sternly that 'no-one should have any doubts about the common determination of the fraternal countries to protect the socialist gains of the Polish people from any infringement by counter-revolution, internal or external' (Bykov 1981: 5). This was an unambiguous restatement of the Brezhnev Doctrine.

The declaration of martial law made it unnecessary for theorists to explain how this common determination fitted with the equality, respect for sovereignty and non-interference inherent in social internationalism. They did not attempt to demonstrate that martial law was consonant with the leading role of the Party.

CONCLUSION

If one examines the historical development of the use of the concepts of proletarian and socialist internationalism by Soviet theorists from Lenin onwards, it becomes clear that Lenin, while promoting the right to self-determination and supporting the freedom to secession, expected that individual socialists and socialist parties would rise above the bourgeois appeal of nationalism and place the interests of internationalism above those of their own parties. The union that followed the revolution would be voluntary. When his optimism proved ill-founded during the Civil War, the assertion of the *right* to secede was retained in respect of the border nations of Russia, but the *freedom* to do so became questionable.[24] Stalin was far more explicit in identifying international interests with the interests of the Soviet Union. But the context in which the term proletarian internationalism was used was primarily in connection with the relations between nations within multi-ethnic states.

It was only after Stalin's death that proletarian internationalism was promoted to a fundamentally new type of international relations and the organizing principle of relations between socialist states. But there were theoretical problems in applying the concept to inter-state relations. In its new capacity it was called socialist internationalism, and to begin with it seemed to imply that the other socialist states would be allowed a certain measure of independence and equality. But the interventions in Hungary in 1956 and Czechoslovakia in 1968 demonstrated that the extent of their room for manoeuvre would be defined by the Soviet leadership (increasingly supported by the more conformist leaders of other socialist states). As a result, the term socialist internationalism began to have far more sinister connotations than those who first used it had intended. The reaction to events in Poland from the middle of 1980 to the end of 1981 seemed to confirm that the equality and sovereignty allowed by socialist internationalism were limited.

The high point of theoretical activity in the field of inter-socialist relations occurred in the 1950s and 1960s. In the post-Czechoslovak period most of the writing referred to the 1957, 1960 and 1969 declarations and repeated earlier definitions and analyses.[25] After the events of 1968 it was admitted that conflict was possible within the socialist commonwealth and some attempt began to be made to analyse it. The possibility of 'divergences' was mentioned in the 1969 declaration, but a book on international conflict published soon afterwards (Zhurkin and Primakov 1972) did not include inter-socialist conflict in its elaborate typology (see Ch. 8). Later Soviet scholars began to distinguish between acute political conflicts, which retarded development and were foreign to socialism, and non-antagonistic conflicts which could be found in the socialist system and which were caused by specific differences (in level of socio-economic development, historical traditions, vestiges of national hostility, geographical position). Non-antagonistic conflicts of this type were said to aid mutual understanding (Butenko 1975: 255–8). In fact, they were harking back to a distinction drawn by Zhdanov, who posited that in the case of non-antagonistic conflict, development could occur through criticism and self-criticism (as opposed to the struggle which resulted from antagonistic conflict). (Zhdanov 1947b: 21). Criticism and self-criticism was now called 'fraternal exchange of experience and opinion', but since there has also been a plea for more theoretical work on the subject (Butenko 1975: 270), Soviet scholars seem to recognize that they have yet to find a way to resolve non-antagonistic conflict amicably.

As far as proletarian and socialist internationalism are concerned, the definitions have remained unchanged. Socialist internationalism has its own entry in a 1980 political dictionary, but the reader is referred to the entry for proletarian internationalism, where socialist internationalism is defined as:

the application and the development of the principles of proletarian internationalism both in the relations between nations and nationalities who have started on the path of socialism and between sovereign socialist states.

(Onikov and Shishlin 1980: 335)

Proletarian internationalism is said to include both the independence of parties and their answerability to the people of their own country and to the toilers of other countries (Onikov and Shishlin 1980: 335). No published theoretical writing or political statement has ever included guidelines about how to resolve the issue when a conflict is perceived between answerability to the people of a particular country and answerability to the toilers of other countries, except to imply that unity always takes precedence. It is difficult, therefore, not to conclude with Brzezinski that Marxism-Leninism is 'rich in guidelines for coping with enemies, but that it offers little scope for resolving conflicts and organizing relations among Communist states' (Brzezinski 1967: 267).

If one examines the conflicts which have occurred in the bloc since 1945, three of them (Yugoslavia, Albania and Poland before 1956) were related to leadership of the national Party, one of them (China) concerned the leadership of the communist world and six of them had to do with the nature of domestic society and its relationship with the Soviet Union (East Germany in 1953, Poland after 1956, Hungary, Romania, Czechoslovakia and Poland 1980). With the exception of the Polish case, the first and second types of conflict led to excommunication from the bloc and had little positive influence on theory. Indeed, there was a deleterious effect as mutual insults took the place of creative theoretical development.

In the third type of conflict, the national parties lost the battle in all cases (in Poland not because of external intervention, but because of regression of the national leadership after 1956 and martial law in 1981), but they did not lose the war entirely. In other words, theoretical development resulted from the conflicts. More importantly, in most cases there were also significant changes in political practice both domestically and in relation to the Soviet Union (although in the case of Czechoslovakia it is the other bloc members, rather than Czechoslovakia, which have benefited). Since the late 1960s there have been attempts to reconcile differences and to change the nature of inter-bloc relations, but there has been very little theoretical change.

It would seem that the concepts of proletarian and socialist internationalism have been stretched as far as they can go. If the recognition of national differences is extended to its logical conclusion, it must also include the kind of diversity proposed in Czechoslovakia or Poland. Similarly, equality logically means that individual members of the socialist system no longer need to tailor their interests to those of the Soviet Union or the other socialist states where the two are perceived to be in conflict. In theory and in practice, however, diversity and equality, like sovereignty, are limited. Removing the limits would lead to the legitimation of the very national communisms that the theory has been concerned to prevent.

In essence, the theoretical dilemma resembles the difficulties with the concept of peaceful coexistence which were described in Chapter 3. Proletarian internationalism refers to class relations, while socialist internationalism subsumes both class and state relations. As long as no clash is perceived between class and national interests there is no problem. Any limitation to diversity, equality and sovereignty is voluntary and therefore does not infringe the normal legal status of international relations. But when a conflict exists (or is perceived to exist) between the two, class interests take precedence in theory and in practice. The question of who it is that defines what the class interest is becomes extremely important. If the definition is not accepted by those who perceive that a contradiction exists, the voluntary nature of the aid and cooperation inherent in socialist internationalism is called into question. And in that case, the respect for international legal norms which is also said to be inherent in socialist internationalism seems no more than a convenient fiction.

The cases of Yugoslavia, Albania and China illustrate another inadequacy in proletarian and socialist internationalism. The concepts are neither broad enough to explain relations between all socialist states or between all socialist parties nor acceptable to all socialist leaders. Soviet theorists implicitly recognized this by accusing China of having a foreign policy which had nothing in common with internationalism. But there was a far more explicit recognition in Brezhnev's offer to the Chinese of relations based on peaceful coexistence (see Ch. 3, n. 16). If Soviet relations with some socialist states can be based on peaceful coexistence, however, there seems to be no logical reason why the relations between all socialist states should not be based on that principle.

As for the claim that socialist international relations are a new type of relations, it is fairly clear from an analysis of both events and theory that they are, in fact, a very old type of relations, a mixture of coercion and conciliation, based on a changing (and often not shared) perception of national and system interests. The most novel element, perhaps, is that they are so frequently and so insistently called new.

NOTES

1. Lowenthal contends that it was the need to sort out relations with China in the first place that prompted Khrushchev's internationalism, and that its application to Yugoslavia was merely a by-product (Lowenthal 1964: 9).

2. Even more disconcerting to the non-Soviet analyst is the method sometimes used of insisting that the new theory (or the new policy) has been in use all the time.

3. For an account of the Polish October and the Hungarian Revolution, see Brzezinski (1967, Chs. 10 and 11). One legitimate reason for complaint may perhaps have been thought to be the term 'people's democracy', which implied a status inferior to socialism. The term gradually disappeared from use after 1956. The People's Democracies were referred to as socialist states, members of the socialist world, camp or commonwealth.

4. Suslov did not mention the role of the Soviet army in suppressing the revolution, but other commentators have consistently maintained that the Soviet army provided aid at the request of the new Hungarian government (see, for example, Farberov 1957: 5). At the time there was no mention of the Warsaw Treaty which had been signed the previous year (for an account of its origins, see Remington 1971, Ch. 2). But later versions have maintained that 'the Hungarian people, with the help of other socialist states . . . routed the counter-revolutionary forces' and that, 'acting in accordance with Article 5 of the Warsaw Treaty, the USSR helped the revolutionary Workers' and Peasants' Government of Hungary' (Sanakoyev 1972: 205).

5. For China's role in reconstructing communist unity, see Brzezinski (1967: 271–308) and Fejtö (1974: 124–37).

6. A lively account of the Yugoslav position as reported personally by various Yugoslavs is given by Lowenthal (1964, Ch. 4).

7. This list of ten general laws was much more comprehensive than the four laws which Suslov had enumerated in 1956 (see Suslov 1956: 3). Earlier in 1957 some of the unique characteristics had been described in an authoritative article: there were national differences in the form taken by the dictatorship of the proletariat, in the franchise restrictions which had been required, in the number of political parties which could be permitted to function, in the existence of broad national fronts, in the way in which private ownership had been eliminated, in the speed and manner of introducing collectivized agriculture and in the way in which the national question had been dealt with (Farberov 1957: 42–8).

8. Most Western scholars agree that although unity was reimposed at the November 1957 conference, it was qualitatively different from the unity imposed by Stalin. Skilling called it 'pluralistic monism', a system which combined autonomy of action with voluntary solidarity, and allowed for policy differences within the bounds of common action and reforms (Skilling 1964: 12–13). Brzezinski called it 'divergent unity' and pointed out that although revisionism was

defeated, 'many of its assumptions had penetrated, informally . . . as part of the prevailing climate of political opinion' (Brzezinski 1967: 367).

9. For a detailed analysis of the draft programme, see Brzezinski (1967: 322–37).

10. Those People's Democracies which were considered to have entered the period of building developed socialism had been promoted particularly rapidly. In 1957 all the People's Democracies were still said to be at a transitional stage from capitalism to socialism (Farberov 1957: 42). Moreover, although Lenin's law of uneven development meant that the capitalist stage could be skipped, the socialist stage was considered essential, since communism was merely a higher form of socialism. In fact, the discussion about the transition to communism should be understood in the context of Soviet reactions to the Chinese Great Leap Forward initiated in 1958, with its claim that China would be the first to attain communism. Soon afterwards Khrushchev began to make detailed calculations to show that the Soviet Union would reach communism in 1980. For reactions to the Great Leap Forward, see Lowenthal (1964, Ch. 6) and for Khrushchev's equally extravagant claims and calculations, see Medvedev (1982: 199–202).

11. 81 Communist and Workers' Parties attended the conference (the 1957 conference had been restricted to ruling parties). The difficulty in reconciling opposing views is demonstrated by the three weeks it took for agreement to be reached.

12. Lowenthal points out that inadequate Soviet aid prompted the Great Leap Forward (Lowenthal 1964, Ch. 6). It was a radical attempt to modernize rapidly without the necessary financial means. Moreover, Khrushchev had increasingly shown that Chinese interests were low in his priorities. Lowenthal deduces that 'the conflict was not "about ideology": it was a clear conflict of national interest which took ideological forms' (Lowenthal 1964: 216).

13. It should be stressed that there were a number of important contentious foreign-policy issues in the disagreements between the Soviet Union and the CPR. The Chinese resented the inadequate support given by the Soviet Union in the 1958 Taiwan Straits crisis and the neutral position adopted in relation to the Sino-Indian border dispute in 1959. They were deeply offended by the way Khrushchev reneged on the nuclear aid he had promised. When China began to lobby for allies within the international movement, Khrushchev responded in July 1960 by reducing Soviet economic assistance to China and withdrawing Soviet technical advisers (see Griffiths 1964).

14. The countries which belonged to the world socialist system were listed as Albania, Bulgaria, China, Hungary, East Germany, North Vietnam, North Korea, Mongolia, Poland, Romania and Czechoslovakia, together with the Soviet Union.

15. Albania had been opposed to the Soviet rapprochement with Yugoslavia, and upset by the secret speech at the Twentieth Congress of the CPSU.

16. These letters and a number of documents which record the Soviet-

Albanian dispute and the positions taken by other Communist Parties are translated in Dallin (1963). For a Yugoslav analysis of Chinese attacks on revisionism, see Kardelj (1961).

17. Dallin, for example, categorized the issues dividing the international communist movement at this time as (1) organizational problems of the international movement (role of the Soviet Union and CPSU; relevance of Soviet experience; polycentrism; membership of the international movement; forms of interparty behaviour; fractionalism) and communist perspective and strategy (whether revisionism or dogmatism was the greatest danger); (2) problems of world affairs (nature of the epoch; war and peace; peaceful coexistence; relations with the national bourgeoisie; economic aid to underdeveloped nations); (3) problems in domestic policy (personality cult and the role of Stalin; stages in building socialism and communism; dictatorship of the proletariat and the class struggle; importance of Soviet economic development; affluent communism; freedom and controls; peaceful transition to socialism) (Dallin 1963: xxviii–xxxvii). After some years, and when the dispute was more mature, Brzezinski divided the issues into (1) ideological (role of CPSU; revisionism or dogmatism; nature of the epoch; war or peace; peaceful transition to socialism; dictatorship of the proletariat and the class struggle; nature of the communist society; Stalin; Albania and the bloc; interparty polemics); (2) foreign-policy issues (grand strategy; national-liberation struggle; détente; test-ban treaty; neutrality on Indian frontier issue and continued aid to India); (3) conflicts of interest (military assistance; economic assistance; territorial claims) (Brzezinski 1967: 398–403). In fact, long though these lists are, they do not exhaust all the causes—neither, for example, include historical reasons or pure geopolitics (i.e. the theory that neighbouring great continental powers are bound to be rivals).

18. For a discussion of Soviet typologies of conflict, see Chapter 8. Chinese accusations that the Soviet Union had ceased to be socialist predated the reverse charge. In 1964 they already maintained that capitalism was being restored in Russia. But they believed then that Khrushchev was the culprit. In 1965, disappointed that the new leadership had changed Soviet policy so little, they renewed the charge (Brzezinski 1967: 424–7). Soviet theorists, on the other hand, have vacillated (often in one and the same book or article), sometimes calling the Chinese Trotskyite and anti-Leninist, sometimes claiming that their socialism is anti-Marxist and anti-scientific. It is also chauvinistic, nationalistic and the Chinese are left-wing opportunists (see Zagladin 1973: 414 and *passim*). Just before Brezhnev's death, when serious efforts began to be made to improve relations, China began to be classified as a socialist state again. For an analysis of the Sino-Soviet polemics prior to this, see Low (1976).

19. Although the impetus for integration is usually credited to Khrushchev, Brown has pointed out that the integration and specialization proposals were initiated by Czechoslovakia in 1958 and accepted by Khrushchev only after 1960 (Brown 1966: 205–6). In fact,

evidence suggests that the idea was accepted in the Soviet Union before 1960. In his report to the Twentieth Party Congress, for example, Khrushchev spoke of the coordination of economic plans and the advantages of industrial specialization based on utilizing the most favourable natural and economic conditions in particular countries (Khrushchev 1956a: 30).

20. For the full test of the CMEA Charter, see Szawlowski (1976): 181–9). Szawlowski has pointed out that the 1962 amendments were illegal (as has been the subsequent incorporation of Mongolia, Cuba and Vietnam) because Albania, still formally a member, was not present at the session when they were adopted and the statutes require ratification by all members (Szawlowski 1975: 50–2).

21. For accounts of Soviet–Romanian relations in the Khrushchev era, see Fetjö (1974) and Skilling (1964).

22. A discussion of the programme and its implementation can be found in Szawlowski (1976: 71–102).

23. There are many accounts of the Prague Spring, and anlayses of why and how the decision was made to intervene. See, for example, Windsor and Roberts (1969); Remington (1971); Skilling (1976); Valenta (1979); Dawisha (1980), to name but a few.

24. As we have seen in Chapter 6, both Lenin and Stalin were clear that there were times when unity took precedence over secession, or proletarian interests over the interests of separatist movements. Soviet attitudes towards secession movement in post-independent Africa (e.g. Tshombe's movement in the Congo, the Biafran declaration of independence and Eritrean separatism after the Ethiopian coup) have always been negative.

25. See Lynch (1984: 248–65) for the argument that there is little serious Soviet theory relating to socialist internationalism.

8 Changes in the International System I: War, Neutrality and Peace

All states and statesmen advocate peace, and the Soviet Union and its leaders are no exception. But few other states have put as much effort into public peace campaigns as the Soviet Union, and few statesmen and scholars have been so frequently insistent that theirs is a policy of peace. Yet Marxist-Leninist teaching has always maintained that war is an endemic feature of capitalist society and that therefore it will only disappear when there is universal socialism. According to the Leninist version of the theory, imperialism is implacably hostile to socialism. A war launched by imperialist against socialist states was, therefore, particularly to be expected and feared.

Soviet policy-makers and theorists have seemed to retain both beliefs, the necessity for peace and the inevitability of war, with equal firmness and equal sincerity. Yet there is a contradiction between the two. From the practical point of view, the problem has been to invest in peace while preparing, both psychologically and militarily, for inevitable war. It has entailed convincing the external world of the peaceful nature of Soviet foreign policy, while maintaining a level of domestic tension high enough not only to promote cohesion but also, particularly in the early years of Soviet history, to act as an exhortation to greater effort in strengthening the economic and military potential of the state. Theoretically, the dilemma has concerned two images central to Soviet Marxism-Leninism: the depiction of international relations as a struggle between capitalism and socialism and the characterization of imperialism as inherently aggressive. Neither image is consonant with promoting peace. Moreover, the dichotomy of the first image leaves little conceptual leeway for a third force like non-alignment, which dissociates itself from both capitalism and socialism.

The practical problems have led to a tendency (not, of course, unique to the Soviet Union) to talk, or even to act, in two voices. Thus in the 1920s, for example, while the Commissariat for Foreign Affairs (Narkomindel) pursued the adroit diplomacy which resulted first in the Rapallo Treaty in 1922 and then in *de jure* recognition by other capitalist states, Stalin constantly warned of the imminence of a capitalist attack. Similarly, Soviet participation in the League of Nations Disarmament Conference in 1928, and Litvinov's radical disarmament proposals at that time and his enthusiastic response to the Kellogg–Briand pact, were accompanied by a scathing denouncement of both conference and pact by the Communist International (Degras 1960, vol. 2: 449). At the Sixth Comintern Congress in 1928 the world was said to be 'pregnant' with both inter-imperialist wars and war against the Soviet Union (*Communism and the International Situation* 1928: 5–32). These contradictory attitudes and the preparations for possible war produced (and their modern analogues still produce) accusations that Soviet peace offers have always been empty propaganda. In fact, the contradictions epitomize the difficulties of preaching revolutionary theory while practising traditional diplomacy.

This chapter considers the way in which Soviet theory about war, neutrality and peace has dealt with the dilemmas and evolved to accommodate the changing nature of war, the growth of the phenomenon of non-alignment and the need for a prolonged peace in which to construct communism. It is divided into three parts. The first examines Soviet thinking about war. Lenin's theories about the inevitability, causes and types of war, and the relationship of war to revolution are described first; and then the changes in each of these aspects are examined.

The second part of the chapter concentrates on the period after the Second World War and considers how the growth and growing authority of the phenomenon of neutralism has impinged on Soviet theorists, forcing them to incorporate a third zone of peace in their world view. The third part of the chapter deals with peace and points to the prevalence of peace campaigns and the dearth of peace theory. The chapter concludes by considering why there should be such an imbalance between war theory and peace theory.

WAR

The Marxist-Leninist theory of war
Although Marx and Engels were primarily concerned with relations within states, rather than between states, issues of war and peace and the effects of war on the class struggle were not matters they could ignore. Later Soviet writers credit them with laying the foundations for dividing wars into just and unjust wars and discovering that war is caused by antagonistic formations and exploitation (Petrenko and Popov 1981: 46–7). In fact, although they wrote a great deal about particular wars, as Carr has pointed out, they were rather vague about what the socialist attitude to war in general should be (Carr 1966, vol. 3: 541–9). Engels, in particular, wrote extensively on military affairs, gaining considerable expertise in military strategy and leaving a body of work to which Trotsky and later Soviet strategists have referred. But Soviet theory distinguishes between military strategy which, 'starting from general considerations, develops and investigates concrete problems' (Sokolovskiy 1963: 42), and military doctrine, to which it is subordinate and which is 'a scientifically based system of views on the nature and character of war . . . and on the preparation of the country and the Armed Forces for repulsing any possible aggression' (Ogarkov 1981: 85).[1] Military doctrine has two aspects—technical and political—and it is the political aspect which is the concern of this chapter.

The inevitability of war
The authority to whom modern Soviet theorists refer most in writing about military doctrine is Lenin. When the First World War began, most European socialists supported their own national war efforts, ignoring the 1907 decision of the Second International that any future war would be an imperialist war and should, therefore, not be supported. Lenin, on

the other hand, contended that a policy of national defeatism would turn the imperialist war into civil war, speeding up the disintegration of capitalism and bringing the socialist revolution closer (Lenin 1915b: 158–64). He argued that war was bound to be a constant feature of monopoly capitalism: once the world had been divided up into colonies and semi-colonies, the only way in which the imperialist states could compete for markets, raw materials and investment opportunities was through a re-division which would provoke inter-imperialist wars (Lenin 1916d: 189–90). War between imperialist powers was thus inevitable. But it would serve to weaken them and therefore to hasten the revolution.

Lenin believed that monopoly capitalism inevitably engendered a second kind of war, since the new international exploited class, the indigenous peoples of the colonies, would fight for their independence (Lenin 1916d: 297). Wars of national liberation, like inter-imperialist wars, would weaken an already moribund capitalism, speeding up the disintegration of capitalist society and the subsequent socialist revolution. It was clear, therefore, that metropolitan socialists should practise national defeatism in respect of inter-imperialist wars and support colonial peoples in their wars of national liberation.

It was only later in 1916 that Lenin began to predict a third kind of inevitable war: war between socialism and capitalism. As we have seen in previous chapters, Lenin argued that the uneven development of capitalism would make possible the existence of one or a few socialist countries. In an attempt to crush the proletarian revolution, the bourgeoisie of other countries were likely to attack the socialist countries. This kind of war would, like the other two types of inevitable war, disappear only after the bourgeoisie of the entire world had been vanquished and expropriated (Lenin 1916e: 77–93). Lenin's categorization of inevitable wars remained an active component of Soviet theory until the 1950s.

The causes of war

The cause of war, according to Marxist thinking, was economic conflict. In the age of imperialism it was almost always the desire for conquest which motivated monopoly capitalists to take up arms. This desire was foreign to socialists. Thus the international socialist revolution would be followed by the disappearance of classes and class conflict within societies, and the elimination of war between societies.

Although Lenin was firm about the economic bases of war, he was deeply impressed by Clausewitz's dictum that war is the continuation of politics by other means. The 1914–18 war, he said, was the continuation of the imperialist policies of two groups of Great Powers. But policies of colonial struggle against oppression, and policies of proletarian struggle against the bourgeoisie, could similarly produce wars which would be a continuation of these policies (Lenin 1916e: 80). For this reason, Lenin was against disarmament before the victory of the international revolution (Lenin 1916b: 94—104) and against pacifism, both of which could prevent the proletariat 'turn[ing] its guns against *its own* governments' (Lenin 1917a: 186). Socialists could not be opposed to *all* wars, since some of them 'in their social content and implications, *serve* the cause of democracy, and *consequently* socialism (Lenin 1917f: 23).

Types of war
Which wars served the cause of socialism could be determined, Lenin thought, by evaluating the politics of which the war was the continuation. He distinguished between just (or progressive) and unjust wars. The former were to be supported by socialists, the latter opposed. The questions which should be asked were: '*What issues* are at stake in the war, *which* classes are waging it, and with *what* political objectives' (Lenin 1916a: 33). Colonial or national wars, civil wars which were an intensification of the class struggle, and defensive wars fought by socialists against attempts to crush socialist states were just wars from the point of view of the colonial peoples, the exploited classes and the socialist states (Lenin 1916e: 77–9). As we shall see, Soviet theorists have continued to divide wars into those fought for just aims which are deserving of support (e.g. wars of national liberation), and reactionary, unjust wars fought for predatory purposes which are sometimes to be resisted and always to be condemned.

Lenin did not conceive of wars between socialist states, civil wars against socialist regimes, or wars between ex-colonies, so he did not include them in his categories of just and unjust wars. Subsequent theorists have had considerable difficulty in applying Marxist-Leninist criteria to such wars.

War and revolution

Whether revolution can occur without violence has always been a contentious issue in Marxist-Leninist theory and practice. Marx himself seemed to change his mind on the matter (see, for example, the discussions in McLellan 1971: 210–2; Bottomore *et al.* 1985: 574) and the social-democratic wing of the socialist movement has preferred his later, non-violent evolutionary opinion. Lenin added an element of voluntarism to Marxist historical determinism: it was not that revolution would not occur when the correct historical conditions occurred, but properly organized revolutionaries need not wait for history to take its course. Revolutionary moments should be seized. He defined a revolutionary situation as one in which the lower classes no longer wanted to, and the upper classes no longer could, live in the old way, in which the suffering of the oppressed class was more acute than usual and, as a result, it was drawn into independent historical action (Lenin 1915a: 213–4). From 1914 to 1917 he grew increasingly certain that the war had brought about such a situation. The revolution which occurred in February 1917 in Russia confirmed his view.

Lenin believed that imperialist wars acted as the 'locomotive of history' and the forcing house of revolution (Lenin 1917d: 330). If socialists practised national defeatism during imperialist wars, bourgeois society would disintegrate and revolution take place. But he did not rule out revolution via civil wars which were 'the natural, and under certain conditions, inevitable, continuation, development and intensification of the class struggle' (Lenin 1916e: 77–8). Nor did he think revolution via external intervention impossible, as the decision to continue the Polish War in 1920 attests (see Carr 1966, vol. 3: 167–9, 213–20 for an account of Polish War).

The Polish War occurred at a time when Lenin and his fellow Bolsheviks still believed and hoped that the revolutionary moment existed and that international revolution was imminent. Its failure, and the need for a breathing space for domestic reconstruction, served to make both Leninist revolutionary theory and Soviet international practice more cautious. The task of encouraging international revolution was left to the Comintern, while *Narkomindel* became pre-occupied with more traditional diplomatic concerns.

War after Lenin

Stalin repeatedly warned of an immiment capitalist attack on the Soviet Union. Indeed, as one Western theorist has pointed out, capitalist encirclement and the danger of a capitalist war against the Soviet Union became the corollary of Stalin's doctrine of socialism in one country (Burin 1963). Towards the end of the 1920s the expectation of war was used to explain the need for rapid industrialization. In urging that the tempo of the first five-year plan be increased, Stalin maintained that if the Soviet Union did not catch up with the advanced countries in ten years, it would be crushed (Stalin 1931: 366). Stalin thus clearly subscribed to Lenin's theory of inevitable war, although he did not really add to it. The Comintern issued a set of theses on war in 1928 which followed Lenin's analysis very closely (Eudin and Slusser 1966: vol. 1: 124–41).

Yet by 1935, when efforts to create a collective-security system were launched in earnest, Stalin had begun to emphasize the avoidability of war rather than its inevitability. Comintern members were instructed to struggle for peace and for the defence of the Soviet Union by forming united people's fronts. The teaching about inevitable war was not entirely abandoned, however. The Comintern pointed out that it was an illusion to believe that war could be eliminated while capitalism existed. None the less, communists would 'exert every effort to prevent war' (Degras 1965, vol. 3: 372–8, quote on p.378). When the long predicted war began, Soviet theorists classified it as an unjust, predatory, imperialist war until June 1941. Once the Soviet Union had been attacked, however, it became a just war by the anti-fascist forces against the menace of Nazi aggression. This has remained the way it is characterized (see, for example, Milovidov 1977: 27). But after the Second World War the Soviet theory of war gradually began to change.

The avoidability of war

Once the destructive power of nuclear weapons was recognized, it was difficult to continue believing in the inevitability of a war that was certain to destroy both sides. As we have seen, Lenin saw war as the forcing house of revolution because it would lead to socialist revolutions in the belligerent capitalist powers. But the destruction caused by nuclear weapons would leave no capitalist society to undergo revolution. Moreover, the military victory of socialism was unlikely in a war between the two camps, since the Soviet teaching about peace held that the imperialists would start the war.

Stalin is often accused of failing to understand this. He is also said to have underestimated the potential of atomic weapons. It is true that he continued stressing the importance of the five 'permanently operating features' of war (Stalin 1942).[2] He also denied that surprise was a vital element in modern warfare, or that nuclear weapons would be the decisive factor in a future war (Stalin 1946a: 56). None the less, there is considerable evidence that he understood how dangerous nuclear war would be and how important it was to avoid such a war. In a zealously pro-Stalin book, for example, it is claimed that:

Now, when capitalism has ceased to be the only all-embracing world economic system, when the camp of socialism is becoming more and more united and powerful, *war engendered by capitalism has ceased to be a fatal, inevitable phenomenon.* War can and must be avoided now.
(Korovin 1951: 595; my emphasis)

Similarly, another author pointed out that although the principle of the inevitability of war in the era of imperialism was correct for some historical conditions, it could not 'be transferred unreservedly to new historical conditions' (Seleznev 1951: 37).

In 'The Economic Problems of Socialism' Stalin himself strongly implied that although intra-imperialist wars were inevitable, war between socialism and capitalism was avoidable, both because the capitalists realized that it would mean the demise of capitalism, and because they knew that the Soviet Union would not attack them (Stalin 1952a: 469–73). In his brief speech at the Nineteenth Congress of the CPSU he maintained that although the contradictions between the socialist and capitalist camps were greater than intra-imperialist contradictions, it was within the capitalist world that war continued to be inevitable (Stalin 1952b: 7–8).[3]

Despite these hints of doctrinal change, the idea that war was no longer inevitable did not gain wide currency immediately. The de-Stalinization of Soviet military doctrine is said to have played a role in the power struggle between Malenkov and Khrushchev and was the subject of a long controversy amongst Soviet strategists (documented in Dinerstein 1962). As late as 1955 some theorists were still maintaining that although war could be avoided, 'as long as capitalism exists, wars are inevitable' (*Marksizm-leninizm o voine, armii i voennoi nauke* [MVAVN] 1955: 30). But there was a caveat: the peace movement could prevent particular wars (MVAVN 1955: 37–40).

Thus Khrushchev's announcement at the Twentieth Party Congress in 1956 that war was not a fatal inevitability was not a complete innovation (Khrushchev 1956a: 37). What was new was the way that Khrushchev blurred the distinction between different kinds of war, implying that *all* wars had ceased to be fatally inevitable: the forces of peace in the world camp of socialism had the moral and material means to prevent aggression. But the danger of war would continue as long as imperialism existed. Three years later Khrushchev still maintained that 'the conclusion drawn by the Twentieth Party Congress that war is not fatally inevitable has been completely justified' (Khrushchev 1959b: 58). Because of the new balance of forces in the world, world war could be excluded from the life of society before the complete triumph of socialism. Once again he made no distinction between different kinds of war. By the following year, however, Chinese objections to this formulation had caused him to modify the doctrine. World war could be prevented, but national liberation could involve armed struggle. Moreover, there was a possibility that the transition to socialism would not be peaceful ('Statement of the Meeting of Representatives of the Communist and Workers' Parties' 1960: 8–14). At the Twenty-Second Congress Khrushchev reiterated that war between states had ceased to be inevitable. Soviet power had deterred the imperialists from unleashing war (Khrushchev 1961: 42–3).

The phrases 'war is not fatally inevitable' and 'the elimination of world wars from the life of society' were used constantly during Khrushchev's tenure of office. But it was made increasingly clear that what was avoidable was war between socialism and capitalism. Sokolovskiy, for example, listed possible new wars of conquest by imperialists; wars between imperialist countries; revolutionary wars to bring about socialism; and national-liberation wars (Sokolovskiy 1963: 176–7). He maintained that 'despite the unrelenting struggle of the Soviet Union and the entire socialist camp—as well as all men of good will—for peace, the occurrence of wars is not excluded' (Sokolovskiy 1963: 202–3). The emphasis on Soviet power as the means of averting world war increased. In 1956 Khrushchev had mentioned the moral and material means to prevent war. By 1959 the new balance of forces was said to prevent war, and in 1961 it was Soviet power. Sokolovskiy attributed the avoidance of war to the increasing defence potential of the Soviet Union and other socialist countries (Sokolovskiy 1963: 49). The moral means (in other words, the peace movement) was not excluded, but there was a distinct shift in the balance of emphasis.

When Brezhnev came to power he endorsed the formulations of the Twentieth, Twenty-First and Twenty-Second Congresses (Brezhnev 1965: 154). But from the beginning of the 1970s there was a distinct change in terminology. From time to time, theorists still used the formulation that world war was no longer inevitable (see, for example, Milovidov 1977: 18), but Brezhnev began to stress the need to avert war, the danger of the arms race, the positive benefits of arms negotiations and the peaceful nature of Soviet foreign policy, often omitting whether war was inevitable (Brezhnev 1971, 1976, 1981). The avoidability of war was explained in the 1961 edition of *Marksizm-leninizm o voine i armii* (MVA) in these words:

Thus wars do not emerge spontaneously or automatically. They are prepared and unleashed by the conscious and organized action of particular parties and governments in the imperialist states. Therefore when there are sufficiently powerful and well-organized forces within society struggling to maintain peace, it is quite possible that wars can be avoided, even if the majority of countries have a bourgeois system. Wars are not fatally inevitable.

(MVA 1961: 37)

In subsequent editions the formulations had been reduced to, 'Thus wars emerge neither spontaneously nor automatically. They are deliberately prepared and unleashed by definite parties and governments of the imperialist states' (MVA 1965: 21; 1968: 20; 1972: 25).[4] The omission of the avoidability of war seemed to coincide with the contemplation within the Soviet Union of the possibility of winning nuclear war. Already in 1962 Sokolovskiy had contradicted Khrushchev by claiming that the chances of attaining decisive political goals in a modern war had been enormously increased and that communism would be victorious in such a war (Sokolovskiy 1963: 170, 203). But other writers were graphic in portraying the hollow victory that this would represent:

Without a doubt, if the imperialists were to launch a new world war, the result would be that the whole system of capitalism would find its grave in it. But will socialist states and the struggle for socialism throughout the world gain from that war? Of course it will not. The revolutionary transition of peoples to socialism and the building of communism are incompatible with thermonuclear war.

(MVA 1965: 88)

By 1977 peace was still said to advance the cause of revolution more effectively than war, but there was said to be

profound error and harm in the disorienting claims . . . that there will be no victor in a thermonuclear world war . . . The existence of sophisticated hardware making possible the annihilation of hundreds of millions of people by no means signifies the irrevocable doom of mankind if a nuclear war erupts.

(Milovidov 1977: 17, 128)

It was almost as if Soviet theorists had begun to 'think the unthinkable' for which they criticized the Chinese in the 1950s and 1960s and Herman Kahn later (Shakhnazarov 1984: 170–1). Nuclear war should be averted. But if it could not be averted, there were still grounds for optimism, because socialism would emerge victorious. More than any other aspect of Soviet theory of war, this reflected the problem of putting the dictum 'If you want peace, prepare for war' into practice in the nuclear age. The problem was not, however, unique to the Soviet Union. It was inherent in the concept of deterrence. If the price of peace was the demonstration that war would if necessary be fought, then the armed forces and people had to be prepared for war. And to prepare them, they had to believe that war could be won. Moreover, they had to be convinced that it would be a war worth winning.

The causes of war

Although war seemed to become more inevitable as Soviet military doctrine shifted towards the need to be prepared to fight and win a future war, Soviet theorists and policy-makers have remained adamant that any future war would be caused by imperialism and not by socialism. The cause of the First and Second World Wars was thought to be the uneven development of capitalism. It was the most likely stimulus of any future world war, since it had already caused many existing military conflicts (MVA 1965: 34).

Contradictions within the capitalist system and the imperialist struggle for world domination were further causes of war. There was also a danger of accidental war (Sokolovskiy 1963: 183), although this had decreased with the establishment of the hot line and the beginning of Soviet–American negotiations. But Soviet theorists recognized that the most likely cause of nuclear war was the escalation of international crises: 'The danger of slipping to the edge of a general war as a result of attempts of the aggressors to take revenge for their failures, thus increasing the scale of the conflict, has become more likely' (Zhurkin and Primakov 1972: 19). It was thought to be the contradictions within imperialism which led to international crisis and conflict. Moreover, the increasing complexity of the world had increased the number of possible contradictions. The main contradictions were, first, those between the capitalist and socialist worlds; second, contradictions between imperialism and the national-liberation movement; third, intra-imperialist contradictions; fourth, contradictions between imperialist states and developing countries and, fifth, between countries of the Third World. A new danger of crisis arose from the divisive, chauvinistic forces in China (Zhurkin and Primakov 1972: 15).

According to Soviet theorists, the world became a far more dangerous place at the end of the 1970s because the intra-imperialist contradictions which were the root cause of war had become more acute. The intra-imperialist struggle for markets, raw materials and energy had increased, and so had the aggressive, adventurist tendencies of imperialism (Petrenko and Popov 1981: 171–2).[5]

No Soviet theorists have ever suggested that socialist policies (apart from the deviant policies of China) could cause war. Imperialism has always been seen as the sole instigator of war and armed conflict. As proof of this fact, theorists and politicians have repeatedly pointed out that war is inimical to the aims of socialism. The general consensus on this matter is aptly reflected in the following:

The Soviet Union, like the other countries of real socialism, do not need war . . . because it brings death and suffering to the toilers . . . because the construction of a new social system demands the concentration of the material and spiritual forces of society on the resolution of tasks of a completely peaceful nature: the building of a material-technical base sufficient to create a surplus of material goods and the transition to distribution according to need. They do not need war because the two other main tasks of building communism—the construction of entirely just and harmonious relationships between people and the educating of a new, completely developed individual—can also only be successfully completed in conditions of peace.

(Petrenko and Popov 1981: 154)

Types of war
The Leninist division of wars into just and unjust has been retained by all subsequent theorists. Just wars have been defined as those the population regards as just, or 'any war which is waged by the people in the name of freedom and social progress, for liberation from exploitation and national oppression, in defence of state independence against an aggressive attack' (MVA 1965: 70–1). But Soviet writers have tended to equate just wars with those that serve the interests of the proletarian class struggle or the interests of the Soviet Union. The characterization of the Second World War as an unjust war until the Soviet Union participated in it is an example of this.

The justness of a war has been said by Soviet theorists to influence the 'moral factor' in war. Just wars are supported by the population and therefore they generate energy, enthusiasm and high morale, cementing society into a single, monolithic whole (Grechko 1977: 164–5). When the moral-

political factor is high, the population displays the 'readiness
. . . to endure the extremely heavy trials of modern warfare
without losing the will to fight and to defeat the enemy' (MVA
1968: 275). The reason why this has been considered particularly important is that the moral-political and psychological
capabilities of both population and army are considered to be
one of the seven factors which determine the outcome of the
war (the other six are the qualitative and quantitative correlation of military forces at the beginning of the war; the
correlation of military potentials; the political content of the
war; the correlation of military-economic capabilities; the
correlation of economic capabilities and the correlation of
scientific potential—MVA 1974: 89–99). Since socialism, by
definition, only fights just wars, and imperialism almost
invariably wages unjust wars, socialists are thought to be
superior to imperialists in this respect.

Although socialists do not initiate war, it has always been
considered that it is their duty to support the just wars of
oppressed peoples, whether these are colonial wars of
national liberation or civil wars between the proletariat and
the bourgeoisie (*Problems of War and Peace* 1972: 97).
Historically, the requirement to support just war has been the
cause of some embarrassment to the Soviet leadership. There
have been occasions when the Soviet Union has lacked the
material and logistic means to offer more than verbal support.
At other times verbal and/or material support have contradicted the particular image the Soviet leadership wished to
project.[6] With increasing Soviet military potential and logistic
capability, military aid became an important instrument of
foreign policy in the 1970s, although, as we saw in Chapter 5,
this has sometimes been at the expense of other, higher-
priority foreign-policy goals. This dilemma has not been
explicitly discussed in the literature, but it must figure prominently in Soviet foreign-policy decision-making.

Soviet theorists are inordinately fond of typologies. Lenin's
initial categories have been elaborated and expanded to cover
a wide range of theoretically possible wars. Sokolovskiy listed
three possible types: world war between socialist and capitalist camps; small imperialist wars either against national-
liberation forces or between capitalist countries; and other
popular wars (Sokolovskiy 1963: 178). The editors of the 1965

edition of *Marksizm-leninizm o voine i armii* divided Soko-lovskiy's second and third types into civil wars; national-liberation wars; and wars between bourgeois states (MVA 1965: 80–1).

Gantman (in Zhurkin and Primakov 1972: 34–6) offered a more ambitious typology, dividing conflicts into three main categories. The first category, caused by the struggle between the two socio-economic systems, contained six sub-types: conflict between individual North Atlantic Treaty Organiza-tion (NATO) and Warsaw Treaty Organization (WTO) members; between the two alliances; between the two super-powers; conflict caused by an imperialist power interfering in the domestic affairs of a WTO member; conflict resulting from blockade or the threat of aggression against a non-WTO socialist state; and finally, conflict resulting from direct aggression by an imperialist state against a non-WTO socialist state. There were five possible sub-types in Gantman's second category, conflict resulting from imperialist attempts to suppress the national-liberation movement: conflict could be caused by attempts to suppress a national-liberation revolu-tion by economic, political or military means; or it might be caused by the export of counter-revolution to a socialist-oriented state. The imperialists could support expansionism on the part of medium and small capitalist-oriented states or, as colonial and neocolonial forces, they could cause conflict in areas not yet liberated. The fifth possibility would arise from imperialist attempts to set Third World countries against one another. Gantman's third main category reflected intra-imperialist contradictions. It contained three possible sub-types: conflict resulting from economic, political or military conflict between large imperialist powers; between medium and small NATO members; or between NATO members and neutral countries.

Although Gantman did not claim that his categories were exhaustive, he clearly did not think that the omission of a category for inter-socialist conflict was significant. He con-tended that inter-socialist conflict (caused, for example, by China) was an isolated phenomenon and therefore did not require a category in his typology. Grechko offered a less ambitious typology, classifying wars according to socio-political character (four types which correspond to those listed in *Marksizm-leninizm o voine i armii* and mentioned above); political aims (just and progressive or unjust and reactionary) and geographic scope (local, confined to a few countries or world wars) (Grechko 1977: 267–77).

In the Khrushchev era the term 'local war' was reserved for small, unjust, imperialist wars. Later it was extended to include civil wars and national-liberation wars, which meant that the term also included wars that were considered just. But Soviet theorists in general have been increasingly conscious of the danger that local wars can escalate into East–West confrontation:

History has shown that limited wars serve as the prelude to world wars and hasten their occurrence. . . .[G]iven the tense and complex international situation, the complex system of mutual treaty obligations among the states of the different camps and the rapid advance in nuclear technology, there is always the danger that [local conflict will develop into a world conflict], especially where nuclear weapons are employed.

(*Problems of War and Peace* 1972: 90–1)

Although the idea of a limited conventional war for limited political objectives has gradually become more acceptable, Soviet theorists have continued to point out that 'there exists no insurmountable barrier between a limited war and a world war' (Milovidov 1977: 48).

The concept of a limited *nuclear* war, however, has been completely rejected and roundly condemned by Soviet theorists and politicians. Sokolovskiy's assertion that a nuclear war would spread instantaneously over the entire globe has been reaffirmed over and over again (Sokolovskiy 1963: 189). When President Reagan seemed to support the view that a limited nuclear war was possible (*Guardian*, 21 October 1981), Soviet fears that they were dealing with someone who did not understand the danger of global conflagration were greatly heightened.

Few theorists have grappled in print with the problem of conflicts which do not easily fit into a Marxist-Leninist schema. The tendency has been either to ignore them or to attribute them to imperialist intervention. Conflicts between developing countries (the 1971 Indo-Pakistan war, for example) are usually attributed to imperialism, not only because the roots of these conflicts lie in the colonial past, but also because of the imperialist tendency to form military blocs, arm and encourage chauvinistic and adventurist circles within the developing countries and aggravate existing conflicts (Zhurkin and Primakov 1972: 139–40). Occasionally, it has been admitted that not all Third World conflicts fit into the existing Marxist-Leninist typology and the need for a new Leninist analysis has been voiced (Milovidov 1977: 33–4). But there has been little evidence in the literature of new Marxist-Leninist analyses of Third World conflicts.

Those theorists who have admitted and discussed intra-socialist conflict have blamed chauvinistic, nationalistic tendencies in the case of the Sino-Soviet dispute (Sanakoyev and Kapchenko 1973: 49–53) and the Chinese–Vietnamese war (Gantman 1981: 303–4). Conflict within the Warsaw alliance, as we saw in the previous chapter, has usually been blamed on forces of internal and external reaction. As a result, Soviet intervention in Hungary in 1956 and WTO intervention in Czechoslovakia in 1968 have been considered defensive and just. Neither intervention has been defined as a case of war. As far as Afghanistan is concerned, the standard explanation is that the Soviet Union acted in fulfilment of its treaty obligations. The intention was to help the Afghan government to defend its 'national sovereignty, freedom and independence . . . against external armed actions' (Petrenko and Popov 1981: 173). While the need to analyse intra-socialist conflict has been recognized, a new analysis does not yet exist. In the same way that the existence of a doctrine of limited sovereignty has always been refuted vehemently (Sanakoyev and Kapchenko 1973: 58–9 and see Chapter 7 above), it has been inconceivable to Soviet theorists that intervention within the WTO or the socialist system can be classified as a war by the Soviet Union or the WTO against the country in which the intervention has taken place.

Clearly, if Soviet theorists and policy-makers see imperialism as the cause of war always and everywhere, then the overt or hidden hand of imperialism must also be responsible for intra-socialist dissent. This is no more than a mirror image of the tendency in the West to attribute domestic strife, terrorism and foreign conflict to the hidden hand of Moscow. But in the West there is almost always a parallel attempt to establish a less simplistic cause-and-effect relationship.

Similar attempts probably occur in the secret corridors of power in the Soviet Union, but they do not often reach the public ear.

War and revolution

In the early years after the October Revolution there seemed little question that revolution would be violent. Indeed, the purpose of the twenty-one conditions of admission to the Third International (Degras 1956, vol. 1: 166–72) was to ensure that the Bolshevik model would prevail. Although the Comintern tactics changed often, the expectation that revolution would probably require violent struggle remained constant. In 1924, for example, the Comintern theses on tactics maintained that the job of true adherents to the proletarian revolution was 'to mobilize the proletarian army for irreconcilable revolutionary struggle' (Degras 1960, vol. 2: 147). At the sixth, more radical, Comintern Congress in 1928, armed insurrection at the correct revolutionary moment was called 'the highest form of struggle' which followed 'the rules of the art of war' (Degras 1960, vol. 2: 522).

The desire for collective security in the 1930s and the need to project a peaceful image turned revolution into a secondary issue. The Comintern concentrated on forming popular fronts to govern bourgeois states, rather than revolution. When war broke out in 1939, Molotov called it an imperialist war (Degras 1953, vol. 3: 390). But there was little talk of turning it into a revolutionary, civil war. The connections examined earlier in this chapter that Lenin had made between war and revolution seemed to have been forgotten. When Germany attacked the Soviet Union, European communists were instructed to fight for democracy against fascism, rather than for socialism and international revolution.

The coming of socialism to Eastern Europe occurred gradually and without the violent overthrow of bourgeois regimes. There has been no suggestion in Soviet literature that the presence of the Red Army was responsible in any coercive way, although according to the 1980 *Dictionary of Scientific Communism* (translated in 1984), 'following World War II old reactionary governments were overthrown (by armed forces at home or with the assistance of the Soviet army)' (Rumyantsev 1984: 14). Soviet power has also been discounted as a reason for the establishment of socialism in Latvia, Lithuania and Estonia and the incorporation of these countries into the Soviet Union (Narochnitsky *et al.* 1979: 110–25). Whatever the facts might have been, the principle was thus established for non-violent revolution. Once again it was Khrushchev who turned this principle into an articulated tenet of Soviet theory.

As we have seen in Chapter 7, at the Twentieth Congress of the CPSU Khrushchev announced that there were many possible roads to socialism, not excluding the election of communist governments in democratic elections (Khrushchev 1956a: 37–8). Although by 1960 he no longer excluded violent revolution, the peaceful transition to socialism remained a possibility. Subsequent policy-makers and theorists have continued to allow for both peaceful and violent revolution:

> Revolutionary class violence is the law and method by which [socialist] revolutions are brought about. But the forms in which they are brought about can also be varied, both peaceful and non-peaceful.
>
> (Butenko 1975: 306)

As far as the indirect effects of war were concerned, the Second World War was thought to have been instrumental in creating the requisite domestic turmoil for the countries of Eastern Europe to become 'national democracies' (Malenkov 1952: 106). Since both the First and the Second World Wars had caused parts of the globe to become socialist, it seemed logical to assume that a third world war would cause the collapse of the entire capitalist system (Malenkov 1952: 106). Although, as we have seen, this formulation fell out of use in the late 1950s and 1960s, once it was posited that socialism could emerge victorious from a future nuclear war, nuclear war, too, had the potential for making what was left of the world socialist. None the less, Soviet theorists have stressed that there is no necessary connection between war and revolution:

> Although at particular stages of historical development wars accompany revolution . . . the revolutionary situation itself comes about as a result of the maturing of internal conditions. It is indicative that the third stage of the

general crisis of capitalism developed not in connection with a new war, but
in conditions of peaceful coexistence.

(Butenko 1975: 317)

In other words, it was decolonization, not war, that had
prompted the third stage of the general crisis of capitalism. In
any case, it was recognized that far from always acting as a
catalyst for revolution, in some circumstances war postponed
it because it stimulated nationalism in the working class. It
could also provoke the ruling class to repress the workers'
movement (Lebedev *et al.* 1981: 27–8).

Soviet theorists and policy-makers have consistently
refuted the idea that war by itself causes revolution or that
revolution can be exported. A revolution can only occur when
the necessary material requisites for it have matured within
society (Zagladin 1973: 168). Therefore socialism can neither
be transferred from one country to another by means of
military force (Brezhnev 1973: 128), nor made to order or be
given a push (Butenko 1975: 307). In fact, Soviet scholars see
no need for outside intervention. There has been a distinct
move back from Leninist voluntarism to Marxist determinism
in Soviet thinking. History itself will ensure that revolution
takes place, since 'the transition from capitalism to communism is an objectively determined, natural historical
process' (Petrenko and Popov 1981: 154).

The most dramatic change which occurred in Soviet thinking about war was, of course, the shift from inevitable to
avoidable war. But the other adaptations have been significant. The change in the nature of war made adaptation
essential. Nuclear weapons and the danger of escalation to
nuclear war have rendered war an irrational means of politics
and an impossible way to spread revolution. As one Western
scholar has expressed it, nuclear weapons have severed the
connection between war and revolution (Lynch 1984: 310).
The only wars that can now be envisaged are wars in defence
of the revolution.

NEUTRALITY AND NON-ALIGNMENT

There was very little in Marxist-Leninist theory to help post-war Soviet theorists explain and accept the phenomenon of neutralism or non-alignment. Neutrality was a recognized phenomenon. Lenin had been rather contemptuous of it, calling it:

The petty striving of petty states to hold aloof, the petty-bourgeois desire to keep as far away as possible from the great battles of world history, to take advantage of one's relatively monopolistic position in order to remain in hidebound passivity.

(Lenin 1961e: 86)

But Soviet international lawyers have always accorded legal status to neutrality and recognized permanent neutrality. The latter was believed to limit sovereignty and to be incompatible with membership of international organizations (Pashukanis 1935). Permanent neutrals should not even belong to a customs union, since 'there is no doubt that customs unions to a considerable extent determine the nature of the whole economic policy of a country and, consequently, its international conflicts' (Korovin 1926: 57). But permanent neutrality and non-alignment did not really become issues in Soviet theory until after the Second World War.

The initial response was to dismiss the phenomenon. There was no room for neutrality in the two-camp image of the world which had replaced Stalin's pre-war theme of an encircled Soviet Union. The national-liberation movements were believed to belong to the same camp as the Soviet Union. Neutralism was merely an imperialist device. National leaders who wished 'to "remain on the sidelines' in relation to . . . the "ideological conflict" between the USSR and the USA, in fact form a bloc with the reactionary bourgeoisie in slandering the USSR and are actively helping the imperialists' (Zhukov 1949: 58). But the new neutral nations were soon seen to be a source of potential support, and the neutralization of Germany and Austria seemed a possible solution to the problems of Europe. Although it was Khrushchev who translated this realization into policy, a change in Soviet attitudes was already perceptible in the speeches made at the Nineteenth Party Congress in 1952 (Gruliow 1953). Moreover, the offer of a reunited neutral Germany was made in 1952, before Stalin's death.[7]

By 1955 Austria had joined Switzerland and Sweden as permanent neutrals with Soviet approval. Whether or not the bargain of German reunification in return for German neutrality was sincere, as Ginsburgs (1960) pointed out, the prospect of a united Europe had made neutralism a more palatable option. When the Soviet–Finnish Friendship Treaty was renegotiated in 1955, assurances were given that the treaty was based on respect for Finish neutrality, a foreign policy which, it was said, had increased Finland's international authority.[8] Verbal approval was followed by appropriate deeds—the Soviet naval base at Porkala was returned to Finland (Ambartsumov 1956). That this did not imply blanket approval for all neutrality was made abundantly clear in October 1956 when, in response to Nagy's declaration that Hungary was opting for neutrality rather than membership of the Warsaw Treaty Organization, Soviet troops invaded Hungary.[9]

But it was the policies of the newly independent ex-colonies that prompted theoretical work on permanent neutrality.

The zone of peace and non-alignment

Although neutralism was not an option for Soviet allies, Soviet theory had already begun to change. In his report to the Twentieth Congress in February 1956 Khrushchev extended Stalin's two-camp world to include a third 'zone of peace'. In part the innovation was aimed at the new nations of Africa. But Khrushchev also hoped to attract Yugoslavia back into the Soviet sphere and he was aware of Tito's authority in the Third World. Moreover, the Bandung Conference had impressed him deeply: since both the socialist countries and the newly independent nations were anti-imperialist and believed in peaceful coexistence, they must be natural allies. He praised the 'peace-loving European and Asian states which have proclaimed non-participation in blocs as a principle of their foreign policy' (Khrushchev 1956a: 34). He promised Soviet support to countries which refused to be involved in military blocs. Friendly relations with Finland, Austria and other neutral countries would be developed and strengthened (Khrushchev 1956a: 38).

Soviet theorists began to explain that the existence of the socialist world was the *sine qua non* for the establishment of what they variously called neutralism, active neutrality, positive neutrality and non-alignment. The new correlation of forces and the certainty that the Soviet Union would counter Western aggression persuaded the imperialists to tolerate neutralism (see Modjoryan 1956; Khabirov 1973; Etinger 1981). It was thought that neutralism had become a widespread aspiration after the Second World War because of the danger of becoming involved in a nuclear war. Refusal to participate in aggressive military blocs exemplified the higher political consciousness of the ex-colonial peoples (Melnikov, 1956).

Khrushchev had insisted in 1956 that the people in the zone of peace were only opposed to imperialist military alliances (Khrushchev 1956a: 33). If that was the case, it might be thought that a more effective counter to Western aggression would have been to join the Soviet bloc. One Soviet theorist explained that:

the only sensible course of action would have been to join the camp of peace-loving states, but because of reasons of an internal and international nature, some states cannot do this. In such cases the only real policy which serves the interests of peace and security is non-participation in military blocs and coalitions.

(Galina 1958: 203)

Later a less evasive explanation accepted that some countries genuinely wished to distance themselves from both capitalism and socialism:

on the one hand, anti-imperialist tendencies and on the other, an unwillingness to co-operate too closely politically or economically with the socialist states and fear of the prospect of genuine socialist development.

(Etinger and Melikyan 1964: 10–11)

The difference between the new neutralism and traditional permanent neutrality was seen to be, first, that it was based on the principles of peaceful coexistence (see Ch. 3, n. 1). Second, it was anti-imperialist, active, and based on broad popular interests. Third, the new neutrals refused to own nuclear weapons. Like the traditional neutrals, they prohibited foreign military bases or the use of their territory by foreign aircraft (Tyulpanov 1961). These prohibitions were interpreted as applying only to imperialist countries since socialist countries did not seek military bases on foreign territory (Tiyunov 1965: 35).

Soviet theorists were, to begin with, divided about whether permanent neutrals could belong to international organizations. The debate concerned Austria, rather than Third World neutrals, but it became clear that behaviour considered unacceptable for European neutrals would be allowed to Third World states. In 1951 Korovin had maintained that membership of collective-security organizations was incompatible with neutral status. By 1958 he had changed his mind. A second writer on neutrality thought that *classical* neutrality was incompatible. New neutrals, however, could belong to the United Nations without infringing international law, providing they accepted the precedence of the UN Charter (Galina 1958). A third objected, pointing out that it was the responsibility of the Security Council to respect the obligations of neutrals, once admission to the United Nations had been recommended (Mikheev 1960). By 1977 non-alignment was said not only to be compatible with UN membership, but also to enhance the concept of collective security (Bobrov and Lukichev 1977).

By this time many other forms of participation were considered compatible with non-aligned status, but unacceptable for the European neutral states. The association agreements of ex-colonies with the European Economic Community (EEC), for example, produced no objections. And although an influential Soviet authority on the Third World (Ul'yanovsky 1972) continued to maintain that neutralism was unsuitable for states following the non-capitalist path of development, socialist-orientation and non-alignment were soon seen as being compatible.[10] Neither Soviet military aid nor association with the Council for Mutual Economic Aid (CMEA) were thought to transgress their non-aligned status. It was averred that friendship and cooperation treaties between the Soviet Union and members of the non-aligned movement did not infringe non-aligned status because Soviet foreign policy was based on the same principles of peaceful coexistence (Tuzmukhamedov 1981).[11]

Soviet theorists and politicians hoped that the presence

within the non-aligned movement of Cuba and socialist-oriented states like Angola, Mozambique, Ethiopia, the People's Democratic Republic of Yemen and Afghanistan would bring about a shift in non-aligned policy. Two themes prominent in the movement at the beginning of the 1970s caused them particular concern. The first was the concept of 'equidistance' from the superpowers. It was firmly rejected as being irrelevant to current problems:

Life urgently requires not 'equidistance' from imperialism and socialism, but mutual action and co-operation of the non-aligned movement and the socialist commonwealth in the business of ensuring peace and national liberation.

(Artem'ev 1981: 69)

It was hoped that the socialist-oriented states within the movement would oppose the concept (Tuzmukhamedov 1976). The second disturbing theme was the demand for a New International Economic Order. As we have seen in Chapter 5, there was great indignation when the non-aligned movement included the socialist commonwealth among the countries which were expected to redress the economic wrongs of centuries.[12]

That the Soviet leadership had misjudged the principles of non-alignment became clear in the wake of the invasion of Afghanistan in December 1980. Members of the non-aligned movement voted against the Soviet Union in the United Nations. They also discussed Afghanistan at the New Delhi Non-Aligned Summit in 1983 in spite of pressure from the Soviet Union to remove the topic from the agenda (for an account of the non-aligned response to the intervention, see Fullerton 1983). Although the criticism was attributed to the 'manoeuvres of imperialist forces, Pakistan and some non-aligned nations under their influence' (Artem'ev 1981: 64), the Soviet Union had been served notice that the non-aligned movement expected the principle of non-interference to be honoured.

European neutralism
The European neutrals have featured far less frequently in Soviet specialist literature and political speeches. But, with the exception of Finland's relations with the Soviet Union,

Soviet theorists are more stringent in their interpretation of the demands of European neutralism than they are about non-alignment. The exact nature of the difference between Afro-Asian neutrality and imperialist neutrality has not really been made clear by Soviet theorists. European neutrality was thought to be akin to traditional permanent neutrality, primarily military, and therefore inferior to the positive neutralism of the Third World. Although one theorist suggested that 'a change from Atlantic status to neutrality would be a move which would strengthen peace and security' (Korovin 1958a: 39), neutrality has rarely been proposed as a viable option for individual European countries. Despite Western fears that the Soviet Union would like to 'Finlandize' Western Europe, a European collective-security system has always been considered a superior and more reliable means of preserving peace.

The compatibility of collective security and neutralism was finally accepted by Soviet theorists when Austria joined the United Nations. But membership of other international organizations caused more problems. The argument arose over the possibility of Austria joining the EEC. Although Austrian membership of the European Free Trade Area and the Council of Europe had not been criticized, the Common Market was seen to be the economic arm of NATO. In the process of arguing the case against Austrian membership, Soviet theorists broadened their definition of European neutralism. It was no longer primarily military, but was a policy with 'military, political, economic and even ideological aspects' (Tyulpanov 1961: 33), each of which was equally important. Association with the EEC was particularly unacceptable because the Rome Treaty was seen as the preparatory stage for political union. In any case, association would make an even-handed economic policy towards third countries impossible (Osnitskaya 1962). Soviet fears about the consequences of Austrian membership seem to have been sincere, but since the association agreements of the non-aligned states had not produced any such outcry, it seemed that it was not Austrian neutrality that was at issue, but the intense distrust Soviet leaders felt for the EEC and their anxiety about any enlargement of the Western bloc.

As the advantages of East–West trade began to outweigh

ideological objections, Soviet attitudes softened. Finland was allowed to sign a free-trade agreement with the EEC in 1972, in return for a similar agreement with CMEA. Irish membership of the EEC was treated less generously, but Irish neutrality had always been treated with the same scepticism with which Finnish neutrality was regarded by the West.

The European neutral which has always presented Soviet politicians and theorists with the greatest difficulty is Yugoslavia. Yugoslavia has usually been ignored in discussions of non-alignment, and Tito's role in founding both the concept and the movement has been passed over in silence, credit being given to Sukarno, Nasser and Nehru (see, for example, Etinger and Melikyan 1964; a rare exception is Tuzmukhamedov 1976, who praised Tito's contribution). When Soviet–Yugoslav relations have been bad, non-alignment has been a stick with which Soviet leaders have tried to beat Yugoslavia. Khrushchev, for example, maintained that Yugoslav neutrality 'carries a distinct odour of the American monopolies which nourish "Yugoslav socialism" ' (Khrushchev 1959b: 62). The statement issued by the November 1960 meeting of eighty-one Communist and Worker's Parties accused Yugoslavia of using the pretext of being outside blocs to 'engage in activities which prejudice the unity of all the peace-loving forces and countries' ('Statement of the Meeting of Representatives of the Communist and Workers' Parties' 1960: 15). On the other hand, when Soviet–Yugoslav relations have been good, the subject of Yugoslav non-alignment has been tactfully ignored (e.g. Brezhnev 1981).

As we have seen, it was hoped that Cuba's presence and that of the socialist-oriented states would set the non-aligned movement on a more pro-Soviet course. Yugoslavia blocked the attempt. But Soviet policy-makers have a longer-standing reason for worrying about Yugoslavia's non-alignment. It represents a threat to socialist unity, in that it offers an alternative model to other European socialist states.

Non-alignment and national liberation
An intriguing feature of the Soviet treatment of non-alignment and neutralism is the difference between the language which has been used in the specialist literature and that uttered or written in political statements and speeches.[13]

Soviet political speeches, reports, statements and programmes have, since Stalin's death, commended the adoption
of the principles of coexistence by Third World countries,
their stand against war and for peace, their anti-imperialism
and anti-colonialism and, most particularly, their refusal to
participate in imperialist military blocs and alliances. But the
praise has almost always been given to the Afro-Asian nations
or to the forces of national liberation and rarely to the non-
aligned movement.

At the Twentieth Party Congress, for example, Khrushchev spoke of the countries which stand for peace and refuse
to be involved in military blocs (Khrushchev 1956a). In his
report to the Twenty-First Congress, he mentioned neutrality
and non-alignment only to criticize Yugoslavia (Khrushchev
1959b: 60–2). At the Twenty-Second Congress he maintained
that the countries of Asia, Africa and Latin America were 'by
no means neutral when it comes to the fundamental question
of the day—the question of war and peace' (Khrushchev
1961b: 49). The programme of the CPSU adopted at that
Congress referred to the 'growing number of countries that
adhere to a policy of neutrality and strive to safeguard themselves against the hazards of participation in aggressive
military blocs' ('Programme of the Communist Party of the
Soviet Union' 1961: 84–5). In contrast, a vast amount of space
was allotted in those speeches to the national-liberation
movement and the break-up of colonial empires, both of
which were said to have contributed to the third stage in the
final crisis of capitalism.

Brezhnev, too, showed a marked preference for the term
'national-liberation movement'. Neither non-alignment nor
neutralism rated an entry in the index to the 1973 collection of
his speeches, although there were seventy-seven entries for
the national-liberation movement (Brezhnev 1973).

Soviet theory has attempted to adjust to the reality of the
non-aligned movement and of the active neutralism of the
European neutrals, but it has had difficulty in incorporating
them within the Marxist-Leninist world view. The European
neutrals (apart from Yugoslavia and Albania) are capitalist.
They should be filled with conflict and prone to war. Yugoslavia, a socialist state, cannot both be socialist and affiliated
to a separate group of states. The non-aligned movement,

anti-imperialist though it may be, is a detour in the linear progression of history envisaged by Marxist–Leninist theory. Lenin predicted that the national-liberation movement would progress towards socialism. He did not expect it to turn into a third force, one that does not always identify itself with the position and actions of the leading socialist power. In using the terms neutral or non-aligned, it is this unpredicted and ahistorical aspect of the movement which is emphasized. As long as it is called the national-liberation movement, it seems to be a more hopeful phenomenon.

PEACE

The desire for peace was skilfully used by the Bolsheviks in the period following the February revolution in their slogan 'Peace, Bread, Freedom'. It was immediately translated into the first foreign-policy act of the new regime. The Peace Decree, issued on 8 November 1917, offered a just peace without annexations or reparations (Degras 1951, vol. 1: 1–3). Although one Western theorist has interpreted it and the accompanying armistice offer as 'instrumentalities for the transformation of world war into a series of civil, revolutionary wars which . . . would bring about communist peace by extending social revolution to new areas' (Taracouzio 1940: 66), it had little to do with Leninist theories of revolution. Peace was essential for the survival of the state, irrespective of the regime.

Lenin understood the urgency rather better than his fellow Bolsheviks. It was only after the failure of Trotsky's 'no peace, no war' strategy at Brest-Litovsk and the advance of the German army that he managed to persuade them that whatever his own theory predicted, there was no other option but to accept the terms offered by the Germans. The survival of the Soviet state was given priority over the immediate advance of international revolution. As we have seen, before long the future of the international revolution was to be interpreted in terms of the survival of the Soviet state.

The peace-loving nature of Soviet foreign policy has been a persistent theme of policy statements, specialist literature and political speeches from 1917 onwards. Over the years a number of national and international campaigns have been launched in support of peace. Soviet disarmament and collective-security proposals have been made in the name of peace. Yet there has been curiously little theory which deals with peace.

The Soviet peace policy

It is almost as if the meaning and content of peace have been taken for granted by Soviet theorists. Neither the 1961 nor the 1985 diplomatic dictionaries (Gromyko *et al.* 1961, 1985) contained entries for peace, although both had entries for peaceful coexistence. Nor did it appear in the 1980 *Dictionary of Scientific Communism* (Rumyantsev 1984). To find a Soviet definition of peace, the analyst has to consult the literature on the Soviet peace policy. The aim of the Soviet peace policy is to exclude war (with the exception of just wars of independence and national liberation) from the life of humankind (Shakhnazarov 1984: 21). Peace, therefore, is the absence of war. Khrushchev distinguished between peace and peaceful coexistence, and it was clear from his definition that peaceful coexistence was more positive than peace:

Peace and peaceful coexistence are not quite the same thing. Peaceful coexistence is not simply the absence of war, not an unstable truce between wars. It is the coexistence of two opposing social systems, founded on the mutual renunciation of war as a means of settling disputes between states.

(Khrushchev 1961b: 49)

The problem for Soviet theorists in constructing a more positive theory of peace is, perhaps, that peace is an unattainable ideal before international revolution. According to Marxist-Leninist theory, it is only then that perfect peace will occur, because it is only then that class antagonisms will disappear, and with them, conflict and war. Marx predicted that 'in contrast to old society, a new society is springing up, whose International rule will be *Peace*, because its national ruler will be everywhere the same—*Labour*' (Marx 1871: 490). Modern theorists believe that peace is 'a social ideal which can only be fully realized in a classless society . . . and fully guaranteed when communism has finally achieved universal victory' (Petrenko and Popov 1981: 154). But before the ideal is realized, peaceful relations provide the best 'external conditions for the successful building of socialism and communism' (Korovin 1951: 574). In part this is because peace creates the opportunity for domestic social and economic development. But peaceful relations are also required because 'in conditions of peace . . . the superiority of the socialist social system is revealed most fully' (Narochnitsky *et al.* 1979: 22).

Peace, like war, is said to be the continuation of politics, but by non-violent means (*Problems of War and Peace* 1972: 72). And like war, peace can be just or unjust, depending on the particular historical circumstances, on the class whose policy it is, on the kind of peace which is proposed and to whom it is advantageous (Petrenko and Popov 1981: 153–4). Certain kinds of peaceful relations, those which 'strengthen [Soviet] class positions and favour the development of the world revolutionary process' make the transition to socialism in other countries more likely (Butenko 1975: 307–8).

As we have seen, even at the most optimistic period of Khrushchev's assertion that there was no fatal inevitability of war, the danger of war was said to remain. It has always, therefore, been considered essential that the Soviet Union possesses a defence potential capable of deterring any imperialist attack, while pursuing policies and making proposals to further the peaceful aims of Soviet foreign policy. It has also always been considered important to mobilize the forces for peace. Khrushchev pointed out that 'Wind from words won't turn windmills . . . still less can the war machine of the aggressors be held in check with talk of peace. Decisive and vigorous action is needed' (Khrushchev 1961b: 50).

There are three ways in which Soviet politicians believe that their decisive and vigorous action has always promoted peace: by mobilizing world opinion in favour of peace; by pursuing policies which enhance peace; and by ensuring that the level of Soviet armaments is sufficiently high to prevent military conflict between the two blocs, counter-revolutionary attacks against individual bloc members or against the national-liberation movement, and the escalation of local wars into world war. All three aspects have been considered important, although more and more reliance seems to have been placed on the efficacy of Soviet power.

Since propaganda has always been an important aspect of

Marxist activity,[14] the efforts which have been put into peace propaganda are not surprising. The 1917 Decree on Peace has been invoked by subsequent Soviet theorists and politicians as concrete proof of the early origins of the Soviet peace policy (see, for example, Zhurkin and Primakov 1972: 218). It was addressed both to the peoples of the belligerent countries and to their governments. Its purpose was thus as much propaganda as a practical proposal for ending the First World War. It has been followed over the years by countless declamations on the theme of peace and the peaceful nature of Soviet foreign policy. To point out that these statements are directed both towards moulding Soviet public opinion in favour of government policy and towards influencing world public opinion in favour of the Soviet Union is not to make any judgement about their sincerity. But calling them declamations draws attention to the fact that they tend to be assertions, with very little reference to Marxist-Leninist theory. That 'the Soviet Union is a profoundly peace-loving state' (Grechko 1977: 22) is uttered and must be accepted as a basic article of faith. Proof tends to be offered in terms of past and present actions, rather than theory, the very reverse of the usual case in Soviet political discourse, where theory (often contradicted by reality) bears the brunt of proof. In 1940 a Western scholar pointed out that 'In comparison with proletarian policies in regard to war, Marxian dogmas relative to practical peace efforts not only occupy less space in communist writings, but also are much less definite' (Taracouzio 1940: 59). The position is very similar in post-war Soviet writings on international relations and problems of war and peace.[15]

One of the actions which was initiated by the Soviet Union to strengthen the forces for peace after the Second World War was to sponsor a World Peace Movement. The Stockholm Appeal against atomic weapons attracted 660 million signatures (Korovin 1951: 590–5). Peace conferences and congresses have been funded which have aimed at bringing together various parties and groups interested in peace. The popularity of the movement has fluctuated rather like that of Western anti-nuclear movements. The Soviet Committee for Peace is a prestigious, well-funded organization and the size and discipline of the marches for peace it organizes would be the envy of the organizers of any similar Western event. Its domestic functions include the mobilizing of Soviet public opinion and the formation of a sense of cohesion around Soviet peace proposals. Given the belief that Soviet military strength is the cornerstone of peace, it is perhaps not surprising that the call is always for a reduction in Western nuclear weapons and no mention is made of Soviet arms. And given the nature of the Soviet political system, there is little tolerance of independent peace groups.

At the Twenty-Fourth Congress of the CPSU in 1971, Brezhnev proposed a peace programme (Brezhnev 1971). It was reaffirmed in 1976 at the Twenty-Fifth Congress (Brezhnev 1976) and updated for the 1980s at the Twenty-Sixth Congress in 1981 (Brezhnev 1981; see Sanakoyev and Kapchenko 1977: 260, 271, and Petrenko and Popov 1981: 180). All three programmes list the current international problems which need to be resolved if there is to be peace. Each lists in rather general terms measures which, in the opinion of the Soviet leadership, will enhance peace. Most of these measures have been proposed in more detail to the West and are usually mentioned in any discussion of the peaceful intentions of Soviet foreign policy. They concern arms control and the establishment of collective-security systems.

From the 1920s onwards the Soviet Union has alternated proposals for general and complete disarmament with arms control and reduction suggestions. These have been rejected by the West regularly, and Western counter-proposals have been rejected equally regularly by the Soviet Union. Whether or not Soviet theorists genuinely believe that the Soviet proposals are practicable, books on Soviet foreign policy (both theoretical and historical) describe them and indicate that Western counter proposals have intended to undermine Soviet security.[16] They are used as evidence of the persistent efforts made by the Soviet government to ensure peace and reduce the danger of world war. The few treaties which have been negotiated successfully (e.g. the 1963 Partial Test Ban, the 1968 Non-Proliferation Treaty and the SALT agreements of the 1970s) have been acclaimed as proof of the success of the Soviet peace policy. Every acceleration in the arms race, on the other hand, has been reported with alarm. The Soviet Union has also proposed atom-free and nuclear-free zones, agreements on the non-use of force and on no first use of nuclear weapons. Rejection of these proposals has been interpreted as evidence of the continuing aggressive intentions of imperialism, and of the need to ensure that the West, particularly the United States, is never in a position to negotiate from a position of strength.

A further series of proposals to enhance peace has concerned the establishment of collective-security systems, particularly in Europe. The failure of Soviet attempts to form a collective-security system against Nazi Germany in the 1930s has been attributed to British and French hopes that Germany would attack Soviet Russia (see Light 1983: 74–8 for an elaboration of the charges). After the war proposals for a European collective-security agreement were resumed. Soviet scholars regard the Conference on Security and Cooperation in Europe in 1973 as the final successful outcome of these proposals. Although much less than a European security system was achieved, Soviet theorists have expressed themselves well satisfied with the early results of the Helsinki Agreement of 1975 (see, for example, Narochnitsky *et al.* 1979: 201–2). The slowdown in the Helsinki process thereafter was interpreted as a further signal of imperialist aggression.

The limited success of disarmament proposals and ideas about collective security have enhanced an already prevalent belief that Soviet power brings about peace by deterring imperialism from launching war. (The West has been equally sure that its power has prevented both war and the onward march of communism.) Stalin had used the threat of war to exhort the populace to greater productive feats in the industrialization drives of 1928–39. The Soviet victory against Germany was attributed to these efforts. When war ceased to be considered inevitable, this was thought to be due to a considerable extent to Soviet military power. Sokolovskiy pointed out that 'the struggle for peace . . . demands above all the steadfast strengthening of the military power of the Soviet Union and the entire socialist camp' (Sokolovskiy 1963: 179). Although some credit has been given to the active struggle of those in favour of peace (see, for example, Brezhnev 1973: 12), it has primarily been thought that the constantly growing military might of the Soviet Union was responsible for peace.

The generally accepted view on the efficacy of Soviet power in bringing about peace is aptly summed up in the statement 'The stronger we are, the stronger peace is, and the greater the possibility of preventing war' (Milovidov 1977: 262). In other words, the Soviet view, like that of the West, is the time-honoured 'If you want peace, prepare for war'.

CONCLUSION

The most obvious feature of Soviet thinking about war and peace is imbalance. There are innumerable books dealing with the theory of war, while very little has been written about peace theory. It should be noted, however, that a similar situation pertains in the West. Although peace theory can be identified as a recognizable branch of Western international relations theory, it is very small compared to strategic studies. Moreover, it is often considered politically suspect both by lay people and by professional international relations scholars. There is no comparable branch of Soviet international relations theory. The primary reason is probably that peace belongs to the millennial future of communism. There is equally little theory or even speculation about what an international communist system will be like (see, for example, how little speculation there is about it in Shakhnazarov 1984).

There is, however, another problem about peace theory. International communism (and therefore absolute peace) is only attainable via international revolution, but there has been a return to a deterministic view of how this revolution will occur. Since the Soviet Union does not launch war, it certainly cannot come about through a Soviet-inspired revolutionary war. In any case, the risk that local war will escalate into nuclear war makes revolutionary war an extremely dangerous concept. And if peace is necessary for the construction of communism within the existing socialist bloc, logically war would retard that development. But the absence of war also retards the development of a revolutionary situation within capitalist states. Peace, therefore, promotes the transition from socialism to communism in states that are already socialist, but it is unlikely to promote the transition from capitalism to socialism in other states. The theoretical problems are similar to those which became evident when peaceful coexistence was discussed in Chapter 3.

As far as the theory of war and neutralism are concerned, there has been more evidence of the impact of the real world on Soviet thinking in these fields than in any other area of Soviet international relations theory. War between socialism and capitalism has ceased to be considered inevitable, because it would be fatal to both. Although the theory still holds that national-liberation war is inevitable and will be supported, in practice the limiting factor to socialist support has been the likelihood of other nuclear powers becoming involved. In other words, the risk of small wars escalating to nuclear war has meant that all wars have ceased to be a rational means of policy. The other theoretical changes, including the separation of revolution and war, stem from this central fact.

The other major adaptation in Soviet theory is the depiction, grudging at times, hopeful at others, of a third camp, neither socialist nor capitalist, or at least able to accommodate both capitalist-oriented, socialist-oriented and socialist states. Both the avoidability of war and the emergence of the non-aligned movement are attributed to Soviet power and this, too, represents a change. Soviet theorists object to Western deterrence theory, but they quite explicitly believe that Soviet power deters imperialist aggression.

The conviction that Soviet power is a deterrent is, perhaps, merely a mirror image of Western deterrence theory. But Soviet theorists have three other reasons for insisting that the Soviet Union must possess military power which is at least equal to that of the West. First, the need stems from the Marxist-Leninist theory of war, which holds that it is in the nature of imperialism to cause war. Even though war is no longer inevitable, the danger remains. Although good sense may prevail to prevent it, something must prompt that good sense. It is clearly not dictated by selflessness or by a belief in peace, particularly since peace, according to the theory, gives socialism an advantage over capitalism. It can only be that the risk of defeat is too high. It is Soviet military power which is thought to create that unacceptable risk.

Second, although Soviet peace campaigns contribute to creating a sense of cohesion and common purpose within

Soviet society and a belief in the ultimate justness of Soviet political goals, it would be dangerous if this led to relaxation and a lack of vigilance. Soviet society has for so long been held together by the threat of the enemy within and the danger of the external enemy, that it would be surprising if there was not some fear that it would disintegrate without this kind of tension. And it is not just the multinational society of the Soviet Union which must cohere, but an alliance which has shown frequent signs of stress. Invoking the continuing danger and emphasizing the defence effort which must be made to combat it, retains the tension and promotes cohesion.

Finally, the communist millennium promises distribution based on need. This requires an abundance which is clearly beyond the present scope of the economy. Moreover, the goal seems to have been retreating, and the higher the investment in defence, the further away it must seem. On a less ideological level, consumer expectations have been disappointed and, even in the Soviet Union, explanations are required for budgetary allocations. If the peace which is required to build a communist society is thought to be bought at the price of heavy investment in arms, the Soviet consumer will accept the level of military spending more easily.

It seems clear that the contradiction of investing in peace while preparing for war is more apparent than real. As in many other countries, the preparation for war has been seen in the Soviet Union as a major part of the investment in peace. The change from Khrushchev's formulation of the non-inevitability of world war to a greater emphasis on the need to avert war made it natural to concentrate on the means that would enable it to be avoided. The shift also corresponded to reality, in that it coincided with the attainment of the nuclear parity which Soviet theorists and politicians have believed essential for equal security.

Preparing for war and explaining why this is necessary and propagandizing peace fulfil different functions in Soviet society. The former maintains vigilance and promotes the belief that war can be survived. The latter, on the other hand, supports faith in the ultimate justness of the Soviet regime. Most other societies use war and peace in this way, although perhaps less stridently and less overtly. Nuclear weapons have produced a paradox for Soviet theorists and policy-makers, but it is one that is shared by other nuclear powers. The citizens of nuclear countries must believe that a nuclear war can be won, or else their morale will affect any preparation for surviving such a war. The deterrent effect of nuclear weapons relies on the opposing side believing it too. On the other hand, encouraging peace movements in antagonistic countries and persuading antagonistic governments to negotiate arms control agreements requires emphasizing that nuclear war can neither be won nor survived. How to convey both views with conviction is an insoluble problem. In the Soviet case the result has been the two voices referred to at the beginning of this chapter. The outcome is probably that neither audience is entirely convinced.

NOTES

1. Soviet theory also distinguishes between strategy and 'operational art', defined as 'the theory and practice of preparing for and conducting combined and independent operations by major field formations or major formations of the services' (*Dictionary of Basic Military Terms*, nd: 144). A further distinction is made, in both military and political thinking, between strategy, 'the fundamental political line for an entire historical (strategical) stage' (Zagladin 1973: 33) and tactics which derive from strategy and are subordinated to them and which determine 'current policies in a given concrete situation' (Zagladin 1973: 40–1).
2. The features which were said to determine the outcome of any war were (1) the stability of the rear; (2) army morale; (3) the quantity and quality of divisions; (4) the armaments; and (5) the organizational ability of the army commanders (Stalin 1942: 39).
3. Dinerstein maintains that although Stalin limited his discussion to war between imperialists, he meant, and was read to mean, that as long as capitalism exists, war involving the Soviet Union was inevitable (Dinerstein 1962: 66). It is equally plausible, however, that his subtext was meant to imply the reverse and that he was harking back to the 1935 Seventh Comintern Congress formulation mentioned above.
4. A further demonstration of the progressive omission of the formulation that war is no longer inevitable can be found in Petrenko and Popov (1981). In an account of how the CPSU and the Soviet state has developed Marxist-Leninist teaching on war and peace, the authors quoted extensively and sequentially from the Twentieth and all subsequent Party Congresses. They also quoted from Brezhnev's speeches and those of other Politburo members. They themselves used the 'not fatally inevitable' formulation when talking about the period 1956–66,

and then ceased using it, dwelling instead on the danger of war and Soviet attempts to reduce it (Petrenko and Popov 1981: 142–93 and *passim*).

5. As a rule, Soviet theorists criticize Western studies of the causes of war for neglecting the class nature of war. In an extensive survey of Western conflict theory, for example, American research was characterized in general as 'conservative'. Quincy Wright ignored the class interests which determine the character of wars (although his contribution to bourgeois political science was recognized). Scholars who study war from a socio-psychological perspective were accused of hiding the role of imperialism in international conflict, while John Burton was said to 'psychologize', to be influenced by Freud and to formalize his research, ignoring class and political aspects of conflict (Gantman *et al.* 1976: 334–82).

6. The Soviet Union, for example, offered little more than verbal support to the post-war national-liberation movements in Africa and very little aid was given to the Allende government in Chile. The Spanish Civil War and Stalin's attitude to the Greek communists in 1944 and later are graphic examples of cases where support would have contradicted the peaceful image projected by the Soviet Union.

7. Vigor has maintained that this offer proves that the Soviet Union only favours 'beneficial neutrality' (Vigor 1975: 187). In fact, this is hardly unique to the Soviet Union. Western responses to non-alignment were no less self-interested. There is some controversy about whether the offer of a neutral Germany was sincere. See, for example, Ulam (1974: 535–7).

8. When the treaty had first been signed in 1948, Finnish foreign policy was called independent, but there was no mention of neutrality ('Soviet–Finnish Treaty' 1948).

9. Korovin quoted the General Secretary of the Netherlands Communist Party to explain the Soviet attitude to Hungarian neutrality: 'For those countries over which America at present rules, neutrality guaranteed by both world camps, would be *a step forward* towards national independence. For a socialist country neutrality would be a *step backwards* towards subordination to American imperialism and its sphere of influence'. He went on to say that as long as Western military alliances existed 'not one of the [socialist countries] can hope to ensure its security from imperialist aggression by a declaration of neutrality' (Korovin 1958a: 29).

10. For an explanation of these terms, see Chapter 5.

11. Treaties were signed with India and Egypt in 1971, with Iraq in 1972, Somalia in 1974, Mozambique in 1977, Angola, Afghanistan, Ethiopia and Vietnam in 1978, South Yemen in 1979 and Syria in 1980. Egypt and Somalia both later abrogated their treaties (Tuzmukhamedov 1981).

12. In fact, these issues were dividing the non-aligned movement itself. Cuba supported the Soviet position while Yugoslavia insisted that there should be a return to the original principles of non-alignment. The Yugoslav view carried the day at the Havana Summit in 1979 and

Soviet hopes for a better understanding with the movement were dashed (Burton *et al*. 1984: 75–9).

13.   Vigor maintained that the terms 'non-alignment' and 'neutralism' went out of vogue at the beginning of the 1970s, when it became clear that there was little advantage to be gained from the phenomenon (Vigor 1975: 191). In fact, the terms have always been used sparingly in programmatic speeches and statements.

14.   The term 'propaganda' (and the activity) does not have the negative connotations in the Russian political vocabulary that it has in the West. The *Bol'shaya Sovetskogo Entsiklopediya* (2nd edn, 1955) defined it as 'the dissemination of a broad spectrum of ideas, theories and teachings which require deep and detailed explanation', and pointed out that it was an integral part of the work of Communist and Workers' Parties. On Soviet propaganda, see Benn (forthcoming).

15.   None the less, it is difficult to agree with Vigor's contention that the word 'peace' is never used by Soviets in our positive 'peace and goodwill' meaning, but only in a negative, absence of war, sense (Vigor 1975: 166–70). Nor is he correct in asserting that the word 'peace-loving' refers to the situation after the victory of communism. He may doubt the *sincerity* with which the word is used, but it is frequently employed to refer to past, present and future Soviet policy.

16.   The 1981 edition of the second volume of Gromkyo and Ponomarev (eds) *Istoriya vneshnei politiki SSSR, 1945-1980*, for example, contains three whole chapters and two sections of other chapters devoted to the subject.

9 Changes in the International System II: The Correlation of Forces

In 1974 a seminar was held at the Institute of World Economy and International Relations (IMEMO) in Moscow, the first of a series of meetings between members of the Centre for the Analysis of Conflict (CAC) and members of the International Theory section of IMEMO. At one moment in the heated discussion about international relations theory, John Burton, leader of the British team, drew a diagram on the board depicting schools of theory. Pointing to the quadrant which represented power theory, he informed the Soviet scholars that if they really meant what they had been saying, they belonged in that quadrant, together with Morgenthau. The Soviet scholars were both genuinely surprised and rather angry at the accusation. Four years later, on a second visit to Moscow, CAC presented a paper which argued that there is a systemic process which leads great powers, including the Soviet Union, to be expansionist, irrespective of their political philosophy. This idea was rejected as preposterous. A few years later a similar but more elaborate theory was put forward by Ashley to explain the triangular Chinese–Soviet–American relationship (Ashley 1980).[1]

Attempts like these by Western scholars to explain Soviet political behaviour in terms of power or to equate it with Western political behaviour infuriate Soviet scholars, even when the explanations are not offered with particularly anti-Soviet motives.[2] Large numbers of Soviet books have been written to criticize and refute Western theories, particularly those which purport to explain Soviet foreign policy in terms of power politics and geopolitics and which suggest a continuity between pre-revolutionary Russian policy and Soviet policy.[3]

Yet throughout this discussion of current Soviet international relations theory, it has been clear that Soviet theorists place considerable emphasis on the efficacy of power. It has also been evident that there is an explicit belief that Soviet power acts as a deterrent. Indeed, since Soviet theorists deny that the Soviet Union would ever use its power except in defence, it is particularly for its ability to deter, that power is considered essential to the present well-being and future progress of socialist society.

The sincerity with which the belief is held that it is only the deterrent power of the Soviet Union that prevents an otherwise inevitable imperialist attack is perhaps best illustrated by the anathema that unilateral Soviet disarmament represents to Soviet theorists and politicians. As Wettig has pointed out, the size and activity of the international peace movement is considered one of the signs that the correlation of forces has changed and one of the factors which have a moderating influence on Western decision-makers (Wettig 1984: 45). As we have seen in Chapter 8, there is a parallel, quasi-independent Soviet peace movement which often demonstrates against nuclear weapons. It would add to the credibility of the Soviet movement if it campaigned not only for Western but also for Soviet disarmament. However, since Soviet weapons are defined as defensive and the only deterrent against imperialist aggression, official Soviet peace campaigners do not protest against their own arsenal. The few dissidents who have taken up the issue of Soviet nuclear weapons have been accused of anti-Soviet behaviour.

Parallel with the belief that Soviet power acts as a deterrent is the equally strongly held conviction that Soviet theory and policy do not rely on the concept of power in the way that Western theory and policy do. Contemporary Soviet theorists maintain that there is a world correlation of forces which is changing inexorably in favour of socialism. The theory of the correlation of forces, according to Soviet theorists, differs from balance of power theory. It is held to be a better reflection of reality, depicting a dynamic world which is changing inevitably in a particular direction, in contrast to the static and status quo oriented model of balance of power. It is also claimed to be more scientific: the correlation at any particular time can be scientifically determined and precisely computed.

However, although many Soviet writers indicate what kinds of factors must be taken into account in analysing the correlation of forces in a particular historical epoch, none provides evidence to corroborate the claim that the correlation can be computed more scientifically than the balance of power, or that it is a more precise concept and a better guide to action (imprecision and weakness in prescriptive power are criticisms that both Soviet and Western theorists level at power theories). Soviet theorists are unanimous in claiming that the correlation has changed and is still changing, that the change favours socialism and that it is therefore detrimental to capitalism. In other words, the correlation of forces, like the balance of power, is essentially a zero-sum concept—a gain to the socialist world automatically represents a loss to imperialism.[4]

The concept of the correlation of forces is by no means new, but in the same way that peaceful coexistence has become primarily associated with Khrushchev, so the change in the correlation of forces belongs essentially to the Brezhnev era, in the sense that it was then that it became something to which theorists and politicians constantly alluded. None the less, it had been in use long before Brezhnev became leader of the Soviet Union. Similarly, power is a concept which is as old in Marxism-Leninism as Marxism-Leninism itself is. But the acquisition of power by the Soviet Union, and the point at which the correlation of forces is thought to have changed, belong very clearly to modern times, specifically to the period from 1945 onwards.

Despite Soviet claims to be able to measure power precisely, one of the central problems of considering both the Soviet and the Western versions of the concept is the many different (and often loose) ways in which the word and the concept are used. Does it mean political power or military power, for example, or a combination of the two? Clearly, when we say 'the Bolsheviks took power in 1917' or 'Khrushchev fell from power in 1964', we do not mean the same as when we talk of the power of the Soviet Union. Yet the two are not entirely unrelated. Soviet theorists (and their classical predecessors) similarly talk of the proletariat seizing power during a revolution and do not mean exactly the same as the power that is required to defend the revolution. Yet once again the two are not entirely unrelated. For example, the political power inherent in the state is, according to Marxist theory, the power of coercion to establish and sustain the interests of the dominant class in society. Yet it is clearly not relative amounts of this coercive ability that are being compared in Soviet discussions of the correlation of forces.

Another related difficulty in considering the Soviet concepts of power and the correlation of forces and how they relate to Western concepts concerns translation. The Russian word for correlation, *sootnoshenie*, has been translated into English variously over the years as correlation, alignment, distribution, arrangement, and so on. In the last few years, however, when the term has been used far more frequently, it has usually been translated as correlation, the word which will be used throughout this chapter. But Soviet authors use a number of Russian words to denote power. The term 'correlation of forces' is *sootnoshenie sil*. *Sili* both means 'forces' in this rather abstract sense and 'forces' as in 'armed forces' (*vooruzhennye sili*). But it is also sometimes used to mean power, and at other times it means strength. Balance of power, for example, is usually translated as *balans sil*, and the much-hated American policy 'from a position of strength' is rendered as *s pozitsii sil*. The word *vlast'* is usually used to denote political power. To make it even more complicated, there is another word *nasilie*, which is sometimes used to mean power, although its dictionary meaning is violence, force or coercion.[5]

The result of this linguistic profusion is that there is a danger of misrepresentation and misunderstanding on both sides. It is not always easy, for example, to establish whether a Soviet theorist is distinguishing between political power and military power, or whether an implicit distinction between the two by Western writers is understood by Soviet commentators. However, whatever terms are used, there seems to be unanimity amongst Soviet scholars that Western and Soviet motives for possessing power differ. Soviet power is defensive, whereas in the West the intention is aggression.

The purpose of this chapter is to examine the concepts of

power and the correlation of forces in Soviet theory and to investigate the claim that the correlation of forces is both different from, and also better, more scientific and more valid than Western theories of power and balance of power. The chapter is divided into four sections. In the first the use of the concept of a correlation of forces by Marx, Engels and Lenin is examined. As in previous chapters, particular attention is paid to those works which are most frequently cited by modern theorists to validate contemporary usage. Stalin and his colleagues used the term 'correlation of forces' in an almost identical way to its later use. In the second part of the chapter Stalin's concept of power is considered.

The third section of the chapter deals with the new correlation of forces. It focuses on Soviet definitions of the correlation, why Soviet scholars believe that it has changed in favour of socialism, and what they consider to be the effects of that change. The similarities in and differences between balance of power and correlation of forces are examined. In the concluding part of the chapter the new correlation of forces and the analysis of power in international relations are compared to Western theories, in particular with respect to the claim that the Soviet concepts are more scientific than the Western.

THE CORRELATION OF FORCES IN MARX AND LENIN

Contemporary Soviet scholars neither claim to have invented the theory of correlation of forces nor to be the first to recognize the need for power. These aspects of Soviet international theory, like all other aspects, are traced back to Marx, Engels and Lenin, although original sources are quoted less frequently than is usually the case with other political concepts. In referring to the classical writers, similar problems are encountered to those found when considering other international relations concepts. It is not so much that Marx, Engels and Lenin did not use the concepts, as that they envisaged a different kind of world when they used them.

Whereas modern theorists prefer to concentrate on the way in which the mere possession of power by the socialist world will lead to peaceful revolutionary change elsewhere, Marx and Engels were more concerned with the revolutionary process than with conditions after the revolution. Consequently, they dealt with the need for power and the use of power in effecting and completing the revolution. They did not consider a prolonged situation of political stalemate after the revolution when power would be required as a deterrent. Lenin was forced to consider such a situation, but by then, as we have seen, it was day-to-day policy rather than theory that concerned him. But the event that has cast most doubt on the usefulness of both the theory and the possession of power, the invention of a power of such magnitude that it is too destructive and dangerous to be used, could not, of course, be envisaged by any of the classical Marxist thinkers. None the less, both power and the correlation of forces are concepts which can be found in their works.

Marx and Engels on power

Marx and Engels were profoundly concerned with power in two ways: first, they analysed its origins in the economic base of society; second, they believed in the inevitable conquest of power by the proletariat. Although they thought that this conquest should and would be universal (see, for example, Marx's belief that 'the Hungarian shall not be free, nor the Pole, nor the Italian, as long as the worker remains a slave', Marx, 1850b: 163), it was essentially power within states that interested them rather than power between states, since 'in form, though not in substance, the struggle of the proletariat against the bourgeoisie is primarily national' (Marx and Engels 1848: 45). Political power would be seized by revolution and, since the ruling class would not forfeit its position voluntarily, force would probably have to be used. According to Marx, 'force is the midwife of every old society pregnant with a new one' (Marx 1867: 916).

Following a successful socialist revolution, there would be a dramatic change in the correlation of forces as the victorious proletariat used the political power it had captured to transform the means of production into state property (Engels 1877: 150). In the interim period before class distinctions finally disappeared, coercive power would be required to prevent the dispossessed bourgeoisie from trying to regain its position of pre-eminence. But as soon as class differences had been eliminated there would be no further need for power and coercion: in a classless society or world there would be no antagonisms or conflicting interests, and therefore no need for coercive organs. Together with the withering away of the state, political power would wither away.

Amongst the institutions that would disappear with the state would be both the army and the police. The absence of conflict within a communist society would do away with their domestic functions, and the army would not be required for external purposes since 'in proportion as the antagonism between classes within the nation vanishes, the hostility of one nation to another will come to an end' (Marx and Engels 1848: 51). Marx admired the abolition of the standing army by the Paris Commune and its replacement by the 'armed people' (Marx 1871: 519).

Later, however, Engels accepted that if the revolution did not spread immediately, it would need to defend itself, and that it would require an army rather than a people's militia to do so. In his capacity as a military historian and commentator, he observed that military power depended on more than the number of guns or men available—social and economic formations, means of production, level of development and the nature and class structure of the productive forces played an important part in determining relative military power (see his military writings in Marx and Engels 1856–63). But in this analysis Engels was primarily concerned with military affairs and how military power functioned when there was overt inter-state conflict. He did not consider the role of military power in international relations in times of peace.

In many ways Marx and Engels cast new light on the concept of power, as they did on so many other aspects of political analysis. The fact that it seems self-evident today that political power within a society is held by the class that controls the economic base, or that military power is closely related to the level of economic development, is to a large extent due to the way in which they drew attention to categories which had previously been neglected in historical, social and political analysis. Their theories have had an intellectual impact not only on Soviet political and international relations theory but also on Western theories. Soviet theorists, however, tend to believe that it is only Marxism-Leninism which has been informed by classical Marxism.[6] In fact, the relationship between the original theories of Marx and Engels and the modern theory of the world correlation of forces is rather distant. Marx and Engels did not consider the use of power as deterrent—power was an instrument to bring about change. Once the change had been effected, there would be no further use for it.

Lenin, power and the correlation of class forces
Non-Soviet scholars of Leninism disagree about whether Lenin was a true Marxist, or whether he corrupted the original doctrine. In part this is a debate about the extent to which he was a power politician and political realist. On the one hand, it has been of practical interest because the Bolshevik Revolution took place at all (the wrong revolution in the right country or the right revolution in the wrong country), particularly since in many ways it seemed to produce the very antithesis of the society envisaged by Marx. On the other hand, the interest has been theoretical, provoked by the particular way in which Lenin adapted Marxism.

Some of Lenin's ideas derived from the Russian revolutionary tradition which had first influenced him. Power and revolutionary violence were strong elements in that tradition. Those who see him as a corrupt Marxist believe that the elements of revolutionary violence and terrorism outweigh historical and economic analysis in his work and that he was, above all, bent on achieving power. He has been accused of being 'a determinist in words and a Realpolitiker in action' (Kolakowski 1978, vol. 2: 494), or at least of basing his international theory on class analysis only until about mid-1920, when he changed to a realist or Machiavellian view (Harding 1981, vol. 2: 244–7). There is perhaps some justice in these accusations, but what they really point to is that it is one thing to theorize about revolution, another to foment it and yet a third to secure it.

It is, of course, true that Lenin added a new and strong element of voluntarism to Marxism (and that this was, in part at least, due to the influence of the Russian Narodnik tradition), but it is difficult to see what 'a determinist in action' would have done in his place. Lenin's revolutionary party differed from the kind of party envisaged by Marx and Engels, but he was constructing a party in a country in which other political parties had easily been repressed and in a society which had a small and relatively new working class. It may be accurate to describe Bolshevism as 'how to make a revolution in an economically backward country having a despotic government' (Wright Mills 1963: 132), but when Lenin urged the Bolsheviks to take power in 1917 it was not because he thought that Russia had the correct capitalist economy for a revolution, but in the conviction that the Russian Revolution would serve as the spark for international revolution. The Third Communist International was to be the international institution to direct that revolution. It was when the hope of an immediate revolution elsewhere began to fade that the need to retain power became the pre-eminent domestic concern, and the relative power of Soviet Russia compared to that of the capitalist countries became an urgent matter. By then Lenin had little time for theory, both because these matters were so demanding and because he fell terminally ill quite soon afterwards. Consequently, there is really very little Leninist theory which deals with the problems of retaining political power with a minority government in a hostile world.

Lenin believed that a combination of military power, moral force and business acumen would save Soviet Russia from the hostility of capitalism. In the absence of international revolution the only alternative to believing this would have been to give up the political power which had been gained by the Bolsheviks in October 1917. What Lenin gave up instead was the idea that revolution could be exported from Russia to other countries. He reverted (in 'Left-Wing Communism: An Infantile Disorder' 1920a: 17–118, for example) to a longer-term programme for the Bolshevik Party and the international movement. A revolutionary mood alone was insufficient for a successful revolution. A careful analysis of class forces, a 'sober and strictly objective appraisal of *all* the class forces in a particular state (and of the states that surround it, and of all states the world over) as well as of the experience of revolutionary movements' (Lenin 1920a: 63) would determine whether the moment was right for revolution. But in saying this Lenin was returning to his original view of the requirements for a successful revolution (see

Lenin 1915a: 213–14 and the discussion in Ch. 8 above), a view he had momentarily discarded in the excitement of the initial victory in the Polish War. He had always held that power without historical process was useless. In other words, like Marx and Engels, he believed that the rule of capitalism would only end when the conditions of revolution had matured within society: 'no power could destroy capitalism if it were not sapped and undermined by history' (Lenin 1917i: 417).[7] What he had misjudged in Poland was the extent to which the existing system had been undermined. In other words, the power of the Red Army would, he thought, initiate the revolution, but it was the seizure of political power by the Polish proletariat that would be the essence of that revolution.

It was in the context of the Civil War and the diplomatic needs of the new Soviet state after the war that Lenin first considered the world correlation of forces, a term he had until then used to prescribe the method of analysing the relative strength of political forces within societies. Once the Civil War had begun, it had become clear that the armed masses which Lenin had envisaged as combining the functions of army and militia (Lenin 1917d: 318–19) were neither sufficiently disciplined nor experienced enough to deal with the White Armies. The Red Army was established under Trotsky (and it soon acquired the ranks and discipline of a professional army). The relationship of its strength to that of the White Armies, and of Soviet Russia to that of the capitalist countries was vitally important. The correlation was clearly not in favour of socialism.

Lenin was, therefore, enormously encouraged when foreign intervention in the Civil War was abandoned. Since Russia was incomparably weaker than the capitalist powers from the point of view of military strength, he believed that the failure of intervention was due to disintegration within the Entente (Lenin 1920b: 411). It would clearly be to the advantage of Russia to encourage divisions within the capitalist world. An assessment of the correlation of forces within capitalism, how they were grouped against one another and how they were deployed, would enable the Bolsheviks 'to draw the proper conclusions concerning our policy in general, and our immediate tasks in particular' (Lenin 1921c: 273). Marxism provided a methodology to make 'a strictly exact and objectively verifiable analysis of relations of classes and of the concrete features peculiar to each historical situation' (Lenin 1917e: 43). Each situation could thus be correctly understood, and the tasks of foreign policy could then be formulated and solved.

Power was not entirely synonymous with military strength in Lenin's analysis. It was not only that the Bolsheviks could, with skilful diplomacy, exploit the contradictions which existed between capitalist states. Socialism was also morally superior, and Soviet Russia had the enormous advantage of being able to count on the support of the proletariat in other countries:

Materially—economically and militarily—we are extremely weak; but morally—by which of course, I mean not abstract morals, but the alignment of the real forces of all classes in all countries—we are the strongest of all.
(Lenin 1921a: 151)

Another factor which contributed to the strength of socialism was sheer numbers. One of the reasons why Lenin began to believe that revolution was inevitable in the East and why it would be successful was the numerical superiority of the population of the East: 'In the last analysis, the outcome of the struggle will be determined by the fact that Russia, India, China, etc., account for the overwhelming majority of the population of the globe' (Lenin 1923a: 317–18).

It can be seen from this brief summary that although contemporary Soviet theorists are correct in maintaining that the concept of power was of theoretical and urgent practical concern to Lenin, there was very little in his work about power in international relations. Moreover, while they quote him accurately as recommending the analysis of the correlation of forces as an exact and precise Marxist method, he did not explain how this was to be done. A theory of the world correlation of forces may, perhaps, be extrapolated from his writings, but they do not contain a theory of a changing correlation of forces except in the loosest sense of his expectation that the revolution would spread.

When the international revolution failed to occur, Lenin certainly thought that the Soviet state should rapidly acquire the accoutrements of power, but this was a matter of survival

and not the outcome of theory. It may be the case, as contemporary theorists claim, that he wanted strong military
power both to win the Civil War and to bolster the Soviet
international position, and that he understood that power
involved economic and political power as well as military
power (Gromyko 1962: 34). But as we have seen in Chapter 2,
it was profit rather than power which Lenin expected would
induce the capitalist countries to maintain relations of peaceful coexistence with the Soviet state.

STALINISM AND POWER

Stalin had no doubt about the importance of power, both
domestically and in international relations. 'Socialism in one
country' could only become a reality if that one country
developed the economic power necessary to construct
socialism and had sufficient military power to defend itself.[8]
The 'revolution from above' was designed to take care of
these requirements, and Stalin was quite explicit that failure
to overcome economic backwardness would result in the
defeat of the revolution (Stalin 1931: 366; see Ch. 8 above).

In order to retain his position as leader of the Revolution,
Stalin quite soon bypassed the legal and political processes of
the Soviet state and the Bolshevik Party and relied for his
domestic authority entirely on brute force, coercion and the
fear they produced. Moreover, he proved the efficacy of
power: socialism (though many may argue that this is not what
either Marx or Lenin intended by socialism) did develop in
one country, the Soviet Union acquired sufficient military
power to defeat its enemies and Stalin retained supreme
political power and survived to die a natural death.

But Stalin also used Soviet military power to further the
international revolution, which, although it still did not occur
in the countries predicted or prescribed by Marx, Engels and
Lenin, none the less contributed to a new sense that their
predictions had been correct. Ironically, Western statesmen
seemed to be even more convinced of this than perhaps Stalin
was. As a result, alliances were forged to contain Soviet
expansionism. The first priority in the foreign and military
policy of the industrialized West became the possession of

sufficient power to deter the Soviet Union from further fulfilling those predictions. Since it seemed (and seems) inconceivable to successive Soviet leaders that this can be the only purpose of Western power, it has seemed no less essential for the Soviet Union to own an equal and opposite power, lest containment be replaced by roll-back.

Stalin and power before the war

As we have seen in Chapter 6, before the Revolution Lenin had been sure that the proletarian state would disappear gradually, but that the process would begin immediately. In Stalin's theory, however, there was no question of the process beginning before the final attainment of a classless society not only in Russia but internationally. In 1939 he updated Engels' theory of the state to conform to the conditions of the 1930s, reproaching Soviet propagandists and ideologists for expecting classical Marxist writers to have been able to foresee every zigzag of history so that their descendants 'might calmly doze at the fireside and munch ready-made solutions' (Stalin 1939: 659). The bourgeois state had both external and internal coercive functions, he maintained. After 1917 the new proletarian state had similarly performed the domestic function of suppressing the overthrown classes and the external function of defending the country from external attack. The exploiting classes had now disappeared, and therefore the Soviet state had no further domestic function. But the external function remained and would continue to be vital until the capitalist encirclement had been eliminated and there was no further danger of foreign military attack. An army, navy, punitive organs and an intelligence service were required to fulfil this external function (Stalin 1939: 660–2).

From the reasons that Stalin had given ten years previously for the urgency of Soviet industrialization, it seems clear that he never had any doubt that the proper execution of the external function of the Soviet state depended upon economic and military power. Like Lenin, he maintained that a successful policy required an accurate analysis of class forces (Stalin 1927f: 176). But his initial interest in the way in which the October Revolution had 'raised the strength, the relative weight, the courage and the fighting preparedness of the oppressed classes of the whole world' (Stalin 1927c: 202) was soon replaced by the more urgent preoccupation with the contribution made to Soviet power by the international working class.

By the mid-1930s there was an undisguised preoccupation with Soviet national interest, and the interests of the oppressed classes in other countries and of the international revolution were now considered to be identical to those of the Soviet Union. This was evident from the way in which the Comintern changed its policies. Stalin emphasized that

Our orientation in the past and our orientation at the present time is towards the USSR, and towards the USSR alone. And if the interests of the USSR demand rapprochement with one country or another which is not interested in disturbing peace, we take this step without hesitation.

(Stalin 1934: 484)

It was Soviet power which served the national interest, and therefore the international interest of the working class. Soviet power acted as a deterrent. The Comintern was told by Kuusinen:

the rapid growth of the power of the Soviet Union has, up to now, been the principal, although not the only obstacle (contradictions between imperialist countries are also important) which has restrained the imperialists from a piratical attack upon the land of the proletarian dictatorship.

(Eudin and Slusser 1967, vol. 2: 555)

Soviet power was, however, more than a deterrent. It was also a factor for peace. The invitation to join the League of Nations, for example, was explained partly in terms of sharpening contradictions within the imperialist camp, but mostly as due to the greatly increased power of the Soviet Union. Soviet power served diplomatic interests as well. Since it was no longer 'the custom to give any consideration to the weak', the growth of the 'strength and might of the USSR' had persuaded countries like Poland and France to adopt a more reasonable policy towards the Soviet Union (Eudin and Slusser 1967, vol. 2: 670).

The international situation in the late 1930s aggravated Stalin's perception of capitalist encirclement and the urgent need for sufficient military power to deter an attack or to defend the Soviet Union if war could not be avoided. According to Stalin's public pronouncements, Soviet foreign policy relied for its success upon a number of factors: growing economic, political and cultural might; moral, political and national unity and amity within the Soviet Union; the Soviet army and navy; a policy of peace; the moral support of the international working class and the good sense of those countries which did not want to violate peace (Stalin 1939: 629). But the anxious attempts to negotiate a collective-security agreement with Great Britain and France or, if that failed, to ensure that Germany would not attack the Soviet Union first, indicated rather less confidence in some of these factors than his public speeches suggested. Within a very short time, when the Great Patriotic War began and the last three factors proved to be unreliable, the survival of the Soviet Union became totally dependent on the first three: Soviet economic and political power, unity and amity within the country, and military force. Stalin's emphasis on the acquisition of economic and military power seemed to be vindicated.

It is Stalin rather than Lenin who is the progenitor of contemporary Soviet theory about power in international relations. From 1917 until Lenin died the central issue was the survival of Soviet Russia. Survival remained Stalin's prime concern. But he lived long enough to preside over vast changes in the Soviet Union and in the international political system. Both Lenin and Stalin believed that survival required power. The Soviet Union did more than survive, however; it became one of the two greatest powers in the world. None the less, the world did not become socialist. The inevitable war had occurred, but it had neither resulted in the collapse of capitalism nor in the defeat of socialism. If Soviet theorists had not been inclined to 'doze by the fireside and munch ready-made solutions' (as Stalin had reproached them in 1939) they might have used Marxist methods of analysis to examine why this was so. But they could not afford to do so because Stalin had produced his own ready-made solutions for them.[9]

Lenin had explained the failure of Marxist predictions with his theory of imperialism. Stalin went on predicting that imperialism would eventually disintegrate. But from the mid-1930s onwards the future collapse was explained not so much as being caused by internal contradictions as by a consequence of Soviet power. Soviet power would not be used actively to produce the collapse. It would be a force for peace, it would deter the imperialists from attacking socialism and merely by existing it would encourage revolutionary change within capitalist societies. After 1943 (when the Comintern was disbanded) an international communist institution to promote revolutionary change was no longer considered necessary. These functions of power have, as we have already seen in previous chapters, remained important elements of modern Soviet concepts of international relations.

Stalinism and the post-war correlation of forces

It is sometimes asserted in the West that Soviet theorists and politicians date the change in the correlation of forces from the achievement of rough parity with the United States in nuclear weapons (see, for example, Mitchell 1982: 60).[10] In fact, while it is true that the concept became far more popular in the 1970s, most Soviet *mezhdunarodniki* began claiming immediately after the war that there had been profound changes in the correlation of forces. This had led to changes in the international system, and a new role for the Soviet Union in that system. As we shall see in the next section, further reasons were given later for the new correlation of forces, but the starting point of the change has remained the outcome of the Second World War.

It has also been suggested that the very imagery of capitalist encirclement was a reflection of Stalin's pessimistic belief that the distribution of power between the socialist and capitalist worlds would inevitably remain weighted in favour of capitalism until its eventual demise (see, for example, Marantz 1982: 221–4). It is certainly true that the victory over Nazi Germany and the establishment of buffer states in Eastern Europe did little to change the depiction of an embattled and threatened socialist world surrounded by an implacably hostile imperialism. There were considerable advantages in playing up the dangers of capitalist encirclement. It served to explain why great sacrifices were required to reconstruct the Soviet economy quickly, and why it was important to continue strengthening Soviet defence capacities (see, for example, Malenkov 1952: 104). It was also an excellent pretext for reimposing a hard ideological line after the relative relaxation during the war.

Despite the reinstated spectre of hostile encirclement, however, great credit was given to the growth in Soviet power and its ability to defend socialism. Soviet military power was acclaimed for defeating the German army (as little credit was given to the Soviet Union's allies for this defeat as was given by popular Western historians to the Soviet army). Although the establishment of socialist regimes in Eastern Europe was not directly attributed to the Red Army, Soviet military power had liberated these countries and therefore made it possible for them to choose socialism. Whatever Stalin's private perceptions were about the balance of power, his public utterances and those of his colleagues paid fulsome tribute to the quantity and quality of Soviet military power and political authority.

The Second World War was seen to have changed the correlation of forces in several different ways. The peace which, it was hoped, would soon be signed, would need to take these changes into account and reflect

the gigantic changes in the correlation of forces between states, in the correlation of forces between democracy and reaction, in the correlation of forces between classes which have taken place in the international arena and within particular countries in the course of and as a result of the un-precedentedly extensive Second World War.

(Lemin 1946: 21–2)

Within the imperialist camp a change in the correlation of forces was perceived in favour of the United States and to the detriment of Great Britain. As far as the Soviet Union itself was concerned, it had not only won the war, but had emerged stronger in all respects. It had regained the territories it had lost when it was weak and become a great sea power (Lemin 1946: 26–7). Soviet theorists insisted, however, that the aims and principles of Soviet foreign policy remained unchanged: the Soviet Union stood, as always, for peace. All that had changed was the means of translating aims into reality.

The change was attributed, above all, to 'the undeviating growth of power and might of the Soviet state itself' (Korovin 1947: 26). It was not that the Soviet Union intended using that power. Indeed, 'the use of force had never been seen by the Soviet state as a necessary attribute of sovereign power'

(Korovin 1947: 12). But it was thought that the strength of the Soviet Union would deter the imperialist powers from attempting aggressive policies. War engendered by capitalism would no longer, therefore, be a fatal, inevitable phenomenon (as we have seen in Chapter 8, this particular formulation predated Khrushchev's historic emendations to Soviet theory by several years) because 'the great and mighty Soviet Union heads the camp of peace and democracy, because the camp of democracy has Stalin as its wise and experienced leader' (Korovin 1951: 593).

The role played by the Soviet Union in the military defeat of the fascist states, together with the fact that the war was a war of liberation from fascism, explained the alteration in the correlation between the capitalist system and the socialist system in favour of socialism (Zhdanov 1947a: 2). But other factors were thought to contribute to this change. First, the withdrawal from the capitalist system of the People's Democracies had initiated the second stage in the general crisis of capitalism (the first had occurred during the First World War, when Russia became socialist). Inevitably, the crisis would weaken capitalism and contribute to the change (Stalin 1952a: 481). Second, the development of the people's democratic regimes and the successes of the colonial national-liberation movement were, it was thought, particularly important in strengthening the peace-loving, democratic forces in the world arena (Korovin 1947: 21). The Soviet Union was no longer the isolated, sole defender of peace in the world (Korovin 1951: 593). Since these countries represented 'new links' which had fallen out of the imperialist chain, the imperialist camp had grown weaker (Korovin 1951: 590).

The People's Democracies and the national-liberation movement were considered both cause and effect in the changing correlation. On the one hand, they formed part of the detectable change in the correlation of forces. On the other hand, the change that had already taken place, particularly the growth in Soviet state power, had made them possible. Thus, Zhukov, for example, claimed that the new successes of the national-liberation movement were due to:

the changes in the correlation of class forces on the world level in favour of democracy and socialism and to the detriment of imperialism. It is the result of an increase in the power of the USSR.

(Zhukov 1949: 56)

It can be seen from this that the change in the correlation of forces was perceived in zero-sum terms. Anything which weakened capitalism contributed by definition to the strength of socialism (or the camp of democracy or of peace—the terms tended to be used interchangeably), and any increase in Soviet power implied an equal and opposite loss in the power of the capitalist camp. But the change was also seen as a continuous process which had been initiated by the Second World War, and was continuing inexorably in line with the laws of historical development (Seleznev 1951: 37).

Certain phenomena within the capitalist states were thought to contribute to the change in favour of the camp of peace. Western communist parties were increasing in strength and so were 'non-partisan democratic peace forces' who were demanding the prevention of a new war. It was feasible that war could be avoided since 'the present ratio of forces between the camp of imperialism and war and the camp of democracy and peace' made this prospect quite real (Malenkov 1952: 104). None the less, the Soviet Union would 'tirelessly . . . strengthen the defense power of the Soviet state and increase preparedness to deal any aggressors a crushing rebuff', (Malenkov 1952: 106). Warmongers were warned of the inevitable outcome of a new war:

facts show that as a result of the first world war Russia seceded from the capitalist system and that as a result of the second world war a whole series of countries in Europe and Asia seceded from the capitalist system. There is every reason to believe that a third world war would cause the collapse of the world capitalist system.

(Malenkov 1952: 106)[11]

It can thus be seen that the concept of a changing correlation of forces was prevalent after the war in the statements made by Soviet politicians and theorists. But although the term 'correlation of forces' was used widely, there was very little theoretical analysis of it or of the nature of power. It was not until the Khrushchev era, when political science and international relations became respectable areas of academic study, that both topics became the subject of serious analysis.

THE NEW CORRELATION OF FORCES

It took some time after Stalin's death for Soviet theorists to develop the self-confidence to analyse subjects which had previously been considered the domain of Party ideologists. But gradually, as Soviet political science and international relations emerged as academic disciplines, theoretical discussions about power grew increasingly sophisticated. The use of the term 'world correlation of forces' increased noticeably in the 1970s. This section considers the various causes to which the change in favour of socialism has been attributed. The constituent elements of the correlation and how they might be measured are examined before considering what the effects of the change are thought to be. In the concluding part of this section the claim by Soviet theorists that the correlation of forces is a superior theory to that of balance of power is analysed.

The causes of the change in the correlation of forces

Soviet scholars have differed slightly in what they consider the main contributing causes to the change in the correlation of forces, according to when they believe the change began. In general, however, the change is thought to be intimately tied to the general crisis of capitalism. According to Soviet theory, the first stage of the crisis occurred during the First World War, in particular in 1917. The crisis itself, and the exacerbation of socio-economic contradictions, are thought to have weakened capitalism, and consequently strengthened socialism, thus initiating a change in the correlation of forces. (Sanakoyev 1974: 46). But Russia's departure from the capitalist world system after the October Revolution is thought to have contributed even more to the general crisis of capitalism. It marked the first substantial change in the world correlation of forces:

Socialism came out into the world arena not only as an ideological and political force, but also as a state force. This led to radical changes in the

correlation of conflicting forces in the world arena in favour of socialism.
(Il'ichev *et al*. 1958: 76)

The existence of a socialist state is thought to have changed the very nature of international relations (Il'ichev *et al*. 1958: 17). States began to personify classes rather than nationalities; political, economic and ideological factors became more important in calculating the correlation of forces; and the balance of power could no longer be reduced to a balance between great powers. Smaller states began to influence international relations. Other international actors like international political movements and international organizations began to be important factors in a 'complex parallelogram' of forces (Shakhnazarov 1974: 77–82).

Despite these modifications in the nature of international relations, however, imperialism retained its dominating position (Gromyko 1962: 3). The economic and military balance still favoured it (Kortunov 1979: 38), although the balance of moral and political forces had begun to favour the Soviet state and to deter imperialism. With the revival of the Soviet economy, industrialization and the re-arming of the Soviet army, Soviet economic power and defence potential became important factors in the correlation (Sergiyev 1975: 104–5).

Soviet theorists believe that the second stage of the general crisis of capitalism occurred at the end of the Second World War and caused a more dramatic change in the correlation of forces:[12] 'One of the most significant features of the international situation was the radical change that had taken place in the balance of forces in the world arena, in favour of socialism and to the detriment of capitalism' (Ponomarev 1960: 606). Once again, it was not only the crisis which caused the change. More important was the formation of a world socialist system which changed the correlation of economic and political forces in the world arena dramatically (Gromyko 1962: 52). One of the more obvious indications of the change was the great increase in the geographic extent of socialism (Il'ichev 1958: 119). A second sign was the increased population which now lived under socialism, from 8 per cent between the wars to 35 per cent after the success of the revolution in China (Kuusinen 1961: 322). But the continual crises in all spheres of bourgeois life, as well as within the imperialist alliances, and the contradictions between imperialist states, are thought to have continued to weaken the capitalist system and strengthen socialism:

The permanent economic, political and social crises are factors which directly influence the economic potential, military might and the home and foreign policies both of imperialism as a whole and of individual countries or groups of countries in the Western world. Consequently, they decisively influence the alignment of class and political forces.

> (Sanakoyev and Kapchenko 1977: 233–4)[13]

The very reverse is claimed for socialism: close economic and political cooperation between the socialist countries and the absence of crises multiplied their power (Il'ichev *et al.* 1958: 84).

The disintegration of the colonial system marked a new stage in the general crisis of capitalism. Soviet scholars explained decolonization as being a result of the change in the correlation of forces which had already occurred:

The most favourable conditions for the development and success of the national-liberation movement were created by the new balance of forces in the international arena resulting from the defeat of German fascism and Japanese imperialism, the consolidation of the power of the Soviet Union and the emergence of the People's Democracies. . . . [T]he crisis of colonialism entered its final stage—the stage of the break-up of the colonial system.

> (Kuusinen 1961: 495)

Moreover, the fact that this particular stage of the crisis had been initiated without war was attributed to the changes which had already taken place (Gromyko 1962: 63). But decolonization also contributed to the change. It was a symptom of the continuing and accelerating disintegration of imperialism (Sanakoyev 1974: 47). Even when newly independent countries did not adopt the path of non-capitalist development, they tended to support Soviet peace policies. Thus the zone of peace was growing, shifting the correlation even further away from imperialism (Khrushchev 1959a: 7–8).

Various other positive economic, scientific and military developments within the socialist world were considered important contributory factors to the change in the correlation of forces. The fact that the socialist system would win the economic competition between socialism and capitalism was in itself symptomatic of the ineluctable nature of the changes which were taking place. More generally, the economic and cultural achievements of socialism, particularly in comparison with the bankruptcy of capitalism, were said to demonstrate to the peoples of the world that the socialist path of development was the only possible way forward. This enhanced the influence of the working people in the capitalist countries, contributing to the change in the correlation of *class* forces (Sanakoyev 1974: 49).

In other words, the correlation was seen to be not just between two blocs of countries, but between two systems. Thus it was neither confined to the increasing military and economic strength of the socialist world, nor to the increasing influence of communist parties within capitalist countries. And although the formation of new socialist states was important, the change was not entirely dependent on this. Support for Soviet peace policies by newly independent countries, or from within the capitalist world by peace-loving forces and realistically minded bourgeois politicians were also contributory factors (Sanakoyev 1974: 49).

This is not to suggest that economic and military developments have been considered unimportant in bringing about the new correlation. Amongst the achievements in the military field which have been thought particularly significant are the elimination of the American atomic monopoly in 1949, the explosion of a Soviet hydrogen bomb in the early 1950s, the launching of the first Soviet sputnik in November 1957 and, more generally, the change in the strategic balance (Butenko 1975: 346). More important than the actual achievements, however, was their recognition, in particular by the United States (Shakhnazarov 1974: 85).

One could sum up what Soviet theorists believe to have caused the change in the correlation of forces as a combination of economic, political, social and scientific and technical factors. The change was initiated by the formation of the first socialist state but only really became significant when socialism spread to a number of other countries. It was (and is) enhanced by the close cooperation of those countries and by their increasing economic and military strength. They also possess a moral force which has the power of attracting further members to the socialist system or, at least, support for its policies. Soviet military strength is thought to have contributed to the changing correlation in three ways: directly, by increasing the sum total of socialist power; and in two indirect ways, by acting as a deterrent and preventing any attempt to stem or reverse the change, and by forcing a change of attitude in some sections of the population in capitalist countries.

Other contributory factors to change are thought to have been upheavals within the imperialist world, ranging from the perpetual economic and political crises which arise from the inherent contradictions within imperialism, to the sense of self-preservation which makes ordinary people want peace and therefore support the Soviet Union. As a result, bourgeois politicians are persuaded to adopt more rational policies *vis-à-vis* the Soviet Union. In general the change has been considered historically inevitable, 'the natural process of development of society in the modern epoch' (Il'ichev *et al.* 1958: 329). Moreover, it is said to be irreversible, although the process takes place 'at different rates and in some periods may even include phenomena which contradict the general tendency' (Shakhnazarov 1974: 86).

The constituent elements and how to measure them

The constituent elements of the correlation which are identi-fied by Soviet theorists are closely related to the perceived causes of change. Because there are believed to have been a variety of causes, both temporal and occurring at different levels of domestic and international society, the elements are extremely complex. All Soviet theorists agree that the units between which there is a correlation of forces are not coter-minous with countries or alliances. Consequently, the corre-lation cannot be reduced to mere military power. As one theorist has expressed it:

In the present time the relationship of power between capitalism and socialism is produced by numerous factors, mostly economic and social. It can on no account be taken as equivalent to the sum of military power.

(*Problems of War and Peace* 1972: 198)

A second theorist has identified the elements which are correlated as economic, moral, political and military (Kapchenko 1975: 5). A third defined them as 'a combination of economic, socio-political, scientific and technical, military-strategic, ideological, international and other factors taken in their quantitative and qualitative correlation' (Butenko 1975: 345).

To complicate the issue, various states, parties and political forces are said to have united into groups or coalitions, based on common class or state interests. As a result, the factors which constitute the correlated forces consist not only of the resources of individual countries, but depend also upon 'the existence of allies, national contingents of congenial classes, mass international movements and other political forces' (Sergiyev 1975: 103). Thus in modern times the correlation of forces

> implies not only the correlation of forces between individual states, but first and foremost, the correlation of contemporary class forces, namely the international working class and the bourgeoisie, the forces of progress and those of reaction.
>
> (Sergiyev 1975: 103)

Marxism-Leninism is said to demand that '*all* the available class forces, *all* the factors, both material and moral' be considered in assessing the correlation of forces (Sanakoyev 1974: 41). This requires an analysis of 'the *class* forces and the struggle of classes . . . taking into account the *real* forces— economic, political, moral and others—which stand behind these classes' (Sanakoyev 1974: 42).

Bourgeois scholars have been taken to task by Soviet theorists for concentrating on economic and military factors alone, although there is general agreement that these factors are very important elements in the correlation, since 'economic potential and military might . . . form the material base of the policy of a state, including its foreign policy' (Sanakoyev and Kapchenko 1977: 224). As far as military power is concerned, Soviet theorists and politicians all agree that there is rough parity between American and Soviet strength. It is considered imperative to retain the equilibrium. The balance is delicate and 'even a relatively brief superiority by the United States over the Soviet Union . . . could exert a destabilizing influence on the international situation throughout the entire world' (Kulish 1972: 226).

Notwithstanding this complexity, all Soviet theorists have pointed to the importance of an objective and accurate assessment of the correlation at any particular historical period. It is essential in working out the strategy or political line of the entire international communist movement, since 'a change in the alignment of class forces can lead to a change in the general line, in the entire strategy of the world communist movement' (Zagladin 1973: 36). It is also required so that the correct tactics for a particular task are adopted (Zagladin 1973: 40–1).[14] It is considered equally important for Soviet foreign policy: a precise analysis of the current state of affairs and an objective estimation of the correlation and interaction of forces is required to elaborate long-term policy and to work out immediate practical tasks (Sergiyev 1975: 99). Moreover, it is not just the correlation between the systems that is important. The correlation within the camps needs to be studied, so that differences between groups or parties can be exploited (Zagladin 1973: 37).

Despite the intangible nature of many of the factors which are thought to contribute to the correlation of forces, Soviet theorists have always insisted that it is an objective category. It is not static, however, since it expresses changing variables (Petrenko and Popov 1981: 261). While it is relatively easy to find criteria for measuring the economic, political or military balance, Soviet scholars have admitted that the general correlation is far harder to calculate, both because of the number of factors and because of the difficulty of measuring many of them. None the less, it is vital that the assessment be made on a scientific basis. One scholar has maintained that:

An analysis of the combination of phenomena of international life in historical context and from the point of view of the laws discovered by Marxism–Leninism of social development allow an objective evaluation of the odds on the class forces opposing one another in the world arena.

(Shakhnazarov 1974: 86)

When it comes to explaining how this objective evaluation is done in practice, however, very little indication has been given.

Despite the constant stress on the scientific nature of the Marxist-Leninist approach to international relations in general, and the correlation of forces in particular, the correlation has usually been described in traditional terms. The list of important factors ranges rather more widely than the variables which a traditional Western power theorist might give, but in all other respects it bears a remarkable resemblance. There is no suggestion of any mathematical values which might be accorded to the various factors, nor is any formula offered to suggest how they might combine, or of a possible hierarchy of factors, or of the relative weight of each factor. Indeed, mere mathematical means have been said to be inadequate—what is required is a 'system of coordinates' (Shakhnazarov 1984: 18). But in essence the system of coordinates offered by this theorist comprises a list of important factors without any real indication of how it could be applied to measure the correlation in a precise way. Nor have any concrete examples been given.

Moreover, although Soviet theorists constantly emphasize the importance of methodology, there has been no detailed explanation of what methodology is used apart from the reminder that Marxist-Leninist scholars must proceed 'from an account of all factors in their dialectical interconnection and determination' (Sanakoyev 1974: 49). In fact, the accounts given by Soviet scholars usually consist of very general descriptions of the changes which have taken place in the correlation, followed by the claim that what has been given are 'some of the considerations pertaining chiefly to the methodology of determining the correlation of forces in the world' (Sanakoyev 1974: 49). The similarity to early decision-making models in Western literature is striking (e.g. Snyder *et al.* 1962). It is useful to have a checklist, but this in itself does not constitute a methodology.

In the absence of any demonstration of scientific method, it is difficult not to conclude that the correlation of forces, like power in Western literature, is assessed by Soviet theorists and decision-makers in a rather impressionistic way and that scholars may strive for objectivity, but they suffer as much risk of being subjective as they would if their starting point were some other political philosophy. Furthermore, and again this resembles the treatment of power in Western literature, what is called analysis often turns out to be description.[15]

The effects of the changing correlation of forces

Whether or not Soviet theorists succeed in measuring the correlation at any given moment, the way in which it has changed is perceived to have brought immense benefits to the international political system. Although military power has always been accorded a low priority in the lists drawn up by Soviet theorists of the causes and the constituent elements of the changing correlation of forces, many of the beneficial effects of the change have been said to be the result of Soviet power. As one Western analyst puts it:

the only acknowledgeable reasons for which the capitalists are ever said to do anything praiseworthy are that their profits will increase, that their system will be strengthened, or that they have been compelled to do so.

(Hough 1980: 527)

In modern Soviet theoretical literature and political statements, however, profit has been considered less important. Compulsion has become the standard explanation for any modification in Western behaviour since the Second World War. Moreover, most of the other postive changes which have occurred in the international system have been attributed to the *possession* of power by the Soviet Union. In other words, the deterrent nature of Soviet power has been a common theme in the writings of contemporary Soviet *mezhdunarodniki*.

As far as the general effects of the post-war change in the correlation of forces are concerned, one of the major results of the growth in socialist might has been that the Soviet Union has become sufficiently strong and authoritative to influence the nature of international relations. According to Soviet theorists, this fulfils Lenin's predictions that this would occur (Gromyko 1962: 22). Soviet policy-makers and theorists reiterate that there can no longer be a situation where one country dictates to others (see, for example, Sanakoyev 1974: 46). The entire system of international relations has been restructured as a result of the change in the world correlation of forces. The reason, it is stressed, is not that the nature of imperialism has changed, but that imperialism has been weakened ('Statement of the Conference of the Communist and Workers' Parties of Europe' 1976: 25–6). The series of treaties and agreements signed by the Soviet Union and other socialist countries with the principal capitalist states in the 1970s are thought to be the products of the new correlation. They 'amount to official recognition and establishment, in the norms and principles of international law, of the new balance of forces . . . and its establishment in the international-legal super-structure' (Sergiyev 1975: 106).

Since imperialism has not, and cannot, change its nature, imperialist aggression remains what it has always been: the greatest threat to world peace. As we have seen in Chapter 8, Soviet theorists and politicians believe implicitly that Soviet power has been responsible for the maintenance of peace. The main task from 1917 onwards has been to force peace on capitalism and compel it to abandon any attempt to destroy socialism by war. However, history has taught that aggressors cannot be appeased by concessions (Khrushchev 1961: 49). Nor are they dissuaded by 'the force of theoretical argument' (Arbatov 1973: 264). Remonstrations and invocations are insufficient to restrain imperialist aggression. The only thing that imperialists have always understood has been character-ized as 'the language of power . . . economic, political and particularly military power' (Gromyko 1962: 58). Thus military power has always been required by the Soviet state to counter aggression.

At one end of the spectrum of coercion, Soviet power has been said to render impossible any resort to political or economic pressure as a means of changing Soviet policy (Kapchenko 1978: 13). At the other end of the spectrum, the power of world socialism has prevented (and continues to prevent) thermonuclear war:

Imperialism . . . would have nothing against checking the advance of history by means of a thermonuclear war against the socialist countries. Fortunately for mankind, however, imperialism is today obliged to take into account the revolutionary forces standing opposed to it, and, first and foremost, the world socialist system. The might of socialism is a strong curb on the aggressive designs of imperialism.

(Zagladin 1973: 50)

Soviet theorists have never, however, believed in the

balance of terror. They believe that if thermonuclear war is to be averted forever, nothing short of complete and general disarmament will be sufficient. The problem is that disarmament cannot depend on 'the bourgeoisie voluntarily renouncing their weapons' (Zagladin 1973: 182). Soviet power is thought to have compelled them to enter into arms negotiations.[16] But until the negotiations are successful, the combination of Soviet deterrent power and the growth in the number of people who wish to avert war has made it possible to exclude world war from society even before the final disappearance of capitalism ('Programme of the Communist Party of the Soviet Union' 1961: 13). There is also the possibility that local wars can be avoided (Gromyko 1962: 53–4).[17] In essence, Soviet power is thought to have prevented the competition between the two systems, the main feature of modern international relations, from turning into armed conflict (Khrushchev 1961b: 42). Soviet theorists hope that it will continue to make possible the resolution of contradictions between the two systems without recourse to war (Kortunov 1979: 38).

Soviet power is credited with much more than the mere avoidance of war. In Chapter 3 it became clear that peaceful coexistence has been attributed, above all, to Soviet and socialist power and the change in the correlation of forces or, to quote Brezhnev, 'the passage from cold war . . . to détente was primarily connected with changes in the correlation of world forces' (Brezhnev 1976a: 20). One Western scholar has described the relationship between the theme of the changing correlation of forces and the theme of peaceful coexistence in Soviet perceptions as follows:

The first theme represents a historical process, the second theme a political strategy. . . . The relations between the two are such that it is the first which makes the second possible and fruitful, and the second which reinforces the tendency represented by the first.

(Bialer 1982: 243)

The way in which peaceful coexistence was made possible is sometimes described as persuasion. As a result of the new correlation of forces, 'sober-minded representatives' of the Western powers began to take a more realistic approach to international relations (Kapchenko 1975: 8). Thus 'realistically-minded bourgeois politicians' have understood that they need to create 'a stable network of international relations' (Shakhnazarov 1974: 87–8). But more often than not, the process has been depicted by Soviet writers less in terms of a dawning realization of the benefits of peaceful coexistence than as the outcome of compulsion (see, for example, Sanakoyev 1974: 43).

Another effect of the changing correlation of forces has been to assist the national-liberation movement. The very existence of the first socialist state has always been said to have inspired the movement. But the victory over Germany in the Second World war, the establishment of socialist regimes in Eastern Europe and, more importantly, Asia, and the ability of the socialist world to deter imperialist aggression have been thought to have been of particular benefit to national-liberation revolutions (Lebedev 1982: 129–30). Soviet scholars note 'an intimate connection between the growing might of the world socialist system and the successes of the revolutionary struggle for national liberation' (Zagladin 1973: 91). On the one hand, the increasing strength of socialism has been accompanied by a weakening of imperialism, making it less able to resist national liberation. On the other hand, because the contradiction between socialism and capitalism is the main feature of the present age, imperialist forces have been diverted away from the newly independent countries. Furthermore, the imperialist monopoly of international economic relations has been broken. The imperialists have thus been forced to make political and economic concessions to the less-developed countries (Gromyko and Ponomarev 1980: 273).

By the mid-1950s all these factors had caused a further stage in the general crisis of capitalism. What was unique about the third stage of the crisis was that, unlike the previous two stages, it had taken place 'not as a result of the world war, but in conditions of competition and struggle between the two systems, an increasing change in the balance of forces in favour of socialism' ('Statement of the Meeting of Representatives of the Communist and Workers' Parties' 1960: 4). There was, however, a dangerous aspect to the crisis and the change in the correlation of forces. It had provoked fear in the imperialist camp for the fate of the capitalist system and the burning hatred of international imperialist reaction towards the socialist states and towards all progressive forces of the world.

(Gromyko 1962: 52)

This fear and hatred explained why imperialists tried to prepare for and unleash a new world war against the socialist world, and more particularly, against the Soviet Union.

It should be noted there has never been any suggestion by Soviet policy-makers or theorists that the Soviet Union needs its military power in order to use it, or even to threaten to use it. On the contrary, they have always been unanimous that the use of force is alien to the nature of socialism (see, for one of the innumerable examples, Shakhnazarov 1974: 88). Power, according to Soviet theory, can be used in various ways. Imperialists use it to enslave people and unleash wars. But in the hands of socialists it can be an instrument of liberation and a means of curbing the forces of war and aggression. Thus socialism has transformed power into a positive phenomenon:

the birth of socialism . . . the development of socialist states and their community . . . has turned force as a definite socio-economic concept into an instrument of progress, into an instrument of safeguarding peace and delivering mankind from the threat of war and all kinds of military ventures.

(Sanakoyev 1974: 50)

Where socialism has been forced to use its power, it has never been for purposes of aggression, but 'exclusively with the aim of counteracting the provocative acts of imperialist circles or the intrigues of counter-revolutionary elements' (Karenin 1971: 29).

It can thus be seen that Soviet theorists have attributed to the changed and changing correlation of forces all the improvements which have been attained in international relations since 1917. Moreover, by deterring aggression, the correlation facilitates further change. It is this dynamic feature of the correlation which is thought to distinguish it from Western balance of power theories.

The correlation of forces and the balance of power
Earlier in the discussion it became clear that there is a close resemblance between many of the constituent elements which, according to Soviet theorists, make up the forces

which must be correlated, and those which Western theorists consider important in calculating the power of a state. Although Soviet theorists are universally critical of Western concepts of power and dismissive of the usefulness of the balance of power, there is, in fact, a marked similarity between the Soviet concept of correlation and the traditional Western concept of balance. Yet Soviet theorists devote considerable energy to pointing out the weaknesses and misguided nature of the Western concepts, contrasting them to the strength and usefulness of the correlation of forces.

Their most serious objection to the Western concept of power, and to the realist and idealist schools of thought, is that power theorists assume that power is the single most important factor in politics and the main means by which all social and international problems can be solved (Il'ichev *et al.* 1958: 312). They claim that Marxists have a more plural approach to the nature and use of power. As one theorist has expressed it:

Marxists do not deny that force plays a role in politics. But at the same time they emphasize that it constitutes only part of the political process, and that it is not the entire process. Let us take the example of such a thoroughly political phenomenon as a socialist revolution. If the reactionary classes actively oppose the popular uprising . . . the suppression of counter-revolution is connected with the use of force. However . . . the proletarian revolutionaries storm the old state machine not for the purpose of winning power as such, but because seizing power is the political means necessary to undertake the economic task of turning capitalist society into socialist.

(Karenin 1971: 26–7)

Western theorists have also been criticized for not distinguishing between types of power and the different ways in which power can be used. It is absurd, for example, to apply the term 'domination' to both the Soviet Union and the United States, since they use their power in completely different ways (Shakhnazarov 1984: 48). Western political realists have been accused of being subjective and ignoring the course of historical development, as well as objective economic laws and the growing role of the popular masses and the vanguard proletariat (Il'ichev *et al.* 1958: 314–25). More importantly, they distort the main essence of international relations, that is 'the historic conflict between two opposing systems, socialism and capitalism' (Petrovsky 1976: 80).

By ignoring socio-economic factors and the class nature of foreign policy, political realists give a completely false picture of the behaviour of states belonging to different social systems. While it is considered to be in the nature of imperialism to strive for world domination,

> the foreign policy of socialist states is determined by the interests of the working class and directed towards ensuring peaceful conditions for building communism, towards exposing and frustrating the actions of aggressive imperialist forces and towards defending socialism, the freedom of other peoples and peace.
>
> (Petrovsky 1976: 80–1)

Soviet *mezhdunarodniki* claim that, while recognizing that politics is a 'form of relations which is directly or indirectly connected with the manifestation of power and the wielding of power', Marxist political scientists have never, as Western sociologists have always done, ignored the class content of power (Burlatsky and Galkin 1974: 15–16). Furthermore, they have not made the mistake often found in Western theory of equating power with military and economic power (Sergiyev 1975: 100–1). Power is a far more complex category than Western theorists realize, particularly when it is applied to the study of international relations. Capitalist countries, for example, are said to have come to terms with Soviet foreign policy:

> not only because of its economic power, the might of its armed forces, but because of the unprecedented ideological, moral and political influence exerted on the peoples of the world by the successful building of socialism within the Soviet Union.
>
> (Kokoshin 1975: 17)

Because they underestimate the ideological and political factors, which in turn is the result of not understanding the socio-economic processes which take place in international relations, Western power theorists, according to their Soviet colleagues, are incapable of comprehending the real nature of power. Their definitions suffer either from 'extreme empiricism, denying the philosophical conception of power, or from abstract sociologization, removing the real content from the concept' (Burlatsky and Galkin 1974: 16).

As far as the balance of power is concerned, the major

Soviet objection to the theory has been that it is directed towards maintaining an equilibrium or the status quo in the international system (Sergiyev 1975: 102). It therefore ignores historical process. The fact that Western decision-makers share the theory, 'attests to a striving of the monopoly bourgeoisie to stem by all means the process of the revolutionary renovation of the world' (Sanakoyev 1974: 44).

Soviet theorists have been particularly critical of the idea that there has been a bipolar balance of power between the Soviet Union and the United States since the Second World War. This view is thought to reduce the entire system of international relations to Soviet–American relations and to underestimate the role played by other states, including the newly liberated states. More importantly, it depicts the main contradiction of the modern era as 'an objectively impersonal struggle of two powers for superiority over one another' and it allows political realists to come to the 'pseudo-scientific conclusion' that the Soviet Union is expansionist (Karenin 1971: 75). On the positive side, the return to balance-of-power thinking amongst Western theorists has reflected

a forced admission . . . of the new realities in world economic, military and political relations, recognition of the role and might of the world socialist system, the world revolutionary and liberation movements and the final bankruptcy of all doctrines and institutions of the Cold War.

(Sanakoyev 1974: 44)

The multipolar balance of power theory, on the other hand, is considered to be slightly more realistic. For one thing, it reflects the fact that new centres of imperialist competition have sprung up. For another it subsumes both the centrifugal tendencies which have become evident in NATO and the effect of the developing countries on the international system (Petrovsky 1976: 193–6). It is therefore thought to amount to 'indirect recognition of the great changes which have taken place in the correlation of forces in the world arena, above all the collapse of American imperialism's plan to dominate the world' (Shakhnazarov 1984: 37).

Compared to the bipolar theory, the multipolar balance is thought to have the advantage of having shifted the emphasis from military confrontation of the two systems to other factors, in particular to the contradictions between the industrially developed and developing states. But the theory of a multipolar balance is suspected of being a tactical move to deflect attention from the totally different foreign policies of socialism and capitalism, and from the radical changes which reflect the objective laws of social development. Moreover, many Western theorists have used the theory of a multipolar balance to attribute to socialism the same problems that afflict capitalism. The result is either distortion, or omission of the reasons for the socio-political changes which have taken place in the world (Petrovsky 1976: 196–9).

In the final analysis the only real differences between bipolar and multipolar concepts, according to Soviet theory, are quantitative. Western international relations specialists who postulate either version have made the same mistake of assuming 'a unitary system of international relations, irrespective of the class nature of the participating national states and other political entities . . . [and] a single set of rules . . . the priority of power' (Shakhnazarov 1984: 39). They have therefore ignored the changes wrought by socialism in the system of international relations.

Soviet objections to Western power theory are colourfully summed up in the following: 'Trying to solve international problems today on the basis of "power" theory, is more or less like trying to calculate the periodicity of the tides on the basis of the Ptolemaic system of the universe' (Shakhnazarov 1984: 45). In essence, the main objections to balance-of-power theories have been that they give a false view of the present state of international affairs and that they lead inevitably to the use of power. Moreover, the theories cannot resolve the global problems which now confront mankind. The theory of the correlation of forces, on the other hand, has been called 'the key to understanding interrelations on the world arena', particularly if it is seen as the application of the class struggle to the sphere of international life, if force is understood to be more than military power and if 'all the contributing factors are taken and assessed in all their dynamism and with all their contradictions' (Burlatsky and Galkin 1974: 260). But the underlying cause of Soviet criticism of balance of power theory is that it posits equilibrium as the ideal state of the international system. It is, therefore, incompatible with a theory that postulates ineluctable and continuing change.

CONCLUSION

Western criticisms of Soviet theory of power and the correlation of forces are legion. It has been maintained by two critics of Soviet international relations theory, for example, that Marxism-Leninism is, above all, about power:

For Marxist-Leninists it is not a question of theory *or* power: for them that theory is most truly Marxist which contributes most to the acquisition and maintenance of power and 'national interests'; ideology, in other words, is neither an apology nor a disguise for power politics. Marxism-Leninist [sic] ideology is all about power politics.

(Kubálková and Cruickshank 1980: 292)

An analogous view implies that the major ideological change in Soviet theory has been the loss of the elements of social and economic reform. In its modern variant 'communism . . . has no social or economic postulates save as they are considered the means of achieving and perpetuating political power' (Ulam 1952: 230). A third view claims that it is not *political* power which is important in contemporary Soviet doctrine, but physical power and its effective organization (Mitchell 1982: 122).

Similar faults have been found in the theory of the correlation of forces. It has been called an elegant theory in that it

has provided a conceptually flexible tool enabling its practitioners to define, pursue and rationalize their policies simultaneously at the complementary levels of ideology and power politics . . . Managing the correlation . . . puts a premium on seizing every possible opportunity to adjust the system— opportunism is built into the concept.

(Pick 1981: 4)

More negatively, it has been accused of being 'dynamic and manipulative, as much a definition of power as a calculus for the application of power' (Dawisha and Dawisha 1982: 149). It has also been implied that it is devious, in that 'it is designed not so much for methodological and cognitive clarity as to send out conflicting signals to separate audiences' (Aspaturian 1980: 12). Despite their insistence that the correlation is between class forces and not between military forces, Soviet theorists are said still 'to regard the employment of military resources and power as the central and even the ultimate factor of international relations' (Bialer 1982: 258). There are some grounds for these criticisms, but they have little to do with the theory itself. None the less the theory of the correlation of forces does have certain shortcomings.

What must be in doubt is, first, the extent to which the correlation of forces differs from balance of power theory and therefore avoids the weaknesses of that theory. Second, there is room for considerable scepticism about the claim that the correlation can be measured. If it cannot, is it really more than a loosely descriptive metaphor (in much the same way that the metaphor of a balance is used)? Third, and this is perhaps the most important criticism in terms of its possible usefulness, the extent to which the theory of a changing correlation of forces reflects the present state of affairs is open to question. If it diverges from reality, does this mean that it functions as a programmatic statement about the future, a modern version of the inevitable international revolution rather than as the theory upon which Soviet foreign policy is based?

There are two obvious similarities between balance of power and correlation of forces. For one thing, both are based on a zero-sum concept of power. For another, they define the components of power in very similar ways. But these are the very features which call into question the usefulness of balance of power, and they must also cast doubt on the theory of the correlation of forces. Even if one accepts the questionable assumption that all politics, including international politics, is motivated by the search for and retention of power, it is clearly not (and never has been) the case that the loss of power by one side means the gain by the other of an equal amount of power, or *vice versa*. In terms of military power, the relative advantage of one side may be increased or decreased by the gain or loss of military power on the other side, but in an age of nuclear overkill this is scarcely relevant. In any case, neither balance of power nor correlation of forces theorists claim that the military factor subsumes the entire theory and, as we have seen, Soviet theorists insist that there is, and needs to be, strategic parity.

With regard to all other components of power, the zero-sum concept clearly does not apply—a fall in the morale of the Western bourgeoisie, for example, is unlikely to cause an equal and opposite rise in socialist morale, and a rise in the

Soviet standard of living does not detract from capitalist wealth. The perceived final capitalist crisis may cause a change in the correlation of forces in favour of socialism, but it is unlikely to do so before the very last stage of that crisis, unless the absolute number of socialists and their political influence within capitalist society increase and unless those socialists are sympathetic to Soviet socialism rather than committed to another variant. Empirical evidence suggests that far from this being the case, there has been a shift to the right in capitalist countries and that even in those countries where socialist parties are influential, they tend to be independent (Halliday 1983: 165–71).

As far as the second similarity is concerned, that is the components which comprise the balance or correlation, many of them are intangible and therefore not susceptible to measurement. As both the American experience in Vietnam and the Soviet position in Afghanistan suggest, measuring what can be measured may give a very false picture. If measurement is impossible or even misleading, it is difficult to see that either theory can be called accurate (far less scientific), or that either can safely be used as a guide to policy. In so far as the theory of the correlation of forces resembles balance of power, therefore, it suffers from similar shortcomings.

But the two theories are also different in at least two important respects. First, the balance of power is based on the premise that the ideal state of the international system is equilibrium (though not necessarily, despite Soviet charges, the existing status quo). The correlation of forces, on the other hand, postulates continual change until the desirable end state—a stateless socialist world—has been reached.[18] But it goes even further than this. It claims that the correlation began to change after 1917, that the process accelerated in 1945 and that it has been continuing.[19] Moreover, it is a change that can both be observed and measured.

It is certainly true that the formation of the first socialist state changed the balance and that the change was particularly marked after 1945. But although there has been an increase in the number of socialist and socialist-oriented states in the last ten years, with a consequent enlargement of the geographic extent of socialism and of the socialist population, it is debatable whether the new socialist states have added very much to the other components of the correlation. They are economically underdeveloped and, in the case of Afghanistan at least, unstable. Moreover, their conversion was preceded by the far more significant defection of China.[20] There is thus little superficial evidence to support the claim that the correlation has continued to change in favour of socialism. Since Soviet theory does not allow for the export of revolution (and disclaims the existence of, or wish for, military superiority), the theory that the change will continue seems to be based more on historical determinism than on hard fact. In other words, the correlation is believed to have changed and to be certain to continue changing because it is an historically inevitable feature of development that this will occur.[21]

It could be argued that Soviet scholars do not claim that the change will occur by linear progression. There may be reverses, for example, and there are 'intermediate sections' of class allies which can vacillate and thus cause the correlation to move first in one direction and then back, at least temporarily (Zagladin 1973: 41). But the overall trend is said to be in the direction of socialism. Moreover, it is never explicitly suggested that a temporary reversal occurred as a result of the Sino-Soviet split. And in this respect the theory seems to take little account of the present situation. It may, of course, still be a guide to action, but if it does not start from a dispassionate assessment of the present state of affairs, it is unlikely to prove a reliable guide.

The second major difference between balance of power and correlation of forces is that balance of power theorists usually use the state as the unit of analysis and compare their national attributes. The correlation of forces, on the other hand, concerns class attributes as well as state attributes. This is why Soviet theorists can claim both military parity and the desire to retain strategic equilibrium and, at the same time, insist that the correlation is changing in their favour. It has already been pointed out that it is debatable whether changes within the capitalist world necessarily benefit socialism. There is, however, another problem. If state attributes are difficult to assess accurately (as Soviet theorists themselves admit), class attributes are almost impossible to pin down. It can, therefore, be no more than an article of faith that the correlation of class forces is changing in favour of socialism. And if that is so, the claim that it is a more accurate model than balance of power is dubious. It is difficult, therefore, not to conclude that the differences between the two theories do not save the correlation of forces from the weaknesses of balance of power.

If class attributes are even more difficult to pin down than state attributes, if there are intermediate forces which vacillate, and if various categories change in importance depending on time and circumstance, then there must be considerable scepticism about the claim that the correlation of forces can really be measured. It may be true, as Soviet theorists maintain, that it is an objective category. But Soviet theorists also point to the importance of subjective factors. They do not indicate how the subjective factors are to be evaluated and nor, as we have seen, do they demonstrate how the measurement might be done. Although most Soviet theorists insist that the correlation of forces is a scientific category and that it can be and is accurately measured, the following, more modest view of the potential usefulness of systems analysis seems to be more likely to reflect the true stage of development of the use of measurement in Soviet political theory:

The identification and analysis from a Marxist viewpoint of the impulses which go from the environment to the system of international relations and back lays the ground for formalizing the process of their interaction as a prerequisite for the wider use of mathematical methods, constructing strict models of the system and gradually moving from qualitative description to quantitative.

(Burlatsky and Galkin 1974: 264)

This was, of course, written more than a decade ago. But it is difficult not to believe that if the move had already been made to quantitative studies of the correlation of forces, there would be more convincing evidence of this in modern literature.

In the absence of accurate measurement, it is open to question whether the correlation of forces is a superior and more reliable theory than balance of power. It must, it would seem, function in very much the same way that balance of theory functions—as a rather loose metaphor of the changing international system, the changes being assessed in an impressionistic and intuitive way. Of course, the point must be made that even as a metaphor, it can still serve as a guide to action. There are many who would argue that this is how all policy is made (or even that this is how the best policy is made). And it could also, as power theory often does, act as a self-fulfilling prophecy (although its function in this respect is limited by the insistence that strategic equilibrium is the ultimate aim of Soviet military policy and that revolution is not for export). The point here, however, is not whether social science can be scientific or whether science can or should serve politics. It is that Soviet theorists claim that it does. But there is no evidence to suggest that a Soviet foreign policy based on the theory of correlation of forces is any more scientific than a Western policy based on balance of power.

NOTES

1. Ashley's ideas were based on the concept of lateral pressure, proposed by Choucri and North. See Choucri and North (1975).
2. I mean to distinguish here between books on Soviet foreign policy which are overtly ideological, whose authors believe *a priori* that Soviet policy is aggressive and expansionist and that communism is spreading and inherently evil, and those books and authors which, though they may have a latent ideology, do not prejudge Soviet behaviour but aspire to understand and explain it.
3. See, for example, Kokoshin (1975); Petrovsky (1976); Chirkin (1980); Shakhnazarov (1984), to mention just a few.
4. Marantz (1982) believes that one of the changes wrought by Khrushchev was a shift from zero-sum thinking to a more flexible stance which allowed for compromise and concessions in East–West relations. While there clearly was a change in the Soviet negotiating posture, power and the correlation of forces continued to be perceived in zero-sum terms.
5. See, for example, Karenin (1971). The title of his book could be translated as 'The Philosophy of Political Coercion' or 'The Philosophy of Political Violence', but in fact 'The Philosophy of Political Power' makes far more sense since it is a critique of the Western school of political realism. Of course, the English word power is also used in more than one sense and this gives Russian writers equal difficulty. Karenin uses not only *vlast'* and *sila*, but also *mogushchestvo* and *moshch* (both meaning might) to explain what political realists mean by power. Still not sure that his readers will understand the concept,

he sometimes simply resorts to using the English word 'power' in inverted commas (Karenin 1971: 30). For a discussion of the polysemy of power, see Burlatsky and Galkin (1974: 15–20).

6. See Wright Mills (1963: 13) on the 'historically provincial' nature of reflective men which leads Western social scientists to deny the influence of Marxism on their disciplines and Soviet social scientists to deny it equally vehemently.

7. Kolakowski accused Lenin of ignoring economic ripeness in his pre-occupation with the existence of revolutionary situations and power (Kolakowski 1978: vol. 2: 494–5). But in one sense the whole of 'Imperialism' was concerned with the economic ripeness of the world of monopoly capitalism. Moreover, in 'War and Revolution' he maintained that the rule of capitalism would end because the whole course of economic development had led to its end (Lenin 1917i: 417).

8. Some Western theorists believe that it was the doctrine of socialism in one country which allowed power to become the prime component of Soviet Marxist thinking and practice. Mayer, for example, maintained that 'the new doctrine of "socialism in one country" permitted political theory to coincide with power considerations, and thus made possible its use in the future development of the USSR' (Mayer 1968: 21).

9. The experience of Varga, of course, proved that analyses which did not endorse Stalin's ready-made solutions would not be acceptable (see Ch. 4, n. 25).

10. Deane, on the other hand, identified three stages in the change in the correlation of forces in Soviet writing: the first in 1917, the second in 1945 and the third in 1969/70, when the Soviet Union achieved rough parity (Deane 1976: 630). As will be seen in the next section, the first two stages can easily be documented in Soviet sources. However, there are several intervening points of change prior to 1969/70 and Soviet authors usually point to the mid-1950s as the beginning of the third stage in the crisis of capitalism, and therefore of the change in the correlation. As far as 1969/70 is concerned, it was not only the *achievement* of parity that was important but also the *recognition* by others, particularly the United States, that it had been achieved.

11. Both war and peace were predicted to cause the collapse of capitalism. Peace was to be preferred, obviously, because there would be less suffering. But at this stage peace was proposed for its own sake, rather than because it would bring about socialism. See Chapter 8.

12. Some Soviet theorists maintained that the existence of the Soviet Union began to change the nature of international relations immediately after 1917, but there was no real change in the correlation of forces until the end of the Second World War. See, for example, Butenko (1975: 336). Others, including those quoted in the preceding section, have claimed that change began immediately after the October Revolution.

13. The permanent crises within the capitalist system and the uneven development which is a feature of imperialism are thought to have led to a change in the correlation of forces within the capitalist system as

well. After the war, for example, Germany and Japan were insignificant, Britain and France had been seriously weakened and the United States emerged as the dominant capitalist power (Kuusinen 1961: 323). For a discussion of the post-war changes in the correlation of forces within the imperialist world, see Butenko (1975: 337–45). Soviet theorists contend that the intra-imperialist correlation has changed in recent years. American dominance has begun to be challenged both because it is less powerful and because it has lost moral authority (Shakhnazarov 1984: 93).

14. For the distinction between strategy and tactics, see Chapter 8, n. 1. Strategy requires 'due account of the alignment and distribution of class forces within a particular country or on the world scene' (Zagladin 1973: 33), while tactics require 'an appraisal of the changes in the alignment of class forces' (Zagladin 1973: 40).

15. The intention here is not to imply that either the correlation of forces or the balance of power can be measured with scientific precision and that what is in question is the standard of Western or Soviet scholarship. Indeed, it is precisely because it is so difficult to define and measure the numerous unpredictable, ineffable and intangible elements of power that the concept is not particularly useful in considering political events either in the domestic polity, or in the international system. For a Western discussion of the Western literature on power, see de Reuck (1985). A Soviet comparison of Western power models and the Soviet model of the correlation of forces can be found in Shakhnazarov (1984: 33–63). On using Western techniques to measure Soviet political power, see Hough (1977, Ch. 10).

16. For a discussion of the dangers of the balance of terror and the need for arms control, see Shakhnazarov (1984: 103–16). Soviet theorists and politicians insist that the change in the correlation of forces does not mean the superiority of Soviet military power. The emphasis in discussions of the strategic balance is on parity and equilibrium and the importance of maintaining both. See, for example, Brezhnev (1976b, 1981).

17. Although Gromyko maintained in 1962 that the new correlation of forces could deter local wars, later some doubt was expressed. As we have seen in Chapters 6 and 8, the shift away from claiming that *all* wars could be avoided was originally made in an attempt to placate Chinese criticisms of the theory that war was no longer inevitable. But presumably the empirical evidence of innumerable local wars, some of them remote from imperialist involvement, also contributed.

18. It should be noted that even here there is a similarity, in that both theories are normative, positing desirable end states.

19. It is ironic (but also almost self-evident) that most credence is given to the claim that the correlation of forces is changing inexorably in favour of socialism by Western politicians and theorists who are least sympathetic to the Soviet Union and most fearful of the Soviet threat, expanding communism and Soviet aggression. They also tend to agree most closely with the Soviet view of the components of the correlation.

Any Third World radical movement, for example, is automatically considered a Soviet client (and often is made one by self-fulfilling prophecy and policy). Similarly, the Western peace movement is considered treacherous precisely because it is thought to contribute to the change in favour of socialism.

20. See Halliday (1983). The thorniest question in the whole theory of the correlation of forces is where Soviet theorists 'weigh' China. Mitchell maintained that China has been classified as part of the imperialist camp since 1971 (Mitchell 1982: 39–47). But the most frequent tendency seems to be simply to omit it from the correlation of forces, while criticizing it for its pro-capitalist policies.

21. Steele quotes Brezhnev asking Carter 'Why pin on the Soviet Union the responsibility for the objective course of history and, moreover, use this as a pretext for worsening our relations?' (Steele 1983: 62).

10 Gorbachev and the New Political Thinking

In March 1985 Gorbachev was elected to the position of General Secretary of the CPSU. He immediately launched reforms aimed at eliminating corruption and overcoming the profound malaise which seemed to have enveloped Soviet society. His programme ranged from domestic economic and political policies to Soviet foreign policy. More important for the subject matter of this book, it included Marxist-Leninist theory and the Soviet theory of international politics.

Each aspect of Gorbachev's reform acquired a term which became a shorthand symbol of his determination and that of most of his colleagues to revitalize Soviet society. In the realm of the economy, the slogan was *uskorenie* (acceleration). With regard to both politics and economics, the term *perestroika* (reconstruction) was applied. *Glasnost'* (openness) became the catchword for the officially condoned more open expression of opinion that applied not only to the social and cultural spheres, but also to current economic and political performance. *Glasnost'*, it was hoped, would counteract corruption and bureaucratic malfunction. A less elliptical term referred to the reform of Soviet foreign policy. It was called the 'new political thinking' (*novoe politicheskoe myshlenie*).

The reform of Soviet foreign policy consisted of four elements: a thorough overhaul of personnel; the adoption of a more flexible and sophisticated diplomatic style; the promotion of more pragmatic policies; and the espousal of new theoretical principles together with an agenda for their further elaboration. Although the first three elements began quite

soon to reflect the new theoretical principles, it is the principles themselves and the projected agenda for the study of
international relations theory which form the subject of this
chapter.[1]

It should be stressed that although the authorship of the
'new political thinking' is frequently attributed to Gorbachev,
the ideas it subsumes had begun to be expressed by academics
from 1983 onwards. Indeed, with regard to Soviet thinking
about the Third World, the re-examination of previous
assumptions had begun even before Brezhnev's death (see,
for example the analyses in Hough: 1986; Valkenier: 1986). In
other words, in the same way that Khrushchev's ideological
revisions can be traced back to the last years of Stalin's life,
many of the constituent elements of the 'new political
thinking' can be found in the scholarly literature published
before Gorbachev became General Secretary of the CPSU.
This is not to discredit Gorbachev or his theoretical acumen,
but to indicate that the 'new political thinking' is more than an
example of Gorbachev's 'spontaneous, untested dreams'
(Glickham 1986: 10).

The 'new political thinking' applies, first and foremost, to
Soviet-American relations and, in particular, to the strategic
and conventional arms balance. In terms of the way in which
Soviet theory has been subdivided in the preceding chapters,
it relates most directly to relations with capitalist states and to
Soviet theory about war and peace. But some of the new
concepts have been extended to Soviet relations with other
countries, particularly LDCs. And although the 'new political
thinking' does not relate directly to relations amongst socialist
states, other members of the socialist commonwealth have
been encouraged to adopt reform programmes of their own,
while participating in a new plan for integrating their tech-
nologies. Moreover, the published theoretical discussions
about inter-socialist relations indicate that here, too, 'new
political thinking' is encouraged. Finally, the 'new political
thinking' seems to have relegated the concept of a changing
correlation of forces to a subsidiary place in the theoretical
agenda.

In general, therefore, the 'new political thinking' has
created an ambience conducive to debate and to a re-examination of the fundamental premises of Soviet international

relations theory. Although it is too soon to judge what the final result of this questioning will be, a brief look at the effect of the 'new political thinking' on relations between socialism and capitalism, Soviet Third World theory, relations among socialists, and Soviet thinking about war and peace will indicate what the theoretical priorities are of the new Soviet leadership.

RELATIONS BETWEEN SOCIALIST AND CAPITALIST STATES

The new edition of the Programme of the Communist Party of the Soviet Union (published in draft form at the end of October 1985 and adopted by the Twenty Seventh Congress of the CPSU in February-March 1986) is the most detailed official statement of Soviet thinking about the international system and the place of the Soviet Union within it which has appeared since Brezhnev's death. Three features of the new Programme deserve mention. First, although it is called a new edition, it has little in common with the previous Party Programme, which was adopted in 1961 (translated in Saikowski and Gruliow 1962) and was very much the product of Khrushchev's euphoric optimism about the future of socialism. Second, judging by the length of time that previous Party Programmes have been considered operative, the new Programme will probably serve as the authoritative statement of the Soviet view of the world for a number of years.[2] The third interesting feature is that there are striking discontinuities between the first, more general, theoretical section of the Programme and the third section which deals in detail with Soviet foreign policy. There are few easily discernible changes from previous formulations in the first rather orthodox section. In the foreign policy section, however, the tone is pragmatic, the outlines of the 'new political thinking' can be discerned and there are practical proposals for improving détente and ensuring international security. These discontinuities may merely reflect the multi-authored nature of the Programme, but they are probably indicative, in the words of one Western analyst, of 'the prevailing ideological confusion' (Shenfield 1987: 80).

In the first part of the Programme familiar formulae are applied to the capitalist world; ever shrinking, it is experiencing profound crisis. Although domestic class struggle has extracted improved work conditions, wages and social security, 'the dialectic of development is such that the very means which capitalism uses to strengthen its positions, inevitably lead to the sharpening of its internal contradictions' ('Programme of the Communist Party of the Soviet Union: New edition' 1986 [Programme 1986]: 4). The idea that the changing correlation of forces compels the capitalist world to accept peaceful coexistence has given way, however, to the logic of nuclear war: given the extreme danger of nuclear war, peaceful coexistence is the only rational or possible form that relations between socialism and capitalism can take. This logic had been set out dramatically by a prominent theorist well before the new programme was published: 'In a situation where the antithesis of peace has become not simply war but a total catastrophe which threatens the survival of the entire human race . . ., [i]n any scale of priorities [peace] must, of course, take first place' (Shakhnazarov 1984a: 63–4).

The tasks of Soviet foreign policy are set out in the third section of the Programme. As far as socialist-capitalist relations are concerned, the common interest of all nations (which is recognized as different from, and implicitly more important than, individual national interests) demands peaceful coexistence between the two systems. Here, again, the dilemma for capitalists is no longer phrased in terms of the changing correlation of forces (nor, as in the earlier, Leninist formulation, does the business acumen of capitalists explain coexistence). Peaceful coexistence is dictated by survival, which is the dominant value for both social systems. It has become an 'historical necessity' (Butenko 1987: 156).

The definition of peaceful coexistence given in the new Programme does not, on the face of it, differ markedly from previous descriptions. Moreover, domestic class struggle within the capitalist system is not depicted here or in other contemporary discussions as incompatible with peaceful coexistence. None the less, Soviet scholars claim that the concept has been expanded substantively to include an indication of how the CPSU envisages the world in a period of 'real, stable peaceful coexistence', when 'good neigh-

bourliness and cooperation prevail, there are broad ex-
changes to the benefit of all nations of the achievements of
science and technology, and of cultural values' (Zagladin
1986: 14). There is some evidence that the theoretical
problem of explaining how peaceful coexistence promotes
revolutionary change has been recognized. There has, for
example, been a call for Marxist-Leninist theoretical work
'applicable to the conditions of the nuclear age' on revolutionary processes and social progress (Dobrynin 1986: 30 and
see the analysis in Shenfield 1987). The relationship between
peaceful coexistence and social progress has been described as
the most complex problem of the nuclear age (Shakhnazarov
1984a). Although the communist movement has always accorded higher priority to avoiding nuclear war than to revolutionary change, 'a careful analysis would probably show that
in some cases due account has not been taken of the acuteness
of the international situation' (Shakhnazarov 1984a: 70). One
prominent journalist maintained that the best maxim for the
nuclear age was the old and banal 'live and let live' (Bovin
1986: 122).

There is a related change in Soviet perceptions of the role of
ideology. As we have seen in Chapter 3, the ideological
struggle has always been considered an integral part of
peaceful coexistence. According to the new Programme,
however, ideological conflict between the two systems should
not be extended to the sphere of peaceful coexistence (Programme 1986: 7). This was probably a response to the harsh
rhetoric and heightened ideological manifestations of the
Reagan administration (see Ch. 3, n. 14). But it has been
accompanied by the recognition that 'psychological war' is but
one step away from hot war (Shakhnazarov 1984a: 72).

The practical proposals for improving détente which were
incorporated into the Party Programme have been reiterated
more forcefully and in greater detail by Gorbachev (Gorbachev 1986 and subsequent speeches). Gorbachev has drawn
particular attention to the urgent common problems facing
mankind, and to the fact that 'together with competition and
conflict between the two systems there is also an increasing
tendency toward the interdependence of all the states in the
world community' (Gorbachev 1986: 3). The common
interests shared by all states have become a prominent theme

in Soviet writing about international relations (see, for example, Bovin 1986: 123).[3] There are two aspects to the new focus on common interests: the view that certain global problems can only be resolved by cooperation, and the related concept of interdependence. Amongst the former are problems of war and peace, ecological problems including the increasing economic gap between developed and developing countries, the peaceful use of outer space and problems connected with modernization and development. Although Soviet theorists have previously recognized that global problems exist (see, for example, Shakhnazarov 1984: Ch. 5), the suggestion that socialism shares the responsibility for causing them and therefore for resolving them (Zagladin 1986) is, essentially, a feature of post-Brezhnev writing.

The term interdependence is used to refer to the inter-relatedness of countries generally and of various aspects of their relations. When applied to global problems, it concerns both the way they spread beyond national boundaries and the way one global problem engenders others. This seems to be the meaning Gorbachev attached to the term in the excerpt from his political report to the Twenty Seventh Congress cited above. It is also the idea behind his call for the creation of a system of international security which would include military security, political measures to resolve conflict and increase mutual trust, a system of economic security, and increased cooperation in the sphere of humanitarian concerns (Gorbachev 1986: 8–9).[4]

Specialist articles published after the Twenty Seventh Congress have suggested avenues for useful future research. As far as capitalism itself is concerned, scholars have been advised to examine the contradictions between the 'centre' of the capitalist world economy and its 'periphery' (terms which have long been used by dependency theorists and others in the West), to explain not only the increasing gap between the developed and the underdeveloped countries but also the phenomenon of the newly industrializing nations of the periphery (Primakov 1986: 8–9). It has also been suggested that Soviet theorists have paid too little attention to the fact that the contradictions within capitalism have served as a source of development, provoking, for example, a new phase in the scientific-technical revolution. The capacity of modern capitalism to innovate and adapt requires study (Abalkin 1985). New technology and phenomena like 'transnational monopoly capital' may lead to a new phase of capitalism (Primakov 1986: 8). Imperialism remains the final *stage* (*stadiya*) of capitalism but within that stage, various successive phases (*etapy*) can be differentiated (Abalkin 1985: 67). The implication is that Lenin's theory of imperialism will be reinterpreted.

THE THIRD WORLD

As we have seen in Chapter 5, an increasing disillusion both with the rate at which LDCs were choosing a non-capitalist path of development, and with the lack of economic and political progress in those that had chosen such a path was noticeable in the work of Soviet academics from the mid 1970s onwards. Internal rebellions (whether or not aided from outside) and the economic plight of the socialist-oriented states (most dramatically of Ethiopia) served to exacerbate the disappointment that socialist orientation was not necessarily irreversible.

The disillusion is reflected in the new Party Programme. Although verbal support is promised to socialist-oriented states and the Soviet Union will 'do what it can' to aid their economic and cultural development (Programme 1986: 7),[5] cooperative relations will also be established with capitalist developing states. The low priority of relations with the LDCs and the national-liberation movement is evident in the little attention paid to the Third World by Gorbachev in his report to the Twenty Seventh Congress (Gorbachev 1986: 8).

The re-examination of previous Soviet assumptions about economic development in the LDCs which preceded the publication of the new edition of the Party Programme is well chronicled in the Western specialist literature (see, for example, Fukuyama 1985, 1986; Hough 1986; Valkenier 1983, 1986). A recent article by a well known Soviet specialist on the Third World, Georgy Mirsky, provides an excellent summary of past misapprehensions and indicates the present direction of Soviet research on the Third World (Mirsky 1987). Mirsky points out that early Soviet assumptions that either the proletariat or the national bourgeoisie would naturally take political power in the ex-colonies ignored the absence of either class in most LDCs. Soviet scholars gradually began to understand the influence and significance of the intermediate strata: the intelligentsia, the bureaucracy, the army. But it took them longer to appreciate that traditional factors like non-class social institutions, tribalism, and deep-rooted ethnic, religious, caste and clan divisions pushed class contradictions into the background.

Mirsky now believes that LDCs were never really faced with a choice between capitalist or non-capitalist development. By the time they achieved independence, various kinds of socio-economic relations which would lead inevitably to capitalism had already sprung up spontaneously. Political leaders could have consciously chosen to establish a political superstructure to overcome this spontaneous development. In fact, it was only when the private sector proved incapable of dealing with the problems of development that a number of countries (Egypt, Algeria, Ghana, Guinea, Mali, Congo, Somalia, Tanzania, Syria, Iraq, Burma) opted for socialist orientation. Mirsky refers to these countries as 'first generation socialist-oriented states' (Mirsky 1987: 72).

Two Leninist concepts were revived by Soviet scholars in their optimism that more LDCs would choose the non-capitalist path of development: first, the possibility that national-liberation revolutions would 'grow over' into socialist revolutions and second, the idea that with the aid of the proletariat of the advanced countries, underdeveloped countries could skip capitalism and move straight to socialism via a Soviet system (Mirsky 1987: 76). It was thought that the support of the victorious proletariat of the socialist countries would compensate for the absence or weakness of an indigenous proletariat. But Mirsky points out that Soviet scholars misunderstood and often misquoted Lenin in two ways. First, in talking of aid from the proletariat of the 'advanced' countries, Lenin was referring to the proletariat of the colonial powers and hypothesizing about the situation after a future successful socialist revolution in Europe. In fact, it was only in Russia that a victorious proletariat emerged to lead the underdeveloped periphery of the empire to socialism. The first generation socialist-oriented states gained independence

from colonial empires in which there was no victorious proletariat. They remained part of the world capitalist economy.
Most of their credits came from the West and they traded
primarily with their former metropolitan countries. Credits
and trade were accompanied by Western, capitalist values.
Socialist aid was primarily political and although it served to
weaken capitalist influence, it could not entirely neutralize it.
Furthermore, the private sector dominated small scale production, agriculture, trade and the service industry, giving
birth to a petty bourgeois peasantry and a new urban bour-
goeisie. Not surprisingly, it proved well nigh impossible in
those circumstances for the socialist superstructure to bring
about the necessary changes in the economic base.

The private sector had made similar gains in the Soviet
Union during the New Economic Policy in the 1920s. But
there was no external capitalist influence on Russia. Moreover, the gains were attenuated by the existence of a dictatorship of the proletariat. This leads to the second way in which
Mirsky believes that modern Soviet theorists have, until
recently, misunderstood Lenin. Lenin envisaged national-
liberation revolution 'growing over' to socialism via a Soviet
system. In other words, the gains made by the private sector
could be neutralized by a Soviet system or, more broadly, 'by
national democratic power based on the principles of scientific socialism which . . . leads the revolution from below and
not merely from above' (Mirsky 1987: 77). But few first generation socialist-oriented states enjoyed this advantage. As a
result, the masses did not develop a revolutionary consciousness, capitalist relations increased in the base of society and
the socialist oriented superstructure rested entirely on
political will (often the will of a single leader). When that will
weakened, or when the leader disappeared, socialist orientation could be reversed with little or no opposition (as
happened in Ghana, Mali and Egypt). Socialist orientation
has proved more resilient only in those countries where there
is a vanguard party based ideologically and theoretically on
scientific socialism (Mirsky 1987: 78).

Amongst the socialist-oriented states, Mirsky distinguishes
a 'national democratic' subgroup (he gives as examples
Angola, Mozambique, Congo, Ethiopia and South Yemen)
in which there are vanguard parties based on scientific

socialism. In those countries the political superstructure is qualitatively different from the superstructure of first generation socialist-oriented states. A new, revolutionary state apparatus controls capitalist tendencies and actively cooperates with socialist countries. A combination of factors made this possible. From the very beginning of the revolution these states contained a leading nucleus of revolutionaries predisposed to accepting the ideology of scientific socialism. At decisive moments this nucleus could rely on the masses. Moreover, when these countries became independent, their level of economic development was particularly low. As a result capitalist relations and a bourgeois or petty bourgeois ideology were not widespread within these societies (Mirsky 1987: 78–9). In other words, national democratic states tend to be extremely poor and backward, but they enjoy good prospects for the future because they have vanguard parties.

In recent years other Soviet specialists have been less optimistic about socialist-oriented vanguard parties, pointing, first, to the gap between socialist orientation and socialism, and second, to the danger that 'declarative radicalism' may exacerbate already unstable conditions by provoking internal opposition (Ul'yanovsky 1984: 27 and see the discussion in Fukuyama 1985). These specialists believe that the gap between the ruling group and the masses often makes effective communication difficult. As a result, vanguard parties cannot always rely on the masses (see, for example, Butenko 1982, cited together with other examples in Valkenier 1986). Perhaps the most striking evidence of growing disillusion with the efficacy of vanguard parties is the encouragement given to the Afghan regime to seek popular legitimacy by including non-Party figures in the government.

Mirsky's article ends with the question 'whither the Third World'? Most Third World countries will remain capitalist. Acceptance of this fact is, in itself, symptomatic of 'new political thinking' in Soviet Third World theory. But the present acceptability of previously criticized analyses of Third World capitalism is even more significant, indicating, as one Western specialist points out, 'the degree to which the deterministic Marxist interpretation of history is being qualified with factors that belie the rigid socioeconomic scheme' (Valkenier 1986: 427). Third World capitalism is now seen to be an unorthodox, 'Eastern' variant, different from European, Russian or Japanese capitalism (Mirsky 1987, quoting extensively from Simoniya's contribution to Reisner and Simoniya 1984). Diverse political superstructures can be found, ranging from monarchies (as in Saudi Arabia) to fundamentalist Islamic republics (as in Iran). But however unorthodox, Eastern capitalism causes the same ills in Third World society that the traditional form does in developed countries. Why, then, will the Third World remain predominantly capitalist? The reasons are partly internal: the passivity of the peasantry, the absence of a proletarian class consciousness, and the fact that national, ethnic and religious problems tend to override class contradictions. But there is also an important external reason: the poor economic and social achievements of the socialist-oriented states do not offer a convincing alternative model (Mirsky 1987: 75).

Despite Mirsky's optimistic assessment of the efficacy of vanguard parties in some socialist-oriented states, he is gloomy about the prospects for socialist orientation. Socialist-oriented states are prey to dangerous negative tendencies. Traditional values and divisions are still prevalent. Bad management, bureaucratism, low productivity and profitability, inadequate food supplies and a low standard of living are common. The socialist path of development is therefore likely to be extremely difficult (Mirsky 1987: 79).

There are indications that although the re-examination of the premises underlying Soviet Third World theory predates the 'new political thinking', *glasnost'* is making it easier for scholars to discard previous shibboleths. But the 'new political thinking' also relates more directly to Third World issues. As we have seen, the problems of underdevelopment have been categorized as one of the urgent global issues requiring both study and urgent international solutions (Zagladin 1986: 4). And although it is unlikely that Gorbachev's proposal that superpowers redirect money saved on arms expenditures to the Third World (see, for example, Gorbachev 1986: 8) will come to anything (or, if it does, that it will amount to enough to resolve the endemic problems of underdevelopment), it is none the less a sign that the Soviet leadership no longer believes that the cure for underdevelopment lies entirely with the capitalist world. A significant recent practical illustration of this change of heart is the OECD report that the Soviet Union gave a greater proportion of its national income in development aid in 1986 than either Britain or the United States (see the report in *The Independent*, 3 September 1987).

RELATIONS AMONG SOCIALISTS

The new edition of the Party Programme holds no surprises in its treatment of relations between socialist countries (Programme 1986: 3, 7). Gorbachev has strongly urged the deepening of socialist economic integration, particularly in the field of science and technology.[6] He has also encouraged socialist countries to undertake their own programme of *perestroika*. But little has been said by policy-makers to suggest that the 'new political thinking' applies to socialist international relations. And yet the work that Soviet *mezhdunarodniki* are doing on the nature of relations among socialists seems to indicate change.

Two aspects of this work are particularly interesting. The first concerns the definition of national interest and how to deal with existing and potential conflicts of interest between member states of the socialist commonwealth. It also concerns the vexed problem of the relationship between national and international interests. The second and related issue consists of elaborating the concept of a 'partnership' relationship. Of course, both topics can be seen to have an important practical application. Closer economic integration within the socialist commonwealth has long been the declared aim of the CPSU and the Soviet government. The perception that integration is an economic necessity is more acute now than ever before. But the obstacles to integration seem to be as intractable in the 1980s as they were when the idea was first mooted under Khrushchev. Theoretical work on the nature of the obstacles may make it easier to overcome them and achieve the *sblizhenie* or 'drawing closer' that will make integration a natural process. But whatever the practical application, the theoretical work is engendering innovative ideas about political processes within the bloc.

At a domestic level the very nature of socialism is thought

to provide the prerequisites for harmonizing individual economic interests to obtain a genuine national interest and eliminate antagonism. In the process of this harmonization, social progress and economic development occur. None the less, it is recognized that conflicts of interest do occur and that they are not resolved automatically. One theorist warns against the common mistake of conceiving of a hierarchy of interests in which lower order, individual interests must be subordinated to higher general interests. A mechanism is required for harmonizing individual interests and for making sure that individual sections of the economy understand the needs of the economy as a whole and the interdependence of its various sections. Involving the workers themselves in the process of economic management is an important step in this direction (Bogomolov 1985, 82–9).

Transposing these ideas to the economy of the socialist commonwealth as a whole implies the recognition that, although the fundamental economic interests of the member countries coincide and there is no basic difference between their various national interests and the general international interest, 'each socialist country . . . aims to achieve . . . specific interests which are characteristic of that country alone and which, therefore, may not coincide with the interests of other countries' (Bogomolov 1985: 90–1). Two processes appear to be occurring simultaneously. On the one hand, as integration proceeds, the core of common interests expands. This expansion entails a greater interdependence between individual members of the socialist economic system, so that change in any one element of the system affects other elements and leads to change in the system as a whole (Novopashin 1986: 5–6). On the other hand, specific and individual interests by no means disappear. In the past Soviet theorists have assumed that specific individual interests cannot engender conflict in a socialist system. Contradictions have always been seen as subjective and transient (Kuznetsova and Lapshin in Novopashin 1985: 34). In fact, objective contradictions can and do exist. The point is to prevent them reaching a state of conflict (Novopashin 1986: 15).

In the international sphere, as at the domestic level, Soviet theorists now point out that it is a mistake to conceive of a hierarchy of interests in which common or international interests take precedence over specific ones or respect for sovereignty is subordinated to the principle of unity (Novopashin 1985: 60).[7] Some theorists maintain that specific and common interests must be harmonized by patiently working together to produce mutually acceptable decisions (Novopashin 1986: 5). The economic mechanisms of cooperation must be improved and the participants in the economic system of the socialist commonwealth must perceive that their individual economic interests will be served by intensifying cooperation and deepening their level of integration (Bogomolov 1985: 92–3). Others believe that rather than 'agreeing' interests or 'harmonizing' them, it would be more accurate to see the process as 'combining interests, which presupposes the agreement not of the interests themselves, but of policies aimed at realizing them' (Kulish, in Novopashin 1986: 168).

The attempt to define 'socialist partnership', the dominant form of relations in the commonwealth, forms part of the move away from simplistic assumptions about inter-socialist relations. It is defined as: 'a form of international relations based not only upon comradely solidarity and mutual aid but also . . . upon an equality of rights and obligations . . . [although] elements of objective inequality are retained under socialism' (Novopashin 1985: 59). Implementing socialist partnership is no easy matter. In part this is because the principle of democratic centralism which regulates social relations *within* each socialist society cannot operate in the relations between them. Although democratic centralism presupposes broad democratic participation in working out problems and options, the responsibility for taking decisions and supervising their implementation is hierarchical and lower bodies are strictly subordinated to higher ones. In socialist inter-state relations, however, where states are sovereign and enjoy 'formal' equality, there can be no hierarchy and no subordination in decision making (Novopashin 1985: 60). Marxist-Leninist theory has not really come to grips with the implications of this fact. Its founders expected that the drawing closer of socialists would follow the pattern it has taken within the Soviet Union. In fact, it rests on the existence of separate sovereign states and has given rise to a series of new practical problems. Moreover, the situation is unlikely to change in the foreseeable future. In fact, more complications are likely to arise as a result of integration. It will lead to an increase in the internationalization of production, with a paradoxical and contradictory tendency towards strengthening the sovereignty of individual socialist states. This makes theoretical work on the nature of socialist partnership all the more important (Novopashin 1985: 63–4).

It would be wrong, of course, to imply that this is the first time that Soviet *mezhdunarodniki* have recognized the existence of potentially conflicting national interests. Nor is the realization that *sblizhenie* cannot be coerced new. But Soviet theorists seem less inclined to assume that their desired goal, voluntary cohesion, has already been achieved. Moreover, the problems which arise within the bloc are no longer automatically attributed to vestiges of the capitalist past or to the malign interference of imperialism. Some problems are recognized to be the product of political and economic processes within the bloc. The 'new political thinking' is making it possible to undertake the serious study of these processes.

WAR AND PEACE

Most of the specialist articles which have been published under the rubric of the 'new political thinking' have dealt primarily with issues of war and peace in a nuclear age. It is usually these issues that Soviet spokesmen have in mind when they refer to the 'new political thinking' and the measures which have been taken to make it effective. What is the 'new political thinking' about war and peace and what implications does it have for previous theory?

Six interrelated principles can be extrapolated from the expositions of the 'new political thinking' which have been offered by various Soviet spokesmen. The first concerns the interdependence of survival in the nuclear age and the fact that, in the event of a nuclear conflict, the fate of all states would be inextricably bound together. The second principle emphasizes that it is important to reduce the level of military confrontation between the two superpowers and their military alliances while retaining the principle of equality and equal security. The third principle recognizes that security cannot be achieved by military–technical means alone: security is a political problem which requires political solutions. Moreover, according to the fourth principle, security is essentially collective—there can be no national security unless there is international security. The last two principles flow from the first four: given the nature of security in the nuclear age, flexibility and the readiness to compromise are necessary attributes of foreign policy. Moreover, the achievement of international security is a complex problem which requires a complex and comprehensive approach, so that military, economic, political and humanitarian problems are resolved to remove the sources and causes of tension, mistrust and hostility.[8]

As we have seen in Chapter 8, the belief that war is, and must continue to be, avoidable is by no means new. Nor are suggestions about how war can be averted, or warnings about the dangers of nuclear war. It could, however, be argued that these issues have been contended more passionately and more persuasively by Gorbachev and his colleagues than by any previous Soviet leader. At one level the reason for the passion is the Soviet domestic reform programme. *Perestroika* requires the redirecting of human and material resources from the defence to the civilian sectors of the economy. It is clearly vital, however, that this must neither leave the Soviet Union vulnerable, nor detract from the hard earned nuclear parity with the United States.[9] But immediate economic interests are not the sole reason for the 'new political thinking'. The impetus has also come from the recognition of the awful consequences of nuclear war, together with a belief that parity at present levels of nuclear weapons, and the possible invention of new weapons systems (whether 'defensive', like the Strategic Defence Initiative, or 'offensive'), make war more likely and detract from the security of both socialism and capitalism. It is not, of course, that policy-makers are prepared to abandon parity, but that they advocate moving down to parity at a far lower level of arms (see, for example, Gorbachev 1986: 8).

When the 'new political thinking' about war and peace is compared with previous Soviet thinking, four features are particularly striking. The first is that there is far less emphasis on the deterrent effects of Soviet power. The change in the correlation of forces is still said to be responsible for advances in 'social progress, democracy, national independence and peace' (Programme 1986: 3). But the implication of reducing the level at which there is parity is to downgrade the military dimensions of the correlation (see the discussion in Shenfield 1987: Ch. 9). Second, the 'new political thinking' removes any ambiguity about whether a nuclear war can be survived (and it certainly does not allow for the possibility of socialism emerging victorious). Soviet theorists who write about the 'new political thinking' maintain that nuclear war threatens the existence of civilization itself and the whole of life on earth (see, for example, Krasin 1986: 3).[10]

The third striking feature in the 'new political thinking' is the recognition that security is a political issue for which political solutions must be found and the acceptance that the solutions must be mutual. The fourth is a shift from zero sum to positive sum thinking; in other words, a move from the belief that more security for one side implies less for the other to the view that an enhancement of one side's security will be accompanied by an increase in the security of the other side. Positive sum thinking has always been implicit in the Soviet insistence on equal security and the denial that fruitful negotiation is possible 'from positions of strength'. But the 'new political thinking' spells out the advantages of positive sum thinking far more explicitly.

These features of the 'new political thinking' about war and peace have important implications for previous Marxist-Leninist theories about war and the nature of imperialism, as well as for the possibility of achieving lasting peace before capitalism is abolished. Soviet theorists have only begun to deal with the theoretical reformulations which are required. Although there is general agreement about the main principles of the 'new political thinking', an uneasy mix between old and new thinking is evident in the way its implications are discussed.

An example of this mix is the attempt to reinterpret the inherently aggressive nature of imperialism. Imperialism has always been believed to be the prime cause of war. Even when war ceased to be considered inevitable, the perception of imperialist aggression was retained. The avoidability of war was first attributed to the growth of the forces standing for peace. But the peace movement soon took second place to Soviet power, which was thought to deter imperialist aggression. Now, however, it is not coercion, but a combination of persuasion and rationality which is thought to restrain imperialism. It is assumed that imperialist policy-makers will share the 'new political thinking' out of rational self-interest and the instinct for survival (Kapchenko 1987: 16). There are also thought to be countervailing factors to imperialist aggression (for example, the peace movement) which create the prerequisites for 'constructive dialogue and rational compromise on questions of war and peace' (Krasin 1986: 7). But Soviet theorists have not really yet explained why, if imperialism remains inherently aggressive, its leaders should be convinced by the logic of the 'new political thinking'.

It has proved relatively easier to discard Lenin's division of war into just and unjust (depending upon the policy of which it is a continuation), at least in relation to nuclear war. There is general agreement that nuclear war cannot be a rational means of continuing policy. There are no political aims which can justify using means which could lead to nuclear war (see, for example, Shakhnazarov 1984a: 73; Bykov 1986: 30). The distinction between just and unjust wars is said to make sense only to the living: if history ends so does the difference between just and unjust wars (Bovin 1986: 117). If there are no political aims which can justify the risk of provoking nuclear war, it is clearly unthinkable to use force to promote revolutionary change. Force can no longer be considered the midwife of history, since in the nuclear age it can too readily turn from midwife into gravedigger (Plimak, in *Pravda*, 14 November 1986, quoted in Shenfield 1987: 43). The logic of this reasoning is perfectly clear, but it leads to difficulties in the perceived relationship of peace and socialism which provide further examples of the mix between old and new thinking.

A major issue for Soviet theorists is whether a stable peace is attainable before the establishment of international socialism. Orthodox Soviet theory holds that peace is an attribute of communism. Because of the contradictions inherent within and between capitalist states, it cannot be achieved as long as capitalism exists (see Ch. 8). But if, as most Soviet theorists now agree, the goal of peace has the highest (or even an absolute) priority, the logical way to achieve it is to promote revolutionary change which will lead to socialism. In the past, however, this has had negative consequences for détente. It has entailed the risk of confrontation with the United States. It thus runs counter to the 'new political thinking'. Orthodox theory therefore implies that socialism cannot promote its own expansion and that stable peace is unattainable. The best that can be achieved is the temporary absence of war. And yet the 'new political thinking' and the proposals which are based upon it are clearly intended to establish something more substantial than the mere absence of war. The logical implication is that the orthodox theory about whether peace can be attained while capitalism still exists requires revision. The debate about the possibility of peace before international socialism has not yet been settled, but there is an increasing tendency to separate the struggle for peace from the struggle for socialism and to accord higher priority to peace (Shenfield 1987: Ch. 6).

The 'new political thinking' about war and peace clearly calls into question many long-held tenets. Theoretical work is required both on the new concepts and on the practical issues which arise from them. The agenda which has been suggested for future international relations research includes many of these issues (Primakov 1986: 10–12). It also includes the task of working out a military strategy 'based on the policy of preventing nuclear war' (Yakovlev 1987: 18).

CONCLUSION

The connection between theory and practice discussed in the introduction to this book has been re-established by Soviet policy-makers since Gorbachev introduced his reforms. Soviet theorists have been encouraged to undertake the theoretical work which can underpin the reforms and make them more successful. It has also been suggested that the social sciences have hitherto been hampered by outdated ideology. The *perestroika* must be extended to the scientific institutes themselves since 'neither the practical output of the social sciences, nor their position in society, nor the state of the subject itself can be called satisfactory from the point of view of the needs of our time' (Yakovlev 1987: 5). To some extent this merely reiterates the kinds of demands that have always followed Party Congresses, when specialists are called upon to consider the implications of the Congress for their particular fields of endeavour. However, after the Twenty Seventh Party Congress, Soviet scholars were told to concentrate on themes which seemed to promise the breaking of new ground in Soviet international relations theory. The 'new political thinking' is not, it seems, to rest with the enunciation of a set of principles. It is to be elaborated into a new theory even if this entails rejecting some of the fundamental assumptions of the Marxist-Leninist theory of international politics.

But the 'new political thinking' involves more than theory. It has expanded into the realm of practice. A panoply of policy proposals, predominantly concerned with arms control, has been launched. To some people these proposals seem to be nothing more than a revigoration of the recurring disarmament and cooperation proposals which have characterized Soviet foreign policy since the days of Khrushchev. Why should Gorbachev's proposals and the projected agenda for 'new political thinking' be taken more seriously than previous offers and revisions of Soviet theory?

There are self-interested practical reasons for responding to the 'new political thinking'. It is accepted in both the West and the Soviet Union that the consequences of nuclear war would be catastrophic. Any political thinking designed to reduce tension and confrontation deserves encouragement and response. A second reason for responding is that some of Gorbachev's proposals are genuinely innovative. They are certainly worth testing. If they are empty offers and mere propaganda ploys, this will soon become obvious. There is nothing to lose and a great deal to gain from taking the 'new political thinking' seriously.

As far as Soviet theory is concerned, there is evidence in Soviet writing about international relations of a genuine theoretical questioning, of a search for explanations that go beyond mere formulae, and of a new freedom to question in print some of the tenets of Marxism-Leninism which have previously been held sacred. The leadership's encouragement of Soviet scholars to break new theoretical ground has not yet given way to a new version of received truth. The 'new political thinking' cannot easily, therefore, be dismissed as nothing more than a fresh, clever move in the battle for propaganda advantage. It promises interesting times both for Soviet scholars and for those who study Soviet theory.

It is too soon to judge whether a new theory will emerge, and whether it will be consistent and convincing. Nor can one say whether it will be able to fulfil the function of serving as a guide to action. Any assessment of the role that theory plays in the Soviet Union must, perforce, be based on the 'old political thinking'. The following and final chapter turns to this assessment.

NOTES

1. For this author's assessment of the changes in personnel, style and the content of Soviet foreign policy under Gorbachev, see Light 1987. At the same time that an agenda was set for theoretical development, 'old forms of thinking' were criticized. The criticism of Brezhnev's foreign policy was even more explicit. In his political report to the Twenty Seventh Party Congress, for example, Gorbachev pointed out that 'continuity in foreign policy has nothing in common with the simple repetition of what has gone before' (Gorbachev 1986: 8). At a conference of foreign policy officials held in May 1986, Gorbachev is officially reported to have examined critically 'the experience of Soviet diplomacy' (see *Summary of World Broadcasts* SU/8269/B/1: 27 May 1986).

2. There have only been three previous programmes of the CPSU. The first was approved in 1903, the second in 1919, and the third, of which the present programme is said to be a revised edition, was adopted in 1961.

3. Perhaps even more interesting than the emphasis given to common interests is the recognition that countries have legitimate *different* interests which should be studied. This requires understanding their perceptions and their legitimate concerns (Primakov 1986: 13).

4. For the development of Soviet 'globalistics', see Glickman 1986 and Shenfield 1987: Chapter 8. Shenfield also discusses the debate on interdependence. The term interdependence is also used more narrowly by Soviet theorists to refer to interactions between national economies and between the economic systems of socialism and capitalism. For an analysis of the concept of economic interdependence in Soviet Third World theory, see Valkenier 1983, 1986.

5. This formulation is taken directly from a speech made by Andropov in 1983. See Fukuyama 1986: 719.

6. For the 'Comprehensive Programme of Scientific and Technical Co-

operation' which was adopted by the CMEA summit on 18 December 1985, see *Pravda*, 19 December 1985.

7. One theorist criticizes the communiqués issued after the 1957 and 1960 international meetings of Communist Parties (see Chapter 7 for the contexts in which they were composed and their content) for representing relations within the system as 'without contradictions and conflict-free' (Kulish, in Novopashin 1986: 140). Another maintains that the mistaken view that there is a hierarchy of interests and values has been reached by means of using the Marixist-Leninist classics in a dogmatic way, 'that is by taking citations out of context and using them as arguments' (Novopashin 1985: 61). It is noteworthy, however, that the Soviet discussion about nuclear war posits a hierarchy of values and the necessary precedence of survival and peace over all other values (Shakhnazarov 1984a: 63–4).

8. Many of these principles can be deduced from Gorbachev's political report to the Twenty Seventh Party Congress (Gorbachev 1986). They were reiterated by other Soviet policy-makers and expanded by many high-ranking theorists. For some examples see Bovin 1986; Dobrynin 1986; Petrovsky 1986. Although Bovin is best known as a political journalist, he is reported to be a gifted theoretician. Dobrynin is head of the International Department of the Central Committee, while Petrovsky was appointed a deputy foreign minister in May 1986.

9. My intention is not to impugn the sincerity of the 'new political thinking' but to indicate that there are important domestic goals which are served by it. Moreover, a number of efforts have been made to turn the 'new political thinking' into concrete policy. Both the domestic goals and the concrete policy proposals make it unlikely that the 'new political thinking' is merely part of the Soviet propaganda for peace. While propaganda is clearly well served by the 'new political thinking', so is the reform programme.

10. Shenfield (1987: 11–14) provides evidence that the view that nuclear war cannot be survived has met with some resistance in the Soviet Union, particularly amongst the military. Gorbachev seems, however, to have persuaded the military to back his arms control proposals. Marshal Akhromeev, Soviet Chief of General Staff, has publicly expressed the readiness of the Soviet armed forces 'to accept certain compromises to reduce the nuclear threat' (reported in *The Guardian*, 3 March 1987).

11 Conclusion

This study began by posing two questions: what is the theoretical framework which is said to underline Soviet foreign policy and is it powerful enough to fulfil the roles claimed for it?

The preceding chapters have offered a reply to the first question. The claim that there is a substantive philosophy and theory of international relations in the Soviet Union has been amply vindicated, even if only by the length of this description and critique. The number of works consulted and authors cited suggests that writing about Soviet international relations theory is no longer the preserve of a select few. International relations may be a relatively new discipline in the Soviet Union, but the number of people who practise it is sizeable. While many of them are academics, there are influential theorists who work in the Central Committee apparatus. This underlines a connection between theory and politics which bears on some of the functions that theory plays in Soviet society. It also serves to substantiate the assertion by Soviet scholars that there is a relationship between theory and practice. Whether that relationship is the one depicted by Soviet scholars and policy-makers, and whether the theory is sufficiently powerful to fulfil the roles of interpreting the past, guiding the present and forecasting the future are the questions which form the agenda for this concluding chapter.

The assertion that theory dictates policy and that policy, in turn, has a feedback effect on theory is examined in the first section, which concludes that Soviet theory probably cannot fulfil the role claimed for it. But the amount of writing there is on Soviet theory and the seniority of some of the writers suggest that, whether or not policy is based upon it, theory must play some role in Soviet society. Some of those functions are considered in the final section of the chapter.

THEORY AND PRACTICE

There are three striking conclusions which can be drawn from the preceding chapters of this study. First, Soviet theory has changed, although the changes have occurred slowly and with difficulty. It is also clear that while Khrushchev encouraged and publicized the doctrinal changes, he did not initiate all of them. They had begun before Stalin's death. Similarly, the 'new political thinking' attributed to Gorbachev originates in the period before his accession to power. Second, there are theoretical and practical difficulties in combining the basic principles of Soviet foreign policy—proletarian and socialist internationalism and peaceful coexistence. These difficulties affect the coherence of Soviet theory regarding socialist–capitalist relations, relations between socialist states and less-developed countries and the new type of relations which are said to exist in the socialist commonwealth. They also affect Soviet peace theory. The 'new political thinking' indicates that Soviet theorists are aware of the difficulties. Third, Soviet theory has relied increasingly on the concept of power as an explanatory device for past events, the assurance of present security and the promise of future change. Paradoxically, however, the theory seems to have become more deterministic at the same time. It is only now that politics seems to be taking precedence over power. It will be argued that these three conclusions detract from the relationship between theory and practice. The third conclusion, the parallel reliance on power to preserve the status quo and on history as the agent of change, indicates that the Soviet concept of socialist power has concentrated on its use as a deterrent. It is also closely connected to the political function of Soviet theory.

As far as the changes which have taken place in Soviet theory are concerned, there are two related aspects which affect the connection between theory and practice. The first has to do with the relationship of contemporary theory to the writings of Marx, Engels and Lenin. The second and related issue concerns the methodology that is used by Soviet theorists, and the way in which it differs from that employed by their intellectual forbears.

There is some justice in the claim that modern theory is based on the writings of Marx, Engels and Lenin. It demonstrably *is* based on their works, but that does not mean that the Soviet claim is entirely justified. It is not surprising that the classical works are not all relevant to present-day conditions, that some of the original theories have been invalidated by history and that Marx, Engels and Lenin could not have known about the scientific and technical developments which have occurred in the twentieth century. On the other hand, it is clear that if Soviet theory had not taken account of these changes, it would have ceased to bear any relation to reality. In fact, it could be argued that a good theory is one that can be adapted or expanded to reflect new circumstances so that it explains the past, serves as a model of the present and has some predictive value for the future, while at the same time still remaining recognizably itself.

One of the strengths of Marxism-Leninism is said to be the fact that it can change in this way (see, for example, Kosolapov and Oizerman 1984: 46). It is not only officially accepted Soviet theorists who believe this. Roy Medvedev, for example, a dissident Marxist, identifies this ability as the feature which gives Soviet socialist ideology a 'rich inner potential'. But he believes that 'it is precisely the ability of Marxism to develop that is employed very little today' (R. Medvedev 1986b: 32). Instead, he argues, both theory and practice in the contemporary Soviet Union systematically violate the potential of the founding ideology. In regard to practice, 'Many of the forms [of the "real socialism" which exists in the Soviet Union] have nothing in common with genuine Marxism or even with "Marxism-Leninism"' (R. Medvedev 1986b: 9). In regard to theory, he objects to the way critics of Marxism-Leninism selectively cite what Marx, Engels or Lenin said sixty or a hundred years ago to prove that their theories do not accord with contemporary reality. He maintains that outdated or disproved elements are omitted from modern Soviet works not necessarily for tactical reasons but because times have changed. But officially accepted theorists have also begun to object to the selective way the classics have been used (see, for example, Ch. 10 n.7).

There are clear reasons for the situation noted by Medvedev, that Soviet Marxism-Leninism is not developing as it might have. Amongst them is the fact that until very recently those tenets which are still held to be operative have never been challenged. Moreover, outdated tenets have hardly ever been mentioned in modern Soviet texts and there has been little discussion about why they no longer hold true. Modern theorists have not engaged in debate with the old theory. Their omissions, or at least the attitude which leads to them, and therefore to the absence of a visible interplay between old and new theory or between new theorists and old theory, has tended to retard and discourage development and change.

It is also the case that modern Soviet theory is not only based on the theory of Marx, Engels and Lenin, but also quite strikingly on the theories of Stalin and Khrushchev. Neither of them, however, are formally acknowledged as precursors of current theory. It could be argued that neither of them *were* theorists in the way that Marx, Engels and Lenin were. This is undoubtedly true. But, as we have seen in the case of Stalin particularly, this did not prevent their contemporaries from showering them with accolades for their theoretical genius, in the same way that Brezhnev, almost certainly also no theorist, was acclaimed as an original thinker and a creative Marxist-Leninist. It could also be argued that there is no need to acknowledge Stalin's and Khrushchev's contributions, for the very reason that they are integral parts of current theory. Again, there is justice in this argument. But it is not just their names that are omitted. Certain of the events of their times are either glossed over in silence or rewritten. This too has implications for the quality of Soviet theory. In describing the origins of contemporary theory, therefore, Soviet scholars and policy-makers are accurate in saying that modern theory is based on Marxism-Leninism, but they omit their *other* sources. Moreover, the relationship is neither as organic nor necessarily as good for the theory as Soviet theorists imply.

The reason why those aspects of Marxism-Leninism which are irrelevant or wrong cannot be publicly disavowed has partly to do with the status of classical theory. This raises the question of the kinds of evidence used by modern theorists compared to that used by their classical predecessors. The selectivity which is practised in deciding what becomes history must also affect the kind of evidence that Soviet theorists can use. Both the status of classical theory and the nature of the evidence certainly affect what can be called the 'idiom' in which the theory is presented. They also relate to the question of what it is that Soviet theorists do with their evidence and, in particular, what precisely they mean when they talk about the dialectical method. Broadly speaking, these are the four main methodological issues which, it will be argued, reduce both the accuracy and value of the theory, and its usefulness in practical policy-making.

As far as the status of classical theory is concerned, it seems to be the case that classical theory can neither be entirely disregarded, nor used freely. Nor can it be challenged. It can and has been tampered with, however, and it has been argued, most notably by the Chinese, that it has been re-interpreted. This might seem to be contradictory but, to return to the term that was used in Chapter 1 in connection with the question of who makes theory in the Soviet Union, the principle of democratic centralism seems to determine the way in which the classical theory can be used. It is never left to individual theorists to tamper or reinterpret. At any one moment there is an acceptable interpretation and deviations from it are unacceptable and unlikely. But the accepted for-mulation seems then to acquire the status almost of proof. The form in which theorists can use classical works is limited, therefore, and they seem sometimes to adduce Marx, Engels and Lenin as if their works were, in themselves, infallibly accurate and therefore proof that modern theory is equally infallible. But if Soviet scholars have inherited a mode of analysis from the classical writers, there is no visible sign of them using it to test the current validity of classical theory. Nor, as we shall see later, do they seem to use it to develop new theory. The test of the 'new political thinking' may well be whether theorists will be permitted to use the classics freely or whether democratic centralism will continue to operate.

A closely related issue concerns the quality and quantity of evidence used by Soviet theorists. The Soviet predilection for rewriting history is well known. It has serious implications for the kinds of historical evidence that can be used to formulate theory or test it for accuracy. It also probably accounts for what sometimes appear to be tendentious interpretations of history. There are limitations, too, on the kinds of contemporary data that can be used. This may explain why the reader frequently finds unsubstantiated assertions in Soviet theoretical writing which, on the face of it, could easily be proved, amended or disproved by using empirical data.[1]

It could be argued, first, that the unconscious rewriting of history is universally practised[2] and, second, that the role of the theorist is to write theory, and that there is no need for evidence to be produced or visibly used. After all, there are many Western international relations theorists who do not seem to use empirical data. But two of the claims that Soviet scholars make for their theory are relevant here: if it is to be considered a *scientific* theory, there are implications for the use of data. And if Soviet theory claims direct descent from classical theory, Marx, Engels and Lenin all used a great deal of empirical data which they published as part of their theoretical work.[3]

A third problem connected with methodology was referred to above as the 'idiom' of Soviet theory. In other words, it concerns the style in which Soviet theory is presented. First, there is frequently less argument and analysis than description and typology, the underlying theory being offered as self-evident truth. Second, when there is an attempt at substantiation, it often takes the form of quotations from the classical writers or the present leaders. Third, there is a marked absence of criticism of previous or present Soviet theory or policy (except in cases like the Varga controversy to which reference has been made several times, where the argument about theory acquired a political dimension). On the other hand, Soviet theory is often very polemical, particularly with regard to Western authors, who are frequently cited, paraphrased and criticized.

A polemical style and frequent recourse to quoting and extolling the classics might well seem to have been inherited from the classical writers themselves. Engels, for example, published many commentaries on Marx's theories (see his prefaces to later edition of Marx's works, for example, in

Marx 1851: 245–6). Lenin cited long passages from Marx and Engels (in, for example, 'The State and Revolution', Lenin 1917g: 381–492) and often engaged in published polemics, particularly with the colleagues he regarded as deviant socialists or even 'renegades'. But in these cases, citations and polemics were accompanied by argument, and the use, expansion and acknowledgement of ideas, both original and borrowed. These accompaniments are rarely found in modern Soviet theory.

Objecting to presentational style might seem to be an exercise in literary criticism, misplaced in a work of social science. But style, absence of evidence and the curious status of classical theory all contribute to the fourth methodological problem. Given that theoretical writing tends to be descriptive rather than analytical, that little evidence is offered and that the classics are used in specific, limited ways, it is difficult to understand what Soviet theorists mean when they say that they use the dialectical method. As we saw in Chapter 1, the way in which Soviet theorists define the dialectical method is not very illuminating. And it has become evident from an examination of various aspects of Soviet theory that little further clarification can be gained from examining the theoretical work itself. As a result, the dialectical method at times seems to mean no more than that two mutually exclusive principles do not necessarily produce cognitive dissonance, or that it is expected that a synthesis will eventually be found for them.

These four methodological problems seem to cast doubt on the pratical usefulness of Soviet international relations theory. If the classics can only be used selectively, if significant aspects of historical and contemporary data cannot be used, if there is little analysis and if the method which has been used to reach the conclusions is not clear, then the reliability of the theory as an aid to making day-by-day decisions must be questionable. But it is still conceivable that the theory itself could be sufficiently coherent and comprehensive to act as a general guide for Soviet policy. The next task, therefore, is to examine whether it is.

One way to investigate whether Soviet theory really does have an impact on policy is to inquire whether there is a connection between particular foreign-policy actions and the relevant theory. But in practice, no scholar seems to have evolved a way to conduct this test efficiently. It is quite possible to take one and the same action and argue convincingly both for and against. For example, aid to bourgeois national-liberation movements is consonant with Leninist precepts but has often adversely affected local socialists, and therefore seemed to be counter to the interests of international revolution.

A second method of assessing whether there is a close connection between Soviet theory and practice would be to consider the relationship of theory to reality as a whole. Soviet theory is said to reflect reality and, indeed, it is difficult to see how an effective foreign policy could be based upon it if it were a poor reflection of the real world. Since events in the real world are, according to Marxism-Leninism, the products of the objective laws of history, Soviet scholars contend that their theory reflects these objective laws.

But as we saw in Chapter 1, theory is also said to influence the objective laws, thereby actively affecting the course of historical development. Indeed, Medvedev points out that one of the things that distinguishes Marxism from other ideologies is that it claims not only cognition of the world but also the ability to change the world by changing people's consciousness (and, once political power has been attained, the productive relations which determine that consciousness) (R. Medvedev 1986b: 50). It is, in consequence, difficult to judge either the effect of Soviet theory on reality or its effect on the objective laws of historical development. It is less difficult to consider whether the theory is a good reflection of reality. If it is not, Soviet foreign policy must be based upon something other or more than theory (or one could conclude that Soviet foreign policy is ineffective and, while it is clearly not as successful as either Soviet theorists or staunch opponents of the Soviet Union claim, it cannot be accused of being entirely ineffective).

A third way to investigate the possible impact of theory on policy is to look at the inner logic of the theory itself. If it lacks coherence and contains internal contradictions or incompatibilities, then it is unlikely that the relationship between policy and theory can be as close as Soviet scholars and policy-makers both insist it is. Coherence, or the lack of it, will also affect the kind of reflection the theory contains of reality.

Throughout this work an attempt has been made to evaluate each aspect of the theory as it has been discussed. It should perhaps be stressed that the intention has not been to imply that any other theory is better (in fact, little comparison has been made with other theories), but to assess whether Soviet theory really can play the role claimed for it. It has become clear in respect of most of the areas of theory investigated that there are unresolved theoretical problems which probably detract from the usefulness of the theory. It would be otiose to repeat in detail the criticisms which have already been made.

But the most intractable problem arises when the areas of theory are put together and looked at as a whole. As we have seen, the external relations of the Soviet Union are held to be governed by two major principles, proletarian internationalism and its new form, socialist internationalism and peaceful coexistence. Proletarian internationalism is the principle underlying Soviet relations with the international working *class*, as well as relations between the Communist Party of the Soviet Union and other Communist and Workers' Parties. Socialist internationalism, on the other hand, although it is derived from proletarian internationalism, refers, like the other major principle, peaceful coexistence, to inter-*state* relations. Peaceful coexistence defines relations between socialist and capitalist states, while socialist internationalism is the principle upon which relations among socialist states are constructed.

The crux of the problem is that in respect of the three major types of relations which have been examined in this work, socialist–capitalist, socialist–LDC and socialist–socialist, both class and state principles pertain. There is a section of the international working class in all three kinds of state (reflected by the existence of Communist, Socialist or Workers' Parties in most of them) and the Soviet Union has extensive inter-state relations with a variety of countries. What causes the problem is that the two kinds of relations, and the principles on which they rest, are incompatible, or at least not always congruent. That there are dilemmas in practice must, of course, be self-evident to Soviet policy-makers and theorists because of the disputes within the socialist system, as well as the difficulty caused by the vulnerability of East–West détente to Soviet policies in the Third World. Dilemmas are also evident from time to time in bilateral Soviet relations with the less-developed countries. The practical difficulties, in short, are numerous, and significant. The 'new political thinking' indicates that Soviet scholars are beginning to accept that there is a basic theoretical problem.

There is a legal component to the lack of congruency between class and state relations. Inter-state relations are based on the principles of international law and the acceptance of sovereignty (and this is frequently acknowledged by Soviet scholars and policy-makers). The concept of sovereignty is entirely alien to class relations, however, since Soviet analysts still rely on the assumption that 'the working men have no country' (Marx and Engels 1848: 51), which logically requires that workers can have no interests and no loyalty outside of their class. While the goals of the state are to defend sovereignty and, by definition, separateness, the goals of the class are (or should be) to abolish national distinctions.

But it is not just the goals of the two types of relations that are incompatible but also the kinds of behaviour that Soviet policy-makers and theorists have expected from the subjects of each. While Stalin's definition of an internationalist ('one who is ready to defend the USSR without reservation', Stalin 1927d: 53) would probably no longer be proclaimed publicly, a certain loyalty still seems to be expected from those with whom the Soviet Union has proletarian class relations. In part this is because it is taken for granted that class interests are internationally identical. But it is also because the Soviet Union is considered to be *the* state of the proletarian class and therefore no distinction is made between Soviet state interests and the interests of the Soviet working class. The class interests of the international proletariat are therefore usually assumed to be identical not only to the interests of the Soviet working class but also to Soviet state interests.

The problems arise when this assumption is not shared by other contingents of the international proletariat (theoretically it is possible that the Soviet proletariat itself could challenge the assumption) or when it is not entirely clear what the international class interest is. Who is to be judge or arbiter? No theoretical answer has been offered, although the concept of 'socialist partnership' (see Ch. 10) indicates that the question is preoccupying Soviet theorists. In practice the answer has usually taken the form of the imposition of the Soviet interpretation (as in Czechoslovakia in 1968) or schism (as in the Sino-Soviet dispute). In the theory, however, the possibility of a clash of interests is held to be relatively unimportant because the conflict that arises is non-antagonistic. In the case of antagonistic conflict, considerable theoretical effort has been devoted to finding a way to resolve it without violence. Peaceful coexistence displaces the conflict to the less dangerous levels of economics and ideology. Soviet theory has not yet found a parallel way of displacing non-antagonistic conflict. Nor has it found a means of resolving the legal quandary that if class relations are extended across national borders, the principles on which state relations are based are automatically eroded. If the theory tends to deny the existence of manifest problems, it cannot serve as a guide to resolving the problems.

The methodological problems discussed above, and the lack of internal compatibility when the separate components are put together, suggest that if Soviet international relations theory serves as a guide to action, it is probably not a very reliable guide. In discussing both sets of problems, the answer to the question whether Soviet theory reflects reality as closely as its proponents contend has begun to be clear. If there are restrictions on the kinds of evidence that can be adduced and if manifest problems are ignored, theory can at best offer only a partial reflection of reality. Recent criticisms of Soviet science suggest that policy-makers have begun to demand a better reflection of reality (Yakovlev 1987). If theory only contains a partial reflection of reality, policy must be based on something more than the articulated theory.

The difficulties which would arise if Soviet theory were the only basis of day-to-day decision-making are apparent. But this is not to say that theory has no effect at all on Soviet policy. Marxism-Leninism affects Soviet foreign policy at what might be called a more abstract level because of the other functions that theory has in Soviet society. This work will conclude with a brief look at some of those functions.

THE FUNCTIONS OF THEORY

The fact that so many people are concerned with Soviet theory and that it is not just theorists who claim that it is important but also policy-makers, suggests that it must serve some important functions in society, even if they are not the functions of analysis or scientific forecasting claimed for it. One of the most obvious of these functions is to legitimize leaders and their policies. The use of theory for purposes of legitimation has a long and powerful history in the Soviet Union. Indeed, if theory had not been used in this capacity, Marxism-Leninism would probably never have evolved from Marxism. In disapproval of what had been done with his theory, Marx claimed not to be a Marxist. Lenin might well have wanted to deny that he was a Leninist, but the opportunity never arose because Leninists were only invented after his death. And the term was invented not as a mark of reverence but rather as an instrument in the power struggle. Its purpose was to make the Zinoviev–Kamenev–Stalin triumvirate the true heir to the leadership of the Bolshevik Party and thereby to deprive Trotsky of the mantle. It succeeded in its aim—Trotskyism became the worst kind of deviance and the claim to Leninism a mark of the highest authority.

Subsequent Soviet leaders have similarly claimed and been accorded the role of disciple and have thereby gained legitimacy. But the use of theory to perform the function of legitimation became particularly important once Stalin had died and de-Stalinization had begun. At a superficial level there was a vacuum to be filled in speeches and in written works, since, as we have seen, in the last years of the Stalin cult nothing was written or said without reference and fulsome tribute to Stalin. At a deeper level, there were urgent political reasons for invoking past theory and theorists. The authority of the Party and its leadership had to be re-established and a crisis of legitimacy avoided. In the process of de-Stalinization, the slogan became the return to the proper norms of Leninism. And this meant that policy had to be seen to accord with those norms and had to be explained in terms of theory. Although de-Stalinization (in the sense of admitting the past and rehabilitating the victims of Stalinism) did not last for very long, the use of theory to legitimize policy has been retained.

The borderline between using theory to legitimize and using it to justify is delicate. Justification is most required when policy seems furthest from theory. Yet it could be argued that in respect of foreign policy, one of the major functions of Soviet theory is to justify. The reason is that although Soviet state interests and the interests of the international working class (or, for that matter, the interests of the international communist movement or of the socialist commonwealth) are usually said by Soviet theorists to be identical, it is not necessarily the case that this is obvious either to the Soviet public or to other members of the international working class. When it is not universally perceived to be the case, theory has a vital role in explaining how the international interest is best served. The use of theory to explain the intervention in Czechoslovakia in 1968 falls into the category of justification.

Theory is used not only to legitimize and to justify. It also acts as a cohesive device.[4] Its usefulness in this capacity has always been important in a multi-ethnic country such as the Soviet Union and it has become equally important in the multi-national socialist system. The establishment of the Third Communist International and the adoption of its twenty-one conditions of admission (Degras 1956, vol. 1: 166–72) was primarily intended to ensure ideological purity and cohesiveness, the two things the Second International had failed to bring about. The Communist Information Bureau, as its name suggests, was also conceived as a means of propagating a uniform theory. The difficulty for successive Soviet leaders since the Cominform was disbanded has been to retain cohesion and ideological conformity in the bloc without an international institution. The statements issued at the 1957, 1960 and 1969 international meetings of representatives of Communist and Workers' Parties were successively longer attempts to set out the theory for that particular stage of historical development. It became apparent, however, that unless cohesion already existed, international meetings of that kind could produce the very opposite effects to what was intended. They were replaced by Brezhnev's meetings with bloc leaders in the Crimea, which may have been useful in terms of agreeing policy, or even for informing leaders of the member countries of the socialist commonwealth what the general line was on particular issues. But they did not help with the function of propagating theory more generally. Although most published theoretical works carry less authority than an analysis issued by an international meeting, they perform a useful function in disseminating theory. If the theory is generally accepted and adhered to, cohesion will follow.

To talk about theory as a legitimizing or cohesive device or as something that is used to justify policy may make it seem as if theory is only used cynically. That is not the case, however. Although there probably are some people who use it cynically, for the vast majority of people there is by now no other language in which to talk about politics or international relations. The role of theory goes deeper than language, however. It affects mental frameworks. Theoretical categories have been internalized, and there is no other set of concepts which can be used to explain policy. It is this, above all, that determines the role which theory must play in relation to practical policy, domestic and foreign, at a more abstract level. For while it seems unlikely that the relationship of theory to practice is the one depicted by Soviet theorists, if there is no other language in which to think or talk about politics and if theoretical categories have been internalized, then theory must determine how the world is perceived.

What this means is that even if Soviet theory cannot easily be applied to concrete issues, it influences the way those issues are interpreted, the way the world is categorized, the evaluation of past and present actions and the range of options which are available to the policy-makers. But these are the effects of all theory, of course, and by no means unique to Soviet theory. It is for this reason that theory can present a major obstacle in attempts to turn relations of enmity into relations of amity.

It can be argued that there are particular features about Soviet theory that make it an inappropriate source of amicable relations. For one thing, one of the main features of the present age is seen to be a struggle between socialism and capitalism. This is an inauspicious basis for peaceful co-existence. For another, the reliance on Soviet power as an explanatory device for the past and the basis of present security fits uneasily with the insistence that Soviet foreign policy is peace-loving. These features seem to be related to a function that Soviet theory plays which makes it rather different from other international relations theories. It arises from the close connection between theory and politics in the Soviet Union. The distinction that Easton makes between government and politics is useful in understanding this function (Easton 1965). Theory, as we have seen, is primarily the preserve of the Party Central Committee and not the state Ministry of Foreign Affairs. As a result, its function is not only to serve state policy, but also Party policy. In terms of government policy, theory serves to legitimize. In relation to politics, however, its purpose is to identify issues, resolve differences and raise support, particularly from Party members, but arguably in a one-party state, also from the populace as a whole.

In its relationship to the Communist Party of the Soviet Union, international relations theory has similar functions to those played by Party political programmes or manifestoes elsewhere. It is the Party's programme and plan of action, a means of rallying the electorate to the Party's cause. It has more to do with the future than the present in this capacity, and its visionary qualities are particularly important. But it also needs to explain why, if past promises have not been kept, international socialism is still the inevitable agenda for the future. Lenin's theory of uneven development provides the escape clause explaining why the past has not followed the pattern predicted by Marx and Lenin. It makes it theoretically possible to postpone the achievement of the final goals of socialism and communism. Soviet power explains why the predictions will come true in the future. It is not that Soviet power will be used to promote progress. Its function is to prevent regression. History will take care of the future. The function of Soviet theory and of Soviet power is to keep socialism intact while history takes its course.

NOTES

1. Soviet scholars have often found it easier to analyse their own society indirectly by examining other societies critically and leaving their readers to draw inferences about the Soviet Union. For an analysis of the relevance of the study of China to Soviet sociology and political science, for example, see Rozman (1985) and for an account of post-Mao China which could be read as a historical parable on the post-Stalin Soviet Union, see Burlatsky (1982).

2. I am endebted to A. V. S. de Reuck for this observation.

3. The question arises whether Soviet policy-makers suffer from inadequate or tendentious information. In other words, does hard evidence exist in the Soviet Union and if it does, who has access to it? Clearly it must exist—Soviet foreign-policy decisions could not be based on the flimsy evidence presented by theorists. Roy Medvedev (1986b: 76) describes the enormous volume of information which is collected in the Soviet Union and the way in which it is channelled both upwards and downward. He does not believe that there is any information lacking to the members of the Politburo, the General Secretary of the Central Committee of the CPSU and their special advisers. Some of the information will be available to theorists too, but that does not mean that it can necessarily be used in published works on international relations and foreign policy. Whether there are unpublished theoretical works using this information for the guidance of decision-makers, as there are said to be unpublished and more accurate economic statistics (Z. Medvedev 1987) must remain speculation.

4. Theory performs similar functions to those fulfilled by inverted traditions which 'use history as a legitimator of action and cement of group cohesion' (Hobsbawm and Ranger 1983: 12). For other techniques of promoting cohesion, see Lane (1981).

Bibliography

The Cambridge University system of transliteration has been used for Russian names and titles except where there is a conventional English spelling of Russian names. For the convenience of the reader in consulting the Bibliography, the sources have been amalgamated into a single list. The Harvard system has been slightly adapted in that the sources are listed in order of year whether or not they have been authored or edited and irrespective of the number of authors. A single dash in a reference following a multi-author work indicates only the author named first in the preceding reference.

Abalkin, L. (1985) Leninskaya teoriya imperializma v svete sovremennoi real'nosti. *Miroraya ekonomika i mezhdunarodnye otnosheniya* 5: 61–73.

Airapetyan, M. and G. Deborin (1959) The Guiding Force of Socialist Foreign Policy. *International Affairs* 11: 34–9.

Akopyan, G. (1975) Ob antiimperialisticheskoi napravlennosti natsionalizma razvivayushchikhsya stran. *Mirovaya ekonomika i mezhdunarodnye otnosheniya* 9: 77–87.

Alekseeva, T., V. Babak and A. Kokeev (1982) Tekushchie problemy mirovoi politiki. *Mirovaya ekonomika i mezhdunarodnye otnosheniya* 1: 84–102.

Ambartsumov, Evgeny A. (1956) *Sovetsko-Finlyandskie otnosheniya*. Moscow: Gospolitizdat.

Anderson, Richard D. Jr (1982) Soviet Decision-Making and Poland. *Problems of Communism* XXXI, 2 (Mar–April): 22–36.

Arbatov, Georgi (1973) *The War of Ideas in Contemporary International Relations*. Moscow: Progress Publishers.

Artem'ev, P. (1981) Neprisoedinenie—vazhny faktor mirovoi politiki. *Mirovaya ekonomika i mezhdunarodnye otnosheniya* 3: 61–72.

Arzumanyan, A. A. (1961) Novy etap obshchego krizisa kapitalizma. *Mirovaya ekonomika i mezhdunarodnye otnosheniya* 2: 3–19.

Ashley, Richard K. (1980) *The Political Economy of War and Peace: The Sino-Soviet-American Triangle and the Modern Security Problematique.* London: Frances Pinter.

Aspaturian, Vernon (1980) Soviet Global Power and the Correlation of Forces. *Problems of Communism* XXIX, 3 (May–June): 1–18.

Avakov, R. and L. Stepanov (1963) Sotsial'nye problemy natsional'no-osvoboditel'noi revolyutsii. *Mirovaya ekonomika i mezhdunarodnye otnosheniya* 5: 46–54.

Avineri, Shlomo (1969) Introduction. In Shlomo Avineri (ed.) *Marx on Colonialism & Modernization. His Despatches and Other Writings on China, India, Mexico, the Middle East and North Africa.* New York: Anchor Books, 1–25.

Azizyan, A. K. (1953) Velikaya sila idei proletarskogo internatsionalizma. *Voprosy filosofii* 5: 3–20.

—— (1956) On Proletarian Internationalism. *Current Digest of the Soviet Press* VIII, 51: 14–16.

Baginyan, K. A. (1956) Postoyanny neitralitet, pravo na samooborony i sistema regionalizma v svete Ustava OON. *Sovetskoe gosudarstvo i pravo* 6: 102–9.

Baratshvili, D. I. (1963) Pozitivny neitralitet v sovremennom mezhdunarodnom prave. *Sovetskoe gosudarstvo i pravo* 6: 95–103.

Benn, David W. (forthcoming) *Persuasion and Communication in the USSR: A Reassessment.* Oxford: Blackwells.

Berki, Ralph N. (1971) On Marxian Thought and the Problems of International Relations. *World Politics* XXIV, 1 (Oct.), 80–105.

Bialer, Seweryn (1980) *Stalin's Successors: Leadership, Stability and Change in the Soviet Union.* Cambridge: Cambridge University Press.

Blishchenko, Igor (1970) *Vneshniye funktsii sotsialisticheskogo gosudarstva.* Moscow: Yuridesheskaya literatura.

Bobrov, R. L. and M. Lukichev (1977) Indiiskaya politika neprisoedineniya i sovremennoe mezhdunarodnoe pravo. *Vestnik Leningradskogo universiteta* 23, Seriya: Ekonomika, filosofiya, pravo, Vypusk 4, 136–42.

Boersner, Demetrio (1982) *The Bolsheviks and the National and Colonial Question 1917–1928.* Westport Connecticut: Hyperion

Press.
Bogomolov, O. T. (1967) *Teoriya i metodologiya mezhdu-narodnogo sotsialisticheskogo razdeleniya truda.* Moscow: Mysl'.
—— Soglasovanie ekonomicheskikh interesov i politiki. *Kommunist* 10: 82–93.
Bol'shaya Sovetskaya Entsiklopediya (1955) (2nd ed) Moscow: Gosnauchizd-vo 'Bol'shaya Sovetskaya Entsiklopediya'.
Borkenau, Franz (1962), *World Communism: A History of the Communist International.* Ann Arbor: University of Michigan Press.
Bottomore, Tom, Laurence Harris, V. G. Kiernan and Ralph Miliband (1985) *A Dictionary of Marxist Thought.* Oxford: Basil Blackwell.
Bovin, A. (1986) Novoe myshlenie—trebovanie yadernogo veka. *Kommunist* 10: 113–24.
Brandt Commission I (1980) Report of the Independent Commission on International Development Issues. *North-South: A Programme for Survival.* London: Pan.
Brandt, Conrad (1958) *Stalin's Failure in China, 1924–1927.* Cambridge, Mass.: Harvard University Press.
Brezhnev, L. I. (1965) Velikaya pobeda sovetskogo naroda. In *Leninskim Kursom*, vol. 1. Moscow: Izd-vo politicheskoi literatury, 1970, 118–55.
—— (1966) Iz otchetnogo doklada tsentral'nogo komiteta KPSS XXIII s''ezdu Kommunisticheskoi partii Sovetskogo Soyuza. In L. I. Brezhnev, *O vneshnei politike KPSS i Sovetskogo gosudarstva.* Moscow: Izd-vo Politicheskoi literatury, 1973, 36–67.
—— (1969) Za ukreplenie splochennosti kommunistov, za novy pod ''em antiimperialisticheskoi bor'by. In L. I Brezhnev, *O vneshnei politike KPSS i Sovetskogo gosudarstva.* Moscow: Izd-vo Politicheskoi literatury, 1973, 144–93.
—— (1971) *Otchetny doklad Tsentral'nogo Komiteta KPSS XXIV s''ezdu Kommunisticheskoi partii Sovetskogo Soyuza.* Moscow: Izd-vo politicheskoi literatury.
—— (1973) *O vneshnei politike KPSS i Sovetskogo gosudarstva: Rechi i stat'i.* Moscow: Izd-vo politicheskoi literatury.
—— (1976a) *Report of the CPSU Central Committee and the Immediate Tasks of the Party in Home and Foreign Policy.* Moscow: Novosti Press Agency.
—— (1976b) Speech to Conference of the Communist and Workers' Parties of Europe, June 1976. *New Times* 28: 17–23.
—— (1981) *Report of the CPSU Central Committee and the Immediate Tasks of the Party in Home and Foreign Policy.* Moscow: Novosti Press Agency.

Brown, J. F. (1966) *The New Eastern Europe: The Khrushchev Era and After*. London: Pall Mall Press.
—— (1975) *Relations between the Soviet Union and its Eastern European Allies*. Santa Monica, Ca.: Rand Corporation for United States Air Force.
Brutents, K. N. (1965a) O nekotorykh osobennostyakh sovremennogo natsional'no-osvoboditel'nogo dvizheniya. *Voprosy filosofii* 1: 16–27.
—— (1965b) O nekotorykh osobennostyakh sovremennogo natsional'no-osvoboditel 'nogo dvizheniya. *Voprosy filosofii* 6: 26–37.
—— (1972a) Pravyashchaya revolyutsionnaya demokratiya: nekotorye cherty prakticheskoi deyatel'nosti. *Mirovaya ekonomika i mezhdunarodnye otnosheniya* 11: 104–17.
—— (1972b) Pravyashchaya revolyutsionnaya demokratiya: nekotorye cherty prakticheskoi deyatel'nosti. *Mirovaya ekonomika i mezhdunarodnye otnosheniya* 12: 115–29.
—— (1977) *National Liberation Movements Today* (2 vols). Moscow: Progress.
Brzezinski, Zbigniew (1967) *The Soviet Bloc: Unity and Conflict*. Cambridge, Mass.: Harvard University Press.
Burdzhalov, E. (1948) O mezhdunarodnom znachenii istoricheskogo opyta partii bol'shevikov. *Bolshevik* 17: 34–56.
Burin, Frederic S. (1963) The Communist Doctrine of the Inevitability of War. *American Political Science Review* LVII, 2 (June): 334–54.
Burlatsky, Fyodor M. (1970) *Lenin, gosudarstvo, politika*. Moscow: Nauka.
—— and Galkin, Aleksandr A. (1974) *Sotsiologiya, politika, mezhdunarodnye otnosheniya*. Moscow: IMO.
—— (1982) Mezhdutsarstvie ili khronika vremen Den Syapina. *Novy mir* 4: 205–28.
Burton, John, A. J. R. Groom, Margot Light, C. R. Mitchell and Dennis J. Sandole (1984) *Britain between East and West: A Concerned Independence*. Aldershot: Gower.
Butenko, A. P. (1964) Revolyutsionnye preobrazovaniya v stranakh Tsentral'noi i Yugo-Vostochnoi Evropy. *Mirovaya ekonomika i mezhdunarodnye otnosheniya* 9: 15–29.
—— (ed.) (1975) *Sotsializm i mezhdunarodnye otnosheniya*. Moscow: Nauka.
—— (1982) Nekotorye teoreticheskie problemy perekhoda k sotsializmu stran s nerazvitoi ekonomikoi. *Narody Azii i Afriki* 5: 70–9.
—— (1984) *Sotsializm kak mirovaya sistema*. Moscow: Politizdat.
—— (1987) *Theory and Practice of Real Socialism: Questions and*

Answers. Sofia: Sofia Press Agency.

Bykov, Oleg (1981) Putevodnaya nit' v budushchee. *Mirovaya ekonomika i mezhdunarodnye otnosheniya* 5: 3–15.

—— (1986) Vseobshchaya bezopasnost'- vlastnoe trebovanie vremeni. *Mirovaya ekonomika i mezhdunarodnye otnosheniya* 3:28–39.

Carr, Edward Hallett (1966) *The Bolshevik Revolution* (3 vols). Harmondsworth, Middlesex: Penguin.

—— (1970–2) *Socialism in One Country (3 vols). Harmondsworth, Middlesex: Pelican.*

Chekhutov, A. (1981) Razvitie finansovo-ekonomicheskogo sotrudnichestva sotsialisticheskikh i osvobodivshikhsya stran. *Mirovaya ekonomika i mezhdunarodnye otnosheniya* 4: 50–62.

Chicherin, Georgy V. (1961) *Stat'i i rechi po voprosam mezhdunarodnoi politiki*. Moscow: Izd-vo sotsial'no-ekonomicheskoi literatury.

Chirkin, Veniamin E. and Y. Yudin (1978) *A Socialist Orientated State*. Moscow: Progress Publishers.

—— (1980) *Burzhuaznaya politologiya i deistvitel'nost' razvivayushchikhsya stran: Kritika kontseptsii 'politicheskoi modernizatsii'*. Moscow: IMO.

Chistyakov, A. (1954) Razvitie ekonomicheskogo sotrudnichestva stran sotsialisticheskogo lagerya. *Kommunist* 15: 45–60.

Choucri, N. and R. C. North (1975) *Nations in Conflict: National Growth and International Violence*. San Francisco: Freeman.

Clarkson, Stephen (1978) *The Soviet Theory of Development: India and the Third World in Marxist-Leninist Scholarship*. London: Macmillan.

Claudin, Fernando (1975) *The Communist Movement*. Harmondsworth, Middlesex: Penguin.

Communism and the International Situation (1928) Theses on the International Situation and the Tasks of the Communist International adopted at the Sixth World Congress of the Communist International. London: Modern Books.

Communist Party of the Soviet Union (CPSU) (1971) *24th Congress of the Communist Party of the Soviet Union: Documents and Resolutions*. Moscow: Novosti Press Agency Publishing House.

—— (1976) *25th Congress of the Communist Party of the Soviet Union: Documents and Resolutions*. Moscow: Novosti Press Agency Publishing House.

Conference of Communist and Workers' Parties (1969) Documents. *International Affairs* 8: 3–23.

Conference of Communist and Workers' Parties of Europe (1970) For Peace, Security, Co-operation and Social Progress in

Europe. *New Times* 28: 24–32.

Constitution (Fundamental Law) of the Union of Soviet Socialist Republics (1985) Moscow: Novosti Press Agency Publishing House.

Council for Mutual Economic Aid (1971) *Comprehensive Programme for the Further Extension and Improvement of Co-operation and the Development of Socialist Economic Integration*. Moscow: CMEA.

Current Soviet Policies V (1973) Documentary Record of the 23rd Congress of the Communust Party of the Soviet Union. Columbus, Ohio: American Association for the Advancement of Slavic Studies.

Current Soviet Policies VI (1973) Documentary Record of the 24th Congress of the Communist Party of the Soviet Union. Columbus, Ohio: American Association for the Advancement of Slavic Studies.

Current Soviet Policies VII (1976) Documentary Record of the 25th Congress of the Communist Party of the Soviet Union. Columbus, Ohio: American Association for the Advancement of Slavic Studies.

Current Soviet Policies VIII (1981) Documentary Record of the 26th Congress of the Communist Party of the Soviet Union. Columbus, Ohio: Current Digest of the Soviet Press.

Dallin, Alexander with Jonathan Harrison Grey Hodnett (eds) (1963) *Diversity in International Communism: A Documentary Record, 1961–1963*. New York/London: Columbia University Press.

Dallin, David J. (1962) *Soviet Foreign Policy after Stalin*. London: Methuen.

Daniels, Robert V. (ed) (1984) *A Documentary History of Communism* (2 vols, rev. edn). Hanover and London: University Press of New England for the University of Vermont.

Dawisha, Adeed and Karen Dawisha (eds) (1982) *The Soviet Union in the Middle East: Policies and Perspectives*. London: Heinemann for the Royal Institute of International Affairs.

Dawisha, Karen (1980) *The Kremlin and the Prague Spring*. London and Berkeley, Ca.: University of California Press.

—— and Philip Hanson (eds) (1981) *Soviet–East European Dilemmas: Coercion, Competition and Consent*. London: Heinemann for the Royal Institute of International Affairs.

—— and Valdez, Jonathan (1987) Socialist Internationalism in Eastern Europe. *Problems of Communism* XXXVI, 2: 1–14.

Deane, Michael J. (1976) The Soviet Assessment of the Correlation of World Forces: Implications for American Foreign Policy.

Orbis 20, 3 (Fall): 625–36.

Debo, Richard (1979) *Revolution and Survival: The Foreign Policy of Soviet Russia 1917–18*. Toronto and Buffalo: University of Toronto Press.

Deborin, G. A. (1956) Leninskaya politika mirnogo sosushchest-vovaniya dvukh sistem—general'naya liniya vneshnei politiki SSSR. *Voprosy ekonomiki* 4: 16–29.

—— (ed.) (1958) *Mezhdunarodnye otnosheniya i vneshnyaya politika Sovetskogo Soyuza, 1945–1949*. Moscow: IMO.

—— and A. Manusevich (1965) Istorichesky opyt pervoi russkoi revolyutsii. *Kommunist* 3: 29–37.

—— I. I. Gaglov, L. N. Kornev, I N. Ksenofontov and G. Z. Lekomtsev (1982) *Razryadka protiv antirazryadka*. Moscow: Politzdat.

Declaration of the Conference of Representatives of Communist and Workers' Parties of Socialist Countries (1957) *Current Digest of the Soviet Press* IX, 47: 3–7.

Degras, Jane (ed.) (1951–3) *Soviet Documents on Foreign Policy, 1917–1941* (3 vols). London: Oxford University Press.

—— (ed.) (1956, 1960, 1965) *The Communist International, 1919–1943: Documents* (3 vols). London: Oxford University Press.

de Reuck, A. V. S. (1985) Power, Influence and Authority. In Margot Light and A. J. R. Groom (eds), *International Relations: A Handbook of Current Theory*. London: Frances Pinter, 113–20.

Dictionary of Basic Military Terms: A Soviet View (n.d.) Washington, DC: US Government Printing Office.

Dimitrov, G. (1949) Report of Comrade G. M. Dimitrov to the 5th Congress of the Bulgarian Workers' Party (Communists). *For a Lasting Peace, for a Peoples' Democracy*, Jan. 1, 3–4.

Dinerstein, H. S. (1962) *War and the Soviet Union: Nuclear Weapons and the Revolution in Soviet Military and Political Thinking* (2nd rev. edn). New York and London: Praeger.

Discussion of the Character and Effect of People's Democracy in the Orient (1951) *Current Digest of the Soviet Press* IV, 20: 3–7, 43.

Djilas, Milovan (1969) *Conversations with Stalin*. Harmondsworth, Middlesex: Pelican.

Dobrynin, A. (1986) Za bez"yaderny mir, navstrechu XXI veku. *Kommunist* 9: 18–31.

Dokumenty Vneshnei Politiki SSSR (1957–82) (vols 1–21). Moscow: Politizdat.

Donaldson, Robert H. (ed.) (1981) *The Soviet Union in the Third World: Successes and Failures*. London: Croom Helm; Boulder, Colo.: Westview Press.

Dudinsky, Ilya V. (1952) Industrializatsiya—osnovnoe zveno stroitel'stva fundamenta sotsializma v evropeiskikh stranakh narodnoi demokratii. *Voprosy filosofii* 5: 132–48.

—— (1976), *Sotsialisticheskoe sodruzhestvo: osnovnye tendentsii razvitiya*. Moscow: Mysl'.

—— (1980) Socialist Internationalism in Action. *International Affairs* 2: 8–17.

Duncan, W. Raymond (ed.) (1980), *Soviet Policy in the Third World*. New York, Oxford: Pergamon Press.

Durdenevsky, V. N. (1956) The Five Principles. *International Affairs* 3: 45–50.

—— (1957) Neitralitet v sisteme kollektivnoi bezonasnosti. *Sovetskoe gosudarstvo i pravo* 8: 81–91.

XX S"ezd Kommunisticheskoi partii Sovetskogo Soyuza i zadachi izucheniya sovremennogo Vostoka (1956) *Sovetskoe Vostokovedenie* 1: 3–12.

XXIII S"ezd Kommunisticheskoi partii Sovetskogo Soyuza, 29 March to 9 April (1966), Stenografichesky otchet. Moscow: Izd-vo politicheskoi literatury.

XXV S"ezd Kommunisticheskoi partii Sovetskogo Soyuza, 24 February to 5 March (1976) Stenografichesky otchet. Moscow: Izdatel'stvo politicheskoi literatury.

XXVI S"ezd Kommunisticheskoi partii Sovetskogo Soyuza, 23 February to 3 March (1981) Stenografichesky otchet. Moscow: Izdatel'stvo politicheskoi literatury.

Dvorzhak, Ladislav (1965), *Mirovaya sistema sotsializma i razvivayushchiesya strany*. Moscow: Mysl'.

Easton, David (1965) *A Framework for Political Analysis*. Englewood Cliffs, NJ: Prentice Hall.

Egorov, Valery N. (1971) *Mirnoe sosushchestvovanie i revolyutsionny protsess*. Moscow: IMO.

Engels, Frederick (1864) Letter to Weydemeyer. *Marx-Engels Selected Correspondence*, 1980, 140–1.

—— (1866) Letter to Marx. *Marx Engels Selected Correspondence*, 1980, 169–70.

—— (1877) Socialism: Utopian and Scientific. *Marx Engels Selected Works*, vol. 2. Moscow: Foreign Languages Publishing House, 1962, 93–155.

—— (1882) Letter to Kautsky in Vienna. *Marx Engels Selected Correspondence*, 1980, 330–1.

Eran, Oded (1979) *The Mezhdunarodniki: An Assessment of Professional Expertise in the Making of Soviet Foreign Policy*. Ramat Gan, Turtledove.

Erickson, John (1962) *The Soviet High Command: A Military-*

Political History, 1918–1941. London: Macmillan.
Ermolenko, Dmitrii V. (1977), *Sotsiologiya i problemy mezhdunarodnykh otnoshenii.* Moscow: IMO.
The Essential Left: Four Classic Texts on the Principles of Socialism (1960) London: Unwin Books.
Etinger, Yakov Ya. and Ovanes Melikyan (1964) *Neitralizm i mir: Neitralistskaya politika stran Azii i Afriki.* Moscow: Mysl'.
—— (1981) Dvizhenie neprisoedineniya: aktual'nye problemy. *Narody Azii i Afriki* 6: 3–13.
—— (1983) Vazhny faktor mira i mezhdunarodnoi bezonasnosti. *Mirovaya ekonomika i mezhdunarodnye otnosheniya* 3: 41–50.
Eudin, Xenia J. and Robert C. North (1957) *Soviet Russia and the East, 1920–1927: A Documentary Survey.* Stanford: Stanford University Press.
—— and Robert M. Slusser (1966, 1967) *Soviet Foreign Policy 1928–1934: Documents and Materials* (2 vols). University Park and London: Pennsylvania State University Press.

Farberov, N. P. (1948) Obshchestvennoe i gosudarstvennoe ustroistvo stran narodnoi demokratii (konstitutsii narodno-demokraticheskikh respublik). *Bolshevik* 24 (Dec): 30–43.
—— (1949) *Gosudarstvennoe pravo stran narodnoi demokratii.* Moscow: Yuridicheskoi literatury.
—— (1957) O edinstve sotsialisticheskikh gosudarstv i svoyeobrazii ikh politicheskikh form. *Sovetskoe gosudarstvo i pravo* 6: 40–51.
Fedoseyev, Anatolii A. (1974) *Politika kak ob"ekt sotsiologicheskogo issledovaniya: Kritika metodologicheskikh osnov sovremennoi burzhuaznoi politologii.* Leningrad: Izd-vo Leningradskogo universiteta.
Fedoseyev, P. N., I. Pomelov and V. Cheprakov (1958a) O proekte programmy Souza Kommunistov Yugoslavii.*Kommunist* 6 (Apr): 16–39 (Trans. in *Current Digest of the Soviet Press* X, 18: 3–11).
—— (1958b) Problema mirnogo sosushchestvovaniya v sotsiologicheskikh issledovaniyakh i v prepodavanii sotsiologii. *Voprosy filosofii* 4: 3–14.
—— and I. Pomelov (1959) O razvitii mirovoi sotsialisticheskoi sistemy k kommunizmu. *Kommunist* 5 (Apr.): 27–43.
—— (1969) Marxism and Internationalism. *International Affairs* 3: 3–8.
Fedotova, Evelina M. (1975) *SShA i neprisoedinivshiesya strany.* Moscow: Nauka, Glavnaya redaktsiya vostochnoi literatury.
Fejtö, François (1974) *A History of the Peoples' Democracies.* Harmondsworth, Middlesex: Penguin.
Figurnov, P. K. (1954) O dvukh etapakh razvitiya narodnodemo-

kraticheskogo stroya v evropeiskikh stranakh narodnoi demokratii. *Voprosy fiilosofii* 5: 124–37.

Fitzpatrick, Sheila (1982) *The Russian Revolution.* Oxford/New York: Oxford University Press.

Franklin, Bruce (ed.) (1973) *The Essential Stalin: Major Theoretical Writings 1905–52.* London: Croom Helm.

Fukuyama, Francis (1985) The Rise and Fall of the Marxist-Leninist Vanguard Party. *Survey* Vol. 29, 2 (125): 116–35.

—— (1986) Gorbachev and the Third World. *Foreign Affairs* Vol. 64, 4: 715–31.

Fullerton, John (1983) *The Soviet Invasion of Afghanistan.* Hong Kong: Far Eastern Economic Review.

Galina, A. (1958) Problema neitraliteta v sovremennom mezhdunarodnom prave. In *Sovetskii ezhegodnik mezhdunarodnogo prava 1958.* Moscow: Izd-vo Akademii Nauk SSSR, 1959, 200–29.

Galkin, I. S. (1953) K. Marks o klassovoi bor'be v burzhuaznom obshchestve i diktature proletariata. *Voprosy istorii* 5: 3–29.

Gantman, Vladimir I. (ed.) (1976) *Sovremennie burzhuaznye teorii mezhdunarodnykh otnoshenii: kritichesky analiz.* Moscow: Nauka.

—— (ed.) (1981) *Razryadka mezhdunarodnoi napryazhennosti i ideologicheskaya bor'ba.* Moscow: Nauka.

Ganyushin, B. V. (1958) *Sovremenny neitralitet. Moscow: IMO.*

Garthoff, Raymond L. (1966) *Soviet Military Policy: A Historical analysis.* London: Faber & Faber.

Gati, Charles (ed.) (1976), *The International Politics of Eastern Europe.* New York: Praeger.

Gati, Toby Trista (1980) The Soviet Union and the North–South Dialogue. *Orbis* 24, 2 (Summer): 241–70.

Gellner, Ernest (1978) Soviets against Wittfogel. Unpublished paper.

Generalov, V. F. (1950) Ob osnovnykh chertakh mezhdunarodno-pravogo sotrudnichestva Sovetskogo Soyuza i stran narodnoi demokratii. *Sovetskoe gosudarstvo i pravo* 7: 14–26.

Ginsburgs, George (1960) Neutrality and neutralism and the tactics of Soviet diplomacy. *American Slavic and East European Review* XIX, 4: 531–60.

Glickham, Charles (1986) New Directions for Soviet Foreign Policy. *Radio Liberty Research Supplement* 2/86.

Golikov, V. (1965) Vazhny printsip leninskoi vneshnei politiki. *Kommunist* 18: 91–9.

Goormaghtigh, John (1974) International Relations as a Field of Study in the Soviet Union. *Yearbook of World Affairs, Volume*

28. London: Stevens & Sons, 250–61.

Gorbachev, M. S. (1986) Politichesky doklad Tsentral'nogo Komiteta KPSS XXVII S"ezdu Kommunisticheskoi partii Sovetskogo Soyuza. *Pravda,* 26 February 1986.

Goulet, Denis (1973) *The Cruel Choice: A New Concept in the Theory of Development.* New York: Atheneum.

Grechko, Andrei A. (1977) *The Armed Forces of the Soviet Union.* Moscow: Progress Publishers.

Griffith, William E. (ed.) (1964) *The Sino-Soviet Rift.* London: George Allen & Unwin.

Griffiths, Franklyn (1964) The Origins of Peaceful Coexistence: A Historical Note. *Survey* 50 (Jan.): 195–201.

Grigoryan, S. N. (ed.) (1966) *Ideologiya sovremennogo natsional'no-osvoboditel'nogo dvizheniya.* Moscow: Nauka.

Gromyko, Anatoly A. (ed.) (1981) *African Countries' Foreign Policy.* Moscow: Progress.

Gromyko, Andrei A., C. A. Golunsky and V. M. Khvostov (eds) (1960–4) *Diplomatichesky slovar'* (3 vols.). Moscow: Politicheskoi literatury.

—— (ed.) (1962) *Mirnoe sosushchestvovanie—Leninskii kurs vneshnei politiki Sovetskogo Soyuza.* Moscow: IMO.

—— and B. N. Ponomarev (eds) (1971, 1976, 1981) *Istoriya vneshnei politiki SSSR* (2 vols.; 1st edn ed. B. N. Ponomarev, A. A. Gromkyo and V. M. Khvostov). Moscow: Nauka.

—— A. G. Kovalev, P. P. Sevos"yanov and S. L. Tikhvinsky (eds) (1984–5) *Diplomatichesky slovar'* (4th edn, 2 vols, 3rd has not yet appeared). Moscow: Nauka.

Gruliow, Leo (ed.) (1953) *Current Soviet Policies I.* The Documentary Record of the Nineteenth Communist Party Congress and the Reorganization after Stalin's Death. New York: Praeger.

—— (ed.) (1957) *Current Soviet Policies II.* The Documentary Record of the 20th Communist Party Congress and its Aftermath. London: Atlantic Press, distributed by Thames & Hudson.

—— (ed.) (1960) *Current Soviet Policies III.* The Documentary Record of the Extraordinary 21st Communist Party Congress. New York: Columbia University Press.

Gudymenko, S. and B. S. Starostin (1981) Traditsii i obshchestvenny progress v razvivayushchikhsya stranakh. *Mirovaya ekonomika i mezhdunarodnye otnosheniya* 9: 119–28.

Hakovirta, Harto (1983) The Soviet Union and the Varieties of Neutrality in Western Europe. *World Politics* XXXV, 4 (July): 563–85.

Halliday, Fred (1983) *The Making of the Second Cold War.* London: Verso.

—— (1987) Vigilantism in International Relations: Kubálková, Cruickshank and Marxist Theory. *Review of International Studies* Vol. 13, 3: 163–75.

Harding, Neil (1977) *Lenin's Political Thought* (2 vols). London: Macmillan.

—— (ed.) (1984) *The State in Socialist Society*. London: Macmillan in association with St Antony's College, Oxford.

Heldman, Dan C. (1981) *The USSR and Africa: Foreign Policy under Khrushchev*. New York: Praeger.

Herod, Charles C. (1976), *The Nation in the History of Marxian Thought: The Concept of Nations with History and Nations without History*. The Hague: Martinus Nijhoff.

Herspring, Dale R. (1980) The Warsaw Pact at 25. *Problems of Communism* XXXIX, 5 (Sept.–Oct.): 1–15.

History of the Communist Party of the Soviet Union (Bolsheviks): Short Course (1939) Moscow: Foreign Languages Publishing House.

Hobsbawm, Eric and Terence Ranger (eds) (1983), *The Invention of Tradition*. Cambridge: Cambridge University Press.

Hoffmann, Erik P. and Frederic J. Fleron, Jr (eds) (1980), *The Conduct of Soviet Foreign Policy*. New York:Aldine Publishing Company.

Hosmer, Stephen T. and Thomas W. Wolfe (1983) *Soviet Policy toward Third World Conflicts*. Lexington, Mass./Toronto: Lexington Books/D. C. Heath.

Hough, Jerry F. (1977) *The Soviet Union and Social Science Theory*. Cambridge, Mass./London: Harvard University Press.

—— (1980) The Evolution in the Soviet World View. *World Politics* XXXII, 4 (July): 509–30.

—— (1986) *The Struggle for the Third World: Soviet Debates and American Options*. Washington, DC: Brookings Institution.

Il'ichev, L. F., Sh. P. Sanakoyev, M. A. Kharlamov, D. E. Mel'nikov (1958) *Voprosy vneshnei politiki SSSR i sovremennykh mezhdunarodnykh otnoshenii*. Moscow: Gospolitizdat.

Irkhin, Yu. V. (1982) Avangardnye revolyutsionnye partii trud-yashchikhsya v osvobodivshikhsya stranakh. *Voprosy istorii* 4: 55–67.

Israelyan, V. (1967) The Leninist Science of International Relations. *International Affairs* 6: 46–52.

Ivanova, Inessa M. (1965) *Mirnoe sosushchestvovanie i krizis vneshnepoliticheskoi ideologii imperializma SShA*. Moscow: IMO.

Jamgotch, Nish Jr (1968) *Soviet–East European Dialogue: Inter-*

national Relations of a New Type? Stanford: Hoover Institution on War, Revolution and Peace, Stanford University.

Jones, Christopher D. (1975) Just Wars and Limited Wars: Restraint on the Use of the Soviet Armed Forces. *World Politics* XXXVIII, 1 (Oct.): 44–68.

—— (1981) *Soviet Influence in Eastern Europe: Political Autonomy and the Warsaw Pact.* New York: Praeger.

Joravsky, David (1970) *The Lysenko Affair.* Cambridge, Mass: Harvard University Press.

Kanet, Roger E. (ed.) (1974) *The Soviet Union and the Developing Nations.* Baltimore: Johns Hopkins Press.

Kanet, Roger E. and Donna Bahry (eds) (1975) *Soviet Economic and Political Relations with the Developing World.* New York/ Washington/London: Praeger Special Studies in International Politics and Government.

Kapchenko, N. (1975) Socialist Foreign Policy and the Restructuring of International Relations. *International Affairs* 4: 3–13.

—— (1978) Leninist Foreign Policy: A Transformative Force. *International Affairs* 10: 3–13.

—— (1987) Politicheskaya filosofiya mira v raketno-yaderny vek. *Mezhdunarodnaya zhizn'* 2: 12–24.

Kardelj, Edvard (1961) *Socialism and War: A Survey of Chinese Criticism of the Policy of Coexistence.* London: Methuen.

Karenin, Aleksei (1971) *Filosofiya politicheskogo nasiliya: Kritika nekotorykh antikommunisticheskikh kontseptsii v oblasti vneshnei politiki SShA.* Moscow: IMO.

Kaser, Michael (1965) *COMECON: Integration Problems of the Planned Economies.* London: Oxford University Press, under the auspices of the Royal Institute of International Affairs.

Katushev, Konstantin (1973) Ukreplenie edinstva sotsialisticheskikh stran-zakonomernost'razvitiya mirovogo sotsializma. *Kommunist* 16: 17–31.

Katz, Mark N. (1982) *The Third World in Soviet Military Thought.* London/Canberra: Croom Helm.

Kautsky, Karl (1970) Ultraimperialism. *New Left Review* 59: 40–8.

Kechek"yan, S. F. (1952) Znachenie truda I.V. Stalina 'Marksizm i voprosy yazykoznaniya' dlya istorii politicheskikh uchenii. *Sovetskoe gosudarstvo i pravo* 3: 6–16.

Kennan, George F. [X] (1947) The Sources of Soviet Conduct. *Foreign Affairs XXV, 4 (July): 566–82.*

—— (1961) *Russia and the West under Lenin and Stalin.* New York and Scarborough, Ontario: Mentor.

Khabirov, V. G. (1973) O mezhdunarodno-pravovykh aspektakh neprisoedineniya'', *Sovetskoe gosudarstvo i pravo* 12: 111–17.

Kharin, Yu A. (1981) *Fundamentals of Dialectics*. Moscow: Progress Publishers.

Khrushchev, Nikita S. (1956a) Report of the Central Committee of the Communist Party of the Soviet Union to the 20th Party Congress. In L. Gruliow (ed.) *Current Soviet Policies II*. The Documentary Record of the 20th Communist Party Congress and its Aftermath. London: Atlantic Press, distributed by Thames & Hudson, 1957, 29–62.

—— (1956b) Secret Speech. In L. Gruliow (ed.) *Current Soviet Policies II*. The Documentary Record of the 20th Communist Party Congress and its Aftermath. London: Atlantic Press, distributed by Thames & Hudson, 1957, 172–88.

—— (1959a) On Peaceful Co-existence. *Foreign Affairs* 38, 1 (Oct.): 1–18.

——(1959b) Report of the Central Committee to the 21st Extraordinary Congress. In L. Gruliow (ed.) *Current Soviet Policies III*. The Documentary Record of the Extraordinary 21st Communist Party Congress. New York: Columbia University Press, 1960, 41–72.

—— (1961a) For New Victories for the World Communist Movement. *World Marxist Review* 1: 2–27.

—— (1961b) Report of the Central Committee of the CPSU to the 22nd Party Congress. In C. Saikowski and L. Gruliow (eds) *Current Soviet Policies IV*. New York and London: Columbia University Press, 1962, 42–77.

—— (1962) Vital Questions of the Development of the Socialist World System. *World Marxist Review* 9: 2–18.

Khvoinik, P. (1980) Mirovoi kapitalizm i razvivayushchiesya gosudarstva (O doklade komissii V. Brandta). *Mirovaya ekonomika i mezhdundarodnye otnosheniya* 10: 44–57.

Kim, G. (1962) O gosudarstve natsional'noi demokratii. *Aziya i Afrika segodnya* 10: 2–5.

—— (1980) Social Development and Ideological Struggle in the Developing Countries. *International Affairs* 4: 65–75.

Kiva, A. (1975) O nekotorykh osobennostyakh kapitalisticheskogo razvitiya v 'tret'em mire'. *Mirovaya ekonomika i mezhdunarodnye otnosheniya* 3: 113–23.

Knorr, Klaus and James M. Rosenau (eds) (1969) *Contending Approaches to International Politics*. Princeton, NJ: Princeton University Press.

Kokoshin, Andrei A. (1975) *Prognozirovanie i politika*. Moscow: IMO.

—— (1978) *O burzhuaznykh prognozakh razvitiya mezhdunarodnykh otnoshenii*. Moscow: IMO.

Kolakowski, Leszek (1978) *Main Currents of Marxism: Its Origins,*

Growth and Dissolution (3 vols). Oxford: Oxford University Press.

Konoplev, E. (1975) Spetsifika protsessa vosproizvodstva v mnogoukladnoi ekonomike. *Mirovaya ekonomika i mezhdunarodnye otnosheniya* 2: 101–6.

Korionov, Vitalii and Nikolai N. Yakovlev (1961) *SSSR i SShA dolzhny zhit' v mire: Sovetsko-amerikanskie otnosheniya: proshloe i nastoyashchee*. Moscow: Izd-vo politicheskoi literatury.

Korovin, E. A. (1926) *Sovremennoe mezhdunarodnoe publichnoe pravo*. Moscow, Leningrad, Gosudarstvennoe izdatel'stvo.

—— (1947) *Osnovnye printsipy sovetskoi vneshnei politiki*. Moscow: Izd-vo 'Pravda'.

—— (ed.) (1951) *Mezhdunarodnoe pravo*. Moscow: Izd-vo Yuridicheskoi literatury.

—— (1956) The Five Principles— A Basis for Peaceful Coexistence. *International Affairs* 5: 46–59.

—— (1958a) The Problem of Neutrality To-day. *International Affairs* 3: 36–40.

—— (1958b) Proletarian Internationalism in World Relations. *International Affairs* 2: 23–30.

Kortunov, V. (1979) The Leninist Policy of Peaceful Coexistence and Class Struggle. *International Affairs* 5: 85–94.

Kosolapov, R. I and T. I. Oizerman (1984) Ideologiya voskhodyashchego klassa. *Kommunist* 13: 45–57.

Kovalev, Professor (1968) Sovereignty and the Internationalist Obligations of Socialist Countries. In R. A. Remington (ed.) *Winter in Prague: Documents on Czechoslovak Communism in Crisis*. Cambridge, Mass.: MIT Press 1969, 412–6.

Kozhevnikov, F. I. (1951) Nekotorye voprosy mezhdunarodnogo prava v svete truda I. V. Stalina 'Marksizm i voprosy yazykoznaniya'. *Sovetskoe gosudarstvo i pravo* 6: 25–36.

Krasin, Yu. (1986) Strategiya mira—imperativ epokhi. *Mirovaya ekonomika i mezhdunarodnye otnosheniya* 1: 3–12.

Krylov, C. B. and V. N. Durdenevsky (eds) (1957) *Mezhdunarodno-pravovye formy mirnogo sosushchestvovaniya gosudarstv i natsii*. Moscow: IMO.

Kubálková, Vendulka and Albert A. Cruickshank (1978) The Soviet Concept of Peaceful Coexistence: Some Theoretical and Semantic Problems. *Australian Journal of Politics and History XXIV, 2 (Aug.): 184–98.*

—— and Albert A. Cruickshank (1980) *Marxism-Leninism and Theory of International Relations*. London: Routledge & Kegan Paul.

—— and Albert A. Cruickshank (1985) *Marxism and International Relations*. Oxford: Clarendon Press.

Kuhn, Thomas, S. (1970) *The Structure of Scientific Revolutions* (International Encyclopaedia of Unified Science). Chicago and London: University of Chicago Press.

Kulish, V. M. (1972) *Voennaya sila i mezhdunarodnye otnosheniya.* Moscow: IMO.

Kulski, Wladyslaw W. (1959) *Peaceful Co-existence: An Analysis of Soviet Foreign Policy.* Chicago: Henry Regnery Company (published in cooperation with Foundation for Foreign Affairs, Inc.).

Kuusinen, O. (ed.) (1961) *Fundamentals of Marxism-Leninism.* London: Lawrence & Wishart; Moscow: Foreign Langugages Publishing House.

Lane, Christel (1981) *The Rites of Rulers: Ritual in Industrial Society—the Soviet Case.* Cambridge: Cambridge University Press.

Latso, A. (1974) *Varshavsky dogovor—instrument obespecheniya mira.* Moscow: IMO.

Lazarev, M. I. (1949) Tovarishch Stalin o nevmeshatel'stve vo vnutrennie dela gosudarstva i o ponyatii interventsii. *Sovetskoe gosudarstvo i pravo,* 11: 1–18.

Lazutkin, E. S. (1948) Speech at conference 'O nedostatkakh i zadachakh nauchno-issledovatel'skoi raboty v oblasti ekonomiki' (to criticize Varga). *Voprosy ekonomiki* 9: 102–8.

Lebedev, Nikolai I. (1976) *Novy etap mezhdunarodnykh otnoshenii.* Moscow: IMO

—— N. P. Dracheva and V. B. Knyazhinsky (1981) *Mezhdunarodnie otnosheniya i bor'ba idei.* Moscow: Izd-vo politicheskoi literatury.

—— (1982) *The USSR in World Politics.* Moscow: Progress Publishers.

Leebaert, Derek (ed.) (1981) *Soviet Military Thinking.* London: George Allen & Unwin.

Lemin, I. (1942) Anglo-indiiskie otnosheniya i voina. *Mirovoe khozyaistvo i mirovaya politika* 5–6: 76–84.

—— (1946) Mezhdunarodnye otnosheniya v 1945 godu. *Mirovoe khozyaistvo i mirovaya politika* 1: 20–34.

Lenin, Vladimir I. (1894) The Economic Content of Narodism and the Criticism of it in Mr Struve's Book. *Collected Works,* vol. 1. Moscow: Foreign Languages Publishing House; London: Lawrence & Wishart, 1960, 333–507.

—— (1897) The Tasks of the Russian Social-Democrats. *Collected Works,* vol. 2. Moscow: Foreign languages Publishing House; London: Lawrence & Wishart, 1960, 323–47.

—— (1902) What is to be Done? *Collected Works,* vol. 5: Moscow: Foreign Languages Publishing House; London: Lawrence &

Wishart, 1961, 347–529.

—— (1905) The Two Tactics of Social Democracy in the Democratic Revolution. *Collected Works*, vol. 9. Moscow: Foreign Languages Publishing House; London: Lawrence & Wishart, 1962, 15–140.

—— (1907) The International Socialist Congress in Stuttgart. In V. I. Lenin, *The National Liberation in the East*. Moscow: Progress Publishers, 1980, 17–19.

—— (1908) Inflammable Material in World Politics. In V. I. Lenin, *The National Liberation in the East*. Moscow: Progress Publishers, 1980, 20–6.

—— (1912) Democracy and Narodism in China. In V. I. Lenin, *The National Liberation in the East*. Moscow: Progress Publishers, 1980, 45–51.

—— (1913) Critical Remarks on the National Question. *Collected Works*, vol. 20. Moscow: Foreign Languages Publishing House; London: Lawrence & Wishart, 1964, 17–51.

—— (1914a) The Agrarian Question in Russia. *Collected Works*, vol. 20. Moscow: Foreign Languages Publishing House; London: Lawrence & Wishart, 1964, 375–7.

—— (1914b) The Right of Nations to Self-Determination. *Collected Works*, vol. 20. Moscow: Foreign Languages Publishing House; London: Lawrence & Wishart, 1964, 393–454.

—— (1915a) The Collapse of the Second International. *Collected Works*, vol. 21. Moscow: Foreign Languages Publishing House; London: Lawrence & Wishart, 1964, 205–59.

—— (1915b) On the Defence of the Fatherland Slogan. *Collected Works*, vol. 21. Moscow: Foreign languages Publishing House; London: Lawrence & Wishart, 1964, 158–64.

—— (1915c) On the Slogan for a United States of Europe. *Collected Works*, vol. 21. Moscow: Foreign Languages Publishing House; London: Lawrence & Wishart, 1964, 339–43.

—— (1915d) Socialism and War. *Collected Works*, vol. 21. Moscow: Foreign Languages Publishing House; London: Lawrence & Wishart, 1964, 295–338.

—— (1916a) A Caricature of Marxism and Imperialist Economism. *Collected Works*, vol. 23. Moscow: Foreign Languages Publishing House; London: Lawrence & Wishart, 1964, 28–76.

—— (1916b) The 'Disarmament' Slogan. *Collected Works*, vol. 23. Moscow: Foreign Languages Publishing House; London: Lawrence & Wishart. 1964, 94–104.

—— (1916c) The Discussion on Self-Determination Summed Up. *Collected Works*, vol. 22. Moscow: Foreign Languages Publishing House; London: Lawrence & Wishart, 1964, 320–60.

—— (1916d) Imperialism, the Highest Stage of Capitalism.

Collected Works, vol. 22. Moscow: Foreign Languages Publishing House; London: Lawrence & Wishart, 1964, 185–304.

—— (1916e) The Military Programme of the Proletarian Revolution. *Collected Works*, vol. 23. Moscow: Foreign Languages Publishing House; London: Lawrence & Wishart, 1964, 77–93.

—— (1916f) Reply to P. Kievsky (Y. Pyatakov). *Collected Works*, vol. 23. Moscow: Foreign Languages Publishing House; London: Lawrence & Wishart, 1964, 22–7.

—— (1916g) The Socialist Revolution and the Right of Nations to Self-Determination. *Collected Works*, vol. 22. Moscow: Foreign Languages Publishing House; London: Lawrence & Wishart, 1964, 143–56.

—— (1917a) Bourgeois Pacifism and Socialist Pacifism. *Collected Works*, vol. 23. Moscow: Foreign Languages Publishing House; London: Lawrence & Wishart, 1964, 177–94.

—— (1917b) Concluding Speech following the discussion on the Report on Peace at the Second All-Russian Congress of Soviets. *Collected Works*, vol. 26. Moscow: Foreign Languages Publishing House; London: Lawrence & Wishart, 1964, 254–6.

—— (1917c) Farewell Letter to Swiss Workers. *Collected Works*, vol. 23. Moscow: Foreign Languages Publishing House; London: Lawrence & Wishart, 1964, 367–73.

—— (1917d) Letters from Afar. *Collected Works*, vol. 23. Moscow: Foreign Languages Publishing House; London: Lawrence & Wishart, 1964, 295–342.

—— (1917e) Letters on Tactics. *Collected Works*, vol. 23. Moscow: Foreign Languages Publishing House; London: Lawrence & Wishart, 1964, 42–54.

—— (1917f) One of the Fundamental Questions of the Revolution. *Collected Works*, vol. 25. Moscow: Foreign Languages Publishing House; London: Lawrence & Wishart, 1964, 366–73.

—— (1917g) The State and Revolution. *Collected Works*, vol. 25. Moscow: Foreign Languages Publishing House; London: Lawrence & Wishart, 1964, 381–492.

—— (1917h) The Tasks of the Proletariat in Our Revolution: Draft Platform for the Proletarian Party. *Collected Works*, vol. 24. Moscow: Foreign Languages Publishing House; London: Lawrence & Wishart, 1964, 55–92.

—— (1917i) War and Revolution. *Collected Works*, vol. 24. Moscow: Foreign Languages Publishing House; London: Lawrence & Wishart, 1964, 398–421.

—— (1918a) The Revolutionary Phrase. *Collected Works*, vol. 27. Moscow: Progress Publishers; London: Lawrence & Wishart, 1965, 19–29.

—— (1918b) Speech against Bukharin's Amendment to the Resolution on the Party Programme at the 7th Congress of the RCP(B). *Collected Works*, vol. 27. Moscow: Progress Publishers; London: Lawrence & Wishart, 1965, 147–8.

—— (1919a) Address to the Second All-Russian Congress of the Communist Organizations of the Peoples of the East. In V. I. Lenin, *The National Liberation in the East*. Moscow: Progress Publishers, 1980, 230–41.

—— (1919b) Letter to the Workers and Peasants of the Ukraine Apropos of the Victories over Denikin. *Collected Works*, vol. 30. Moscow: Progress Publishers; London: Lawrence & Wishart, 1965, 291–7.

—— (1919c) The State. *Collected Works*, vol. 29. Moscow: Progress Publishers; London: Lawrence & Wishart, 1965, 470–88.

—— (1919d) The Third International, Its Place in History. *Collected Works*, vol. 29. Moscow: Progress Publishers; London: Lawrence & Wishart, 1965, 305–13.

—— (1919e) To the American Workers. *Collected Works*, vol. 30. Moscow: Progress Publishers; London: Lawrence & Wishart, 1965, 38–9.

—— (1920a) 'Left-wing' Communism—An Infantile Disorder. *Collected Works*, vol. 30. Moscow: Progress Publishers; London: Lawrence & Wishart, 1965, 17–118.

—— (1920b) Our Foreign and Domestic Position and the Tasks of the Party. *Collected Works*, vol. 31. Moscow: Progress Publishers; London: Lawrence & Wishart, 1966, 408–26.

—— (1920c) Preliminary Draft Theses on the National and Colonial Questions. In V. I. Lenin, *The National Liberation in the East*. Moscow: Progress Publishers, 1980, 252–9.

—— (1920d) Report of the Commission on the National and Colonial Questions to the Second Congress of the Communist International. In V. I. Lenin, *The National Liberation in the East*. Moscow: Progress Publishers, 1980, 266–71.

—— (1920e) Report on the International Situation and the Fundamental Tasks of the Communist International. *Collected Works*, vol. 31. Moscow: Progress Publishers; London: Lawrence & Wishart, 1966, 215–34.

—— (1920f) Speech Delivered at a Meeting of Activists of the Moscow Organization of the RCP(b). *Collected Works*, vol. 31. Moscow: Progress Publishers; London: Lawrence & Wishart, 1966, 438–59.

—— (1921a) Report of the All-Russia Central Executive Committee and the Council of People's Commissars to the 9th All-Russia Congress of Soviets. *Collected Works*, vol. 33. Moscow: Progress Publishers; London: Lawrence & Wishart, 1966, 143–77.

—— (1921b) Report on the Tax in Kind. *Collected Works*, vol. 32. Moscow: Progress Publishers; London: Lawrence & Wishart, 1966, 286–98.

—— (1921c) Speech Delivered at the All-Russia Congress of Transport Workers. *Collected Works*, vol. 32. Moscow: Progress Publishers; London: Lawrence & Wishart, 1966, 272–84.

—— (1921d) The Tax in Kind: The Significance of the New Policy and its Conditions. *Collected Works*, vol. 32. Moscow: Progress Publishers; London: Lawrence & Wishart, 1966, 329–65.

—— (1921e) Theses for a Report on the Tactics of the RCP: Third Congress of the Communist International. *Collected Works*, vol. 32. Moscow: Progress Publishers; London: Lawrence & Wishart, 1966, 453–96.

—— (1922a) The International and Domestic Situation of the Soviet Republic: Speech delivered to a meeting of the Communist Groups at the All-Russia Congress of Metalworkers. *Collected Works*, vol. 33. Moscow: Progress Publishers; London: Lawrence & Wishart, 1966, 212–26.

—— (1922b) Interview Given to Michael Farbman, *Observer* and *Manchester Guardian* Correspondent. *Collected Works*, vol. 33. Moscow: Progress Publishers; London: Lawrence & Wishart, 1966, 383–9.

—— (1923a) Better Fewer, but Better. In V. I. Lenin, *The National Liberation in the East*. Moscow: Progress Publishers, 1980, 316–19.

—— (1923b) On Co-operation. *Collected Works*, vol. 33. Moscow: Progress Publishers; London: Lawrence & Wishart, 1966, 467–71.

—— (1960–70) *Collected Works* (trans. from the 4th Russian edn). Moscow: Foreign Languages Publishing House and Progress Publishers; London: Lawrence & Wishart.

—— (1980) *The National Liberation Movement in the East*. Moscow: Progress Publishers.

Levskovsky, Aleksei I. (1970) *Tretii mir v sovremennom mire: nekotorye problemy sotsial'no-ekonomicheskogo razvitiya mnogoukladnykh gosudarstv*. Moscow: Nauka.

Light, Margot (1983) The Soviet View. In Roy Douglas (ed.) *1939: A Retrospect Forty Years After*. London: Macmillan, 74–89.

—— (1987) Foreign Policy. In Martin McCauley (ed.) *The USSR under Gorbachev*. London: Macmillan, 210–29.

Litvinov, Maxim (1934) Speech at the League Assembly on the entry of the USSR into the League of Nations. In Jane Degras (ed.) *Soviet Documents on Foreign Policy* vol. 3. London: Oxford University Press, 1953, 89–96.

—— (1939) *Against Aggression: Speeches Together with Texts of*

Treaties and of the Covenant of the League of Nations. London: Lawrence & Wishart.

Low, Alfred D. (1976) *Sino-Soviet Dispute: An Analysis of the Polemics*. London: Associated University Presses.

Lowe, Donald M. (1966) *The Function of 'China' in Marx, Lenin and Mao*. Berkeley/Los Angeles: University of California Press.

Lowenthal, Richard (1964) *World Communism: The Disintegration of a Secular Faith*. New York: Oxford University Press.

—— (1977) *Model or Ally? The Communist Powers in the Developing Countries*. New York: Oxford University Press.

—— (1982) The Limits of Intra-Bloc Pluralism: The Changing Threshold of Soviet Intervention. *International Journal* XXXVII, 2 (Spring): 263–84.

Lynch, Allen C. (1984) The Soviet Study of International Relations, 1968–1982. PhD Thesis, Columbia University.

MccGwire, Michael (ed.) (1973) *Soviet Naval Developments: Capability and Context*. New York: Praeger.

McKenzie, Kermit E. (1964) *Comintern and World Revolution 1928–1943: The Shaping of Doctrine*. New York: Columbia University Press.

McLane, Charles B. (1958) *Soviet Policy and the Chinese Communists, 1931–1946*. New York: Columbia University Press.

—— (1966) *Soviet Strategies in Southeast Asia: An Exploration of Eastern Policy under Lenin and Stalin*. Princeton, NJ: Princeton University Press.

McLellan, David (1971) *The Thought of Karl Marx: An Introduction*. London: Macmillan.

McNeal, Robert H. (ed.) (1967) *International Relations Among Communists*. Englewood Cliffs, NJ: Prentice-Hall.

Maidanik, K. and G. I. Mirsky (1981) Natsional 'no-osvoboditel'naya bor'ba: sovremenny etap. *Mirovaya ekonomika i mezhdunarodnye otnosheniya* 6: 17–30.

Malcolm, Neil (1984) *Soviet Political Scientists and American Politics*. London: Macmillan.

Malenkov, G. M. (1947) The Activities of the CC CPSU (Bolshevik). *For a Lasting Peace, for a People's Democracy*, 1 December, 3.

—— (1952) Report of the Central Committee of the All-Union Communist Party (Bolshevik) to the 19th Party Congress. In L. Gruliow (ed.) *Current Soviet Policies I*, The Documentary Record of the Nineteenth Communist Party Congress and the Reorganization after Stalin's Death. New York: Praeger, 1953, 99–124.

—— (1953a) Funeral Oration. In L. Gruliow (ed.) *Current Soviet*

Policies I. The Documentary Record of the Nineteenth Communist Party Congress and the Reorganization after Stalin's Death. New York: Praeger, 1953, 249–51.

—— (1953b) Speech before the Supreme Soviet, 8 August 1953. *Current Digest of the Soviet Press* V, 3:3–12.

Mankovsky, B. S. (1949a) Klassovaya sushchnost' narodno-demokraticheskogo gosudarstva. *Sovetskoe gosudarstvo i pravo* 6: 7–17 (summarized in *Current Digest of the Soviet Press* I, 42: 11–15.

—— (1949b) Narodno-demokraticheskaya respublika–politicheskaya forma diktatury rabochego klassa. *Sovetskoe gosudarstvo i pravo* 10: 12–21.

—— (1950) Novy etap v razvitii narodno-demokraticheskikh gosudarstv kak gosudarstv sotsialistichekogo tipa. *Sovetskoe gosudarstvo i pravo* 7: 1–14 (trans. in *Current Digest of the Soviet Press II:* 35: 3–8.

Mann, Esther Kingston (1983) *Lenin and the Problem of Marxist Peasant Revolution*. New York and Oxford: Oxford University Press.

Marantz, Paul (1982) Changing Soviet Conceptions of East–West Relations. *International Journal XXXVII 2 (Spring): 220–39.*

Marcuse, Herbert (1958) *Soviet Marxism: A Critical Analysis*. London: Routledge & Kegan Paul.

Marksizm-leninizm o voine, armii i voennoi nauke (MVAVN) (1955). Moscow: Voenizdat.

Marksizm-leninizm o voine i armii (MVA) (1958, 1961, 1965, 1968, 1972). Moscow: Voenizdat.

Marx, Karl and Frederick Engels (1845a) *The German Ideology*. London: Lawrence & Wishart, 1965.

—— (1845b) Theses on Feuerbach. In Karl Marx, *Early Writings*. Harmondsworth, Middlesex: Penguin, 1975, 421–3.

—— and Frederick Engels (1848) Manifesto of the Communist Party. In *Marx Engels Selected Works*, vol. 1. Moscow: Foreign Languages Publishing House, 1962, 13–65.

—— and Frederick Engels (1850a) Address of the Central Committee to the Communist League. In *Marx Engels Selected Works*, vol. 1. Moscow: Foreign Languages Publishing House, 1962, 106–17.

—— and Frederick Engels (1850b) The Class Struggles in France, 1848–1850. In *Marx Engels Selected Works*, vol. 1. Moscow: Foreign Languages Publishing House, 1962, 118–242.

—— (1851) The Eighteenth Brumaire of Louis Bonaparte. In *Marx Engels Selected Works*, vol. 1. Moscow: Foreign Languages Publishing House, 1962, 243–344.

—— and Frederick Engels (1856–63) *Articles in the New American*

Cyclopaedia. Ed. and with Introduction by Hal Draper. Berkeley, Ca.: Independent Socialist Press, 1969.

—— (1859) Preface to a Contribution to the Critique of Political Economy. In *Marx Engels Selected Works*, vol. 1. Moscow: Foreign Languages Publishing House, 1962, 361–5.

—— (1867) *Capital*. Harmondsworth, Middlesex: Penguin, 1976.

—— (1870) Letter to Meyer and Vogt. *Marx Engels Selected Correspondence. Moscow: Progress Publishers, 1975, 220–4.*

—— (1871) The Civil War in France. In *Marx Engels Selected Works*, vol. 1. Moscow: Foreign Languages Publishing House, 1962, 473–545.

—— (1875) Critique of the Gotha Programme. In *Marx Engels Selected Works*, vol. 2. Moscow: Foreign Languages Publishing House, 1962, 13–48.

—— (1877) Letter to the Editorial Board of the 'Otechestvenniye Zapiski'. *Marx Engels Selected Correspondence*. Moscow: Progress Publishers, 1975, 291–4.

—— (1881) Letter to Zasulich. *Marx Engels Selected Correspondence*. Moscow: Progress Publishers, 1975, 319–20.

—— (1951a) *Articles on India*. Bombay: People's Publishing House.

—— (1951b) *Marx on China; 1853–1860: Articles from the New York Daily Tribune*. Ed. Dona Torr. London: Lawrence & Wishart.

—— and Frederick Engels (1962). *Selected Works* (2 vols.). Moscow: Foreign Languages Publishing House.

—— (1969) *On Colonialism and Modernization: His Despatches and Other Writings on China, India, Mexico, the Middle East and North Africa*. Ed. and with Introduction by Shlomo Avineri. New York: Anchor Books.

—— (1975a) *Early Writings*. Introduced by Lucio Colletti. Harmondsworth, Middlesex: Penguin.

—— and Frederick Engels (1975b) *Selected Correspondence* (3rd edn.). Moscow: Progress Publishers.

Marxism-Leninism on War and the Army (1972) Translation of the 6th Russian edn. Moscow: Progress Publishers.

Maslennikov, V. (1949) O rukovodyashchei roli rabochego klassa v natsional'no-osvoboditel'nom dvizhenii kolonial'nykh narodov. *Voprosy ekonomiki* 9: 62–75.

Mayer, Peter (1968) *Cohesion and Conflict in International Communism: A Study of Marxist-Leninist Concepts and their Application*. The Hague: Martinus Nijhoff.

Meadows, Dennis *et al.* (1972) *The Limits to Growth*. New York: Dutton.

Medovoi, A. and V. Yashkin (1975) Sotsial'no-ekonomicheskaya struktura razvivayushchikhsya stran i ikh mesto v sisteme mirovykh obshchestvennykh otnoshenii. *Mirovaya ekonomika i mezhdunarodnye otnosheniya* 9: 106–16.

Medvedev, Roy (1982) *Khrushchev*. Oxford: Basil Blackwell.

—— (1986a) *China and the Superpowers*. Oxford: Basil Blackwell.

—— (1986b) Ideologiya, informatsiya i vlast' v Sovetskom Soyuze. Unpublished manuscript.

Medvedev, Zhores (1969) *The Rise and Fall of T. D. Lysenko*. New York: Columbia University Press.

—— (1987) *Soviet Agriculture*. New York: Norton.

Meeting of the Representatives of Communist and Workers' Parties (1960) *World Marxist Review* III, 12: 3–28.

Mel'man S. (1942) Polozhenie v India. *Mirovoe khozyaistvo i mirovaya politika* 11-12: 41–7.

Melnikov, D. (1956) Neutrality and the Current Situation. *International Affairs* 2: 74–81.

Mel'nikov, E. (1981) Politicheskie preobrazovaniya v afrikanskikh stranakh sotsialischeskoi orientatsii, *Mirovaya ekonomika i mezhdunarodnye otnosheniya* 12: 121–6.

Mel'nikov, Y. M. (1970) *Vneshnepoliticheskie doktriny SShA: proiskhozhdenie i sushchnost' programmy 'Novykh rubezhei' prezidenta D. Kennedi*. Moscow: Nauka.

Menzhinsky, V. (1969) The Moscow Meeting on the Problem of Peaceful Coexistence. *International Affairs* 10: 44–5.

Mikheev, Yu. Ya. (1960) Vopros o sovmestimosti statusa postoyannogo neitraliteta s obyazannostyami chlena OON. In *Sovetsky ezhegodnik mezhdunarodnogo prava, 1960*. Moscow: Akademii Nauk SSSR, 1961, 167–76.

Milestones in Soviet Foreign Policy, 1917–1967 (1976) Moscow: Progress Publishers.

Miliband, Ralph (1977) *Marxism and Politics*. Oxford: Oxford University Press.

Milovidov, A. S. (1977) *Philosophical heritage of V. I. Lenin and Problems of Contemporary War: A Soviet View*. Washington, DC: USAF Publication.

Mirsky, G. I. (1963) Tvorcheskii Marksizm i problemy natsional— 'no-osvoboditel'nykh revolyutsii. *Mirovaya ekonomika i mezhdunarodnye otnosheniya* 2: 63–8.

—— (1976) Razvivayushchiesya strany i mirovoi kapitalizm. *Mirovaya ekonomika i mezhdunarodnye otnosheniya* 3: 35–46.

—— (1977) Razvivayushchiesya strany v sovremennom mire. *Mirovaya ekonomika i mezhdunarodnye otnosheniya* 1: 139–41.

—— (1979) Sotsial'naya rol' melkoi burzhuazii. *Mirovaya ekonomika i mezhdunarodnye otnosheniya* 5: 139–41.

—— (1987) K voprosu o vybore puti i orientatsii razvivayushchikhsya stran. *Mirovaya ekonomika i mezhdunarodnye otnosheniya* 5: 70–81.

Mitchell, R. Judson (1982) *Ideology of a Superpower: Contemporary Soviet Doctrine on International Relations*. Stanford, Ca.: Stanford University, Hoover Institution Press.

Mitin, M. (1947) Sovetskaya demokratiya i demokratiya burzhuaznaya. *Bolshevik* 6: 23–43.

—— (1961) Nerushimoe edinstvo sotsialisticheskikh stran. *Kommunist* 2: 11–22.

Modelski, George (1960) *The Communist International System*. Princeton, NJ: Princeton University, Center for International Studies Monograph.

Modjoryan, L. (1956) Neutrality. *New Times* 8: 12–15.

Molotov, V. M. (1949) *Problems of Foreign Policy: Speeches*. Moscow: Foreign Languages Publishing House.

Morozov, V. I. (1963) Mnogostoronnie soglasheniya—deistvennaya forma ekonomicheskogo sotrudnichestva sotsialisticheskikh stran. *Sovetskoe gosudarstvo i pravo* 12: 75–85.

The Moscow Meeting and Fundamental Problems of International Relations (1969) *International Affairs* 9: 50–66.

Moshetov, V. and V. Lesakov (1947) O demokraticheskikh preobrazovaniyakh v stranakh novoi demokratii. *Bolshevik* 22: 38–42.

Mshvenieradze, V. (1981) Politika razryadki i krizis burzhuaznoi politologii. *Mirovaya ekonomika i mezhdunarodnye otnosheniya* 2: 108–23.

—— (1985) *Political Reality and Political Consciousness*. Moscow: Progress Publishers.

Narochnitsky, A. L. *et al.* (1979), *Politika mira i sotrudnichestva*. Moscow: IMO.

The National Bourgeoisie and the Liberation Movement (1959a) *World Marxist Review* 8: 61–83.

The National Bourgeoisie and the Liberation Movement (1959b) *World Marxist Review* 9: 66–82.

Nikiforov, V. N. (1975) *Vostok i vsemirnaya istoriya*. Moscow: Nauka.

Nikitin, P. (1959) *Fundamentals of Political Economy: Popular Course*. Moscow: Foreign Languages Publishing House.

North, Robert C. (1953) *Moscow and the Chinese Communists*. Stanford, Ca.: Stanford University Press.

—— and Xenia J. Eudin (1963) *N. M. Roy's Mission to China: The Communist Kuomintang split of 1927*. Berkeley and Los Angeles: University of California Press.

Novopashin, Yu. S. (1978) *Mezhdunarodnye otnosheniya novogo tipa: Voprosy teorii i praktiki razvitiya mirovoi sistemy sotsializma.* Moscow: IMO.

——(1985) Politicheskie otnosheniya stran sotsializma. *Rabochii klass i sovremenny mir* 5: 55–65.

—— (ed.) (1986) *Mezhdunarodnaya sfera sotsialisticheskikh obshchestvennykh otnoshenii: Sbornik nauchnykh trudov.* Moscow: AN SSSR, Institut ekonomiki mirovoi sotsialisticheskoi sistemy.

Ogarkov, N. (1981) Na strazhe mirnogo truda. *Kommunist* 10: 81–91.

O nedostatkakh i zadachakh nauchno-issledovatel'skoi raboty v oblasti ekonomiki (1948) *Voprosy ekonomiki* 9: 52–116.

On Friendship and Co-operation between the Soviet Union and other Socialist States. In L. Gruliow (ed.) *Current Soviet Policies II.* The Documentary Record of the 20th Communist Party Congress and its Aftermath. London: Atlantic Press, distributed by Thames & Hudson, 1957, 230–1 (trans. of an article in *Pravda*, 31 October 1956).

Onikov, L. A. and N. V. Shishlin (1980) *Kratky politichesky slovar'* (2nd edn). Moscow: Politizdat.

On the Character and Attributes of People's Democracy in Countries of the Orient (1951) Report of a Conference at the Oriental Studies Institute, November 12–23. Trans. in *Current Digest of the Soviet Press* IV, 20: 3–7, 43.

Osnitskaya, G. (1962) Neutrality and the Common Market. *International Affairs* 6: 52–5.

Pamyati Akademika Bol'shevika (1949) *Sovetskoe gosudarstvo i pravo* 6: 1–6.

Panfilov, E. G. (1958) Marksizm-leninizm o demokraticheskom i spravedlivom mire. *Voprosy filosofii* 4: 15–27.

Pashukanis, E. (1935) *Ocherki po mezhdunarodnomu pravu.* Moscow: Izd-vo Sovetskoe zakonodatel'stvo.

Paul, David W. and Maurice D. Simon (1981) Poland Today and Czechoslovakia 1968. *Problems of Communism* XXX, 5 (Sept./ Oct.): 25–39.

Pervy s''ezd narodov Vostoka: Stenografichesky otchet (1921). Moscow.

Pervy s''ezd revolyutsionnykh organizatsii Dal'nego Vostoka: Sbornik (1922). Petrograd.

Petrenko, Fyodr F. and Valery V. Popov (1981) *Printsipy rukovodstva Sovetskoi vneshnei politikoi.* Moscow: Mezhdenarodnye otnosheniya.

Petrovsky, Vladimir F. (1976) *Amerikanskaya vneshnepoliti-*

cheskaya mysl'. Moscow: IMO.

—— (1986) Sovetskaya kontseptsiya vseobshchei bezopasnosti. *Mirovaya ekonomika i mezhdunarodnye otnosheniya* 6: 3–13.

Pick, Otto (1981) Introduction: Political and Ideological Aspects. In E. J. Feuchtwanger and P. Nailor (eds) *The Soviet Union and the Third World*. London: Macmillan, 3–11.

Ponomarev, B. N. (ed.) (1958) *Politichesky slovar'* (2nd edn). Moscow: Izd-vo Politicheskoi literatury.

—— *et al.* (eds) (1960) *History of the Communist Party of the Soviet Union*. Moscow: Foreign Languages Publishing House.

—— (1961) O gosudarstve national'noi demokratii. *Kommunist* 8: 33–48.

—— (1980) Sovmestnaya bor'ba rabochego i natsional'no-osvoboditel'nogo dvizhenii protiv imperializma, za sotsial'ny progress. *Kommunist* 16: 30–44.

Potekhin, I. I. (1950) Stalinskaya teoriya kolonial'noi revolyutsii i natsional'no-osvoboditel'noe dvizhenie v tropicheskoi i yuzhnoi Afrike. *Sovetskaya etnografiya*, 1: 24–40.

—— (1960) Kharakternye cherty raspada kolonial'noi sistemy imperializma v Afrike. *Problemy vostokovedeniya* 1: 12–29.

Powell, David E. and Paul Shoup (1970) The Emergence of Political Science in Communist Countries. *American Political Science Review* LXIV, 2: 572–88.

Press Goup of Journalists (1968) *On events in Czechoslovakia*. Moscow: Novosti.

Primakov, E. (1980a) Islam i protsessy obshchestvennogo razvitiya zarubezhnogo Vostoka. *Voprosy filosofii* 8: 60–71.

—— (1980b) Zakon neravnomernosti razvitiya i istoricheskie sud'by osvobodivshikhsya stran. *Mirovaya ekonomika i mezhdunarodnye otnosheniya* 12: 28–47.

—— (1981) Strany sotsialisticheskoi orientatsii: trudny, no real'ny perekhod k sotsializmu. *Mirovaya ekonomika i mezhdunarodnye otnosheniya* 7: 3–16.

—— (1986) XXVII S''ezd KPSS i issledovanie problem mirovoi ekonomiki i mezhdunarodnykh otnoshenii. *Mirovaya ekonomika i mezhdunarodnye otnosheniya* 5: 3–20.

Problems of War and Peace: A Critical Analysis of Bourgeois Theories (1972) Moscow: Progress Publishers.

Programme of the Communist Party of the Soviet Union (1961). In C. Saikowski and L. Gruliow (eds) *Current Soviet Policies IV*. New York and London: Columbia University Press 1962, 1–33.

Programme of the Communist Party of the Soviet Union: New edition (1986) in *Izvestiya* 7 March 1986.

Pukhovsky, Nikolai. V. (1965) *O mire i voine*. Moscow: Mysl'.

Rakowska-Harmstone, T. (1976) Socialist Internationalism and Eastern Europe—A New Stage. *Survey* 22, 1 (98) (Winter): 38–54.

Reisner, L. I. and N. A. Simoniya (eds) (1984) *Evolyutsiya vostochnykh obshchestv: Sintez traditsionnykh i sovremennykh struktur.* Moscow: Nauka.

Remington, Robin A. (ed.) (1969) *Winter in Prague: Documents on Czechoslovak Communism in Crisis.* Cambridge, Mass.: MIT Press.

—— (1971) *The Warsaw Pact: Case Studies in Communist Conflict Resolution.* Cambridge, Mass.: MIT Press.

Remnek, Richard B. (1975) *Soviet Scholars and Soviet Foreign Policy: A Case Study of Soviet policy towards India.* Durham, NC: University of North Carolina Press.

Rozman, Gilbert (1985) *A Mirror for Socialism.* London: Taurus.

Rubinstein, Alvin, Z. (ed.) (1966) *The Foreign Policy of the Soviet Union.* New York: Random House.

Rubinshtein, M. (1947) Bor'ba imperialisticheskogo i anti--imperialisticheskogo lagerya. *Mirovoe khozyaistvo i mirovaya politika* 11, 78–94.

Rumyantsev, A. M. (ed.) (1984) *A Dictionary of Scientific Communism.* Moscow: Progress Publishers.

Safarov, G. (1930a) Na fronte kolonial'noi revolyutsii. *Bol'shevik* 15–16: 63–85.

—— (1930b) Oktyabr' i kolonial'naya revolyutsiya. *Bol'shevik* 19–20: 39–54.

Saikowski, Charlotte and Leo Gruliow (eds) (1962) *Current Soviet Policies IV.* The Documentary Record of the 22nd Congress of the Communist Party of the Soviet Union (from the translations of the *Current Digest of the Soviet Press*). New York/London: Columbia University Press.

Saivetz, Carol R. (1982) *Socialism and Egypt and Algeria, 1960–1973: The Soviet Assessment.* Ann Arbor, Michigan: University Microfilms International.

Sanakoyev, Shalva P. (1964) *Velikoe sodruzhestvo svobodnykh i suverennykh narodov.* Moscow: IMO.

—— (1972) *The World Socialist System: Main Problems, Stages of Development.* Moscow: Progress Publishers.

—— and Nikolai I. Kapchenko (1973) *Teoriya i praktika vneshnei politiki sotsializma.* Moscow: IMO.

—— (1974) The World Today: Problems of the Correlation of Forces. *International Affairs* 11: 40–50.

—— (1975) Foreign Policy of Socialism. *International Affairs* 5: 108–18.

—— and Nikolai I. Kapchenko (1977) *O teorii vneshnei politiki sotsializma.* Moscow: Mezhdunarodnye otnosheniya.

—— and Nikolai I. Kapchenko (1981) *Vneshnyaya politika i bor'ba idei.* Moscow: Mezhdunarodnye otnoshenii.

Sanford, George (1984) The Polish Communist Leadership and the Onset of the State of War. *Soviet Studies* XXXVI, 4 (Nov.): 494–512.

Savkin, Vasily Ye. (1974) *The Basic Principles of Operational Art and Tactics: A Soviet View.* Washington, DC: USGPO for the USAF.

Scott, Harriet Fast and William F. Scott (eds) (1982) *The Soviet Art of War: Doctrine, Strategy and Tactics.* Boulder, Col.: Westview Press.

Sedov, Pavel L. (1981) *Razvivayushchiesya strany i Sovetsky Soyuz.* Moscow: Mysl'.

Selektor, M. Z. (1955) Ob ob"ektivnykh osnovakh mirnoi politiki SSSR. *Voprosy filosofii* 6: 31–44.

Seleznev, I. A. (1951) I. V. Stalin ob opasnosti novoi mirovoi voiny i vozmozhnosti predotvrashcheniya. *Voprosy filosofii* 4: 25–44.

Semmel, Bernard (ed.) (1981) *Marxism and the Science of War.* Oxford: Oxford University Press.

Sergeev, Sergei D. (1964) *Ekonomicheskoi sotrudnichestvo i vzaimopomoshch' sotsialisticheskikh stran.* Moscow: Vneshtorgizdat.

Sergiyev, A. (1975) Leninism on the Correlation of Forces as a Factor of International Relations. *International Affairs* 5: 99–107.

Seton-Watson, Hugh (1961) *The East European Revolution.* London: Methuen.

Shakhnazarov, Georgy (1974) K probleme sootnosheniya sil v mire. *Kommunist* 3: 77–89.

—— (1982) *Futurology Fiasco: A Critical Study of Non-Marxist Concepts of How Society Develops.* Moscow: Progress Publishers.

—— (1984) *The Coming World Order.* Moscow: Progress Publishers.

—— (1984a) Logika politicheskogo myshleniya v yadernuyu eru. *Voprosy filosofii* 5: 63–74.

Shapiro, A. Sovremennaya epokha i ee osobennosti. *Mirovaya ekonomika i mezhdunarodnye otnosheniya,* 11, 13–25.

Shenfield, Stephen (1987) *The Nuclear Predicament: Explorations in Soviet Ideology* (Chatham House Papers 37). London: RIIA and Routledge & Kegan Paul.

Sheptulin, A. P. (1978) *Marxist-Leninist Philosophy.* Moscow: Progress Publishers.

Skilling, H. Gordon (1951a) People's Democracy in Soviet Theory.

Soviet Studies III, 1: 16–33.

—— (1951b) People's Democracy in Soviet Theory. *Soviet Studies* III, 2: 131–49.

—— (1964) *Communism, National and International: Eastern Europe after Stalin.* Toronto: University of Toronto Press in association with the Canadian Institute of International Affairs.

—— (1976) *Czechoslovakia's Interrupted Revolution.* Princeton, NJ: Princeton University Press.

Snyder, R. C. *et al.* (1962) *Foreign Policy Decision Making.* Princeton, NJ: Princeton University Press.

Sobolev, A. (1951) Narodnaya demokratiya kak forma politicheskoi organizatsii obshchestva. *Bolshevik* 19: 25–38.

Sokolovskiy, V. D. (1963) *Military Strategy: Soviet Doctrine and Concepts.* New York: Praeger.

Solodovnikov, V. (1973) Some Aspects of Non-Capitalist Development. *International Affairs* 6: 44–50.

Sovetov, A. (1964) Road to Détente: Possibility and Reality. *International Affairs* 1: 3–11.

Sovetskaya voennaya nauka nakanune Velikoi Otechestvennoi voiny. In *Istoriya Veilikoi Otechestvennoi Voiny Sovetskogo Soyuza 1941–1945 gg.* Moscow: Voennoe Izd-vo, 436–51.

The Soviet–Finnish Treaty (1948) *New Times* 16: 1–3.

Staar, Richard F. Checklist of Communist Parties in 1984. *Problems of Communism* XXXIV, 2 (Mar.–Apr.): 90–101.

Stalin, Joseph V. (1913) Marxism and the National Question. In J. V. Stalin, *Marxism and the National and Colonial Question.* London: Lawrence & Wishart, 1936, 3–61.

—— (1917) Report on the National Question. In J. V. Stalin, *Marxism and the National and Colonial Question.* London: Lawrence & Wishart, 1936, 62–7.

—— (1918a) Don't Forget the East. In Alvin Z. Rubinstein, *The Foreign Policy of the Soviet Union.* New York: Random House, 1966, 358–60.

—— (1918b) The October Revolution and the National Question. In J. V. Stalin, *Marxism and the National and Colonial Question.* London: Lawrence & Wishart, 1936, 68–77.

—— (1921) The National Question Presented. In J. V. Stalin, *Marxism and the National and Colonial Question.* London: Lawrence & Wishart, 1936, 111–16.

—— (1922) The Amalgamation of the Soviet Republics. In J. V. Stalin, *Marxism and the National and Colonial Question.* London: Lawrence & Wishart, 1936, 120–8.

—— (1923) Report on the National Factors in Party and State Development. In J. V. Stalin, *Marxism and the National and Colonial Question.* London: Lawrence & Wishart, 1936, 147–71.

—— (1924a) Foundations of Leninism. In J. V. Stalin, *Leninism*. London: Lawrence & Wishart, 1940, 1–85.

—— (1924b) The National Question. In J. V. Stalin, *Marxism and the National and Colonial Question*. London: Lawrence & Wishart, 1936, 190–9.

—— (1924c) The October Revolution and the Tactics of the Russian Communists (Preface to *On the Road to October*). In J. V. Stalin, *Leninism*. London: Lawrence & Wishart, 1940, 86–117.

—— (1925a) 14th Congress of the CPSU(B): Political Report. In J. V. Stalin, *Works*, vol. 7. Moscow: Foreign Languages Publishing House, 1954, 267–361.

—— (1925b) The Political Tasks of the University of the Peoples of the East. In J. V. Stalin, *Marxism and the National and Colonial Question*. London: Lawrence & Wishart, 1936, 206–20.

—— (1927a) China. In J. V. Stalin, *Marxism and the National and Colonial Question*. London: Lawrence & Wishart, 1936, 232–52.

—— (1927b) The 15th Congress of the CPSU(B). In J. V. Stalin, *Works*, vol. 10, Moscow: Foreign Languages Publishing House, 1954, 277–363.

—— (1927c) The International Character of the October Revolution. In J. V. Stalin, *Leninism*. London: Lawrence & Wishart, 1940, 197–204.

—— (1927d) The International Situation and the Defence of the USSR. In J. V. Stalin, *Works*, vol. 10. Moscow: Foreign Languages Publishing House, 1954, 3–96.

—— (1927e) Notes on Contemporary Themes: China. In Bruce Franklin (ed.) *The Essential Stalin: Major Theoretical Writings, 1905–52*. London: Croom Helm, 1973, 194–219.

—— (1927f) The Party's Three Fundamental Slogans on the Peasant Problem. In J. V. Stalin, *Leninism*. London: Lawrence & Wishart, 1940, 175–86.

—— (1927g) Political Report of the Central Committee. In J. V. Stalin, *Works*, vol. 10, Moscow: Foreign Languages Publishing House, 1954, 277–382.

—— (1930) Deviations on the National Question. In J. V. Stalin, *Marxism and the National and Colonial Question*. London: Lawrence & Wishart, 1936, 256–66.

—— (1931) The Tasks of Business Executives. In J. V. Stalin, *Leninism*. London: Lawrence & Wishart, 1940, 359–67.

—— (1934) Report on the Work of the Central Committee to the Seventeenth Congress of the CPSU(B). In Bruce Franklin (ed.) *The Essential Stalin: major Theoretical Writings, 1905–52*. London: Croom Helm, 1973, 224–43.

—— (1936) *Marxism and the National and Colonial Question*.

London: Lawrence & Wishart, 1936.

—— (1937) O nedostatkakh partiinoi raboty. In J. V. Stalin, *Sochineniya*, vol. 1 (XIV). Stanford, Ca.: Hoover Institute Press, 1967, 189–224.

—— (1938) Dialectical and Historical Materialism. In J. V. Stalin, *Leninism*. London: Lawrence & Wishart, 1940, 591–618.

—— (1939) Report on the Work of the Central Committee to the Eighteenth Congress of the CPSU(B). In Bruce Franklin (ed.) *The Essential Stalin: Major Theoretical Writings, 1905–52.* London: Croom Helm, 1973, 334–92.

—— (1940) *Leninism*. London: Lawrence & Wishart, 1940.

—— (1942) Prikaz narodnogo komissara oborony. In J. V. Stalin, *Sochineniya*, vol. 2 (XV). Stanford, Ca.: Hoover Institute Press, 1967, 36–44.

—— (1946a) Otvety na voprosy zadannye Moskovskim korrespondentom 'Sandei Taims', g-nom A. Bert poluchennye 17-go sentyabrya 1946 g. In J. V. Stalin, *Sochineniya,* vol. 3(XVI). Stanford, Ca.: Hoover Institute Press, 1967, 53–6.

—— (1946–51) *Sochineniya*, vols. 1–13. Moscow: Izd-vo politicheskoi literatury.

—— (1947) Interv'yu s gospodinom Stassenom, 9/4/1947. In J. V. Stalin, *Sochineniya,* vol. 3 (XVI). Stanford, Ca.: Hoover Institute Press, 1967, 75–92.

—— (1950) Marxism and Linguistics. In Bruce Franklin (ed.) *The Essential Stalin: Major Theoretical Writings, 1905–52.* London: Croom Helm, 1973, 407–44.

—— (1952a) Economic Problems of Socialism in the USSR. In Bruce Franklin (ed.) *The Essential Stalin: Major Theoretical Writings, 1905–52. London: Croom Helm, 1973, 445–81.*

—— (1952b) Speech at the 19th Congress of the CPSU. In L. Gruliow (ed.) *Current Soviet Policies I.* New York, Praeger, 1953, 7–8.

—— (1967) *Sochineniya*, vols 1–3 (XIV–XVI). Ed. Robert H. McNeal. Stanford, Ca.: Hoover Institute Press.

—— (1954) *Works.* 10 vols. Moscow: Foreign Languages Publishing House.

Statement of the Meeting of Representatives of the Communist and Workers' Parties (1960) *New Times* 50, Documents Supplement, 1–16.

Statement of Conference of the Communist and Worker's Parties of Europe (1976) For Peace, Security, Co-operation and Social Progress in Europe. *New Times* 28: 24–32.

Steele, Jonathan (1983) *World Power: Soviet Foreign Policy under Brezhnev and Andropov*. London: Michael Joseph.

Stepanov, Lev (1963) Neutralism: Attack Repelled. *New Times* 9: 3–6.

Stepanova. Ol'ga L. (1982) 'Kholodnaya voina': istoricheskaya retrospektiva. Moscow: Mezhdunarodnye otnosheniya.

Suslov, M. A. (1956) 39th Anniversary of the Great October Socialist Revolution. In Current Digest of the Soviet Press VIII, 44: 3–8 (trans. of an address published in Izvestiya, 7 November, 1956).

—— (1963) On the Struggle of the CPSU for the Solidarity of the International Communist Movement. Current Digest of the Soviet Press XVI, 13: 5–16 (trans. of an article published in Pravda, 3 April).

Svyaz' teorii s praktikoi i partiinaya propaganda. (1955) Kommunist 14: 3–12.

Szawlowski, Richard (1976) The System of the International Organizations of the Communist Counties. Leyden: Sijthoff.

Tarabrin, E. (1975) 'Tretii mir' i imperializm: novye v sootnoshenii sil. Mirovaya ekonomika i mezhdunarodnye otnosheniya 2: 12–23.

Tarschys, Daniel (1971) Neutrality and the Common Market. Co-operation and Conflict VI, 2: 65–75.

Taracouzio, T. A. (1940) War and Peace in Soviet Diplomacy. New York: Macmillan.

Tasks at the Present Stage of the Struggle against Imperialism and United Action of the Communist and Workers' Parties and All Anti-Imperialist Forces (1969) New Times 26: 25–39.

Theen, Rolf H.W. (1971) Political Science in the USSR: 'To Be, or Not to Be'. World Politics XXIII, 4 (July): 684–703.

Thorton, Thomas (ed.) (1964) The Third World in Soviet Perspective: Studies by Soviet Writers on Developing Areas. Princeton, NJ: Princeton University Press.

Tichelmann, Fritjof and Irfan Habib (1983) Marx on Indonesia and India. Trier: Schriften aus dem Karl-Marx-Haus.

Tipologiya nesotsialisticheskikh stran (opyt mnogomernogo statisti-cheskogo analiza narodnykh khozyaistv (1976). Moscow: Nauka.

Titarenko, S. (1955) Sotsialistichsky internatsionalizm—ideologiya druzhby narodov. Kommunist 11: 97–110.

Tiyunov, O. I. (1965) O razvitii ponyatiya neitraliteta gosudarstv. In Vestnik Moskovskogo universiteta, Seriya X, Pravo, 4 (oktyabr'-dekabr'). Moscow: Izd-vo Moskovskogo universiteta.

Tolkunov, L. (1961) Novy etap v razvitii mirovoi sistemy sotsializma. Kommunist 3: 14–27.

Trainin, I. P. (1947a) Demokratiya osobogo tipa. Sovetskoe gosudarstvo i pravo 3: 1–15.

—— (1947b) Demokratiya osobogo tipa. Sovetskoe gosudarstvo i pravo 3: 1–14.

Treaty of Friendship, Cooperation and Mutual Aid between the USSR and the Socialist Republic of Czechoslovakia (1970) *New Times* 20: 30–1.

Treaty of Friendship, Cooperation and Mutual Aid between the USSR and the Socialist Republic of Rumania (1970). In Robin Remington (ed.) *Winter in Prague: Documents on Czechoslovak Communism in Crisis*. Cambridge, Mass: MIT Press, 1969, 242–5.

Treaty of Friendship, Cooperation and Mutual Aid between the USSR and the German Democratic Republic (1975) *New Times* 41: 12–13.

Triska, Jan F. (1958) A Model for the Study of Soviet Foreign Policy. *American Political Science Review* 41, 1:64–83.

Trofimenko, G. (1975) Na sterzhnevom napravlenii. *Mirovaya ekonomika i mezhdunarodnye otnoshenii* 2: 3–11.

Trotsky, Leon (1917) Taina diplomatii i tainye dogovory. *Sochineniya*, vol. III. Moscow: Gosizdat, n.d. (?1925), 163, 165, 326.

—— (1962) *The Permanent Revolution and Results and Prospects*. London: New Park Publications.

Trukhanovsky, V. G. (1963) Printsip mirnogo sosushchestvovaniya i ego burzhuaznye kritiki. *Voprosy istorii* 7: 62–96.

—— (1966) Proletarian Internationalism and Peaceful Coexistence. *International Affairs* 8: 54–9.

—— (1968) Proletarian Internationalism and Peaceful Coexistence: Foundation of the Leninist Foreign Policy. *International Affairs* 11: 54–62.

Trush, Mikhail I. (1977) *Sovetskaya vneshyaya politika i diplomatiya v trudakh V.I. Lenina*. Moscow: Mezhdunarodnye otnosheniya.

Tunkin, Grigorii I. (1956) Mirnoe sosushchestvovanie i mezhdunarodnoe pravo. *Sovetskoe gosudarstvo i pravo* 7: 3–13.

—— (1963) Printsip mirnogo sosushchestvovanie—general'naya liniya vneshnepoliticheskoi deyatel'nosti KPSS i Sovetskogo gosudarstva. *Sovetskoe gosudarstvo i pravo* 7: 26–37.

—— (1974) *Theory of International Law* (trans. and with Introduction by William Butler). London: George Allen & Unwin.

Tuzmukhamedov, R. A. (1976) *Neprisoedinenie i razryadka mezhdunarodnoi napryazhennosti*. Moscow: IMO.

—— (1981) Neprisoedinenie: nekotorye voprosy mezhdunarodnogo pravo. *Sovetskoe gosudarstvo i pravo* 6: 113–20.

Tyagunenko, Viktor L. (1965) Budushchee osvobodivshikhsya gosudarstv. *Kommunist* 4: 112–14.

—— (1957) Oktyabr' i sovremennaya natsional'no-osvodboditel'naya revolyutsiya. *Mirovaya ekonomika i mezhdunarodnye otnoshenii* 1: 3–18.

Tyulpanov, S. I. (1961) Problema neitralizma slabo-razvitikh stran v svete reshenii XXII s"ezda KPSS. In *Vestnik Leningradskogo gos. universiteta* 23, Seriya ekonomika, filosofiya, pravo, vypusk 4, 16–34.

Ulam, Adam B. (1952) *Titoism and the Cominform*. Cambridge, Mass.: Harvard University Press.
—— (1974) *Expansion and Coexistence: Soviet Foreign Policy, 1917–73* (2nd edn). New York: Praeger.
Ul'rikh, O. (1975) Gosudarstvenny sektor v sisteme obshchestvennykh otnoshenii razvivayushchikhsya stran. *Mirovaya ekonomika i mezhdunarodnye otnoshenii* 4: 137–45.
—— (1981) Preodelenie otstalosti razvivayushchikhsya stran—global 'naya problema sovremennosti. *Mirovaya ekonomika i mezhdunarodnye otnoshenii* 9: 47–58.
Ul'yanovsky, Rostislav A. (1966) Nekotorye voprosy nekapitalisticheskogo razvitiya. *Kommunist* 1: 109–19.
—— (1972) *Sotsializm i osvobodivshiesya strany*. Moscow: Glavnaya redaktsiya vostochnoi literatury.
—— (1979) O stranakh sotsialisticheskoi orientatsii. *Kommunist* 11: 119–29.
—— (1984) O revolyutsionnoi demokratii, ee gosudarstve i politcheskoi sisterne. *Voprosy filosofii* 4: 26–35.
Unger, Aryeh, L. (1981) *Constitutional Development in the USSR: A Guide to the Soviet Constitutions*. London: Methuen.
US Department of State and Department of Defence (1984) *Grenada Documents: An Overview and Selection*. Washington, DC: DS; DD.
Usachev, Igor' G. (1980) *Mezhdunarodnaya razryadka i SShA*. Moscow: Mysl'.

Valenta, Jiri (1979) *Soviet Intervention in Czechoslovakia, 1968: Anatomy of a Decision*. Baltimore/London: Johns Hopkins University Press.
Valkenier, Elizabeth K. (1979) The USSR, the Third World and the Global Economy. *Problems of Communism*, XXVIII, 4 (July/Aug.): 17–33.
—— (1980) Development Issues in Recent Soviet Scholarship. *World Politics*, XXXII, 4: 485–508.
—— (1983) *The Soviet Union and the Third World: An Economic Bind*. New York: Praeger.
—— (1986) Revolutionary Change in the Third World: Recent Soviet Reassessments. *World Politics* XXVIII, 3: 415–34.
Varga, Evgeny S. (1946) *Izmeneniya v ekonomike kapitalizma v itoge Vtoroi mirovoi voiny*. Moscow: Izd-vo politicheskoi literatury.
—— (1947) 'Demokratiya novogo tipa'. *Mirovoe khozyaistvo i*

mirovaya politika, 3: 3–14.

—— (1953, 1957) *Osnovnye voprosy ekonomiki i politiki imperia-lizma (posle Vtoroi mirovoi voiny)* (2 edns). Moscow: Politi-cheskaya literatura.

Vasil'eva, V. Ya. (1947) Ekonomicheskoe razvitie kolonii v gody Vtoroi mirovoi voiny. *Mirovoe khozyaistvo i mirovaya politika* 5: 51–64.

Velikaya sila leninskikh idei internatsionalizma (1955) *Kommunist* 1: 3–13.

Vigor, Peter H. (1968) The Soviet Conception of Neutrality. *Bulletin XV, 11: 3–18.*

—— and John Erickson (1970) Soviet View of Theory and Strategy of War. *Journal of the Royal United Service Institution* CXV, 658: 3–13.

—— (1975) *The Soviet View of War, Peace and Neutrality*. London/Boston: Routledge & Kegan Paul.

Vinogradov, I. (1959) Ekonomicheskoe sotrudnichestvo sotsialis-ticheskikh stran krepnet i rasshiryaetsya: k desyatiletiyu Soveta ekonomicheskoi vzaimopomoshchi. *Kommunist* 6: 80–91.

Vneocherednoi XXI S"ezd Kommunisticheskoi partii Sovetskogo Soyuza, Stenografichesky otchet (1959). Moscow: Izd-vo politi-cheskoi literatury.

Warren, Bill (1980) *Imperialism: Pioneer of Capitalism*. London: Verso.

Wetter, Gustav, A. (1958) *Dialectical Materialism: A History and Systematic Survey of Philosophy in the Soviet Union* (rev. edn). London: Routledge & Kegan Paul.

Wilbur, C. Martin and Julie Lien-Ying How (eds) (1972) *Docu-ments on Communism, Nationalism and Soviet Advisers in China, 1918–1927*. New York: Octagon Books.

Wettig, Gerhard (1984) The Western Peace Movement in Moscow's Longer View. *Strategic Review (Spring): 44–54.*

Whetten, Lawrence L. (ed.) (1984) *The Present State of Communist Internationalism*. Lexington, Mass./Toronto: Lexington Books.

Windsor, Philip and Adam Roberts (1969) *Czechoslovakia 1968: Reform, Repression and Resistance*. London: Chatto & Windus.

Wittfogel, K. A. (1957) *Oriental Despotism*. New Haven, Conn.: Yale University Press.

Wright Mills, C. (1963) *The Marxists*. Harmondsworth, Middlesex: Penguin.

Yakovlev, A. (1987) Dostizhenie kachestvenno novogo sosto-yaniya sovetskogo obshchestva i obshchestvennye nauki. *Kom-munist* 8: 3–22.

Yudin, P. F. (1948) Centenary of the 'Communist Manifesto'. *For a*

Lasting Peace, for a People's Democracy, 15 February, 2.
—— (1949) Perekhod k sotsializmu v stranakh narodnoi demokratii. *Voprosy filosofii* 1: 40–59.
Zadorozhny, G. P. (1951) Voprosy mezhdunarodnogo prava v trinadtsatom tome Sochinenii I. V. Stalina. *Sovetskoe gosudarstvo i pravo* 9: 1–13.
Zagladin, Vladimir V. (ed.) (1973) *The World Communist System: Outline of Strategy and Tactics*. Moscow: Progress Publishers.
—— (1981) XXVI S"ezd KPSS i mirvoi revolyutsionny protsess. *Mirovaya ekonomika i mezhdunarodnye otnosheniya*, 4: 3–19.
—— (1986) Programmnye tseli KPSS; global'nye problemy. *Voprosy filosofii* 2: 3–15.
Zagoria, Donald S. (1982) *Soviet Policy in Asia*. New Haven, Conn./London: Yale University Press.
Zamostny, Thomas K. Moscow and the Third World: Recent Trends in Soviet Thinking. *Soviet Studies* XXXVI, 2: 225–35.
Zhdanov, Anrei A. (1947a) The International Situation. *For a Lasting Peace, for a People's Democracy*, 10 November: 2–4.
—— (1947b) Vystuplenie na diskusii po knige G. G. Aleksandrova 'Istoriya zapadnoevropeiskoi filosofii', 24 iyunya 1947 goda. *Bolshevik* 16: 7–23.
Zhukov, E. M. (1946) Velikaya Oktyabr'skaya sotsialisticheskaya revolyutsiya i kolonial'ny Vostok. *Bolshevik* 20: 38–47.
—— (1947a) Kolonial'ny vopros posle vtoroi mirovoi voiny. *Pravda*, 7 August, trans. in Alvin Z. Rubinstein (ed.) *The Foreign Policy of the Soviet Union*. New York: Random House, 1966.
—— (1947b) K polozheniyu v Indii. *Mirovoe khozyaistvo i mirovaya politika* 7: 3–14.
—— (1947c) Obostrenie krizisa kolonial'noi sistemy. *Bolshevik* 23: 51–64.
—— (1949) Voprosy natsional'no-kolonial'noi bor'by posle Vtoroi mirovoi voiny. *Voprosy ekonomiki*, 9: 54–61 (trans. in *Current Digest of the Soviet Press* 1, 49: 3–6).
Zhurkin, V. V. and E. M. Primakov (1972) *Mezhdunarodnye konflikty*. Moscow: IMO.
Zimmerman, William (1971) *Soviet Perspectives on International Relations 1956–1967*. Princeton, NJ: Princeton University Press.
Zinner, Paul E. (ed.) (1956) *National Communism and Popular Revolt in Eastern Europe: A Selection of Documents on Events in Poland and Hungary, 1956*. New York: Columbia University Press.
Znachenie trudov I. V. Stalina po voprosam yazykoznanie dlya Sovetskoi istoricheskoi nauki. *Voprosy istorii* 7: 3–9.
Zorin, V., V. Israelyan and Sh. Sanokoyev (1963) Leninisky kurs vneshnei politiki Sovetskogo gosudarstva. *Kommunist* 4: 27–37.

Index